THE LOS ANGELES
OLD-TIME RADIO
SCHEDULE BOOK

VOLUME 2
1938-1945

KEITH D. LEE

The Los Angeles Old-Time Radio Schedule Book — Volume 2, 1938-1945
© 2013 Keith D. Lee. All Rights Reserved.

No part of this book may be reproduced in any form or by any means, electronic, mechanical, digital, photocopying or recording, except for the inclusion in a review, without permission in writing from the publisher.

Published in the USA by:
BearManor Media
PO Box 1129
Duncan, Oklahoma 73534-1129
www.bearmanormedia.com

ISBN 978-1-59393-238-1

Printed in the United States of America.
Book design by Brian Pearce | Red Jacket Press.

TABLE OF CONTENTS

Introduction 5

Listings for 1938 7

Listings for 1939 65

Listings for 1940 123

Listings for 1941 181

Listings for 1942 239

Listings for 1943 297

Listings for 1944 355

Listings for 1945 413

INTRODUCTION

This series of books are a listing of national and local Los Angeles-based OTR shows from Fall, 1929 through Summer, 1954, in an easy-to-read grid format. Each section lists the OTR shows that were playing during that particular calendar season in that particular OTR year. The shows that are listed were on the four major OTR networks (Blue/ABC, CBS, MBS, and NBC) and their local Los Angeles affiliates from 8AM to 11PM Monday through Sunday.

In reading any of the sample chapters, please note the following:

Each cell in the grid represents a fifteen minute block of time.

Each blank cell means that the preceding show is still on. I deferred from using quotation marks because it looked too unreadable.

A slash between the names of two or more daily shows either in the same cell or adjoining cells signifies that those shows shared that timeslot on intermittant days for each week during that particular calendar season. In the case of weekly shows, a slash signifies that the shows shared the same timeslot for part of that particular calendar season.

Such generic show titles as "Songs," "Music," "News," "Public Affairs," "Sports," and "Talk" and any combination thereof are used. In the case of a daily show, such a generic title signifies the type of show on during the week. In the case of a weekly show, the networks or their affiliated stations couldn't find a sponsor for that timeslot and filled it with a generic show of music, talk, etc.

The information printed has been thoroughly checked for absolute correctness based on the OTR sources that still exist; contradictions and errors in them notwithstanding.

The book is the summation of one year of research using the following sources:

JJ's Radio Logs: *http://www.jjonz.us/RadioLogs/*

The New York Old-Time-Radio Schedule Book, Volumes 1-3 by Keith D. Lee. BearManor Media, OK, 2011.

Because there aren't very many OTR sources anymore, and many of them contradict one another, many thanks are necessary to JJ for allowing me access to his wonderfully entertaining and informative Radio Log Web Page. Hopefully, this will inspire the next generations to research even more into the history of OTR.

LISTINGS FOR 1938

EVENING — WINTER, 1938

Sunday

	BLUE	CBS	MBS	NBC
5pm	Detective Stories	Public Affairs	The Epic of America	The Chase and Sanborn Hour
5:15				
5:30	Ernest Gill's California Concert	Earaches of 1938	Sammy Kaye Orchestra	
5:45				
6pm	Vic Lewis Orchestra	The Ford Sunday Evening Hour	Impressions	The Manhattan Merry-Go-Round
6:15				
6:30	The Beaux Arts Trio		The News Testers	The American Album of Familiar Music
6:45			John B. Hughes, news	
7pm	The Reader's Guide	The Zenith Foundation	Louisiana Hayride	Carefree Carnvial
7:15	Dance Orchestra			
7:30	Music	My Secret Ambition	The Old Fashioned Revival Hour	The Hollywood Playhouse
7:45	News			
8pm	The Colonial Quartet	The Park Avenue Penners		Walter Winchell's Jergens Journal
8:15	Irene Rich Dramas			I Want a Divorce
8:30	Henry Busse Orchestra	Cab Calloway Orchestra	Music	The Jello Program, Jack Benny
8:45				
9pm	Dance Orchestra	The Toast of the Town	News	The Night Editor
9:15			Dance Orchestra	Treasure Island
9:30		The Hollywood Melody Shop	Lew Fields Orchestra	One Man's Family
9:45	The University Explorer			
10pm	Phil-Harmonia	The Ten o'Clock Wire	Dance Orchestra	The Richfield Reporter
10:15		Door to the Moon		Trudy Wood, songs
10:30		Dance Orchestra	News	Bridge to Dreamland
10:45			Dance Orchestra	

EVENING — WINTER, 1938

		Monday		
BLUE	CBS	MBS	NBC	
Melody Puzzles	Maurice Winnick Orchestra	Morton Gould Orchestra	Gladys Swartout, songs	5pm
	Charlie Chan			5:15
Sports	Jack Westaway, songs	Lawrence Welk Orchestra	Grand Hotel	5:30
News	Little Orphan Annie			5:45
Philadelphia Symphony Orchestra	The Lux Radio Theater	Jack Armstrong, The All-American Boy	Lum and Abner	6pm
		The Phantom Pilot Patrol	Songs	6:15
		Sports	The Hour of Charm	6:30
		John B. Hughes, news		6:45
Behind Prison Bars	Lady Esther Serenade	The Marines Tell It to You	The Carnation Contented Hour	7pm
				7:15
Music	Brave New World	The Lone Ranger	Burns and Allen	7:30
Hollywood Speaks				7:45
Whatsit Land	US Weather	Henry Weber's Musical Revue	Amos 'n' Andy	8pm
Lum and Abner	Boake Carter, news		Uncle Ezra's Radio Station	8:15
The Colonial Quartet	Pick and Pat	The Townsend Plan	The Voice of Firestone	8:30
Magnolia Blossoms		Music		8:45
Mildred Marsh, songs	Music	News	Fibber McGee and Molly	9pm
The University Explorer		Jimmy Dorsey Orchestra		9:15
A Man Should	Scattergood Baines	Dance Orchestra	Vox Pop	9:30
	Hawaiian Moon			9:45
Phil-Harmonia	The Ten o'Clock Wire		The Richfield Reporter	10pm
	White Fires of Inspiration		Gene and Glenn	10:15
		News	Jimmy Grier Orchestra	10:30
	Dance Orchestra	Dance Orchestra		10:45

EVENING — WINTER, 1938

Tuesday

	BLUE	CBS	MBS	NBC
5pm	Varieties	Big Town	Sammy Kaye Orchestra	Those We Love
5:15				
5:30	Chansonette	Knox Manning, news	Music	Helen Colley, songs
5:45		Little Orphan Annie		Motordom
6pm	The Beaux Arts Trio	Silhouettes	Jack Armstong, the All-American Boys	The Alemite Half-Hour
6:15		Strings	The Phantom Pilot Patrol	
6:30	Alias Jimmy Valentine	Jack Oakie's College	Sports	Mardi Gras
6:45			John B. Hughes, news	
7pm	Hugh S. Johnson, comment	Benny Goodman's Swing School	The Hour of Romance	
7:15	The Kidoodler's Novelty Quartet			
7:30	Celia Gamba, songs	Calling All Cars	Symphonic Strings	Jimmy Fidler, gossip
7:45				Dale Carnegie, inspirational talk
8pm	Whatsit Land	US Weather	Carlton Kelsey Orchestra	Amos 'n' Andy
8:15	Jerry Blaine Orchestra	Screenscoops		Vocal Varieties
8:30	Henry Busse Orchestra	The Lifebouy Program, Al Jolson	Mysteries	Johnny Presents
8:45			Vic Arden Orchestra	
9pm	Preview Tonight	Watch the Fun Go By, Al Pearce	News	Death Valley Days
9:15			Did You Know That	
9:30	Freddy Nagel Orchestra	Scattergood Baines	Isham Jones Orchestra	Good Morning Tonight
9:45	The University Explorer	Buddy Rogers Orchestra		
10pm	Phil-Harmonia	The Ten o'Clock Wire	Ray Pearl Orchestra	The Richfield Reporter
10:15		On the Air	Ozzie Nelson Orchestra	Radiola
10:30			News	Jimmy Grier Orchestra
10:45		Dance Orchestra	Johnny Keating Orchestra	

EVENING — WINTER, 1938

Wednesday

BLUE	CBS	MBS	NBC	
The Roy Shields Revue	Maurice Winnick Orchestra	Ennio Bolognini Orchestra	Stringin' Along	5pm
	Charlie Chan			5:15
Hollywood News	Under the Sea	Music	Tom Sawyer, comment	5:30
News	Little Orphan Annie		The California Safety Council	5:45
Cleveland Symphony Orchestra	Chesterfield Presents	Jack Armstong, the All-American Boys	Lum and Abner	6pm
		The Phantom Pilot Patrol	Four Stars Tonight	6:15
	Ben Bernie, the Old Maestro	Sports	Thrills	6:30
		John B. Hughes, news		6:45
Hugh S. Johnson, comment	Gangbusters	Horace Heidt Orchestra	Your Hollywood Parade	7pm
Lal Chand Mehra, india talk				7:15
Music	Hobby Lobby	The Lone Ranger		7:30
Marching Along				7:45
Whatsit Land	US Weather	Sinfonietta	Amos 'n' Andy	8pm
Lum and Abner	Boake Carter, news		Uncle Ezra's Radio Station	8:15
Fashions	Texaco Town, Eddie Cantor	The Deep South	Hawthorne House	8:30
Raine Bennett, rhymes		Music		8:45
Music	The Cavalcade of America	News	Town Hall Tonight, Fred Allen	9pm
Public Affairs		Guy Lombardo Orchestra		9:15
Busman's Holiday	Scattergood Baines	Dr. McCoy, health		9:30
	Jack Harris Orchestra	Did You Know That		9:45
Phil-Harmonia	The Ten o'Clock Wire	Dance Orchestra	The Richfield Reporter	10pm
	Your Witness	Ozzie Nelson Orchestra	Meet Some People	10:15
		News	The Haven of Rest	10:30
		Dance Orchestra		10:45

EVENING — WINTER, 1938

Thursday

	BLUE	CBS	MBS	NBC
5pm	The Story Store	Maurice Winnick Orchestra	Dance Orchestra	The Royal Gelatin Hour, Rudy Vallee
5:15	Music			
5:30	The March of Time	The Jesters		
5:45		Little Orphan Annie		
6pm	Rochester Philharmonic Orchestra	Major Bowes' Original Amateur Hour	Jack Armstong, the All-American Boy	Good News of 1938
6:15			The Phantom Pilot Patrol	
6:30	America's Town Meeting of the Air		Sports	
6:45			John B. Hughes, newsr	
7pm		Man to Man	The Witch's Tale	The Kraft Music Hall, Bing Crosby
7:15		Leaves in the Wind		
7:30	Music	Showcase	Henry Weber's Musical Revue	
7:45	The Music Parade			
8pm	Whatsit Land	US Weather	Public Affairs	Amos 'n' Andy
8:15	Elza Schallert Interviews	Screenscoops		The Standard Symphony Hour
8:30	Jimmy Grier Orchestra	The Kate Smith Hour		
8:45			Vic Arden Orchestra	
9pm	Dance Orchestra		News	
9:15			Dance Orchestra	I Want a Divorce
9:30	Gar Van Orchestra	Scattergood Baines		Mother In Law
9:45	The University Explorer	Music		The Times Dramatic Program
10pm	Phil-Harmonia	The Ten o'Clock Wire	Joe Reichmann Orchestra	The Richfield Reporter
10:15		The Art of Conversation	Ozzie Nelson Orchestra	Listener-Inner
10:30			News	Dance Orchestra
10:45		Jack Harris Orchestra	Dance Orchestra	

EVENING — WINTER, 1938

Friday

BLUE	CBS	MBS	NBC	
Stringtime	The Hammerstien Music Hall	The Trumpeter	Helen Colley, songs	5pm
		Fashions	Music	5:15
Gladys Swartout, songs	Jack Westaway, songs	The Radio Guild	Know Your Schools	5:30
News	Little Orphan Annie		Moving Stories of LIfe	5:45
Nola Day, songs	Hollywood Hotel	Jack Armstong, the All-American Boy	Lum and Abner	6pm
Linton Welles, news		The Phantom Pilot Patrol	King's Cowboy Revue	6:15
Organ Recital		Sports	Tommy Dorsey Orchestra	6:30
You and Your Government		John B. Hughes, news		6:45
Dance Orchestra	The Song Shop	Twenty Years Ago and Today	The First Nighter Program	7pm
Safety				7:15
Public Affairs		The Lone Ranger	Jimmy Fidler, gossip	7:30
	Public Affairs		Dorothy Thompson, news	7:45
Whatsit Lamd	US Weather	Music	Amos 'n' Andy	8pm
Lum and Abner	Boake Carter, news	Nat Brusiloff Orchestra	Uncle Ezra's Radio Station	8:15
Music	Chesterfield Presents	Music	The Court of Human Relations	8:30
Henry Busse Orchestra				8:45
Nick Harris	Dance Orchestra	News	The Gilmore Circus	9pm
The March of Progress		Room Service		9:15
Music	Scattergood Baines	Music	Four Stars Tonight	9:30
	Music		Ho Hum	9:45
Phil-Harmonia	The Ten o'Clock Wire	Dance Orchestra	The Richfield Reporter	10pm
	What Would You Do	Ozzie Nelson Orchestra	Gene and Glenn	10:15
		News	Jimmy Grier Orchestra	10:30
	Jack Harris Orchestra	Dance Orchestra		10:45

EVENING — WINTER, 1938

Saturday

	BLUE	CBS	MBS	NBC
5pm	Ted Lewis Orchestra	Organ Recital	Pat Barnes' Barnstormers	The Haven of Rest
5:15		Charlie Chan		
5:30	Spelling Bee	Maurice Winnick Orchestra	Olga Baclanova's Continental Revue	Josef Hornik Orchestra
5:45				
6pm	Education Today	A Word for Swing	The Ed Lowry Show	Allen Roth Orchestra
6:15	The California Safety Council			Music
6:30	Music	Saturday Night Serenade	Sports	King's Cowboy Revue
6:45			John B. Hughes, news	Marching Along
7pm	NBC Symphony Orchestra	Your Hit Parade	Indianapolis Symphony Orchestra	Music
7:15				Broadway Bill
7:30				
7:45		The Juvenile Revue		Organ Recital
8pm				The National Barn Dancet
8:15		US Weather	Dance Orchestra	
8:30	Al Donahue Orchestra	Johnny Presents		
8:45				
9pm	Buddy Rogers Orchestra	Professor Quiz	News	Believe It or Not
9:15			Your State	
9:30	Dance Orchestra	Gaylord Carter, organ	Dance Orchestra	The Log Cabin Jamboree, Jack Haley
9:45		Dance Orchestra	Did You Know That	
10pm	Phil-Harmonia	The Hollywood Barn Dance	Joe Reichmann Orchestra	Don Wilkie, songs
10:15			Ozzie Nelson Orchestra	Ted Lewis Orchestra
10:30			News	Raine Bennett, rhymes
10:45		Charlie Parker Orchestra	Burke Orchestra	Dance Orchestra

DAYTIME — WINTER, 1938

Sunday

	BLUE	CBS	MBS	NBC
8am	Music	The CBS Church of the Air	The Comics Weekly Man	The Silver Flute
8:15				
8:30	Felix Knight, songs	Major Bowes' Capitol Family	Music	Angler and Hunter
8:45	The Bill Stern Sports Review			The Church Quarter-Hour
9am	Garden Talk		The Voice of Prophecy	Home Symphony Orchestra
9:15	Pilgrimage			
9:30	The Radio City Music Hall	The Salt Lake Tabernacle Choir	Public Affairs	The University of Chicago Round Table
9:45			News	
10am		The CBS Church of the Air	The Sands of Time	Howard Bell, songs
10:15			Music	Henry Busse Orchestra
10:30	Your Letter Box	Music	The Romance of the Highways	Xavier Cugat Orchestra
10:45	Al Gayle Orchestra	Poet's Gold	Music	John Holmes, sports
11am	The Magic Key of RCA	Walberg Brown Strings	Psychiana	Bob Becker's Dog Talks
11:15			Music	Vagabonds Orchestra
11:30		Music		Music
11:45				
12pm	Cabbage and Kings	New York Philharmonic Orchestra	On a Sunday Afternoon	Gladys Swartout, songs
12:15	Music			
12:30				Sunday Drivers
12:45			The Trail Blazers	
1pm	National Vespers		The Court of Human Relations	The Sunday Special
1:15				
1:30	Music		The Lutheran Hour	The World is Yours

DAYTIME — WINTER, 1938

Monday-Friday

BLUE	CBS	MBS	NBC	
Talk and Music	Houseboat	Music / Merrymakers Orchestra	Margo, songs	8am
	The Jesters Quartet		Aunt Jemima	8:15
Originalities	Kitty Keene, Inc.	Music	News	8:30
Talk and Music	Ma Perkins		The Gospel Singer	8:45
Thought Time	Talk / Mary Margaret McBride, talk	Boy and Girl	Gene and Glenn	9am
News	Edwin C. Hill, news	Music	The O'Neills	9:15
The National Farm and Home Hour	The Romance of Helen Trent	Norma Young, talk	Music	9:30
	Our Gal Sunday	We Are Four	Music / The Homemakers	9:45
	Betty and Bob	The Monticello Party Line	Music	10am
	Hymns of All Churches / Betty Crocker, cooking	The Buckaroos / Dr. A. F. Payne, psychology	Mrs. Wiggs of the Cabbage Patch	10:15
Sue Blake	Arnold Grimm's Daughter	Talk and Music	John's Other Wife	10:30
Talk and Music / Jack and Loretta Clemens, songs	Hollywood in Person	The Voice of Experience	Just Plain Bill	10:45
Talk and Music	Big Sister	Talk and Music	Music / The Standard School Broadcast	11am
Ann Cook, songs	Aunt Jenny's True Life Stories		Ann Warner Chats / The Standard School Broadcast	11:15
Stock Market Reports	The American School of the Air	Lucky Girl		11:30
The National Farm and Home Hour		Songs / Beatrice Fairfax, advice	Music / The Mystery Chef	11:45
Music	Music / Mary Lee Taylor, cooking	Ben Sweetland, comment	Pepper Young's Family	12pm
	Talk and Music	Music	Ma Perkins	12:15
		News	Vic and Sade	12:30
	Music / The Newlyweds	Talk and Music	The Guiding Light	12:45
News	The Story of Myrt and Marge		Talk and Music / Hello, Peggy	1pm
Talk and Music	Pretty Kitty Kelly		The Story of Mary Marlin	1:15
	News		Music / Gloria Gale	1:30

DAYTIME — WINTER, 1938

Sunday

	BLUE	CBS	MBS	NBC
1:45	The Ranch Boys			
2pm	The Metropollitan Opera Auditions	Heinz Magaziine of the Air	Piano	Ry-Krisp Presents Marion Talley
2:15			Rabbi Magnin, religion	
2:30	Dance Orchestra	Dr. Christian	The Shadow	The Mickey Mouse Theater of the Air
2:45	Songs			
3pm	The Catholic Hour	Strange As It Seems	Thirty Minutes in Hollywood, George Jessel	Midwestern Stars
3:15		Songs		
3:30	Senator Fishface and Professor Figgsbottle	Double Everything	Reunion of the Stars	Songs
3:45				Southern Harmony
4pm	Music	Vick's Open House	Help Thy Neighbor	Professor Puzzlewit
4:15				
4:30	Seein' Stars	The Gulf Headliners, Phil Baker	Music	Interesting Neighbors
4:45			Edith Gwynn, songs	

DAYTIME — WINTER, 1938

Monday-Friday

BLUE	CBS	MBS	NBC	
	Talk and Music / Dr. Allen Dafoe, health talk		Music / The Martha Meade Society	*1:45*
The Classic Hour	Follow the Moon	The Johnson Family	Wife vs. Secretary	*2pm*
	The Life of Mary Southern	Talk and Music	Stella Dallas	*2:15*
	Talk and Music		Music	*2:30*
	Hilltop House	The Widder Jones		*2:45*
Talk and Music	Talk and Music	Feminine Fancies		*3pm*
	The In-Laws			*3:15*
	Judy and Jane, songs	Talk and Music	Women's Magazine of the Air	*3:30*
	Lady of Millions			*3:45*
	Fletcher Wiley, talk	News	Talk and Music	*4pm*
		Talk and Music		*4:15*
	Talk and Music		News	*4:30*
	Music / Easy Aces	The Radio Campus	Dick Tracy	*4:45*

DAYTIME — WINTER, 1938

Saturday

	BLUE	CBS	MBS	NBC
8am	Toy Symphony Orchestra	Cincinatti Conservatory Symphony	Corn Time	The Florence Hale Radio Forum
8:15	The Minute Men Quartet			News
8:30	Our Barn		The US Army Band	Music of Ameican Youth
8:45				
9am	Call to Youth	Music	The California Board of Education	Abram Chasin's Music Series
9:15	News	The Federation of Women's Club	This Wonderful World	
9:30	The National Farm and Home Hour	George Hall Orchestra	Two Pianos	Music
9:45			Steve Severn's Pet Club	
10am		The Monitor Children's Program	News	County Medical Association Talks
10:15		Music	Microphone in the Sky	Music
10:30	Club Mattnee, Ransom Sherman	Buffalo Presents	Carnegie Tech Symphony Orchestra	Campus Capers
10:45				
11am	The Metropolitan Opera	Federal Housing Authority Talk	Benay Venuta's Variety Program	Music
11:15		Music		
11:30		Motor City Melody		Your Host is Buffalo
11:45				
12pm		Ann Leaf at the Organ	The Music Hall	Music
12:15				
12:30		Waltzes of the World		Bill Krenz Orchestra
12:45				
1pm		News	International House	Music
1:15		Music		
1:30			Public Affairs	Carlton Kelsey Orchestra
1:45		The Four Clubmen	Music	

DAYTIME — WINTER, 1938

Saturday

	BLUE	CBS	MBS	NBC
2pm	The Classic Hour	The Story of Industry	Sammy Kaye Orchestra	Tophatters Orchestra
2:15				
2:30		Music		The Stamp Club
2:45				Music
3pm		Columbia's Chorus Quest	Harry Owens Orchestra	El Chico
3:15			Aces High	
3:30	Music	Syncopation Piece	The Tercentenary	The Sports Question Bee
3:45			The Charioteers Quartet	Religion in the News
4pm	Message of Israel	The Saturday Night Swing Club	Lawrence Welk Orchestra	Kaltenmeyer's Kindegarten
4:15				
4:30	Jack Meskin Orchestra	The Voice of Niagara	Tango Pancho Orchestra	Alistair Cooke, comment
4:45				The Jean Sablon Show

EVENING — SPRING, 1938

Sunday

	BLUE	CBS	MBS	NBC
5pm	Spy at Large	St. Louis Blues	The News Testers	The Chase and Sanborn Hour
5:15			The Magazine Man	
5:30	Songs We Remember	Musical Gazette	Hawaii Calls	
5:45				
6pm	Joe Sudy Orchestra	The Ford Sunday Evening Hour	The Marines Tell It to You	The Manhattan Merry-Go-Round
6:15				
6:30	The Reader's Guide		The Brown Sisters, songs	The American Album of Familiar Music
6:45	The Southern Harmony Four		John B. Hughes, news	
7pm	Freddy Martin Orchestra	The Hollywood Showcase	The House of Melody	Carefree Carnvial
7:15	News			
7:30	Cheerio's Musical Mosaics	My Secret Ambition	The Old Fashioned Revival Hour	The Hollywood Playhouse
7:45				
8pm	The Colonial Quartet	The Park Avenue Penners		Walter Winchell's Jergens Journal
8:15	Blue Barron Orchestra			Irene Rich Dramas
8:30	Lou Breeze Orchestra	Duke Ellington Orchestra	The River King	The Jello Program, Jack Benny
8:45	The Gilmore Circus			
9pm	Roger Pryor Orchestra	Ted Owen Orchestra	News	The Night Editor
9:15			George Fisher, gossip	I Want a Divorce
9:30	Dance Orchestra	Ted Fiorito Orchestra	Bob Crosby Orchestra	One Man's Family
9:45	The University Explorer			
10pm	Phil-Harmonia	The Ten o'Clock Wire	The Playboys	The Richfield Reporter
10:15		Thanks for the Memory	Jack Johnson Orchestra	Circus on the Move
10:30			News	Bridge to Dreamland
10:45		Nat Brandwynne Orchestra	Johnny Keating Orchestra	

LISTINGS FOR 1938

EVENING — SPRING, 1938

Monday

BLUE	CBS	MBS	NBC	
Melody Puzzles	Maurice Winnick Orchestra	Music	Gladys Swartout, songs	5pm
	Charlie Chan		Songs	5:15
Sports	Songs	Howie Wing	Those We Love	5:30
News	Boake Carter, news	Little Orphan Annie		5:45
Philadelphia Symphony Orchestra	The Lux Radio Theater	Jack Armstrong, The All-American Boy	The Hour of Charm	6pm
		The Phantom Pilot Patrol		6:15
		Sports	Public Affairs	6:30
		John B. Hughes, news		6:45
Behind Prison Bars	Lady Esther Serenade	True or False	The Carnation Contented Hour	7pm
				7:15
Music	The Camel Caravan, Eddie Cantor	The Lone Ranger	Burns and Allen	7:30
Hollywood Speaks				7:45
Music	Scattergood Baines	Dick Tracy	Amos 'n' Andy	8pm
	Lum and Abner	Dance Orchestra	Uncle Ezra's Radio Station	8:15
The Colonial Quartet	Pick and Pat	The Townsend Plan	The Voice of Firestone	8:30
Albert Bergman, legal talk		Dance Orchestra		8:45
Chick Webb Orchestra	You Said It	News	Herbie Kay Orchestra	9pm
The University Explorer		Red Norvo Orchestra		9:15
As a Man Should	Sam Balter, sports	Bob Crosby Orchestra	Vox Pop	9:30
	Music			9:45
Phil-Harmonia	The Ten o'Clock Wire	Tommy Tucker Orchestra	The Richfield Reporter	10pm
	Whte Fires of Inspiration		Ridin' the Range	10:15
		News	Frank Trombar Orchestra	10:30
	Ted Fiorito Orchestra	Dance Orchestra		10:45

EVENING — SPRING, 1938

Tuesday

	BLUE	CBS	MBS	NBC
5pm	Enric Madriguera Orchestra	The KNX Forum	Morton Gould Orchestra	Music
5:15		Maurice Winnick Orchestra		
5:30	It May Have Happened	Knox Manning, news	Howie Wing	Lady Esther Serenade
5:45		Boake Carter, news	Little Orphan Annie	
6pm	Dance Orchestra	Let's Celebrate	Jack Armstrong, the All-American Boys	The Alemite Half-Hour
6:15	Tax Info	Lew White Orchestra	The Phantom Pilot Patrol	
6:30	Alias Jimmy Valentine	Benny Goodman's Swing School	Sports	Fibber McGee and Molly
6:45			John B. Hughes, news	
7pm	Jamboree	Music	Say It with Music	Music
7:15				
7:30		Calling All Cars	The Witch's Tale	Jimmy Fidler, gossip
7:45				Dale Carnegie, inspirational talk
8pm	Music	Scattergood Baines	Dick Tracy	Amos 'n' Andy
8:15		Screenscoops	Fortunes	Vocal Varieties
8:30	Lou Breeze Orchestra	The Lifebouy Program, Al Jolson	Dr, Polyzoides, health	Johnny Presents
8:45			Dance Orchestra	
9pm	Herbie Kay Orchestra	Watch the Fun Go By, Al Pearce	News	Death Valley Days
9:15			Dance Orchestra	
9:30	Francis Craig Orchestra	Big Town	Jack Johnson Orchestra	Good Morning Tonight
9:45	The University Explorer			
10pm	Phil-Harmonia	The Ten o'Clock Wire	Jan Garber Orchestra	The Richfield Reporter
10:15		The Art of Conversation		Radiola
10:30			News	Frank Trombar Orchestra
10:45		Ted Fiorito Orchestra	The Playboys	

EVENING — SPRING, 1938

Wednesday

BLUE	CBS	MBS	NBC	
Motordom	Maurice Winnick Orchestra	Music	Viennese Echoes	5pm
The Roy Shields Revue	Charlie Chan		Tom Sawyer, comment	5:15
Harriet Parsons, gossip	Music	Howie Wing	The Raleigh and Kool Show	5:30
News	Boake Carter, news	Little Orphan Annie		5:45
Tune Types	Chesterfield Presents	Jack Armstong, the All-American Boys	String Symphony	6pm
		The Phantom Pilot Patrol		6:15
Under Western Skies	The Word Game	Sports	Thrills	6:30
		John B. Hughes, news		6:45
Music	Gangbusters	Symphonic Strings	Kay Kyser's College of Musical Knowledge	7pm
				7:15
The NBC Minstrels	The Camera Speaks	The Lone Ranger		7:30
	Jack Shannon, news			7:45
Music	Scattergood Baines	Dick Tracy	Amos 'n' Andy	8pm
	Lum and Abner	Music	Uncle Ezra's Radio Station	8:15
Raine Bennett, rhymes	Ben Bernie, the Old Maestro	Dance Orchestra	Hawthorne House	8:30
				8:45
Preview Tonight	The Cavalcade of America	News	Town Hall Tonight, Fred Allen	9pm
		Tommy Tucker Orchestra		9:15
Cleary and Gillum, songs	Sam Balter, sports	News		9:30
The University Explorer	Music	Lili Russell Orchestra		9:45
Phil-Harmonia	The Ten o'Clock Wire	Jan Garber Orchestra	The Richfield Reporter	10pm
	Your Witness		Ridin' the Range	10:15
		News	Lights Out	10:30
	Charlie Parker Orchestra	The Playboys		10:45

EVENING — SPRING, 1938

Thursday

	BLUE	CBS	MBS	NBC
5pm	The Beaux Arts Trio	Songs	Sinfonietta	The Royal Gelatin Hour, Rudy Vallee
5:15		Maurice Winnick Orchestra		
5:30	Jim Kemper and Company	Twin Pianos	Howie Wing	
5:45	The Music School	Boake Carter, news	Little Orphan Annie	
6pm		Major Bowes' Original Amateur Hour	Jack Armstong, the All-American Boy	Good News of 1938
6:15			The Phantom Pilot Patrol	
6:30	America's Town Meeting of the Air		Sports	
6:45			John B. Hughes, news	
7pm		Man to Man	Dance Orchestra	The Kraft Music Hall, Bing Crosby
7:15		Ditmar and His Organ		
7:30	Music	Music	Henry Weber's Musical Revue	
7:45	The Music Parade			
8pm	Music	Scattergood Baines	Dick Tracy	Amos 'n' Andy
8:15		Screenscoops	Neutral Thousands	The Standard Symphony Hour
8:30		The Kate Smith Hour	Songs	
8:45			Vic Arden Orchestra	
9pm	Elza Schallert Interviews		News	
9:15	Music		Al Goodman Orchestra	The March of Time
9:30	Gar Van Orchestra	Let's Celebrate	Bob Crosby Orchestra	
9:45	The University Explorer	Nat Brandwynne Orchestra		Francis Craig Orchestra
10pm	Phil-Harmonia	The Ten o'Clock Wire	Joe Reichmann Orchestra	The Richfield Reporter
10:15		On the Air		Meet Some People
10:30			News	The Haven of Rest
10:45		Ted Fiorito Orchestra	The Playboys	

EVENING — SPRING, 1938

Friday

BLUE	CBS	MBS	NBC	
Stringtime	Maurice Winnick Orchestra	Music	Helen Colley, songs	5pm
	Charlie Chan		Virginia Fiohri, songs	5:15
Gladys Swartout, songs	Twin Pianos	Topics of the Day	Know Your Schools	5:30
News	Boake Carter, news	Little Orphan Annie	Moving Stories of LIfe	5:45
The Beaux Arts Trio	Hollywood Hotel	Jack Armstrong, the All-American Boy	Gene and Glenn	6pm
		The Phantom Pilot Patrol	King's Cowboy Revue	6:15
The Southern Harmony Four		Sports	Music	6:30
You and Your Government		John B. Hughes, news		6:45
Freddy Martin Orchestra	The Song Shop	Bamberger Little Orchestra	The First Nighter Program	7pm
				7:15
Public Affairs		The Lone Ranger	Jimmy Fidler, gossip	7:30
	American Viewpoints		Dorothy Thompson, news	7:45
Music	Scattergood Baines	Dick Tracy	Amos 'n' Andy	8pm
	Lum and Abner	News	Uncle Ezra's Radio Station	8:15
	Chesterfield Presents	The American Composer Series	Music	8:30
			Ruby Newman Orchestra	8:45
Nick Harris	Arthur Godfrey, songs	News	The Gilmore Circus	9pm
The March of Progress	Dance Orchestra	The Toast of the Town		9:15
Dick Stabile Orchestra	Sports		The Roy Shield Revue	9:30
	Ted Fiorito Orchestra	Music		9:45
Phil-Harmonia	The Ten o'Clock Wire	Jan Garber Orchestra	The Richfield Reporter	10pm
	On the Air		Ridin' the Range	10:15
		Isham Jones Orchestra	Ho Hum	10:30
	Harry Owens Orchestra		Frank Trombar Orchestra	10:45

EVENING — SPRING, 1938

Saturday

	BLUE	CBS	MBS	NBC
5pm	Music	The Columbia Workshop	Contrasts	The Haven of Rest
5:15				
5:30	Heads I Win	Maurice Winnick Orchestra	Pat Barnes' Barnstormers	Music of American Youth
5:45				
6pm	Education Today	Music	The Ed Lowry Show	Allen Roth Orchestra
6:15	The California Safety Council			
6:30	Galleons	Saturday Night Serenade	Sports	King's Cowboy Revue
6:45	The Three Pals		John B. Hughes, news	The Music Parade
7pm	NBC Symphony Orchestra	Your Hit Parade	Chicago Symphony Orchestra	Carlton Kelsey Orchestra
7:15				
7:30				The Family Party
7:45		The Juvenile Revue		
8pm		Silhouettes	Night Skies	The National Barn Dancet
8:15			Abe Lyman Orchestra	
8:30	Horace Heidt Orchestra	Johnny Presents	Jan Garber Orchestra	
8:45				
9pm		Professor Quiz	News	Believe It or Not
9:15			Public Affairs	
9:30	Herbie Kay Orchestra	Let's Celebrate	Bob Crosby Orchestra	Dance Orchestra
9:45		Capitol Opinions		
10pm	Phil-Harmonia	The Hollywood Barn Dance	Joe Reichmann Orchestra	Raine Bennett, rhymes
10:15				Dance Orchestra
10:30			Jan Garber Orchestra	
10:45		Ted Fiorito Orchestra		

DAYTIME — SPRING, 1938

Sunday

	BLUE	CBS	MBS	NBC
8am	Music	The CBS Church of the Air	The Comics Weekly Man	The Silver Flute
8:15				
8:30	Louis Florea, songs	Major Bowes' Capitol Family	Rev. Zoller, religion	America Aboard
8:45	The Bill Stern Sports Review			The Church Quarter-Hour
9am	Garden Talk		The Voice of Prophecy	Home Symphony Orchestra
9:15	The Southernaires Quartet			
9:30	The Radio City Music Hall	The Salt Lake Tabernable Choir	News	The University of Chicago Round Table
9:45			The Sands of Time	
10am		The CBS Church of the Air	Two Pianos	Garden Talk
10:15			Romance of the Highways	Ted Weems Orchestra
10:30	Music	Europe Calling	The Success Doctor	Music
10:45	Al Gayle Orchestra	Poet's Gold	The American Radio Warblers	Health Talk
11am	The Magic Key of RCA	Walberg Brown Strings	Psychiana	The Kidoodlers Novelty Quartet
11:15			Music	Vincente Gomez, guitar
11:30		Rainbow's End		Sunday Dinner at Aunt Fanny's
11:45				
12pm	Cabbage and Kings	New York Philharmonic Orchestra	On a Sunday Afternoon	Gladys Swartout, songs
12:15	Music			
12:30	Souvenirs			Sunday Drivers
12:45	William Primrose, violin		The Blue Plate Special	
1pm	National Vespers		The Court of Human Relations	The Sunday Special
1:15				

DAYTIME — SPRING, 1938

Monday-Friday

BLUE	CBS	MBS	NBC	
Music (7:45AM)	Houseboat	Happy Times / Merrymakers Orchestra	Aunt Jemima	8am
Waltzes	The Wife Saver		Margo, songs	8:15
Music	Kitty Keene, Inc.	Music / Rita Gould, songs	News	8:30
Originalities	Ma Perkins	Music	Music	8:45
Thought Time	Talk / Mary Margaret McBride, talk	Talk and Music	Music / Vaughn de Leath, songs	9am
News	Music / The Newlyweds		The O'Neills	9:15
The National Farm and Home Hour	The Romance of Helen Trent	Norma Young, talk	The Bridge Club	9:30
	Our Gal Sunday	Music	Talk / The Homemakers	9:45
	Betty and Bob	Music / The Happy Gang	Music	10am
	Hymns of All Churches / Betty Crocker, cooking	Microphone in the Sky	Mrs. Wiggs of the Cabbage Patch	10:15
Mother In Law	Arnold Grimm's Daughter	The Widder Jones	John's Other Wife	10:30
Talk and Music / Jack and Loretta Clemens, songs	Valiant Lady	Talk and Music / The Voice of Experience	Just Plain Bill	10:45
Music	Big Sister	Talk and Music	Music / The Standard School Broadcast	11am
Let's Talk It Over	Aunt Jenny's True Life Stories		Ann Warner Chats / The Standard School Broadcast	11:15
Stock Market Reports	Music			11:30
The National Farm and Home Hour			Music / The Mystery Chef	11:45
Music	Talk and Music / Mary Lee Taylor, cooking		Pepper Young's Family	12pm
	Fletcher Wiley, talk		Ma Perkins	12:15
	News		Vic and Sade	12:30
	Songs		The Guiding Light	12:45
News	The Story of Myrt and Marge	Music / Ed Fitzgerald and Company	Talk and Music / Hello, Peggy	1pm
Club Matinee, Ransom Sherman	Pretty Kitty Kelly	Talk and Music	The Story of Mary Marlin	1:15

DAYTIME — SPRING, 1938

Sunday

	BLUE	CBS	MBS	NBC
1:30	Jean Ellington, songs		The Lutheran Hour	The World is Yours
1:45	The Vagabond Quartet			
2pm	There Was a Woman	Heinz Magaziine of the Air	The Musical Steelmakers	Ry-Krisp Presents Marion Talley
2:15				
2:30	The Beaux Arts Trio	Dr. Christian	Rabbi Magnin, religion	The Mickey Mouse Theater of the Air
2:45	Howard Marshall, news		Summer Prindle	
3pm	The Catholic Hour	Strange As It Seems	Thirty Minutes in Hollywood, George Jessel	Musical Camera
3:15		Songs		
3:30	Haven MacQuarrie, songs	Phil Cook's Almanac	Reunion of the Stars	The Beaux Art Trio
3:45				Surprise Party
4pm	Music	The Story of Joan and Kermit	Help Thy Neighbor	Professor Puzzlewit
4:15				
4:30	Seein' Stars	The Gulf Headliners, Phil Baker		Interesting Neighbors
4:45			Dr. Thomas, religion	

DAYTIME — SPRING, 1938

Monday-Friday

BLUE	CBS	MBS	NBC	
	Talk and Music		Hughesreel	1:30
The Classic Hour			Dr. Kate	1:45
	Music / DearTeacher	Talk and Music	Music / The Martha Meade Society	2pm
	Talk and Music		Stella Dallas	2:15
			Music	2:30
	Hilltop House	The Johnson Family		2:45
Talk and Music	Talk and Music	Feminine Fancies	Talk and Music	3pm
	News of Radio Stars		Candid Lady	3:15
	Judy and Jane, songs	Talk and Music	Women's Magazine of the Air	3:30
	Music			3:45
	Fletcher Wiley, talk	Fulton Lewis, Jr., news	Talk and Music / Easy Aces	4pm
		Talk and Music	Talk and Music / Mr. Keen, Tracer of Lost Persons	4:15
	Talk and Music		News	4:30
		The Radio Campus	Way Down East	4:45

DAYTIME — SPRING, 1938

Saturday

	BLUE	CBS	MBS	NBC
8am	Vaughn de Leath, songs	Cincinatti Conservatory Symphony	Corn Time	The Florence Hale Radio Forum
8:15	The Minute Men Quartet			News
8:30	Our Barn		The US Army Band	Music of Ameican Youth
8:45				
9am	Call to Youth	Federal Housing Authority Talk	The California Board of Education	Abram Chasin's Music Series
9:15	News	Romany Trails	This Wonderful World	
9:30	The National Farm and Home Hour		Jazz Nocturne	Rex Battle Orchestra
9:45		The Monitor Children's Program		
10am		Melody Ramblings	Steve Severn's Pet Club	County Medical Association Talks
10:15		Golden Memories	Microphone in the Sky	Music
10:30	The Metropolitan Opera	Buffalo Presents	Carnegie Tech Symphony Orchestra	Your Host is Buffalo
10:45				
11am		Public Affairs	Benay Venuta's Variety Program	Music for Everyone
11:15				
11:30		Motor City Melody		Campus Capers
11:45				
12pm		Merrymakers Orchestra	Music	Golden Melodies
12:15				
12:30		Music		Swingology
12:45				
1pm				Music
1:15			The Butler Rodeo Ramblers	
1:30		News		Tophatters Orchestra
1:45		The All-Year Club	Music	

DAYTIME — SPRING, 1938

Saturday

	BLUE	CBS	MBS	NBC
2pm		The People's Lobby	Tango Pancho Orchestra	Great Plays
2:15				
2:30		Bill McCune Orchestra	Dance Orchestra	
2:45				
3pm	The Tune Twisters	Columbia's Chorus Quest	News	The Art of Living
3:15	The Master Builder		The Business Bureau	Barry McKinley, songs
3:30	Chick Webb Orchestra	News of Radio Stars	Jam and Jive	Paul Douglas, sports
3:45		Artie Shaw Orchestra		Religion in the News
4pm	Message of Israel	Music	Let's Visit	Kaltenmeyer's Kindegarten
4:15				
4:30	Dance Orchestra		Xavier Cugat Orchestra	Alistair Cooke, comment
4:45				Barry McKinley, songs

EVENING — SUMMER, 1938

Sunday

	BLUE	CBS	MBS	NBC
5pm	Joe Sudy Orchestra	The Lewisohn Stadium Concerts (4:30PM)	The Grant Park Concerts	The Manhattan Merry-Go-Round
5:15				
5:30	The Reader's Digest		Music	The American Album of Familiar Music
5:45	The Jingletown Gazette			
6pm	Dance Orchestra		The Marines Tell It to You	Carefree Carnival
6:15				
6:30	Cheerio's Musical Mosaics	Headlines and Bylines	The Goodhwill Hour	Win Your Lady
6:45				
7pm	News	Vincent Lopez Orchestra	The House of Melody	Ben Grauer's Column Quiz
7:15	Music			Irene Rich Dramas
7:30	Abe Lyman Orchestra	Dance Orchestra	The Old Fashioned Revival Hour	Hobby Lobby
7:45				
8pm	Music			I Want a Divorce
8:15				Cabbages and Kings
8:30		Henry King Orchestra	The Sons of the Pioneers	One Man's Family
8:45				
9pm		Public Affairs	News	The Night Editor
9:15			George Fischer, gossip	Music
9:30		Tommy Dorsey Orchestra	Old Letters	Public Affairs
9:45				Music
10pm	Phil-Harmonia	The Times World News	Carl Ravazza Orchestra	The Richfield Reporter
10:15		Thanks for the Memory	The Playboys	Bridge to Dreamland
10:30			Dance Orchestra	
10:45		Dance Orchestra		

EVENING — SUMMER, 1938

Monday

BLUE	CBS	MBS	NBC	
America's Rhythm	The Mercury Theater on the Air	Bob Crosby Orchestra	The Fight Program	5pm
				5:15
		The Baseball Coach	The Grant Park Concerts	5:30
		Fulton Lewis, Jr., news		5:45
True or False	Lady Esther Serenade	Popeye, the Sailor	The Carnation Contented Hour	6pm
		The Phantom Pilot Patrol		6:15
The National Radio Forum	Music	Frank Bull, sports	Burns and Allen	6:30
	American Viewpoints	Howie Wing		6:45
The Sons of Lone Star	Henry Busse Orchestra	The Career Builders	Amos 'n' Andy	7pm
Gentlemen Preferred			Uncle Ezra's Radio Station	7:15
Music	Pick and Pat	The Lone Ranger	The Voice of Firestone	7:30
				7:45
Hollywood Speaks	The Monday Night Show, Henny Youngman	Public Affairs	The Passing Parade	8pm
Music		Music		8:15
	Dick Jurgens Orchestra	The Townsend Plan	Vox Pop	8:30
Albert Bergman, legal talk		The Sons of the Pioneers		8:45
Frank Trombar Orchestra	Let's Celebrate	News	Hawthorne House	9pm
The University Explorer	Bob Grant Orchestra	Music		9:15
Ricardo and His Caballeros	The Camera Club	Lobblies	Leo Reisman Orchestra	9:30
	Whispering Jack Smith, songs		The Steinie Bottle Boys	9:45
Phil-Harmonia	The Times World News	Dance Orchestra	The Richfield Reporter	10pm
	White Fires of Inspiration		Sports	10:15
		Anson Weeks Orchestra	Music	10:30
	Tommy Dorsey Orchestra			10:45

EVENING — SUMMER, 1938

Tuesday

	BLUE	CBS	MBS	NBC
5pm	Now and Then with Frank	Maurice Winnick Orchestra	The Grant Park Concerts	Organ Recital
5:15	Sports			
5:30	Jamboree	Benny Goodman's Swing School	The Baseball Coach	Attorney at Law
5:45			Fulton Lewis, Jr., news	
6pm		James Melton Orchestra	John B. Hughes, news	Believe It or Not
6:15		Jack Meskin Orchestra	The Phantom Pilot Patrol	
6:30	Our Own Music	The Grant Park Concerts	Frank Bull, sports	Jimmy Fidler, gossip
6:45			Howie Wing	Public Affairs
7pm	The Sons of Lone Star	Music	The Right Job	Amos 'n' Andy
7:15	Between the Lines	Screenscoops	The Inside of Sports	Vocal Varieties
7:30	Music	Music	The Green Hornet	Johnny Presents
7:45				
8pm	Erskine Hawkins Orchestra	Fiesta	Public Affairs	King's Cowboy Revue
8:15		Let's Celebrate	Don"t You Believe It	Dance Orchestra
8:30	Leo Reisman Orchestra	Pete Long Orchestra	The Summer School Concert	Sittin' with Sweeten
8:45				
9pm	Charlie Barnet Orchestra	Sports	News	Good Morning Tonight
9:15		Music	Music	
9:30	Glenn Miller Orchestra	Let's Celebrate	Say It With Words	The King's Jesters
9:45		Dick Jurgens Orchestra		Ho Hum
10pm	Phil-Harmonia	The Times World News	Skinnay Ennis Orchestra	The Richfield Reporter
10:15		Studio Party		Jan Garber Orchestra
10:30			Dance Orchestra	Dona Drake Orchestra
10:45		Tommy Dorsey Orchestra		

EVENING — SUMMER, 1938

Wednesday

BLUE	CBS	MBS	NBC	
It May Have Happened	Meet the Champ	Bob Crosby Orchestra	Tones	5pm
		Impressions	Charles Dillon, news	5:15
The National Music Camp	Organ Recital	The Baseball Coach	Virginia Flohri, songs	5:30
	History Behind the Headlines	Little Orphan Annie	Moving Stories of Life	5:45
	Rainbow's End	Popeye, the Sailor	Kay Kyser's College of Musical Knowledge	6pm
		The Phantom Pilot Patrol		6:15
The NBC Minstrels	Carthart and Wood, songs	Frank Bull, sports		6:30
		Howie Wing		6:45
The Sons of Lone Star	The Last Word	The Ed Lowry Show	Amos 'n' Andy	7pm
Boxing Bout	Farm Time		Uncle Ezra's Radio Station	7:15
	Chesterfield Presents	The Lone Ranger	Pull Over, Neighbor	7:30
				7:45
Dance Orchestra	Public Affairs	Music	Town Hall Varieties, Colonel Stoopnagle	8pm
				8:15
Bob Thompson Orchestra	Dance Orchestra	Anson Weeks Orchestra	The Raleigh and Kool Show	8:30
		The Sons of the Pioneers		8:45
Music		News	Dance Orchestra	9pm
		Public Affairs		9:15
		Music		9:30
		Joe Cunningham Orchestra		9:45
Phil-Harmonia	The Times World News	The Playboys	The Richfield Reporter	10pm
	On the Air	Dance Orchestra	Gentlemen Preferred	10:15
		Ted Lewis Orchestra	Bob Grant Orchestra	10:30
	Eddie Durant Orchestra		Larry Lewis, songs	10:45

EVENING — SUMMER, 1938

Thursday

	BLUE	CBS	MBS	NBC
5pm	Pulitzer Prize Plays	Major Bowes' Original Amateur Hour	Public Affairs	Promenade Symphony of Toronto
5:15				
5:30			The Baseball Coach	
5:45			Fulton Lewis, Jr., news	
6pm	People I Have Known	Essays in Music	Public Affairs	The Kraft Music Hall, Bob Burns
6:15			The Phantom Pilot Patrol	
6:30		Americans at Work	Frank Bull, sports	
6:45			Howie Wing	
7pm	The Sons of Lone Star	Music	Music	Amos 'n' Andy
7:15	Elza Schallert Interviews	Screenscoops	The Inside of Sports	Detective Stories
7:30	The California Safety Council	Music	The Green Hornet	Parents on Trial
7:45				
8pm	Bob Grant Orchestra	What is Radio	Public Affairs	King's Cowboy Revue
8:15		Music	Don't You Believe It	The Standard Symphony Hour
8:30	Jan Garber Orchestra	Calling All Cars	Dance Orchestra	
8:45			James Melton, songs	
9pm	Music	Music	News	
9:15		Interviews	Dance Orchestra	Meet Some People
9:30		Dick Jurgens Orchestra	Press Time	
9:45				The Steinie Bottle Boys
10pm	Phil-Harmonia	The Times World News	Dance Orchestra	The Richfield Reporter
10:15		Hatch Sketchbook		The King's Jesters
10:30				Joe Reissman Orchestra
10:45		Jimmy Dorsey Orchestra	Tne Hawaiians	

EVENING — SUMMER, 1938

Friday

BLUE	CBS	MBS	NBC	
Gladys Swartout, songs	Hollywood Showcase	Jimmy Grier Orchestra	Music	5pm
			Know Your Schools	5:15
Armand Girard, songs		The Baseball Coach	The March of Time	5:30
You and Your Government		Fulton Lewis, Jr., news		5:45
Editorial	Edwin Franko Goldman Band	Popeye, the Sailor	The First Nighter Program	6pm
Music		The Phantom Pilot Patrol		6:15
The Grant Park Concerts	Barry Woods, songs	Curtain Time	Jimmy Fidler, gossip	6:30
	American Viewpoints		Jesse Crawford, organ	6:45
The Sons of Lone Star	Henry Busse Orchestra	Dance Orchestra	Amos 'n' Andy	7pm
Motordom		Dr. Polyzoides, health	Uncle Ezra's Radio Station	7:15
Music	Dance Orchestra	The Lone Ranger	The Inglewood Park Concert	7:30
				7:45
The March of Progress	Dance Orchestra	Neutral Thousands	Death Valley Days	8pm
Music	Let's Celebrate			8:15
	Baker's Brain Teasers	Freddy Nagel Orchestra	The Royal Crown Revue, Tim and Irene	8:30
Nick Harris		The Sons of the Pioneers		8:45
Music	Dick Jurgens Orchestra	News	The Gilmore Circus	9pm
		Dance Orchestra		9:15
	Music		Weather or Not	9:30
	Whispering Jack Smith, songs		Jan Garber Orchestra	9:45
Phil-Harmonia	The Times World News	Jimmy Grier Orchestra	The Richfield Reporter	10pm
	The Art of Conversation		The King's Jesters	10:15
		Sterling Young Orchestra		10:30
	Henry King Orchestra		The Fiddler's Three	10:45

EVENING — SUMMER, 1938

Saturday

	BLUE	CBS	MBS	NBC
5pm	Jan Garber Orchestra	Maurice Winnick Orchestra	The Robin Hood Dell Concerts (4:30PM)	America Dances
5:15				
5:30	The Three Pals			
5:45	Glenn Hurlburt, news	Rhythm		
6pm	Recollections	Your Hit Parade	John B. Hughes, news	Crickets
6:15			Frank Bull, sports	
6:30			The River King	Music
6:45		American Viewpoints		
7pm	Music	Dance Orchestra	Jimmy Grier Orchestra	The National Barn Dance
7:15			The Inside of Sports	
7:30	Dance Orchestra	Johnny Orchestra	Russ Carlson Orchestra	
7:45				
8pm	Jack Hawkins Orchestra	Professor Quiz	Rancho Grande	Dance Orchestra
8:15				
8:30	Joe Reissman Orchestra	Plantation Party		
8:45				
9pm	Sittin' with Sweeten	Dan Jurgens Orchestra	News	The Voice of Hawaii
9:15			Dance Orchestra	Between Us
9:30	The King's Jesters	Music		Dance Orchestra
9:45				
10pm	Phil-Harmonia	Bob Grant Orchestra		Joe Sudy Orchestra
10:15				
10:30		Billy Mozet Orchestra		Frank Trombar Orchestra
10:45				

DAYTIME — SUMMER, 1938

Sunday

	BLUE	CBS	MBS	NBC
8am	Sacred Concert	Major Bowes' Capitol Family	The Comics Weekly Man	The Silver Strings
8:15	The Church Quarter-Hour			
8:30	The Radio City Music Hall	The Salt Lake Tabernacle Choir	Strings	Walter Logan's Musicale
8:45				
9am		The CBS Church of the Air	The Voice of Prophecy	Shakesphere's England
9:15				
9:30	Way Down Home	Europe Calling	Men with Wings	Glenn Darwin, songs
9:45		Poet's Gold		
10am	The Magic Key of RCA	Walberg Brown Strings	The Lamplighter	Sunday Dinner at Aunt Fanny's
10:15			Romance of the Highways	
10:30		Summer Session	Handicraft Hobbies	Al Gayle Orchestra
10:45			News	Health Talk
11am	Star Gazing	Everybody's Music	Music	Sunday Drivers
11:15	Dance Orchestra			
11:30	Songs			Melody
11:45	Garden Talk			
12pm	National Vespers	The Farmer Takes a Wife	Benay Venuta's Variety Program	Divin' Wen Yacht
12:15				
12:30	Looks at Books	The Toronto Glee Concerts		The World is Yours
12:45	Nola Day, songs			
1pm	There Was a Woman	America's Music	Dance Orchestra	Ry-Krisp Presents Marion Talley
1:15				
1:30	The Jean Sablonl Show	Oliver Drake, writing talk		The University of Chicago Round Table
1:45	The Master Builder	Organ Recital		

DAYTIME — SUMMER, 1938

Monday-Friday

BLUE	CBS	MBS	NBC	
Talk and Music	Talk and Music	Talk and Music	Talk / Vaughn de Leath, songs	8am
Music / The Kidoodlers Novelty Quartet	RFD #1, Irene Beasley		The O'Neills	8:15
The National Farm and Home Hour	The Romance of Helen Trent	The Haven of Rest	Talk and Music	8:30
	Our Gal Sunday			8:45
	The Goldbergs	The Happy Gang	Talk / The Mystery Chef	9am
	Vic and Sade	Music / Between the Bookends	Music / The Three Romeos	9:15
News	Talk and Music	Norma Young, talk	The Bridge Club	9:30
Talk and Music	Talk / Mary Lee Taylor, cooking	Talk		9:45
	Big Sister	A Woman's World	Betty and Bob	10am
	Aun Jenny's True Life Stories		Arnold Grimm's Daughter	10:15
	Music	Home Town	Valiant Lady	10:30
			Hymns of All Chjurches / Betty Crocker, cooking	10:45
Talk and Music	Talk and Music	Talk	The Story of Mary Marlin	11am
		Strings	Ma Perkins	11:15
	Scattergood Baines	Music	Pepper Young's Family	11:30
Stock Market Reports	Fletcher Wiley, talk	Paul Small, songs	The Guiding Light	11:45
US Agricultural Talk	The Story of Myrt and Marge	Norman Nesbitt, stories	Mary Noble, Backstage Wife	12pm
Club Matinee, Ranson Sherman	Pretty Kitty Kelly	Midstream	Stella Dallas	12:15
	Hilltop House		Hughesreel	12:30
	The Women's Forum	The Hatterfields	Dr. Kate	12:45
Talk and Music	Houseboat Hannah	Music	Tophatters Orchestra / The Martha Meade Society	1pm
Don Winslow of the Navy	The Road of Life	Country Editor	Ann Warner Chats	1:15
News	Kitty Keene, Inc.	Talk	Talk and Music	1:30
Talk and Music	Ma Perkins	The Johnson Family		1:45

DAYTIME — SUMMER, 1938

Sunday

	BLUE	CBS	MBS	NBC
2pm	The Catholic Hour	Strange As It Seems	Music	Music
2:15		Music		
2:30	The Canadian Grenadiers	The Laugh Liners		Joseph Gallichio Orchestra
2:45				It's a Fact
3pm	The Classic Hour	Phil Cook's Almanac	Help Thy Neighbor	Professor Puzzlewit
3:15				
3:30	Budding Talent	The CBS Church of the Air		Interesting Neighbors
3:45			Music	
4pm	Spy at Large	World Dances		The Chase and Sanborn Hour
4:15				
4:30	Songs We Remember	The Lewisohn Stadium Concerts		
4:45				

DAYTIME — SUMMER, 1938

Monday-Friday

BLUE	CBS	MBS	NBC	
	Music	Talk and Music	Talk and Music	*2pm*
The Classic Hour	The Catalina Islander		Candid Lady	*2:15*
	Talk and Music		Women's Magazine of the Air	*2:30*
				2:45
Music	Music / The Heart of Julia Blake	Feminine Fancies	Talk / Easy Aces	*3pm*
	Talk and Music		Talk / Mr. Keen, Tracer of Lost Persons	*3:15*
		Talk and Music	Talk and Music	*3:30*
				3:45
News	Fletcher Wiley, talk		Talk and Music / The Royal Gelatin Hour, Rudy Vallee /	*4pm*
Music				*4:15*
Music / Information, Please	Talk and Music / Charlie Chan		Talk / Those We Love	*4:30*
	Boake Carter, news			*4:45*

DAYTIME — SUMMER, 1938

Saturday

	BLUE	CBS	MBS	NBC
8am	Call to Youth	The Columbia Concert Hall	This Wonderful World	The Music Guild
8:15	The Church Quarter-Hour		Corn Time	
8:30	The National Farm and Home Hour			News
8:45		Federal Housing Authority Talk	Elinor Sherry, songs	Along Gypsy Trails
9am		Enoch Light Orchestra	Meet a Friend	County Medical Association Talks
9:15			Our Quartette	
9:30	News	The Federation of Women's Clubs	The Coach Club	Words and Music
9:45	Ray Kinney Orchestra	The Monitor Children's Program		
10am	Rex Maupin Orchestra	Madison Ensemble	Spotlight Revue	Your Host is Buffalo
10:15				
10:30	Judy and Lanny, songs	Prosperity		Music Internationale
10:45	Dance Orchestra			
11am	Music	Romany Trails	Music	Golden Melodies
11:15		Merrymakers Orchestra		
11:30	Richardo and His Caballeros	The All-Year Club		Swing
11:45		News		
12pm	Club Matinee, Ransom Sherman	Sports		The Stamp Club
12:15		Music		Men of the West
12:30				Allen Roth Orchestra
12:45				
1pm	The Beaux Arts Trio	Syncopation Piece	Dance Orchestra	Tophatters Orchestra
1:15				
1:30	The Classic Hour	Dancepators Orchestra		The Kidoodlers Novelty Quartet
1:45				Commander Hawkes

DAYTIME — SUMMER, 1938

Saturday

	BLUE	CBS	MBS	NBC
2pm		Sports	News	Sports
2:15		Music	Schemes	
2:30			American Legion News	News
2:45		News		The Art of Living
3pm	Message of Israel	The Columbia Workshop	Music	Richard Himber Orchestra
3:15				
3:30	Music	Music		Joe Reissman Orchestra
3:45				
4pm	International Dance	The Saturday Night Swing Club	Bands Across the Sea	Kaltnemeyer's Kindegarten
4:15				
4:30	Original Dramas	Harmony	The Robin Hood Dell Concerts	Safety First
4:45				Barry McKinley, songs

EVENING — FALL, 1938

Sunday

	BLUE	CBS	MBS	NBC
5pm	Out of the West	The Mercury Theater on the Air	The Bach Cantata Series	The Chase and Sanborn Hour
5:15				
5:30			Say It With Words	
5:45				
6pm	Buddy Maleville Orchestra	The Ford Sunday Evening Hour	The Old Fashioned Revival Hour	The Manhattan Merry-Go-Round
6:15				
6:30	The Reader's Guide			The American Album of Familiar Music
6:45	Spaulding Orchestra			
7pm	Horace Heidt Orchestra	Public Affairs	The Goodwill Hour	Carefree Carnvial
7:15				
7:30	Cheerio's Musical Mosaics	I Want A Divorce		The Hollywood Playhouse
7:45		The Night Editor		
8pm	The Chapel Quartet	Ben Bernie, the Old Maestro	The Shadow	Walter Winchell's Jergens Journal
8:15	Johnny Messner Orchestra			Irene Rich Dramas
8:30	Lou Breeze Orchestra	Pendarvis Orchestra	The Sons of the Pioneers	The Jello Program, Jack Benny
8:45			Chicco Orchestra	
9pm	Freddy Martin Orchestra	Lady Esther Sernade	News	Sunday Evening's at Seth Parkers
9:15			World Affairs	
9:30	Dance Orchestra	Sallie Orchestra	Ted Fiorito Orchestra	One Man's Family
9:45	The University Explorer			
10pm	Phil-Harmonia	The Ten o'Clock Wire	Dance Orchestra	The Richfield Reporter
10:15		Thanks for the Memory		Bridge to Dreamland
10:30				
10:45		Dance Orchestra		

EVENING — FALL, 1938

Monday

BLUE	CBS	MBS	NBC	
The Cole Jesters	Maurice Winnick Orchestra	Johnny Murray, songs	Carson Robison's Buckaroos	*5pm*
News	Howie Wing	Contrasts		5:15
Sports	Tea for Two	Dick Tracy	Those We Love	5:30
Ricardo and His Caballeros	Boake Carter, news	Little Orphan Annie		5:45
The Hour of Charm	The Lux Radio Theater	Jack Armstrong, The All-American Boy	Public Affairs	*6pm*
		The Phantom Pilot Patrol		6:15
Grandfather Clock		The Tinkle Toy Band	Eddy Duchin Orchestra	6:30
Cheers		Frank Bull, sports		6:45
True or False	Guy Lombardo Orchestra	Strings	The Carnation Contented Hour	*7pm*
		The Sons of the Pioneers		7:15
The National Radio Forum	The Camel Caravan, Eddie Cantor	The Lone Ranger	Al Pearce and His Gang	7:30
				7:45
Ricardo and His Caballeros	Sam Hayes, sports	The Marines Tell it to You	Amos 'n' Andy	*8pm*
Hollywood Speaks	Lum and Abner	The Townsend Plan	Edwin C. Hill, news	8:15
The University Explorer	Pick and Pat	Chicco Orchestra	The Voice of Firestone	8:30
Albert Bergman, legal talk				8:45
Joe Sudy Orchestra	The Grouch Club	News	Hawthorne House	*9pm*
		Dick Barrie Orchestra		9:15
Dance Orchestra	The Camera Club	Candid Camera	Battle of the Sexes	9:30
	Public Affairs			9:45
Phil-Harmonia	The Ten o'Clock Wire		The Richfield Reporter	*10pm*
	Whte Fires of Inspiration		Dance Orchestra	10:15
		Dance Orchestra		10:30
	Dance Orchestra			10:45

EVENING — FALL, 1938

Tuesday

	BLUE	CBS	MBS	NBC
5pm	Silhouettes	Songs	Jimmy and Gyp, songs	Charles Dillon, songs
5:15	News	Howie Wing	Music	Virginia Fiorhi, songs
5:30	Infomation, Please	Dick Aurandt Orchestra	Dick Tracy	Sweeten Swing
5:45		Boake Carter, news	Little Orphan Annie	
6pm	Who Sang It	We, the People	Jack Armstong, the All-American Boys	Pull Over, Neighbor
6:15			News Dramas	
6:30	Jamboree	Benny Goodman's Swing School	Violin	Fibber McGee and Molly
6:45			Chicco Orchestra	
7pm		Dr. Christian	A Woman's Diary	The Pepsodent Show, Bob Hope
7:15			The Inside of Sports	
7:30	Between the LInes	Maxine, songs	The Green Hornet	Jimmy Fidler, gossip
7:45	The State of the Nation	American Viewpoints		Uncle Ezra's Radio Station
8pm	Eddie Rogers Orchetra	Charles Baum Orchestra	The Philistine	Amos 'n' Andy
8:15	Man Bites Dog	The Farmer's Market	Don't You Believe It	Vocal Vareites
8:30	Nick Harris	Big Town	Salute to the Cities	Johnny Presents
8:45	Novak Orchestra			
9pm	Hollywood Speaks	The Lifebouy Program, Al Jolson	News	Good Morning Tonight
9:15	Radio Logic		Herbie Kay Orchestra	
9:30	The Music Parade	Screenscoops	The Devil's Scrapbook	Stars Tonight
9:45	The University Explorer	Music		Detective Story
10pm	Phil-Harmonia	The Ten o'Clock Wire	Meditations	The Richfield Reporter
10:15		In Town Tonight	Dance Orchestra	Ho Hum
10:30				Dance Orchestra
10:45		Dance Orchestra		

EVENING — FALL, 1938

Wednesday

BLUE	CBS	MBS	NBC	
The Roy Shields Revue	Tea for Two	Johnny Murray, songs	Contrasts	5pm
News	Howie Wing	Cincinatti Music	Moving Stories of Life	5:15
Gladys Swartout, songs	Rainbow End	Dick Tracy	Hobby Lobby	5:30
	Boake Carter, news	Little Orphan Annie		5:45
Now and Then	Columbia Symphony Orchestra	Jack Armstrong, the All-American Boys	Organ Recital	6pm
		The Phantom Pilot Patrol	Sweeten Swing	6:15
The Music Festival	The Texaco Star Theater	The Tinkle Toy Band	Public Affairs	6:30
		Frank Bull, sports		6:45
Magnolia Blossoms		Famous Jury Trials	Kay Kyser's College of Musical Knowledge	7pm
				7:15
The NBC Minstrels	The Ask-It Basket	The Lone Ranger		7:30
				7:45
Aviation	Sam Hayes, sports	Dick Tracy	Amos 'n' Andy	8pm
High School Rally	Lum and Abner	Johnny Keating Orchestra	Edwin C. Hill, news	8:15
Music	Chesterfield Presents	Jimmy Dorsey Orchestra	The Raleigh and Kool Show	8:30
				8:45
Larry Clinton Orchestra	Gangbusters	News	Town Hall Tomight, Fred Allen	9pm
		The Playboys		9:15
Parents on Trial	Public Affairs	Skinnay Ennis Orchestra		9:30
		Joe Cunningham Orchestra		9:45
Phil-Harmonia	The Ten o'Clock Wire	Dance Orchestra	The Richfield Reporter	10pm
	On the Air		The Hot Stove League	10:15
				10:30
	Dance Orchestra		Dance Orchestra	10:45

EVENING — FALL, 1938

Thursday

	BLUE	CBS	MBS	NBC
5pm	Reserve	News	Jimmy and Gyp, songs	The Royal Gelatin Hour, Rudy Vallee
5:15	News	Howie Wing	Morton Gould Orchestra	
5:30	The Eastman School of Music	The Joe Penner Show	Dick Tracy	
5:45			Little Orphan Annie	
6pm		Major Bowes' Original Amateur Hour	Jack Armstong, the All-American Boy	Good News of 1939
6:15	Dr. Harlian Barrows, talk		News	
6:30	Music		We Want a Touchdown	
6:45				
7pm	People I Have Known	Public Affairs	Melody	The Kraft Music Hall, Bing Crosby
7:15			The Inside of Sports	
7:30		Americans at Work	The Green Hornet	
7:45				
8pm	The California Safety Council	Baker's Brain Teasers	The Philistine	Amos 'n' Andy
8:15	Music		Don't You Believe It	The Standard Symphony Hour
8:30	Cleary Gillium, songs	The Kate Smith Hour	Don Wilkie, songs	
8:45			Music	
9pm			News	
9:15	The Voice of Hawaii		Dance Orchestra	Vocal Varieties
9:30	Freddy Martin Orchestra	Let's Celebrate		Ed Dooley, sports
9:45	The University Explorer	Nat Brandwynne Orchestra		Stars Tonight
10pm	Phil-Harmonia	The Ten o'Clock Wire	Meditations	The Richfield Reporter
10:15		The Art of Conversation	Dance Orchestra	Dance Orchestra
10:30				
10:45		Dance Orchestra		

EVENING — FALL, 1938

Friday

BLUE	CBS	MBS	NBC	
Reserve	Chiquito, songs	Johnny Murray, songs	Criminal Case Histories with Warden Lawes	5pm
News	Howie Wing	Sinfonietta		5:15
If I Had a Chance	Tea for Two	Dick Tracy	Know Your Schools	5:30
	Boake Carter, news	Little Orphan Annie	The US Army Band	5:45
Paul Martin Orchestra	Hollywood Hotel	Jack Armstrong, the All-American Boy	Public Affairs	6pm
		The Phantom Pilot Patrol	James Melton, songs	6:15
Melody		Dad and Junior	The March of Time	6:30
		Frank Bull, sports		6:45
Motordom	Grand Central Station	Curtain Time	Lady Esther Serenade	7pm
Music				7:15
Norman Sper, sports	Calling All Cars	The Lone Ranger	Jimmy Fidler, gossip	7:30
The State of the Nation			Public Affairs	7:45
Al Donahue Orchestra	Sam Hayes, sports	Public Affairs	Amos 'n' Andy	8pm
High School Rally	Lum and Abner	Chicco Orchestra	Cabbages and Kings	8:15
Waltz	Burns and Allen	California Caravan	Death Valley Days	8:30
				8:45
The Community Chest	The First Nighter Program	News	The Gilmore Circus	9pm
Dance Orchestra		The Playboys		9:15
Novak Orchestra	The Wonder Show, Jack Haley	Bob Crosby Orchestra	The Inglewood Park Concert	9:30
				9:45
Phil-Harmonia	The Ten o'Clock Wire	Dance Orchestra	The Richfield Reporter	10pm
	I Was There		The Night Editor	10:15
			Dance Orchestra	10:30
	Dance Orchestra			10:45

EVENING — FALL, 1938

Saturday

	BLUE	CBS	MBS	NBC
5pm	News and Views	The Fifth Quarter	Music	Tommy Riggs and Betty Lou
5:15				
5:30	Original Dramas	Tunesmiths		Will Aubrey, news
5:45				Ed Dooley, sports
6pm	Joe Sudy Orchestra	Men Against Death	Hawaii Calls	Public Affairs
6:15				Strings
6:30	Tomorrow's Stars	The Pet Milk Program	George Fisher, gossip	Dances
6:45			The Playboys	King's Cowboy Revue
7pm	NBC Symphony Orchestra	Your Hit Parade	John Conte, news	America Dances
7:15			The Inside of Sports	
7:30			Minstrels	
7:45		The Juvenile Revue		
8pm		The Joe E. Brown Show	The Hollywood Barn Dance	The National Barn Dancet
8:15				
8:30		Johnny Presents		
8:45				
9pm	Larry Clinton Orchestra	Professor Quiz	News	Fred Waring Orchestra
9:15	The Voice of Hawaii		Dance Orchestra	
9:30	Dance Orchestra	Dance Orchestra		Avalon Variety Time, Red Foley
9:45				
10pm	Phil-Harmonia	Dance Orchestra		Dance Orchestra
10:15				
10:30				
10:45				

DAYTIME — FALL, 1938

Sunday

	BLUE	CBS	MBS	NBC
8am	Alice Remson, songs	The West Coast Church	The Comics Weekly Man	The Pine Tavern
8:15	Neighbor Nell			
8:30	The Church Quarter-Hour	Major Bowes' Capitol Family	Los Cumhancheros	Health Talk
8:45	Southern Airs		Food for Thought	Songs
9am	The Radio City Music Hall		The Voice of Prophecy	Dr. Casselbury, health
9:15				It Happened So Quick
9:30		The Salt Lake Tabernable Choir	The Lamplighter	The University of Chicago Round Table
9:45			Touchdown Topics	
10am	Nick Harris	The CBS Church of the Air	Organ Recital	Meridian Music
10:15	Garden Talk		Romance of the Highways	
10:30	Security Steps	Europe Calling	Men with Wings	Benny Rubinoff, violin
10:45		Romany Trails		Bob Becker's Dog Talks
11am	The Magic Key of RCA	Walberg Brown Strings	Psychiana	Sunday Dinner at Aunt Fanny's
11:15			Music	
11:30		Farm Time		The Kidoodlers Novelty Quartet
11:45				Olympic Talk
12pm	Star Gazing	New York Philharmonic Orchestra	On a Sunday Afternoon	Sunday Drivers
12:15	Looks at Books			
12:30	Second Guessers		News	Ranger's Serenade
12:45			Reminiscing	
1pm	National Vespers		Benay Venuta's Variety Program	Music / Public Affairs
1:15				

DAYTIME — FALL, 1938

Monday-Friday

BLUE	CBS	MBS	NBC	
The Church Quarter-Hour	Talk and Music	Financial Service	Musical Clock	8am
Sweethearts		Georgia Crackers	Talk	8:15
The Story of Mo	Brown Berman	The Haven of Rest	News	8:30
Music / The Jingletown Gazette	Sally of Star		Music / The Morin Sisters, songs	8:45
Talk and Music	Music / Mary Margaret McBride, talk	Talk and Music	Dan Harding's Wife	9am
	Her Honor, Nancy James		The O'Neills	9:15
The National Farm and Home Hour	The Romance of Helen Trent	Norma Young, talk	The Bridge Club	9:30
	Our Gal Sunday	Music		9:45
	The Goldbergs	Matinee	Talk and Music / The Mystery Chef	10am
Talk and Music	Vic and Sade		Let's Talk It Over / Ann Warner Chats	10:15
	Music / Ben Sweetland, comment	Talk and Music	Dangerous Roads	10:30
	Yours Sincerely	Talk and Music / The Voice of Experience	Dr. Kate	10:45
Talk and Music / The Standard School Broadcast	Big Sister	Hometown	Betty and Bob	11am
	Aunt Jenny's True Life Stories	Music / As You Like It	Arnold Grimm's Daughter	11:15
Stock Market Reports	The American School of the Air	Music	Valiant Lady	11:30
The National Farm and Home Hour			Hymns of All Churches / Betty Crocker, cooking	11:45
US Agricultural Talk	Talk and Music / Mary Lee Taylor, cooking	Norman Nesbitt, stories	The Story of Mary Marlin	12pm
Music	Fletcher Wiley, talk	Talk and Music	Ma Perkins	12:15
	Scattergood Baines		Pepper Young's Family	12:30
Between the Bookends	Music		The Guiding Light	12:45
Talk	Pretty Kitty Kelly	Talk	Mary Noble, Backstage Wife	1pm
Club Matinee, Ransom Sherman	The Story of Myrt and Marge	Midstream	Stella Dallas	1:15

DAYTIME — FALL, 1938

Sunday

	BLUE	CBS	MBS	NBC
1:30	The World is Yours		The Lutheran Hour	The Court of Human Relations
1:45				
2pm	The Metropolitan Opera Auditions	Strange As It Seems	The Musical Steelmakers	Uncle Ezra's Radio Station
2:15		Buddy Clark's Musical Weekly		Donald Novis, songs
2:30	Vincent Gomez, songs	Back Home	The Nation's Playhouse	Public Affairs
2:45	The Master Builder			
3pm	The Catholic Hour	The Silver Theater	Help Thy Neighbor	Broadway Memories
3:15				
3:30	Music	The Laugh Liners	The Show of the Week	Joseph Gallichio Orchestra
3:45				It's a Fact
4pm	The Other Americas	The People's Platform	Rabbi Magnin, religion	Professor Puzzlewit
4:15			Dick Jurgens Orchestra	
4:30	Organ Recital	Song at Twilight	Dick Barrie Orchestra	The Fitch Bandwagon
4:45				

DAYTIME — FALL, 1938

Monday-Friday

BLUE	CBS	MBS	NBC	
Talk	Hilltop House	Music	Talk and Music	1:30
The Classic Hour	Talk and Music	The Hatterfields	Girl Alone	1:45
	The Women's Forum	Talk and Music	Houseboat Hannah	2pm
	Talk and Music	The Johnson Family	Music	2:15
	The Road of Life	Talk and Music		2:30
	Kitty Keene, Inc.		Art Baker's Notebook	2:45
Talk and Music	Ma Perkins	Feminine Fancies		3pm
	Music / The Heart of Julia Blake		Candid Lady	3:15
	Talk and Music	Talk and Music	Women's Magazine of the Air	3:30
Nola Day, songs / Father and Son				3:45
Talk and Music	Fletcher Wiley, talk	Fulton Lewis, Jr., news	Talk and Music / Easy Aces	4pm
		News	Talk and Music / Mr. Keen, Tracer of Lost Persons	4:15
	Talk and Music	Talk and Music	Talk and Music	4:30
			News	4:45

DAYTIME — FALL, 1938

Saturday

	BLUE	CBS	MBS	NBC
8am	The Church Quarter-Hour	Cincinatti Conservatory Symphony	Financial Service	No School Today
8:15	The Radio City Four		The California Board of Education	News
8:30	Our Barn		The US Army Band	Music for You
8:45				
9am	News	Federal Housing Authority Talk	This Wonderful World	Public Affairs
9:15	Carol Weymann, songs	Music	Collegiate Review	
9:30	The National Farm and Home Hour		Music	Call to Youth
9:45		The Monitor Children's Program	The Gloomchasers	Along Gypsy Trails
10am		The Federation of Women's Clubs	Matinee	See Saw
10:15		Football Souvenir		
10:30	Music	Spprts	The Gloomchasers	Campus Capers
10:45	Sports		Meet a Friend	Sports
11am			Sports	
11:15				
11:30				
11:45				
12pm				
12:15				
12:30				
12:45				
1pm				
1:15				
1:30				
1:45				

DAYTIME — FALL, 1938

Saturday

	BLUE	CBS	MBS	NBC
2pm				
2:15				
2:30				
2:45				
3pm	The Classic Hour			Revue
3:15				
3:30	Dance Orchestra			Strings
3:45				The Art of Living
4pm	Message of Israel			Richard Himber Orchestra
4:15				
4:30	Don Ricardo Orchestra	Organ Recital		
4:45				The Lives of Great Men

LISTINGS FOR 1939

EVENING — WINTER, 1939

Sunday

	BLUE	CBS	MBS	NBC
5pm	Out of the West	This is New York	The American Forum of the Air	The Chase and Sanborn Hour
5:15				
5:30	Dance Orchestra			
5:45				
6pm	The Hollywood Playhouse	The Ford Sunday Evening Hour	The Old Fashioned Revival Hour	The Manhattan Merry-Go-Round
6:15				
6:30	The Reader's Guide			The American Album of Familiar Music
6:45	The Three Cheers			
7pm	Dance Orchestra	The Old Gold Program, Robert Benchley	The Goodwill Hour	The Circle
7:15				
7:30	Cheerio's Musical Mosaics	The Los Angeles Hour		
7:45		Bert Lytell, songs		
8pm	Music	The People's Platform	The Sons of the Pioneers	Walter Winchell's Jergens Journal
8:15			Dr. Polyzoides	Irene Rich Dramas
8:30		Ted Fiorito Orchestra	Faith Music	The Jello Program, Jack Benny
8:45				
9pm	Dance Orchestra	Ben Bernie, the Old Maestro	News	Sunday Evening's at Seth Parkers
9:15			Frank Watanabe and Honorable Archie	
9:30	Herbie Kay Orchestra	Harry Owens Orchestra	Ted Fiorito Orchestra	One Man's Family
9:45	The University Explorer	John B. Hughes, news		
10pm	Phil-Harmonia	Ladies and Gentlemen of the Turf	Jack Harris Orchestra	The Richfield Reporter
10:15				Bridge to Dreamland
10:30			Jimmy Grier Orchestra	
10:45		Dance Orchestra		

EVENING — WINTER, 1939

Monday

BLUE	CBS	MBS	NBC	
Music	News and Sports	Johnny Murray, songs	Carson Robison's Buckaroos	5pm
News	Howie Wing	Contrasts		5:15
Sports	News	Dick Tracy	Those We Love	5:30
Vignettes	Music	Little Orphan Annie		5:45
The Budd Hulick Show	The Lux Radio Theater	Jack Armstrong, The All-American Boy	The Hour of Charm	6pm
		The Phantom Pilot Patrol		6:15
Public Affairs		Dorothy Gordon, songs	Eddy Duchin Orchestra	6:30
The Two Westminster College Choirs		Frank Bull, sports		6:45
True or False	Guy Lombardo Orchestra	Tom Sawyer, comment	The Carnation Contented Hour	7pm
		Music		7:15
The National Radio Forum	The Camel Caravan, Eddie Cantor	The Lone Ranger	Al Pearce and His Gang	7:30
				7:45
Twing Orchestra	Sam Hayes, sports	The Marines Tell it to You	Amos 'n' Andy	8pm
	Lum and Abner		Edwin C. Hill, news	8:15
The University Explorer	Pick and Pat	The Listener Theater	The Voice of Firestone	8:30
Albert Bergman, legal talk				8:45
Freddy Martin Orchestra	The Cavalcade of America	News	Hawthorne House	9pm
		Frank Watanabe and Honorable Archie		9:15
Know Your Schools	Sophie Tucker, songs	Tic-Tac-Toe	Battle of the Sexes	9:30
Ricardo and His Caballeros	John B. Hughes, news	Music		9:45
Phil-Harmonia	The Camera Club	The Devil's Scrapbook	The Richfield Reporter	10pm
	Night Cap Yarns		Ernie Fields Orchestra	10:15
	Mary L. Cook, songs	Malendo and His Tango Orchestra	Joe Sudy Orchestra	10:30
	Clyde McCoy Orchestra			10:45

EVENING — WINTER, 1939

Tuesday

	BLUE	CBS	MBS	NBC
5pm	Gilbert and Sullivan Music	News and Sports	The Airliners	Charles Dillon, songs
5:15	News	Howie Wing	Shafter Parker, comment	Virginia Fiorhi, songs
5:30	Cheers	Dick Aurandt Orchestra	Dick Tracy	Information, Please
5:45	Richardo and His Caballeros	News	Little Orphan Annie	
6pm	What's the Big Idea	We, the People	Jack Armstong, the All-American Boys	Pull Over, Neighbor
6:15			News Dramas	
6:30	Music	Benny Goodman's Swing School	Music	Fibber McGee and Molly
6:45				
7pm	If I Had a Chance	Dr. Christian	A Woman's Diary	The Pepsodent Show, Bob Hope
7:15			The Inside of Sports	
7:30	The Sons of Lone Star	Jimmy Fidler, gossip	The Green Hornet	Uncle Ezra's Radio Station
7:45		American Viewpoints		Music
8pm	Dance Orchetra	The Farmer's Market	Music	Amos 'n' Andy
8:15	Nick Harris	Charles Baum Orchestra	Don't You Believe It	Vocal Vareites
8:30	Music	Big Town	Salute to the Cities	Johnny Presents
8:45				
9pm	Joe Sudy Orchestra	The Lifebouy Program, Al Jolson	News	Good Morning Tonight
9:15			Frank Watanabe and Honorable Archie	
9:30	Radio Logic	The Grouch Club	Mysteries of Life	Carefree Carnival
9:45	The University Explorer		Skinnay Ennis Orchestra	
10pm	Phil-Harmonia	The Ten o'Clock Wire	Jack Harris Orchestra	The Richfield Reporter
10:15		Night Cap Yarns		Ho Hum
10:30		Harry Owens Orchestra	Jimmy Grier Orchestra	Ernie Fields Orchestra
10:45		Clyde McCoy Orchestra		

EVENING — WINTER, 1939

Wednesday

BLUE	CBS	MBS	NBC	
The Roy Shields Revue	Tea for Two	Johnny Murray, songs	Robert Hurd, news	*5pm*
News	Howie Wing	Shafter Parker, comment	Moving Stories of Life	*5:15*
Gladys Swartout, songs	Clark Ross, songs	Dick Tracy	Hobby Lobby	*5:30*
Editorial	News	Little Orphan Annie		*5:45*
Magnolia Blossoms	The Texaco Star Theater	Jack Armstrong, the All-American Boys	Meet Some People	*6pm*
Between the Lines		The Phantom Pilot Patrol	The Music Parade	*6:15*
Wings for the Martin		Helene Daniels, songs	Music	*6:30*
		Frank Bull, sports		*6:45*
People I Have Known	The Los Angeles Hour	Famous Jury Trials	Kay Kyser's College of Musical Knowledge	*7pm*
	Rhapsody			*7:15*
Public Interest in Democracy	The Ask-It Basket	The Lone Ranger		*7:30*
				7:45
Grey Gordon Orchestra	Jimmy Hamilton Orchestra	Frost Warnings	Amos 'n' Andy	*8pm*
	Lum and Abner		Edwin C. Hill, news	*8:15*
Music	Chesterfield Presents	The Answer Game	The Raleigh and Kool Show	*8:30*
				8:45
Verne Osborne, songs	Gangbusters	News	Town Hall Tonight, Fred Allen	*9pm*
		Herbie Kay Orchestra		*9:15*
Parents on Trial	Sophie Tucker, songs	Clyde Lucas Orchestra		*9:30*
	John B. Hughes, news	Elias Breeskin, violin		*9:45*
Phil-Harmonia	Clyde McCoy Orchestra	Jack Harris Orchestra	The Richfield Reporter	*10pm*
	Night Cap Yarns		Baffa Orchestra	*10:15*
	Music	Jimmy Grier Orchestra	The Night Watchman	*10:30*
			Ernie Fields Orchestra	*10:45*

EVENING — WINTER, 1939

Thursday

	BLUE	CBS	MBS	NBC
5pm	The Parade of Progress in Foods	News and Sports	The Airliners	The Royal Gelatin Hour, Rudy Vallee
5:15		Howie Wing	Shafter Parker, comment	
5:30	The Eastman School of Music	The Joe Penner Show	Dick Tracy	
5:45			Little Orphan Annie	
6pm		Major Bowes' Original Amateur Hour	Jack Armstong, the All-American Boy	Good News of 1939
6:15			News	
6:30	America's Town Meeting of the Air		Music	
6:45				
7pm		Tune-Up Time	Tom Sawyer, comment	The Kraft Music Hall, Bing Crosby
7:15			The Inside of Sports	
7:30	The NBC Minstrels		The Green Hornet	
7:45		American Viewpoints		
8pm	The California Safety Council	The Inside Story	Music	Amos 'n' Andy
8:15	The March of Progress		Don't You Believe It	The Standard Symphony Hour
8:30	Music	The Kate Smith Hour	Russ Carlson Orchestra	
8:45			Jimmy Grier Orchestra	
9pm	It's A Curious World		News	
9:15	Shelley Orchestra		Music / Public Affairs	Music
9:30	Dance Orchestra	I Want a Divorce		The Music Parade
9:45	The University Explorer	Bert Lytell, songs		Stars Tonight
10pm	Phil-Harmonia	The Ten o'Clock Wire	Dance Orchestra	The Richfield Reporter
10:15		Night Cap Yarns		Ernie Fields Orchestra
10:30		Dance Orchestra		Baffa Orchestra
10:45				

EVENING — WINTER, 1939

Friday

BLUE	CBS	MBS	NBC	
Gladys Swartout, songs	Chiquito, songs	Johnny Murray, songs	Criminal Case Histories with Warden Lawes	5pm
News	Howie Wing	Shafter Parker, comment		5:15
Jamboree	Tea for Two	Dick Tracy	Know Your Schools	5:30
	News	Little Orphan Annie	The US Army Band	5:45
Paducah Plantation, Red Foley	The Campbell Playhouse	Jack Armstrong, the All-American Boy	You and Your Government	6pm
		The Phantom Pilot Patrol	The Music Parade	6:15
Youth Finds Itself		Dorothy Gordon, songs	Swing with Sweeten	6:30
		Frank Bull, sports		6:45
Motordom	Grand Central Station	Curtain Time	Lady Esther Serenade	7pm
Music				7:15
Horse and Buggy Days	Calling All Cars	The Lone Ranger	Uncle Ezra's Radio Station	7:30
			Jimmy Fidler, gossip	7:45
Music	Sam Hayes, sports	The Philstine	Amos 'n' Andy	8pm
Winter Snow Sports Talk	Lum and Abner	Music	Cabbages and Kings	8:15
Waltz	Burns and Allen		Death Valley Days	8:30
				8:45
Dance Orchestra	The First Nighter Program	News	The Gilmore Circus	9pm
		Nicol Smith, songs		9:15
	The Wonder Show, Jack Haley	The Round Towner	The Inglewood Park Concert	9:30
		Jan Garber Orchestra		9:45
Phil-Harmonia	Sophie Tucker, songs	Jack Harris Orchestra	The Richfield Reporter	10pm
	Night Cap Yarns		John Burton, songs	10:15
	Dance Orchestra	Jimmy Grier Orchestra	Herbie Kay Orchestra	10:30
	Clyde McCoy Orchestra			10:45

EVENING — WINTER, 1939

Saturday

	BLUE	CBS	MBS	NBC
5pm	Music	Sports Broadside	Jazz Nocturne	Tommy Riggs and Betty Lou
5:15				
5:30	Brent House	Bradford Orchestra	Symphonic Strings	Joe Sudy Orchestra
5:45				
6pm	Music	Honolulu Bound, Phil Baker	Hawaii Calls	Dinner Date
6:15				
6:30	The Hall of Fun	The Pet Milk Program	George Fisher, gossip	Rhythm
6:45			The Sons of the Pioneers	King's Cowboy Revue
7pm	NBC Symphony Orchestra	Your Hit Parade	Betty Rhodes, songs	Music
7:15			The Inside of Sports	
7:30			Larry Clinton Orchestra	
7:45		The Night Editor		
8pm		The Joe E. Brown Show	Frost Warning	The National Barn Dancet
8:15			Jimmy Dorsey Orchestra	
8:30	Lou Breeze Orchestra	Johnny Presents	Jimmy Grier Orchestra	
8:45				
9pm	Music	Professor Quiz	News	Fred Waring Orchestra
9:15			Glen Gray Orchestra	
9:30	Freddy Martin Orchestra	Bert Lytell, songs	John Conte, songs	Avalon Variety Time, Red Foley
9:45		John B. Hughes, news	Music	
10pm	Phil-Harmonia	The Los Angeles Hour	Jack Harris Orchestra	The Week in Review
10:15		Capitol Opinions		Joe Sudy Orchestra
10:30		Dance Orchestra	Clyde Lucas Orchestra	Dance Orchestra
10:45				

DAYTIME — WINTER, 1939

Sunday

	BLUE	CBS	MBS	NBC
8am	The Church Quarter-Hour	The West Coast Church	The Comics Weekly Man	Julio Oyanguren, guitar
8:15	Neighbor Nell			Chimney House
8:30	The Southernaires Quartet	Major Bowes' Capitol Family	Raoul Nadeau, songs	Walter Logan's Musicale
8:45			Food for Thought	
9am	The Radio City Music Hall		Organ Recital	Dr. Casselbury, health
9:15				The Madrigral Singers
9:30		The Salt Lake Tabernable Choir	The Lamplighter	The University of Chicago Round Table
9:45			American Wildlife	
10am	Nick Harris	The CBS Church of the Air	Sumner Prindle, news	Health Talk
10:15	Garden Talk		Romance of the Highways	The Music Parade
10:30	Music	Salute to the New York World's Fair	Salute to the New York World's Fair	Salute to the New York World's Fair
10:45	Look at Books			
11am	The Magic Key of RCA	Immigrants All, Americans All	Good Manners	Sunday Dinner at Aunt Fanny's
11:15			Sinfonietta	
11:30		Music	Church	Barry McKInley, songs
11:45				Fables in Verse
12pm	Frank Simon Orchestra	New York Philharmonic Orchestra	On a Sunday Afternoon	Sunday Drivers
12:15				
12:30	Festival of Music		News	Vivian Della Chiesa, songs
12:45			Tony Cabooch, songs	Bob Becker's Dog Talks
1pm	National Vespers		Benay Venuta's Variety Program	Ranger's Serenade
1:15				

DAYTIME — WINTER, 1939

Monday-Friday

BLUE	CBS	MBS	NBC	
The Church Quarter-Hour	Talk and Music	Clipper	Ted White, songs	8am
Virginia Lane, songs			Music	8:15
Music		The Haven of Rest	News	8:30
Originalities	Sally of Star		Music / Optimism Optometrists	8:45
News	Radio Recipes / Mary Margaret McBride, talk	Talk and Music	Dan Harding's Wife / The Martha Meade Society	9am
Music	Her Honor, Nancy James	Hometown	The O'Neills	9:15
The National Farm and Home Hour	The Romance of Helen Trent	Norma Young, talk	The Bridge Club	9:30
	Our Gal Sunday	Music / Strings		9:45
	The Goldbergs	Matinee	John's Other Wife	10am
Talk and Music	Life Can Be Beautiful		Just Plain Bill	10:15
Music / Peables Takes Charge	The Road of Life	Talk and Music / As You Like It	Dangerous Roads	10:30
Music	Tena and Tim / Mary Lee Taylor, cooking	Talk and Music / The Voice of Experience	Dr. Kate	10:45
Talk and Music / The Standard School Broadcast	Big Sister	The National School of the Air	Betty and Bob	11am
	Aunt Jenny's True Life Stories		Arnold Grimm's Daughter	11:15
	The American School of the Air	Eddie Albright, organ	Valiant Lady	11:30
Stock Market Reports		Music / George Fisher, gossip	Hymns of All Churches / Betty Crocker, cooking	11:45
US Agricultural Talk	Fletcher Wiley, talk	Norman Nesbitt, stories	The Story of Mary Marlin	12pm
Music		Talk and Music	Ma Perkins	12:15
	Scattergood Baines	The Cats and the Fiddle	Pepper Young's Family	12:30
Between the Bookends	Music / Yours Sincerely	Music	The Guiding Light	12:45
Club Matinee, Ransom Sherman	Pretty Kitty Kelly	Talk and Music	Mary Noble, Backstage Wife	1pm
	The Story of Myrt and Marge	Midstream	Stella Dallas	1:15

DAYTIME — WINTER, 1939

Sunday

	BLUE	CBS	MBS	NBC
1:30	The World is Yours		The Lutheran Hour	Amanda's Party
1:45				
2pm	The Metropolitan Opera Auditions	Golden Afternoon	The Musical Steelmakers	Uncle Ezra's Radio Station
2:15				Cook's Travelogue
2:30	Music	The Problem Clinic	Rabbi Magnin, religion	
2:45	Charles Sears, news		Elinor Warren, songs	Organ Recital
3pm	The Catholic Hour	The Silver Theater	Help Thy Neighbor	Mirandy's Sociable
3:15				
3:30	Music Celebrities	Gateway to Hollywood	The Show of the Week	Professor Puzzlewit
3:45				
4pm	The Classic Hour	Back Home	The Bach Cantata Series	The Hollywood Playhouse
4:15				
4:30	Organ Recital	The Gulf Screen Guild Show	Jimmy Hamilton Orchestra	The Fitch Bandwagon
4:45				

DAYTIME — WINTER, 1939

Monday-Friday

BLUE	CBS	MBS	NBC	
School News	Hilltop House	Talk and Music	Vic and Sade	*1:30*
Talk and Music	Stepmother	Book a Week	Girl Alone	*1:45*
The Classic Hour	The Women's Forum	Talk and Music	Houseboat Hannah	*2pm*
	Music / Let's Pretend / March of Games	The Johnson Family	Doc Sellers	*2:15*
		Talk and Music	Music	*2:30*
	Kitty Keene, Inc.			*2:45*
Talk and Music	Ma Perkins	Feminine Fancies	Art Baker's Notebook	*3pm*
	Talk / The Heart of Julia Blake			*3:15*
	Talk and Music	Talk and Music	Women's Magazine of the Air	*3:30*
Music / Father and Son				*3:45*
Talk and Music	Fletcher Wiley, talk	Fulton Lewis, Jr., news	Talk and Music / Easy Aces	*4pm*
		Talk and Music	Talk and Music / Mr. Keen, Tracer of Lost Persons	*4:15*
	Talk and Music		Music / Ann Warner Chats	*4:30*
			News	*4:45*

DAYTIME — WINTER, 1939

Saturday

	BLUE	CBS	MBS	NBC
8am	The Church Quarter-Hour	Cincinatti Conservatory Symphony	Revue	Glen Hurlburt, news
8:15	Music Internationale		This Wonderful World	Music
8:30	Our Barn		The US Army Band	News
8:45				Remember
9am	The American Education Forum	Radio Recipes	Collegiate Review	County Medical Association Talks
9:15				Music
9:30	The National Farm and Home Hour	US Agricultural Talk	Organ Recital	Call to Youth
9:45		Music		Along Gypsy Trails
10am		The Monitor Children's Program	Matinee Friend	Radio Pen
10:15		The Federation of Women's Clubs		Rhythm
10:30	The School Harmonies Band	Music	The California Board of Education	Campus Capers
10:45	Music		Hitmakers Orchestra	
11am	The People's Lobby	Men Against Death	The Columbia University Public Discussion	The Metropolitan Opera
11:15				
11:30	Music	Buffalo Presents	Anthony Candelori Orchestra	
11:45		Fran Hines, songs		
12pm		Merrymakers Orchestra	The London Music Hall	
12:15	The Four of Us	Federal Housing Authority Talk		
12:30	Allen Roth Orchestra	Public Affairs		
12:45				
1pm	Club Matinee, Ransom Sherman	Student Takes the Mike	Horse Racing	
1:15				
1:30		Dancepators Orchestra	The Gloomchasers	
1:45				

DAYTIME — WINTER, 1939

Saturday

	BLUE	CBS	MBS	NBC
2pm	Congress Concert	What Price America	International House	
2:15				The Stamp Club
2:30	The Classic Hour	Music	Drama	
2:45				
3pm	Revue	News	Dance Orchestra	Kaltenmeyer's Kindergarten
3:15		Ray Noble Orchestra		
3:30	Renfrew of the Mounted	Swing	Review	Swingology
3:45				Religion in the News
4pm	Message of Israel	Americans at Work	Music	Freddy Martin Orchestra
4:15				
4:30	Don Ricardo Orchestra	The National Golf Open		The Lives of Great Men
4:45			Legion News	The Castilla Twins

EVENING — SPRING, 1939

Sunday

	BLUE	CBS	MBS	NBC
5pm	Leo Spitalny Orchestra	Dance Orchestra	The American Forum of the Air	The Chase and Sanborn Hour
5:15				
5:30	Swing			
5:45				
6pm	Songs	The Ford Sunday Evening Hour	The Old Fashioned Revival Hour	The Manhattan Merry-Go-Round
6:15				
6:30	Organ Recital			The American Album of Familiar Music
6:45	The Three Cheers			
7pm	Jan Savitt Orchestra	The Old Gold Program, Robert Benchley	The Goodwill Hour	The Circle
7:15				
7:30	Cheerio's Musical Mosaics	The Inglewood Park Concert		
7:45				
8pm	Music	Calling All Cars	Highway Patrol	Walter Winchell's Jergens Journal
8:15				Irene Rich Dramas
8:30	Russ Morgan Orchestra	Life Without Regrets	Carl Ravazza Orchestra	The Jello Program, Jack Benny
8:45				
9pm	Dance Orchestra	Ben Bernie, the Old Maestro	News	The Hollywood Playhouse
9:15			Frank Watanabe and Honorable Archie	
9:30	Herbie Kay Orchestra	Dance Orchestra	The Voice of Prophecy	One Man's Family
9:45	The University Explorer	John B. Hughes, news		
10pm	Phil-Harmonia	The March of California	Jack Harris Orchestra	The Richfield Reporter
10:15		The People's Platform		The Chapel Quartet
10:30			Eddie Rogers Orchestra	Bridge to Dreamland
10:45		Capitol Opinions		

EVENING — SPRING, 1939

Monday

BLUE	CBS	MBS	NBC	
Music	News and Sports	News	Music	*5pm*
News	Howie Wing	Johnny Murray, songs		*5:15*
Music	News	Dick Tracy	Miniature Memories	*5:30*
Sagebrush Songs	Eddie Albright, organ	Little Orphan Annie		*5:45*
The Eastman School of Music	The Lux Radio Theater	Jack Armstrong, The All-American Boy	The Hour of Charm	*6pm*
		Speed Gibson of the International Secret Police		*6:15*
The National Radio Forum		Music	Eddy Duchin Orchestra	*6:30*
		Shafter Parker, comment		*6:45*
True or False	Guy Lombardo Orchestra	News Drama	The Carnation Contented Hour	*7pm*
		The Shadow of Fu Manchu		*7:15*
Sports	The Camel Caravan, Eddie Cantor	The Lone Ranger	Music	*7:30*
Music				*7:45*
Mr. District Attorney	Amos 'n' Andy	The Golden Hour	News	*8pm*
Music	Lum and Abner		Art Baker's Notebook	*8:15*
The University Explorer	The Model Minstrels		The Voice of Firestone	*8:30*
Albert Bergman, legal talk				*8:45*
Dance Orchestra	The Cavalcade of America	News	Hawthorne House	*9pm*
		Frank Watanabe and Honorable Archie		*9:15*
Know Your Schools	Sophie Tucker, songs	The California Legislature	Al Pearce and His Gang	*9:30*
The University Explorer	John B. Hughes, news	Tom Sawyer, comment		*9:45*
Phil-Harmonia	Tito Guizar, guitar	The Devil's Scrapbook	The Richfield Reporter	*10pm*
	Night Cap Yarns		Claude Sweeten Orchestra	*10:15*
	Music	Jimmy Walsh Orchestra	Kent Kennan Orchestra	*10:30*
	Clark Ross, songs			*10:45*

EVENING — SPRING, 1939

Tuesday

	BLUE	CBS	MBS	NBC
5pm	Virginia Flohri, songs	Quintette	News	Charles Dillon, songs
5:15	News	Howie Wing	Johnny Murray, songs	Talk
5:30	Freddy Martin Orchestra	Talk	Dick Tracy	Information, Please
5:45		News	Little Orphan Annie	
6pm	Mary and Bob's True Story Hour	We, the People	Jack Armstong, the All-American Boys	Pull Over, Neighbor
6:15			Music	
6:30	Dr. Rockwell's Brain Trust	Benny Goodman's Swing School	Public Information	Fibber McGee and Molly
6:45			Shafter Parker, comment	
7pm	If I Had a Chance	Music	The Phantom Pilot Patrol	The Pepsodent Show, Bob Hope
7:15			The Inside of Sports	
7:30	The Inside Story	Jimmy Fidler, gossip	The Green Hornet	Uncle Ezra's Radio Station
7:45		Talk		Music
8pm	Mr. District Attorney	Amos 'n' Andy	Fulton Lewis, Jr., news	News
8:15	Magnolia Bloossoms	Sam Hayes, sports	Don't You Believe It	Vocal Vareieites
8:30	Nick Harris	Big Town	Exposition Quiz	Johnny Presents
8:45	Music		Music	
9pm		The Tuesday Night Party, Dick Powell	News	Battle of the Sexes
9:15			Frank Watanabe and Honorable Archie	
9:30	The Troubadour	The Grouch Club	Music	Carefree Carnival
9:45	Dance Orchestra		Skinnay Ennis Orchestra	
10pm	Phil-Harmonia	The Ten o'Clock Wire	Jack Harris Orchestra	The Richfield Reporter
10:15		Night Cap Yarns		Ho Hum
10:30		Dance Orchestra	Dance Orchestra	Kent Kennan Orchestra
10:45		Amercan Viewpoints		

EVENING — SPRING, 1939

Wednesday

BLUE	CBS	MBS	NBC	
The National Federation of Music Clubs	Tea for Two	News	Robert Hurd, news	5pm
News	Howie Wing	Johnny Murray, songs	Know Your School	5:15
Music	News	Dick Tracy	Hobby Lobby	5:30
Editorial	Eddie Albright, organ	Little Orphan Annie		5:45
Horse and Buggy Days	The Texaco Star Theater	Jack Armstrong, the All-American Boys	Swing with Sweeten	6pm
		Speed Gibson of the International Secret Police	Meet Some People	6:15
Wings for the Martin		Music	Music	6:30
		Shafter Parker, comment		6:45
Pubilc Affairs	Ninety-Nine Men and a Girl, Hildegarde	Rush Hughes, news	Kay Kyser's College of Musical Knowledge	7pm
		The Shadow of Fu Manchu		7:15
Public Interest in Democracy	The Ask-It Basket	The Lone Ranger		7:30
				7:45
Mr. District Attorney	Amos 'n' Andy	Fulton Lewis, Jr., news	News	8pm
Music	Lum and Abner	Frank Bull, sports	Edwin C. Hill, news	8:15
Horace Heidt Orchestra	Chesterfield Presents	The Answer Game	The Raleigh and Kool Show	8:30
				8:45
Looks at Books	Gangbusters	News	Town Hall Tonight, Fred Allen	9pm
Music		Dance Orchestra		9:15
Shelley Orchestra	Sophie Tucker, songs			9:30
	John B. Hughes, news	Tom Sawyer, comment		9:45
Phil-Harmonia	Tito Guizar, guitar	Jack Harris Orchestra	The Richfield Reporter	10pm
	Night Cap Yarns		The Witch's Tale	10:15
	Dance Orchestra	Eddie Rogers Orchestra		10:30
			Kent Kennan Orchestra	10:45

EVENING — SPRING, 1939

Thursday

	BLUE	CBS	MBS	NBC
5pm	The Parade of Progress in Foods	Quintette	News	The Royal Gelatin Hour, Rudy Vallee
5:15		Howie Wing	Johnny Murray, songs	
5:30	The Eastman School of Music	Dick Aurandt Orchestra	Dick Tracy	
5:45		News	Little Orphan Annie	
6pm		Major Bowes' Original Amateur Hour	Jack Armstong, the All-American Boy	Good News of 1939
6:15	The Radio City Four		Music	
6:30	America's Town Meeting of the Air		Public Information	
6:45			Shafter Parker, comment	
7pm		Tune-Up Time	The Phantom Pilot Patrol	The Kraft Music Hall, Bing Crosby
7:15			The Inside of Sports	
7:30	Music		The Green Hornet	
7:45		Public Affairs		
8pm	Mr. District Attorney	Amos 'n' Andy	Fulton Lewis, Jr., news	News
8:15	The Music Parade	I Want a Divorce	Don't You Believe It	The Standard Symphony Hour
8:30	Music	The Joe E. Brown Show	Exposition Quiz	
8:45			Music	
9pm	It's A Curious World	The Kate Smith Hour	News	
9:15			Music / Public Affairs	Broadway Memories
9:30	Shelley Orchestra			
9:45	The University Explorer			Tax Talk
10pm	Phil-Harmonia	The Ten o'Clock Wire	Jack Harris Orchestra	The Richfield Reporter
10:15		Night Cap Yarns		We Three
10:30		Matty Malneck Orchestra	Eddie Rogers Orchestra	What's the Big Idea
10:45				

EVENING — SPRING, 1939

Friday

BLUE	CBS	MBS	NBC	
Don't Forget	Tea for Two	News	Gladys Swatrtout, songs	5pm
	Howie Wing	Johnny Murray, songs		5:15
Jamboree	News	Dick Tracy	You and Your Government	5:30
	Eddie Albright, organ	Little Orphan Annie	Moving Stories of Life	5:45
Paducah Plantation, Red Foley	The Campbell Playhouse	Jack Armstong, the All-American Boy	Waltz Time	6pm
		Speed Gibson of the International Secret Police		6:15
Remember		Music	The March of Time	6:30
Motordom		Shafter Parker, comment		6:45
Rochester Philharmonic Orchestra	Grand Central Station	Rush Hughes, news	Lady Esther Serenade	7pm
Vocal		The Shadow of Fu Manchu		7:15
Dance Orchestra	Believe It or Not	The Lone Ranger	Uncle Ezra's Radio Station	7:30
			Jimmy Fidler, gossip	7:45
Mr. District Attorney	Amos 'n' Andy	Let's Go Hollywood	News	8pm
Music	Lum and Abner		Cabbages and Kings	8:15
Waltz	Burns and Allen	Author, Author	Death Valley Days	8:30
News				8:45
Gray Gordon Orchestra	The First Nighter Program	News	The Gilmore Circus	9pm
		The Round Towner		9:15
Parents on Trial	Sophie Tucker, songs	Music	Good Morning Tonight	9:30
	Ray Noble Orchestra			9:45
Phil-Harmonia	The Camera Club	Jack Harris Orchestra	The Richfield Reporter	10pm
	Night Cap Yarns		Kent Kennan Orchestra	10:15
	Dick Barrie Orchestra	Eddie Rogers Orchestra	Harry Owens Orchestra	10:30
	Dance Orchestra			10:45

EVENING — SPRING, 1939

Saturday

	BLUE	CBS	MBS	NBC
5pm	Music	Sports Broadside	Music	Tommy Riggs and Betty Lou
5:15				
5:30	Brent House	News and Sports	Fiesta	Dance Orchestra
5:45		Adventures in Science		
6pm	Organ Recital	Honolulu Bound, Phil Baker	The World's Fair Party	Swing with Sweeten
6:15	The March of Progress			
6:30	Stars of Tomorrow	The Pet Milk Program	Music	The Hall of Fun
6:45				
7pm	Public Affairs	Your Hit Parade	Betty Rhodes, songs	King's Cowboy Revue
7:15			The Inside of Sports	Ricardo and His Caballeros
7:30			The Gloomchasers	The Show Songs
7:45		Music		
8pm	Music	Sports	George Fisher, gossip	The National Barn Dancet
8:15		Music	The Sons of the Pioneers	
8:30		Johnny Presents	Dance Orchestra	
8:45				
9pm		Professor Quiz	News	Avalon Variety Time, Red Foley
9:15			Dance Orchestra	
9:30		Ted Weems Orchestra	Eddy Duchin Orchestra	Artie Shaw Orchestra
9:45		John B. Hughes, news		
10pm	Phil-Harmonia	Capitol Opinions	Jack Harris Orchestra	News
10:15		Dick Aurandt Orchestra		Dance Orchestra
10:30		Dance Orchestra	Joe Reichman Orchestra	Nottingham Light Orchestra
10:45				

DAYTIME — SPRING, 1939

Sunday

	BLUE	CBS	MBS	NBC
8am	The Church Quarter-Hour	The West Coast Church	The Comics Weekly Man	News
8:15	Neighbor Nell			Chimney House
8:30	The Southernaires Quartet	Major Bowes' Capitol Family	Music	Tapestry Musicale
8:45			The Canary Pet Shop	
9am	The Radio City Music Hall		Choir	Music for Moderns
9:15			Organ Recital	
9:30		The Salt Lake Tabernable Choir	Book Theater	The University of Chicago Round Table
9:45			Food for Thought	
10am	Great Plays	The CBS Church of the Air	Sumner Prindle, news	Health Talk
10:15			Romance of the Highways	Meditation
10:30		Salute to the New York World's Fair	Salute to the New York World's Fair	Salute to the New York World's Fair
10:45				
11am	The Magic Key of RCA	Immigrants All, Americans All	Music	Sunday Dinner at Aunt Fanny's
11:15				
11:30		Charley Lung, comment		Dr. Casselbury, health
11:45		Organ Recital		Music
12pm	College Choir	New York Philharmonic Orchestra	News	Sunday Drivers
12:15			On a Sunday Afternoon	
12:30	Nick Harris		Sinfonietta	Name the Place
12:45	Music			Bob Becker's Dog Talks
1pm	National Vespers		Benay Venuta's Variety Program	Songs

DAYTIME — SPRING, 1939

Monday-Friday

BLUE	CBS	MBS	NBC	
The Church Quarter-Hour	My Turn Now / It Happened in Hollywood	The Sons of the Pioneers	Ted White, songs	8am
Talk / Crosscuts of the Day	Music	The Haven of Rest	News	8:15
Music / The Jingletown Gazette	Nancy Dixon, talk		The Martha Meade Society / Optimism Optometrists	8:30
Music / Originalities	Martha Moore, news	Mirandy's Garden Patch	Kitty Keene, Inc.	8:45
News	Talk / Mary Margaret McBride, talk	Talk and Music	The Carters of Elm Street	9am
Music	Her Honor, Nancy James		The O'Neills	9:15
The National Farm and Home Hour	The Romance of Helen Trent	Norma Young, talk	Talk and Music	9:30
	Our Gal Sunday	Music / Strings		9:45
	The Goldbergs	Matinee	The Bridge Club	10am
US Agricultural Talk	Life Can Be Beautiful			10:15
Music / Peables Takes Charge	The Road of Life	Music / Katz on Keys	Dangerous Roads	10:30
Talk and Music	Mary Lee Taylor, cooking / The Heart of Julia Blake	Talk and Music / The Voice of Experience	Dr. Kate	10:45
Talk and Music / The Standard School Broadcast	Big Sister	The National School of the Air	Betty and Bob	11am
	Aunt Jenny's True Life Stories		Arnold Grimm's Daughter	11:15
	The American School of the Air	Eddie Albright, organ	Valiant Lady	11:30
Stock Market Reports		Music	Hymns of All Churches / Betty Crocker, cooking	11:45
US Agricultural Talk	Fletcher Wiley, talk	Norman Nesbitt, stories	The Story of Mary Marlin	12pm
Music		Talk and Music	Ma Perkins	12:15
	The Dream Dealer		Pepper Young's Family	12:30
Between the Bookends	David Harum		The Guiding Light	12:45
Club Matinee, Ransom Sherman	Pretty Kitty Kelly		Mary Noble, Backstage Wife	1pm

DAYTIME — SPRING, 1939

Sunday

	BLUE	CBS	MBS	NBC
1:15				Hendrick Van Loon, comment
1:30	The World is Yours		The Lutheran Hour	The Crawford Caravan
1:45				
2pm	Music	World News Roundup	The Musical Steelmakers	Ranger's Serenade
2:15				
2:30	Look at Books	The Problem Clinic	Rabbi Magnin, religion	Organ Recital
2:45	Songs			The National Editor
3pm	The Catholic Hour	The Silver Theater	Help Thy Neighbor	Watson, Flotsom and Jetsam
3:15				
3:30	Jan Savitt Orchestra	Gateway to Hollywood	The Show of the Week	Dance Orchestra
3:45				
4pm	The New York World's Fair	Back Home	The Bach Cantata Series	Professor Puzzlewit
4:15	Eugene Conley, songs			
4:30	The Radio Guild	The Gulf Screen Guild Show	Dance Orchestra	The Fitch Bandwagon
4:45				

DAYTIME — SPRING, 1939

Monday-Friday

BLUE	CBS	MBS	NBC	
	The Story of Myrt and Marge		Stella Dallas	1:15
School News	Hilltop House		Vic and Sade	1:30
Talk and Music	Stepmother	Book a Week	Girl Alone	1:45
The Classic Hour	Scattergood Baines	Talk and Music	Houseboat Hannah	2pm
	The Life and Love of Dr. Susan	The Johnson Family	Talk and Music	2:15
	Sports	Talk and Music		2:30
			Young Dr. Malone	2:45
Talk and Music		Feminine Fancies	Music / Ann Warner Chats	3pm
			I Love a Mystery	3:15
		Talk and Music	Women's Magazine of the Air	3:30
				3:45
Keith Orchestra		Community Hall	Talk and Music / Easy Aces	4pm
Virginia Lane, songs		Let's Play Bridge	Talk and Music / Mr. Keen, Tracer of Lost Persons	4:15
Talk and Music	Fletcher Wiley, talk	So This is Radio	Art Baker's Notebook	4:30
			News	4:45

DAYTIME — SPRING, 1939

Saturday

	BLUE	CBS	MBS	NBC
8am	The Church Quarter-Hour	Cincinatti Conservatory Symphony	Organ Recital	The Musical Clock
8:15	Music Internationale			News
8:30	Our Barn	Nancy Dixon, talk	The US Army Band	The National Federation of Musid Clubs
8:45		The Southern California Symphony Association	Mirandy's Garden Patch	
9am	The American Education Forum	The Music Room	Music	Music
9:15		The Federation of Women's Clubs		
9:30	The National Farm and Home Hour	Let's Pretend	The California Board of Education	Call to Youth
9:45			Walter Flandorf, organ	Along Gypsy Trails
10am		The Monitor Children's Program	Matinee Friend	Radio Pen
10:15		Amercans at Work		The Stamp Club
10:30	The Little Variety Show		Bernie Cummins Orchestra	Campus Capers
10:45		Music	The Radio Garden Club	
11am	The People's Lobby	Men Against Death	The London Music Hall	Music
11:15				
11:30	Music	Ranger's Serenade		The Glee Club
11:45		Federal Housing Authority Talks		
12pm	Up to You	Public Affairs	News	Music
12:15			Music	
12:30	Allen Roth Orchestra	Horse Racing	Organ Recital	KSTP Presents
12:45				
1pm	Club Matinee, Ransom Sherman		Music	Dol Brissett Orchestra
1:15				
1:30	The Classic Hour	Dance Orchestra		Southwestern Stars
1:45				

DAYTIME — SPRING, 1939

Saturday

	BLUE	CBS	MBS	NBC
2pm	Congress Concert	Sports	Herbie Kay Orchestra	Cheers
2:15				Youth Meets the Government
2:30	The Classic Hour		Drama	
2:45				
3pm	Revue		Music	Kaltenmeyer's Kindergarten
3:15				
3:30	Renfrew of the Mounted			Swingology
3:45				Religion in the News
4pm	Message of Israel		Bernie Cummins Orchestra	Herbie Kay Orchestra
4:15		Music		
4:30	Garden Talk	County Seat	Music	The Lives of Great Men
4:45	Music		Legion News	The Castilla Twins

EVENING — SUMMER, 1939

Sunday

	BLUE	CBS	MBS	NBC
5pm	The Sons of Lone Star	The Ford Summer Hour	The Old Fashioned Revival Hour	The Manhattan Merry-Go-Round
5:15				
5:30	Organ Recital			The American Album of Familiar Music
5:45	Dance Orchestra			
6pm	The Voice of Hawaii	Let's Go to the Fair	The Goodhwill Hour	NBC Symphony Orchestra
6:15				
6:30	Cheerio's Musical Mosaics	The Inglewood Park Concert		
6:45				
7pm	Nobel Sissel Orchestra	Spelling Bee	Faith Music	Edwin C. Hill, news
7:15	The Beaux Arts Trio			Irene Rich Dramas
7:30	Isham Jones Orchestra	Henry King Orchestra	Ballads	The Aldrich Family
7:45				
8pm	Will Osborne Orchestra	Al Goodman Orchestra	Author, Author	The Hollywood Playhouse
8:15				
8:30	Dance Orchestra	John B. Hughes, news	Music	One Man's Family
8:45		Music		
9pm		Molenas Orchestra	News	The Night Editor
9:15			Dance Orchestra	Frankie Masters Orchestra
9:30		Ted Weems Orchestra	The Voice of Prophecy	Bunny Berigan Orchestra
9:45				The Bridge Club
10pm	Phil-Harmonia	Tito Guizar, guitar	Joe Reichman Orchestra	The Richfield Reporter
10:15		Organ Recital		Bridge to Dreamland
10:30		Sterling Young Orchestra	Dance Orchestra	
10:45				

EVENING — SUMMER, 1939

Monday

BLUE	CBS	MBS	NBC	
The Magic Key of RCA	Man About Hollywood	News	Tempo	5pm
		Shafter Parker, comment		5:15
Al Gayle Orchestra	Guy Lombardo Orchestra	Buck Rogers of the 25th Century	Horace Heidt Orchestra	5:30
News		The Phantom Pilot Patrol		5:45
True or False	So This is Radio	Speed Gibson of the International Secret Police	The Carnation Contented Hour	6pm
		Detective O'Malley		6:15
Gray Gordon Orchestra	Blondie	Melody	Dance Orchestra	6:30
		News		6:45
Frank Watanabe and Honorable Archie	Amos 'n' Andy	Melody	Chesterfield Time	7pm
Dance Orchestra	Sam Hayes, news	Captain Herne	Uncle Ezra's Radio Station	7:15
Moving World	The Model Minstrels	The Lone Ranger	The Voice of Firestone	7:30
				7:45
Traffic Tribunal	Al Goodman Orchestra	The Golden Hour	Art Baker's Notebook	8pm
Music			Dance Orchestra	8:15
	John B. Hughes, news		Al Pearce and His Gang	8:30
	Ted Weems Orchestra			8:45
Frank Trombar Orchestra	Calling All Cars	News	Hawthorne House	9pm
The University Explorer		Fulton Lewis, Jr., news		9:15
Ricardo and His Caballeros	The Hoosier Hot Shots	The Shadow of Fu Manchu	This is My Slant	9:30
	The Camera Club	Arthur Orchestra	The Steinie Bottle Boys	9:45
Phil-Harmonia	Tito Guizar, guitar	The Devil's Scrapbook	The Richfield Reporter	10pm
	Night Cap Yarns		Ho Hum	10:15
	Ted Weems Orchestra	Garwood Van Orchestra	Dance Orchestra	10:30
				10:45

EVENING — SUMMER, 1939

Tuesday

	BLUE	CBS	MBS	NBC
5pm	Cabbages and Kings	Dance Orchestra	News	The Old Gold Program, Robert Benchley
5:15	Lady Make Believe		Shafter Parker, comment	
5:30	True Story Time	The Camel Caravan	The Stamp Club	Alec Templeton Time
5:45			Organ Recital	
6pm	If I Had a Chance	Geoffrey Waddington Conducts	The Green Hornet	Mr. District Attorney
6:15				
6:30	The Inside Story	Music	Music	Uncle Walter's Dog House
6:45		Sports		
7pm	Frank Watanabe and Honorable Archie	Amos 'n' Andy		Chesterfield Time
7:15	Al Goodman Orchestra	Jimmy Fidler, gossip	The Inside of Sports	Quicksilver
7:30	Moving World	Music	Captain Herne	Johnny Presents
7:45			Dick Jurgens Orchestra	
8pm	Jan Savitt Orchestra	Music	The King Sisters, songs	George Olsen Orchestra
8:15			Scrapbook Stories	
8:30	Nick Harris	We, the People	Exposition Quiz	Battle of the Sexes
8:45	Music		Garwood Van Orchestra	
9pm	Tommy Tucker Orchestra	Sports	News	Good Morning Tonight
9:15			Fulton Lewis, Jr., news	
9:30	The Troubadour		Dance Orchestra	This Is My Slant
9:45	Bunny Berigan Orchestra			Pinky Tomlin Orchestra
10pm	Phil-Harmonia		Lofner-Harris Orchestra	The Richfield Reporter
10:15			Myers Orchestra	Music
10:30			Dance Orchestra	Woodbury Orchestra
10:45		Ted Weems Orchestra		

EVENING — SUMMER, 1939

Wednesday

BLUE	CBS	MBS	NBC	
Horse and Buggy Days	The Lewisohn Stadium Concerts	News	Chesterfield Time	5pm
		Shafter Parker, comment	Music	5:15
Organ Recital		Tom Sawyer, comment	Idea Mart	5:30
News		The Phantom Pilot Patrol		5:45
Music		Music	Kay Kyser's College of Musical Knowledge	6pm
				6:15
	American Viewpoints			6:30
	Music			6:45
Frank Watanabe and Honorable Archie	Amos 'n' Andy	Dance Orchestra	Cabbages and Kings	7pm
The University Explorer	Music	Captain Herne	Chesterfield Time	7:15
News	Chesterfield Presents	The Lone Ranger	The Raleigh and Kool Show	7:30
Music				7:45
Dance Orchestra	Honolulu Bound, Phil Baker	The King Sisters, songs	What's My Name	8pm
		Dance Orchestra		8:15
California Composers	John B. Hughes, news		George Jessel's Celebrity Program	8:30
	Sterling Young Orchestra			8:45
The Encore Theater	Sports	News	Music	9pm
		Fulton Lewis, Jr., news		9:15
Put That in Your Pipe and Smoke It		The Shadow of Fu Manchu	Joe Sudy Orchestra	9:30
The Camera Club		Henry King Orchestra		9:45
Phil-Harmonia		Dance Orchestra	The Richfield Reporter	10pm
		The Rascals	Irving Miller Orchestra	10:15
	Freddy Martin Orchestra	Charles Cascales Orchestra	Jimmy Grier Orchestra	10:30
				10:45

EVENING — SUMMER, 1939

Thursday

	BLUE	CBS	MBS	NBC
5pm	America's Lost Plays	Major Bowes' Original Amateur Hour	News	Promenade Symphony of Toronto
5:15			Shafter Parker, comment	
5:30			The Stamp Club	
5:45			Music	
6pm	One Thousand and One Wives	The Columbia Workshop	The Green Hornet	The Kraft Music Hall, Bob Burns
6:15				
6:30	Music	Americans at Work	Marek Weber Orchestra	
6:45		Sports		
7pm	The Beaux Art Trio	Amos 'n' Andy	Music	Chesterfield Time
7:15	Dance Orchestra	Screenscoops	The Inside of Sports	The Adventures of Q13
7:30		The Joe E. Brown Show	Captain Herne	Dance Orchestra
7:45	Moving World		Ben Bernie, the Old Maestro	
8pm	Now and Then	Pull Over, Neighbor	The King Sisters, songs	Meet Some People
8:15			Henry James Orchestra	The Standard Symphony Hour
8:30	Will Osborne Orchestra	John B. Hughes, news	Exposition Quiz	
8:45		Sterling Young Orchestra	Garwood Van Orchestra	
9pm	The Music Parade	Sports	News	
9:15	Music		Fulton Lewis, Jr., news	Dance Orchestra
9:30	Ran Wilde Orchestra		Press Time	This is My Slant
9:45				Dance Orchestra
10pm	Phil-Harmonia		Lofner-Harris Orchestra	The Richfield Reporter
10:15			Myers Orchestra	Dance Orchestra
10:30		Ted Weems Orchestra	Don Redman Orchestra	
10:45				

EVENING — SUMMER, 1939

Friday

BLUE	CBS	MBS	NBC	
Paducah Plantation, Red Foley	The Musical Comedy Hour	News	Waltz Time	5pm
		Shafter Parker, comment		5:15
Lady Make Believe	The First Nighter Program	Buck Rogers of the 25th Century	Swing	5:30
News		The Phantom Pilot Patrol		5:45
Music	Grand Central Station	Speed Gibson of the International Secret Police	Serenade	6pm
Novelettes		Detective O'Malley		6:15
Hollywood Ladder Fame	Believe It or Not	Congressional Review	Music	6:30
		Russ Hughes, news	King's Cowboy Revue	6:45
Music Talk	Amos 'n' Andy	Dance Orchestra	Chesterfield Time	7pm
Motordom	The Parker Family	Captain Hearn	Cabbages and Kings	7:15
Jimmy Dorsey Orchestra	Johnny Presents Dramatized Short Stories	The Lone Ranger	Richard Himber Orchestra	7:30
Moving World				7:45
Dance Orchestra	I Want a Divorce	The Laugh and Swing Club	Good Morning Tonight	8pm
	Farm Time			8:15
	John B. Hughes, news	Freddy Nagel Orchestra	Death Valley Days	8:30
News	Music			8:45
Skelly Oil Orchestra	Sports	News	Oscar Levant Orchestra	9pm
		Fulton Lewis, Jr., news		9:15
Bunny Berigan Orchestra		The Shadow of Fu Manchu	This is My Slant	9:30
		Music	Dance Orchestra	9:45
Phil-Harmonia		Lofner-Harris Orchestra	The Richfield Reporter	10pm
			Songs	10:15
	Ted Weems Orchestra	Don Redman Orchestra	Pinky Tomlin Orchestra	10:30
				10:45

EVENING — SUMMER, 1939

Saturday

	BLUE	CBS	MBS	NBC
5pm	Music	Sports Broadside	Horse Racing	George Olsen Orchestra
5:15				
5:30	Organ Recital	Russell Brown, songs		Arch Oboler's Plays
5:45	Garden Talk	The Pet Milk Program	George Fisher, gossip	
6pm	Don't You Forget		The World's Fair Party	Dance Orchestra
6:15		The West Remembers		
6:30	Al Donahue Orchestra		Music	Dick Tracy
6:45		Sports Mirror		
7pm	Jimmy Dorsey Orchestra		Betty Rhodes, songs	The National Barn Dance
7:15		Talk	The Inside of Sports	
7:30	The Ranch Boys	Henry Wood Orchestra	Dance Orchestra	
7:45	Moving World			
8pm	Horace Heidt Orchestra	Your Hit Parade	Dance Orchestra	Avalon Variety Time, Red Skelton
8:15				
8:30	Dance Orchestra			Music
8:45		Rowland Greenberg Orchestra		
9pm	Ran Wilde Orchestra	Sports	News	Dance Orchestra
9:15			Garwood Van Orchestra	
9:30	Will Osborne Orchestra		Paul Pendarvis Orchestra	Bunny Berigan Orchestra
9:45				
10pm	Phil-Harmonia		Lofner-Harris Orchestra	The Richfield Reporter
10:15				Tommy Tomlin Orchestra
10:30		Pasadena Dance Orchestra	Dance Orchestra	Dance Orchestra
10:45				

DAYTIME — SUMMER, 1939

Sunday

	BLUE	CBS	MBS	NBC
8am	The Radio City Music Hall	The West Coast Church	The Comics Weekly Man	The Church Quarter-Hour
8:15				Dr. Casselbury, heatlh
8:30		The Salt Lake Tabernacle Choir	Betty and Buddy, songs	On Your Job
8:45			The Canary Pet Shop	
9am	Waterloo Junction	The CBS Church of the Air	The Voice of Prophecy	Music for Moderns
9:15			Don Arres, songs	
9:30	Look at Books	Walberg Brown Strings	Harp Recital	Sunday Symphonette
9:45	Continental Varieities		Food for Thought	
10am	The National Music Camp	Democracy in Action	Music	Health Talk
10:15			Romance of the Highways	
10:30	Treasure Trails of Songs	News and Views	Manhatters Orchestra	The University of Chicago Round Table
10:45			Alice Blue, songs	
11am	Melody	New York Philharmonic Orchestra	Ballads	Chautauqua Symphony Orchestra
11:15	Joseph Jackson, books			
11:30	Al Roth Presents			
11:45				
12pm	National Vespers	So You Think You Know Music	News	John Gunther, war talk
12:15			Music	Serenade
12:30	Nick Harris	St. Louis Orchestra	The Haven of Rest	The World is Yours
12:45	Music			
1pm	H. R. Baukage, news	World News Roundup	Nobody's Children	The Hall of Fun
1:15	Jimmy Dorsey Orchestra			

DAYTIME — SUMMER, 1939

Monday-Friday

BLUE	CBS	MBS	NBC	
The Church Quarter-Hour	Nancy Dixon, songs	The Sons of the Pioneers	Luigi Romanelli Orchestra	8am
Music / The Kidoodlers Novelty Quartet	Her Honor, Nancy James	The Haven of Rest	The O'Neills	8:15
The National Farm and Home Hour	The Romance of Helen Trent		Mirandy's Garden Patch / Optimist Optometrist	8:30
	Our Gal Sunday	Mirandy's Garden Patch	News	8:45
	The Goldbergs	The Happy Gang	The Bridge Club	9am
	Life Can Be Beautiful			9:15
Peables Takes Charge	The Road of Life	Talk and Music	Music / Virginia Lane, songs	9:30
Talk and Music	Mary Lee Taylor, cooking / The Heart of Julia Blake		Dr. Kate	9:45
	Big Sister	Norma Young, talk	Betty and Bob	10am
	Aun Jenny's True Life Stories		Arnold Grimm's Daughter	10:15
	Mr. Hamp Goes to Town	Talk and Music	Valiant Lady	10:30
	When a Girl Marries		Hymns of All Churches / Betty Crocker, cooking	10:45
Talk and Music	Fletcher Wiley, talk	Talk and Music	The Story of Mary Marlin	11am
			Ma Perkins	11:15
	Talk / The Dream Dealer	Eddie Albright, organ	Pepper Young's Family	11:30
Between the Bookends	Singin' Sam, the Barbasol Man	Music	The Guiding Light	11:45
Club Matinee, Ranson Sherman	Pretty Kitty Kelly	Norman Nesbitt, stories	Mary Noble, Backstage Wife	12pm
	The Story of Myrt and Marge	Curtis Springer, health	Stella Dallas	12:15
	Hilltop House	Talk and Music	Vic and Sade	12:30
US Agricultural Talk	Stepmother		Midstream	12:45
Stock Market Reports	Scattergood Baines		Kitty Keene, Inc.	1pm
Music	The Life and Love of Dr. Susan		Houseboat Hannah	1:15

DAYTIME — SUMMER, 1939

Sunday

	BLUE	CBS	MBS	NBC
1:30	Letters Home from the New York World's Fair	Chorus from the World's Fair	Ballads	Music
1:45				
2pm	The Catholic Hour	The Gay Nineties Revue	Music	The Canadian Grenadiers
2:15				
2:30	Music	The Gateway to Hollywood Summer Theater		The Grouch Club
2:45				
3pm	The Classic Hour	The Alibi Club	Help Thy Neighbor	Professor Puzzlewit
3:15				
3:30	The Radio Guild	Life Without Regrets	Music	The Fitch Bandwagon
3:45			Dance Orchestra	
4pm	NBC Symphony Orchestra	The Adventures of Ellery Qyeen	The House of Melody	The Chase and Sanborn Hour
4:15				
4:30			Edwin Franko Goldman Band	
4:45				

DAYTIME — SUMMER, 1939

Monday-Friday

BLUE	CBS	MBS	NBC	
News	Joyce Jordan, Girl Intern		Music / Back Fence Gossip	1:30
Music	David Harum		Music / Ann Warner Chats	1:45
Talk and Music	News	Talk / Let's Play Bridge	Young Dr. Malone	2pm
	Catalina Quiz	The Johnson Family	I Love a Mystery	2:15
The Classic Hour	Sam Hayes, news	News	Women's Magazine of the Air	2:30
	Songs	Manhattan Mother	Meet Miss Julia	2:45
	Talk and Music	Feminine Fancies	Music / Easy Aces	3pm
			Music / Mr. Keen, Tracer of Lost Persons	3:15
		Talk and Music	Music / The Career of Alice Blair	3:30
			Talk and Music	3:45
The Unclassic Hour			Talk and Music / The Royal Gelatin Hour, Rudy Vallee /	4pm
				4:15
Music / Information, Please			Music / Hobby Lobby	4:30
				4:45

DAYTIME — SUMMER, 1939

Saturday

	BLUE	CBS	MBS	NBC
8am	The Church Quarter-Hour	Nancy Dixon, songs	The Gloomchasers	Music
8:15	Music	Women in the World of Tomrrow		
8:30	The National Farm and Home Hour	Let's Pretend	The California Board of Education	Mirandy's Garden Patch
8:45			Mirandy's Garden Patch	News
9am		The Monitor Children's Program	Xavier Cugat Orchestra	Jean Ellington, songs
9:15		The Federation of Women's Clubs		The Stamp Club
9:30	The Little Variety Show	What Price America	Dance Orchestra	Call to Youth
9:45				Variety
10am	Morton Franklin's Notes of Grace	Youth Session	Music	Music
10:15				
10:30	Indiana Indigo	Mr. Hamp Goes to Town	Louisiana Hayride	County Medical Association Talks
10:45	Music Please	Music		Melody
11am	Irving Miller Orchestra	Merrymakers Orchestra	The London Music Hall	Matinee in Rhythm
11:15				
11:30	Music	Federal Housing Authority Talks		Roy Eldridge Orchestra
11:45		Organ Recital		
12pm	Club Matinee, Ransom Sherman	Music / Sports	News	Summertime Swing
12:15			Songs	
12:30			Hits and Bits	Paul La Valle Orchestra
12:45				
1pm	Stock Market Reports		Joe Marsala Orchestra	The National Music Camp
1:15	Music			
1:30	The Classic Hour		Dance Orchestra	
1:45				Music

DAYTIME — SUMMER, 1939

Saturday

	BLUE	CBS	MBS	NBC
2pm		News and Sports	Dance Orchestra	Kaltenmeyer's Kindegarten
2:15				
2:30		Albert Warner, news	Youth Drama	The Art of Living
2:45		Songs		The Colonial Quartet
3pm	Message of Israel	Americans at Work	Music	Dance Orchestra
3:15				
3:30	From Hollywood Today	County Seat	Cats and Jammers	Irving Miller Orchestra
3:45			America Legion News	
4pm	The Unclassic Dance	Music Maestro Please	Fiesta	Strings
4:15				Gladys Swartout, songs
4:30		Professor Quiz	Hawaii Calls	Brent House
4:45				

EVENING — FALL, 1939

Sunday

	BLUE	CBS	MBS	NBC
5pm	Music	The Adventures of Ellery Queen	The American Forum of the Air	The Chase and Sanborn Hour
5:15				
5:30	News			
5:45	Music			
6pm	Dots and Dashes	The Ford Sunday Evening Hour	The Old Fashioned Revival Hour	The Manhattan Merry-Go-Round
6:15				
6:30	Organ Recital			The American Album of Familiar Music
6:45	The Colgate Sports Newsreel, Bill Stern			
7pm	The Chapel Quartet	The Campbell Playhouse	The Goodwill Hour	The Hour of Charm
7:15	The Voice of Hawaii			
7:30	Cheerio's Musical Mosaics			Carefree Carnival
7:45				
8pm	Noble Sissle Orchestra	Hobby Lobby	Music	The Night Editor
8:15				Irene Rich Dramas
8:30	Sweet and Low	European News Roundup	Author, Author	The Jello Program, Music Jack Benny
8:45				
9pm	Mr. District Attorney	Ben Bernie, the Old Maestro	News	Walter Winchell's Jergens Journal
9:15			The Voice of Prophecy	The Parker Family
9:30	News	Mitchell Ayers Orchestra		One Man's Family
9:45	The University Explorer	Tito Guizar, guitar	The Round Towner	
10pm	Music / Public Affairs	The Ten o'Clock Wire	Pomona Symphony Orchestra	The Richfield Reporter
10:15	Phil-Harmonia	Organ Recital		Bridge to Dreamland
10:30		Edith Lorand Orchestra	Jan Garber Orchestra	
10:45				

EVENING — FALL, 1939

Monday

BLUE	CBS	MBS	NBC	
Frank Wantanabe and Honorable Archie	Dance Orchestra	News	Variety	5pm
Tom Mix and His Ralston Straight Shooters	The Dream Dealer	Buck Rogers in the 25th Century		5:15
News	Mary Foster, Editor's Daughter	Jack Armstrong, the All-American Boy	Music	5:30
Music	News	Little Orphan Annie	The Voice of the World	5:45
Traffic Tribunal	The Lux Radio Theater	The Phantom Pilot Patrol	Dr. I. Q., the Mental Banker	6pm
Dance Orchestra		Shafter Parker, comment		6:15
Youth Questions the Headlines		John B. Hughes, news	Alec Templeton Time	6:30
		The Round Towner		6:45
Dance Orchestra	Guy Lombardo Orchestra	Public Affairs	The Carnation Contented Hour	7pm
Public Affairs		European News		7:15
News	Blondie	The Lone Ranger	Music	7:30
Strings				7:45
The Studio Dark Room	Amos 'n' Andy	Pull Over, Neighbor	Chesterfield Time	8pm
	Lum and Abner		I Love a Mystery	8:15
Music	The Model Minstrels	Public Affairs	The Voice of Firestone	8:30
		Hawaiian Music		8:45
True or False	Tune Up Time	News	Sherlock Holmes	9pm
		Dance Orchestra		9:15
	Dance Orchestra	Johnny Davis Orchestra	Hawthorne House	9:30
The Encore Theater	The Camera Club	Fulton Lewis, Jr., news		9:45
	The Ten o'Clock Wire	Dance Orchestra	The Richfield Reporter	10pm
Organ Recital	Sports Roundup		Richard Himber Orchestra	10:15
Phil-Harmonia			Ho Hum	10:30
	Night Cap Yarns		Chuck Foster Orchestra	10:45

EVENING — FALL, 1939

Tuesday

	BLUE	CBS	MBS	NBC
5pm	Frank Wantanabe and Honorable Archie	Dance Orchestra	News	The Aldrich Family
5:15	Tom Mix and His Ralston Straight Shooters	Boulevard Interviews	Strings	
5:30	Sherlock Holmes	Mary Foster, Editor's Daughter	Jack Armstong, the All-American Boy	Pot o' Gold
5:45		News	Little Orphan Annie	
6pm	Music	Second Husband	The Stamp Club	The Old Gold Program, Robert Benchley
6:15			Shafter Parker, comment	
6:30	Meet Edward Weeks	The Camel Caravan	John B. Hughes, news	Fibber McGee and Molly
6:45			European News	
7pm	Music	Calling All Cars	America Looks Ahead	The Pepsodent Show, Bob Hope
7:15	Public Affairs		The Inside of Sports	
7:30	News	Sports	The Green Hornet	Uncle Walter's Dog House
7:45	The Globetrotters	Talk		
8pm	Information, Please	Amos 'n' Andy	Rhythm	Chesterfield Time
8:15		Jimmie Fidler, gossip		I Love a Mystery
8:30	The Aldrich Family	Big Town	Music	Johnny Presents
8:45				
9pm	Strings	The Tuesday Night Party, Dick Powell	News	Good Morning Tonight
9:15			Skinnay Ennis Orchestra	
9:30	News	We, the People	Music	Battle of the Sexes
9:45	The Encore Theater		Fulton Lewis, Jr., news	
10pm		The Ten o'Clock Wire	Jack Harris Orchestra	The Richfield Reporter
10:15	Phil-Harmonia	Edith Lorand Orchestra		Ho Hum
10:30			Jan Garber Orchestra	Chuck Foster Orchestra
10:45		Night Cap Yarns		

EVENING — FALL, 1939

Wednesday

BLUE	CBS	MBS	NBC	
Frank Wantanabe and Honorable Archie	Dance Orchestra	News	Chesterfield Time	5pm
Tom Mix and His Ralston Straight Shooters	The Dream Dealer	Buck Rogers in the 25th Century	Songs	5:15
Music	Mary Foster, Editor's Daughter	Jack Armstong, the All-American Boy	Operator	5:30
	News	Little Orphan Annie	News	5:45
Beyond a Reasonable Doubt	The Texaco Star Theater	The Phantom Pilot Patrol	Music	6pm
Public Affairs		Shafter Parker, comment	Public Affairs	6:15
The University Explorer		John B. Hughes, news	The Hollywood Playhouse	6:30
Music		Maxine Gray Entertains		6:45
Public Affairs	Music	Public Affairs	Kay Kyser's College of Musical Knowledge	7pm
	Public Affairs	European News		7:15
News and Views	Burns and Allen	The Lone Ranger		7:30
				7:45
Public Affairs	Amos 'n' Andy	Quartet	Cabbages and Kings	8pm
The Word Hunters	Lum and Abner	Music	I Love a Mystery	8:15
Quicksilver	Chesterfield Presents	Dick Jurgens Orchestra	Avalon Variety Time, Red Skelton	8:30
				8:45
The University Explorer	Al Pearce and His Gang	News	The Fred Allen Show	9pm
		Guy Lombardo Orchestra		9:15
News	Music	Skinnay Ennis Orchestra		9:30
The Encore Theater		Fulton Lewis, Jr., news		9:45
	The Ten o'Clock Wire	Music	The Richfield Reporter	10pm
Organ Recital	Sports Roundup		Richard Himber Orchestra	10:15
Phil-Harmonia		Jan Garber Orchestra	Enric Madriguera Orchestra	10:30
	Night Cap Yarns			10:45

EVENING — FALL, 1939

Thursday

	BLUE	CBS	MBS	NBC
5pm	Frank Wantanabe and Honorable Archie	Dance Orchdestra	News	Don't Forget
5:15	Tom Mix and His Ralston Straight Shooters	Boulevard Interviews	World Drama	
5:30	Showcase	Mary Foster, Editor's Daughter	Jack Armstong, the All-American Boy	Music
5:45	Talk	News	Little Orphan Annie	News
6pm	Beyond a Reasonable Doubt	Major Bowes' Original Amateur Hour	The Stamp Club	Good News of 1940
6:15	The Voice of Motordom		Shafter Parker, comment	
6:30	America's Town Meeting of the Air		John B. Hughes, news	
6:45			European News	
7pm		Music	America Looks Ahead	The Kraft Music Hall, Bing Crosby
7:15			The Inside of Sports	
7:30	News	Sports	The Green Hornet	
7:45	The Globetrotters	Public Affairs		
8pm	Public Affairs	Amos 'n' Andy	The King Sisters, songs	Chesterfield Time
8:15	Mayor Bowron, comment	The Ballot Box		I Love a Mystery
8:30	The Quiz Club	The Ask-It Basket	Eddy Howard Orchestra	The Standard Symphony Hour
8:45				
9pm	Music	Strange As It Seems	News	
9:15			Skinnay Ennis Orchestra	
9:30	News	Opera		Those We Love
9:45	The Encore Theater		Fulton Lewis, Jr., news	
10pm		The Ten o'Clock Wire	Jack Harris Orchestra	The Richfield Reporter
10:15	Phil-Harmonia	Sports Roundup		Ray Noble Orchestra
10:30			Shorty Baker Orchestra	Carl Ravazza Orchestra
10:45		Night Cap Yarns		

EVENING — FALL, 1939

Friday

BLUE	CBS	MBS	NBC	
Frank Wantanabe and Honorable Archie	Dance Orchestra	News	Organ Recital	5pm
Tom Mix and His Ralston Straight Shooters	The Dream Dealer	Buck Rogers in the 25th Century	Know Your Schools	5:15
News	Mary Foster, Editor's Daughter	Jack Armstong, the All-American Boy		5:30
Tempos	News	Little Orphan Annie	The Voice of the World	5:45
Paducah Plantation, Red Foley	Professor Quiz	Adventure Ahead	Waltz Time	6pm
		Shafter Parker, comment		6:15
Dale Armstrong, songs	The First Nighter Program	John B. Hughes, news	For Men Only, George Jessell	6:30
Rhythm		European News		6:45
Public Affairs	Grand Central Station	Public Affairs	Lady Esther Serenade	7pm
		News		7:15
News	Young Man with a Band	The Lone Ranger	The Quiz Court	7:30
Songs				7:45
Carson Robison's Buckaroos	Amos 'n' Andy	Maxine Gray Entertains	Chesterfield Time	8pm
	Lum and Abner	Public Affairs	I Love a Mystery	8:15
Music	Johnny Presents Dramatized Short Stories	Music	Death Valley Days	8:30
				8:45
Joe Sudy Orchestra	The Kate Smith Hour	News	Public Affairs	9pm
Football Forecast		Dance Orchestra	Meet Some People	9:15
News		Johnnie Davis Orchestra	The University Explorer	9:30
The Encore Theater		Fulton Lewis, Jr., news	Music	9:45
	The Ten o'Clock Wire	Jack Harris Orchestra	The Richfield Reporter	10pm
Phil-Harmonia	Sports	Hawaiian Music	Richard Himber Orchestra	10:15
	Music	Jan Garber Orchestra	Enric Madriguera Orchestra	10:30
	Night Cap Yarns			10:45

EVENING — FALL, 1939

Saturday

	BLUE	CBS	MBS	NBC
5pm	The Unclassic Hour (4:30PM)	The Fifth Quarter	Sinfonietta	The Voice of the World
5:15				Dance Orchestra
5:30	Cal Tinney, news	Wayne King Orchestra	Hawaii Calls	Stop Me If You've Heard This One
5:45	Public Affairs			
6pm	Beyond a Reasonable Doubt	Music	The World's Fair Party	The Hall of Fun
6:15	Know Your Schools			
6:30	Organ Recital		John B. Hughes, news	Fiesta
6:45	Moving Stories of Life	Saturday Night Serenade	Betty Rhodes, songs	King's Cowboy Revue
7pm	NBC Symphony Orchestra		America Looks Ahead	Bob Crosby Orchestra
7:15		Music	The Inside of Sports	
7:30		Sports	Fiesta	Public Affairs
7:45		Songs		
8pm		Americans at Work	George Fisher, gossip	The National Barn Dancet
8:15			The Sons of the Pioneers	
8:30	Public Affairs	Gangbusters	Dance Orchestra	
8:45	Music			
9pm	The Week's Waxes	Your Hit Parade	News	Public Affairs
9:15			Music	Dance Orchestra
9:30	News		Dance Orchestra	Arch Oboler's Plays
9:45	Dance Orchestra	Public Affairs		
10pm	Chuck Foster Orchestra	The Ten o' Clock Wire	Tommy Tucker Orchestra	The Richfield Reporter
10:15	Phil-Harmonia	Sports Roundup		Enric Madriguera Orchestra
10:30		Dance Orchestra	Jan Garber Orchestra	Ray Noble Orchestra
10:45				

DAYTIME — FALL, 1939

Sunday

	BLUE	CBS	MBS	NBC
8am	News	The West Coast Church	The Comics Weekly Man	Melody
8:15	Neighbor Nell			
8:30	The Church Quarter-Hour	Major Bowes' Capitol Family	The Voice of Prophecy	Julio Oyanguren, guitar
8:45	The Southernaires Quartet		The Canary Pet Shop	Dr. Casselbury, health
9am	The Radio City Music Hall		P. E. Gardner, religion	Walter Logan's Musicale
9:15				
9:30		The Salt Lake Tabernable Choir	American Wildlife	On Your Job
9:45			Food for Thought	
10am	Garden Talk	The CBS Church of the Air		Pilgrimage of Poetry
10:15	The Vass Family, songs		Romance of the Highways	
10:30	Norman Cloutier Orchestra	Public Affairs	Harp Recital	From Hollywood Today
10:45			Hits and Bits	
11am	Great Plays	Democracy in Action	The Mystery History Quiz	Wanda Lee, songs
11:15				
11:30		Rhythm	Youth Drama	The University of Chicago Round Table
11:45				
12pm	The Roy Shield Revue	New York Philharmonic Orchestra	News	Music
12:15	Joseph Jackson, books		On a Sunday Afternoon	
12:30	Nick Harris		The Haven of Rest	H. V. Kaltenborn, news
12:45	Al Roth Presents			Bob Becker's Dog Talks
1pm	National Vespers		Nobody's Children	I Want a Divorce
1:15				

DAYTIME — FALL, 1939

Monday-Friday

BLUE	CBS	MBS	NBC	
Financial Services	Nancy Dixon, talk	Victor Lindlahr, health	Music	8am
Oh, Mr. Dinwiddy	Music	News		8:15
The Church Quarter-Hour	Mr. Hamp Goes to Town	A Mutual Friend	News / The Johnny Murray Show	8:30
Organ Recital	My Children	Mirandy's Garden Patch	News	8:45
Talk and Music	Kate Smith Speaks	Talk and Music	The Carters of Elm Street	9am
	When a Girl Marries	Music / The Sons of the Pioneers	The O'Neills	9:15
The National Farm and Home Hour	The Romance of Helen Trent	Patty Jean, songs	The Bridge Club	9:30
	Our Gal Sunday	Music		9:45
	The Goldbergs	Norma Young, talk	Music / The Heart of Julia Blake	10am
Talk and Music	Life Can Be Beautiful		The Story of Ellen Randolph	10:15
	The Road of Life	Talk and Music	Young Dr. Malone	10:30
	Mary Lee Taylor, cooking / The Lanny Ross Show	Talk and Music / The Voice of Experience	Dr. Kate	10:45
Hollywood and Vine	Big Sister	Talk and Music	Betty and Bob	11am
Music	Aunt Jenny's True Life Stories		Arnold Grimm's Daughter	11:15
	Brenda Curtis	Eddie Albright, organ	Valiant Lady	11:30
Stock Market Reports	My Son and I	Music	Hymns of All Churches / Betty Crocker, cooking	11:45
Orphans of Divorce	Joyce Jordan, Girl Intern	News	The Story of Mary Marlin	12pm
News	Society Girl	Curtis Springer, health	Ma Perkins	12:15
Music	The American School of the Air	Music	Pepper Young's Family	12:30
US Agricultural Talk		Let's Play Bridge	The Guiding Light	12:45
Club Matinee, Garry Moore	Pretty Kitty Kelly	Talk and Music	Mary Noble, Backstage Wife	1pm
	The Story of Myrt and Marge		Stella Dallas	1:15

DAYTIME — FALL, 1939

Sunday

	BLUE	CBS	MBS	NBC
1:30	Music		Rabbi Magnin, religion	The World is Yours
1:45			Music	
2pm	The Three Cheers	Columbia's Country Journal	The Musical Steelmakers	Melody
2:15	Four-Star News			
2:30	The Metropolitan Opera Auditions	Spelling Beeliner	Lest We Forget	Music
2:45				
3pm	The Catholic Hour	The Silver Theater	Help Thy Neighbor	Jack Teagarden Orchestra
3:15				Public Affairs
3:30	Public Affairs	Gateway to Hollywood	The Show of the Week	The Grouch Club
3:45				
4pm	The Dinah Shore Show	Tapestry of Life	The Bach Cantata Series	Professor Puzzlewit
4:15	European News			
4:30	Dots and Dashes	The Gulf Screen Guild Show	Shorty Baker Orchestra	The Fitch Bandwagon
4:45				

DAYTIME — FALL, 1939

Monday-Friday

BLUE	CBS	MBS	NBC	
	Hilltop House		Vic and Sade	1:30
	Stepmother	Book a Week	Midstream	1:45
School News	By Kathleen Norris	Talk and Music	Girl Alone	2pm
The Classic Hour	The Life and Love of Dr. Susan	The Johnson Family	Against the Storm	2:15
	It Happened in Hollywood	News	Kitty Keene, Inc.	2:30
	Scattergood Baines	Manhattan Mother	The Career of Alice Blair	2:45
	David Harum	Feminine Fancies	Pictorial	3pm
	Music / Background in Living		Meet Miss Julia	3:15
Talk and Music	Tena and Tim	Talk and Music	Ann Warner Chats	3:30
	European News		Women's Magazine of the Air	3:45
The Unclassic Hour	Fletcher Wiley, talk	Community Hall	Talk and Music / Easy Aces	4pm
		The Haven of Rest	Talk and Music / Mr. Keen, Tracer of Lost Persons	4:15
			Art Baker's Notebook	4:30
		Talk and Music		4:45

DAYTIME — FALL, 1939

Saturday

	BLUE	CBS	MBS	NBC
8am	The Charioteers Quartet	Nancy Dixon, talk	The Model Airplane Club	The Ross Trio
8:15	Music	News	This Wonderful World	Smilin' Ed McDonnell, songs
8:30	The Church Quarter-Hour	Mr. Hamp Goes to Town	News	Hilda Hope, M. D.
8:45	Church and Women	The Saturday Party	Mirandy's Garden Patch	
9am	The American Education Forum		Music	Dol Brisett Orchestra
9:15				
9:30	The National Farm and Home Hour	Let's Pretend		Call to Youth
9:45				County Medical Association Talks
10am		What Price America		Music
10:15				The Stamp Club
10:30	Three-Quarter Time	The Town Crier		Government Reports
10:45		Sports	Sports	Sports
11am	Hollywood at Vine			
11:15	Sports			
11:30				
11:45				
12pm				
12:15				
12:30				
12:45				
1pm				
1:15			News	
1:30			Music	Harry James Orchestra
1:45				

DAYTIME — FALL, 1939

Saturday

	BLUE	CBS	MBS	NBC
2pm	The Classic Hour	Music	News	Music
2:15		Sports	Sports	Sports
2:30				
2:45				
3pm	The Nutshell Playhouse			
3:15				
3:30				
3:45	Music			
4pm	Message of Israel			
4:15				
4:30	The Unclassic Hour		News and Views	
4:45				

LISTINGS FOR 1940

EVENING — WINTER, 1940

Sunday

	BLUE	CBS	MBS	NBC
5pm	Festival of Music	The Adventures of Ellery Queen	The American Forum of the Air	The Charlie McCarthy Show
5:15				
5:30	The Voice of Hawaii			One Man's Family
5:45				
6pm	Joseph Jackson, books	The Ford Sunday Evening Hour	The Old Fashioned Revival Hour	The Manhattan Merry-Go-Round
6:15	Lifelong Planning			
6:30	Organ Recital			The American Album of Familiar Music
6:45	The Colgate Sports Newsreel, Bill Stern			
7pm	The Chapel Quartet	The Campbell Playhouse	The Goodwill Hour	The Hour of Charm
7:15	Jan Savitt Orchestra			
7:30	Cheerio's Musical Mosaics			Carefree Carnival
7:45				
8pm	Ernest Gill Orchestra	Hobby Lobby	George Williams Orchestra	The Night Editor
8:15			Rabbi Magnin, religion	Irene Rich Dramas
8:30	Sweet and Low	The March of California	Lazy Rhapsody	The Jello Program, Jack Benny
8:45		Dance Orchestra		
9pm	Mr. District Attorney	Ben Bernie, the Old Maestro	News	Walter Winchell's Jergens Journal
9:15			Choir	The Parker Family
9:30	News	I Was There		I Want a Divorce
9:45	The University Explorer		Fred Berrens Orchestra	
10pm	Freddy Martin Orchestra	The Ten o'Clock Wire	Dance Orchestra	The Richfield Reporter
10:15	Phil-Harmonia	Dance Orchestra		Bridge to Dreamland
10:30			Fred Berrens Orchestra	
10:45		War News		

EVENING — WINTER, 1940

Monday

BLUE	CBS	MBS	NBC	
Twilight Tales	Teletunes	News	Tommy Riggs and Betty Lou	5pm
Tom Mix and His Ralston Straight Shooters	The Dream Dealer	Music		5:15
News	Music	Jack Armstrong, the All-American Boy	The Voice of Firestone	5:30
The Adventures of Pinocchio	News	Little Orphan Annie		5:45
The Green Hornet	The Lux Radio Theater	Shafter Parker, comment	Dr. I. Q., the Mental Banker	6pm
		War News		6:15
Unemployment Talk		John B. Hughes, news	Alec Templeton Time	6:30
Sports		Paging the Past		6:45
Little Ol' Hollywood	Guy Lombardo Orchestra	Raymond Gram Swing, news	The Carnation Contented Hour	7pm
		This is Magic		7:15
News	Blondie	The Lone Ranger	Larry Clinton Orchestra	7:30
Claude Sweeten Orchestra				7:45
The Studio Dark Room	Amos 'n' Andy	Pull Over, Neighbor	Chesterfield Time	8pm
	Lum and Abner		I Love a Mystery	8:15
Minstrels	The Model Minstrels	Public Affairs	Music	8:30
		Maxine Gray Entertains	Meet Some People	8:45
True or False	Tune Up Time	News	Sherlock Holmes	9pm
		Barber's Beeville		9:15
News	Herbert Straub Orchestra	Laws and Lawyers	Hawthorne House	9:30
Dance Orchestra	The Camera Club	Fulton Lewis, Jr., news		9:45
Enric Madriguera Orchesra	The Ten o'Clock Wire	Author, Author	The Richfield Reporter	10pm
Electric Music	Jimmy Grier Orchestra		The Blue Moonlight	10:15
Phil-Harmonia	Sports	Who is the Latest	Dance Orchestra	10:30
	Night Cap Yarns	Music		10:45

EVENING — WINTER, 1940

Tuesday

	BLUE	CBS	MBS	NBC
5pm	Bud Barton	Teletunes	News	The Aldrich Family
5:15	Tom Mix and His Ralston Straight Shooters	The Dream Dealer	Sinfonietta	
5:30	Sherlock Holmes	The Court of Missing Hers	Jack Armstong, the All-American Boy	Pot o' Gold
5:45			Little Orphan Annie	
6pm	Two-Thousand Four-Hundred Forty A. D.	Second Husband	Shafter Parker, comment	The Cavalcade of America
6:15			War News	
6:30	Meet Edward Weeks	The Camel Caravan	John B. Hughes, news	Fibber McGee and Molly
6:45			Paging the Past	
7pm	The Roy Shields Revue	Moonlight Serenade	Raymond Gram Swing, news	The Pepsodent Show, Bob Hope
7:15		Americans at Work	The Inside of Sports	
7:30	News		Ned Jordan, Secret Agent	Uncle Walter's Dog House
7:45	Piano Recital	Sports		
8pm	Information, Please	Amos 'n' Andy	Rhythm	Chesterfield Time
8:15		Jimmy Fidler, gossip		I Love a Mystery
8:30	The Aldrich Family	Concert in Rhythm	Public Affairs	Johnny Presents
8:45			Trails	
9pm	Beyond a Reasonable Doubt	We, the People	News	The Passing Parade
9:15			Dance Orchestra	Manchester Boddy, news
9:30	News	Jimmy Grier Orchestra	Fred Berrens Orchestra	Battle of the Sexes
9:45	The University Explorer			
10pm	Phil-Harmonia	The Ten o'Clock Wire	Jack Harris Orchestra	The Richfield Reporter
10:15		Sports		Ho Hum
10:30		Dance Orchestra	What's the Latest	Chuck Foster Orchestra
10:45		Night Cap Yarns	Skinnay Ennis Orchestra	

EVENING — WINTER, 1940

Wednesday

BLUE	CBS	MBS	NBC	
Bud Barton	Teletunes	News	Chesterfield Time	5pm
Tom Mix and His Ralston Straight Shooters	The Dream Dealer	Music	Music	5:15
Music	Public Affairs	Jack Armstong, the All-American Boy	Songs	5:30
The Adventures of Pinocchio	News	Little Orphan Annie	The Voice of the World	5:45
The Green Hornet	The Texaco Star Theater	Shafter Parker, comment	Music	6pm
		War News		6:15
Horse and Buggy Days		John B. Hughes, news	The Hollywood Playhouse	6:30
		Paging the Past		6:45
Public Affairs	Moonlight Serenade	Raymond Gram Swing, news	Kay Kyser's College of Musical Knowledge	7pm
	This is Magic	Music		7:15
News	Burns and Allen	The Lone Ranger		7:30
Music				7:45
Breezin' Along	Amos 'n' Andy	Quartet	Cabbages and Kings	8pm
	Lum and Abner	Maxine Gray Entertains	I Love a Mystery	8:15
Quicksilver	Dr. Christian	Public Affairs	Avalon Variety Time, Cliff Arquette	8:30
				8:45
Beyond a Reasonable Doubt	Al Pearce and His Gang	News	The Fred Allen Show	9pm
		Guy Lombardo Orchestra		9:15
News	Public Affairs	Jack Harris Orchestra		9:30
The University Explorer	Vincent Lopez Orchestra			9:45
Jan Garber Orchestra	The Ten o'Clock Wire	Shorty Baker Orchestra	The Richfield Reporter	10pm
Electric Music	Sports	Jan Stuart Orchestra	Chuck Foster Orchestra	10:15
Phil-Harmonia	Jimmy Grier Orchestra	What's the Latest	Enric Madriguera Orchestra	10:30
	Night Cap Yarns	Skinnay Ennis Orchestra		10:45

EVENING — WINTER, 1940

Thursday

	BLUE	CBS	MBS	NBC
5pm	Twilight Tales	Teletunes	News	For Men Only, George Jessel
5:15	Tom Mix and His Ralston Straight Shooters	The Dream Dealer	Tom Sawyer, comment	
5:30	News	News	Jack Armstong, the All-American Boy	Music
5:45	The Voice of Motordom	Music	Little Orphan Annie	The Voice of the World
6pm	Rochester Philharmonic Orchestra	Major Bowes' Original Amateur Hour	Shafter Parker, comment	Good News of 1940
6:15			Music	
6:30	America's Town Meeting of the Air		John B. Hughes, news	
6:45			Paging the Past	
7pm		Moonlight Serenade	Raymond Gram Swing, news	The Kraft Music Hall, Bing Crosby
7:15		The Inglewood Park Concert	The Inside of Sports	
7:30	News		The Shadow	
7:45	Music	Sports		
8pm	Mayor Bowron, comment	Amos 'n' Andy	Alvino Rey Orchestra	Chesterfield Time
8:15	Music	Talk		I Love a Mystery
8:30		Music	Dance Orchestra	The Standard Symphony Hour
8:45				
9pm	Beyond a Reasonable Doubt	Strange As It Seems	News	
9:15	The March of Progress		Dance Orchestra	
9:30		Opera	Fred Berrens Orchestra	Those We Love
9:45	Horace Heidt Orchestra		Fulton Lewis, Jr., news	
10pm	Phil-Harmonia	The Ten o'Clock Wire	Jack Harris Orchestra	The Richfield Reporter
10:15		Sports		Ray Noble Orchestra
10:30		Jimmy Grier Orchestra	What's the Latest	Carl Ravazza Orchestra
10:45		Night Cap Yarns	Skinnay Ennis Orchestra	

EVENING — WINTER, 1940

Friday

BLUE	CBS	MBS	NBC	
Bud Barton	Teletunes	News	Don't Forget	5pm
Tom Mix and His Ralston Straight Shooters	The Dream Dealer	Sinfonietta		5:15
News	News	Jack Armstong, the All-American Boy	Know Your Schools	5:30
The Adventures of Pinocchio	Music	Little Orphan Annie	The Voice of the World	5:45
Paducah Plantation, Red Foley	Professor Quiz	Shafter Parker, comment	Waltz Time	6pm
		Dance Orchestra		6:15
Public Affairs	The First Nighter Program	John B. Hughes, news	Hits and Bits	6:30
		Paging the Past		6:45
Sports	Grand Central Station	Raymond Gram Swing, news	Lady Esther Serenade	7pm
Songs		The Voices of Yesterday	News	7:15
News	Young Man with a Band	The Lone Ranger	The Quiz Court	7:30
Music				7:45
Carson Robison's Buckaroos	Amos 'n' Andy	Music	Chesterfield Time	8pm
	Lum and Abner		I Love a Mystery	8:15
What Would You Have Done	Johnny Presents Dramatized Short Stories		Death Valley Days	8:30
				8:45
The Word Hunters	The Kate Smith Hour	News	Music	9pm
		Barber's Beeville	Manchester Boddy, news	9:15
News		Fred Berrens Orchestra	The University Explorer	9:30
Music		Fulton Lewis, Jr., news	Donald Novis, songs	9:45
Jan Garber Orchestra	The Ten o'Clock Wire	Jack Harris Orchestra	The Richfield Reporter	10pm
Electric Music	Jimmy Grier Orchestra		Chuck Foster Orchestra	10:15
Phil-Harmonia	Harry Owens Orchestra	What's the Latest	Ray Noble Orchestra	10:30
	Night Cap Yarns	Skinnay Ennis Orchestra		10:45

EVENING — WINTER, 1940

Saturday

	BLUE	CBS	MBS	NBC
5pm	The Unclassic Hour (4:30PM)	The Fifth Quarter	Sterling Young Orchestra	Fiesta
5:15				Sweepstakes
5:30	Cal Tinney, news	Wayne King Orchestra	Hawaii Calls	Stop Me If You've Heard This One
5:45	Music			
6pm	The Green Hornet	Calling All Cars	The World's Fair Party	Youth vs. Age
6:15				
6:30	Social Security Talk	Songs	John B. Hughes, news	Traffic Tribunal
6:45	Music	Saturday Night Serenade	Betty Rhodes, songs	King's Cowboy Revue
7pm	NBC Symphony Orchestra		Tropical Serenade, Don Arres	The Camel Caravan
7:15		Public Affairs	The Inside of Sports	
7:30		The Gay Nineties Revue	Imperial Intrigue	What's My Name
7:45				
8pm		Ray Noble Orchestra	George Fisher, gossip	The National Barn Dancet
8:15			The Sons of the Pioneers	
8:30	Eddie LeBaron Orchestra	Gangbusters	Music	
8:45				
9pm	The Marriage Club	Your Hit Parade	News	Arch Oboler's Plays
9:15			Dance Orchestra	
9:30	News			Grand Ole Opry
9:45	Carl Ravazza Orchestra	Nightcap Yarns		
10pm	Phil-Harmonia	By the Way	Jan Stuart Orchestra	News
10:15		Sports		Eddie Fitzpatrick Orchestra
10:30		Dance Orchestra	Dance Orchestra	Ray Noble Orchestra
10:45				

DAYTIME — WINTER, 1940

Sunday

	BLUE	CBS	MBS	NBC
8am	News	The West Coast Church	The Comics Weekly Man	Melody
8:15	Melodic Moods			
8:30	The Book of Books	Major Bowes' Capitol Family	Matinee	Music and American Youth
8:45	The Southernaires Quartet		The Canary Pet Shop	
9am	The Radio City Music Hall		P. E. Gardner, religion	Dr. Casselbury, health
9:15				Meditation
9:30		The Salt Lake Tabernable Choir	American Wildlife	On Your Job
9:45			Songs	
10am	Garden Talk	The CBS Church of the Air	Piano Recital	Pilgrimage of Poetry
10:15	The Vass Family, songs		Romance of the Highways	Health Talk
10:30	Metropolitan Moods	Grand Hotel	Symphony Orchestra	From Hollywood Today
10:45				
11am	Great Plays	Democracy in Action	Music	Ricardo and His Caballeros
11:15				
11:30		Rhythm	Youth Drama	The University of Chicago Round Table
11:45				
12pm	Mischa Mischakoff, violin	New York Philharmonic Orchestra	News and Views	News
12:15	Foreign Policy Association Talks			Organ Recital
12:30	Nick Harris		The Haven of Rest	H. V. Kaltenborn, news
12:45	Music			Yvette Sings
1pm	National Vespers		Nobody's Children	Al Donahue Orchestra
1:15				

DAYTIME — WINTER, 1940

Monday-Friday

BLUE	CBS	MBS	NBC	
Financial Services	Mary Foster, Editor's Daughter	Victor Lindlahr, health	The Johnny Murray Show	8am
Young Dr. Malone	Music / Mr. Hamp Goes to Town	News	News	8:15
The Unclassic Hour	Nancy Dixon, talk	A Mutual Friend	Against the Storm	8:30
Music	My Children	Mirandy's Garden Patch	The Guiding Light	8:45
May I Come In	Kate Smith Speaks	Talk and Music	Strings	9am
Songs	When a Girl Marries		The O'Neills	9:15
The National Farm and Home Hour	The Romance of Helen Trent	Music / Patty Jean, songs	The Bridge Club	9:30
	Our Gal Sunday	The Carters of Elm Street		9:45
	The Goldbergs	News	Music / The Heart of Julia Blake	10am
Talk and Music	Life Can Be Beautiful	Norma Young, talk	The Story of Ellen Randolph	10:15
	The Right to Happiness	Talk and Music	Music / Songfellow	10:30
	Songs / Mary Lee Taylor, cooking		Dr. Kate	10:45
Talk and Music	Big Sister	Talk and Music	Betty and Bob	11am
	Aunt Jenny's True Life Stories		Arnold Grimm's Daughter	11:15
	Life Begins	Eddie Albright, organ	Valiant Lady	11:30
	My Son and I	Music	Hymns of All Churches / Betty Crocker, cooking	11:45
News	Joyce Jordan, Girl Intern	News	The Story of Mary Marlin	12pm
Stock Market Reports	Society Girl	Curtis Springer, health	Ma Perkins	12:15
US Agricultural Talk	The American School of the Air	Dance Orchestra	Pepper Young's Family	12:30
Between the Bookends		Let's Play Bridge	Vic and Sade	12:45
Club Matinee, Garry Moore	Pretty Kitty Kelly	The National School of the Air	The Road of Life	1pm
	The Story of Myrt and Marge		Stella Dallas	1:15

DAYTIME — WINTER, 1940

Sunday

	BLUE	CBS	MBS	NBC
1:30	Look at Books		The Lutheran Hour	The World is Yours
1:45	Richard Himber Orchestra			
2pm	News and Views	Spelling Beeliner	The Musical Steelmakers	Music
2:15				Bob Becker's Dog Talks
2:30	The Metropolitan Opera Auditions	The Adventures of Dr. Hunt	Lest We Forget	Spelling Bee
2:45		Return to Romance	Memory Music	
3pm	The Catholic Hour	The Silver Theater	Help Thy Neighbor	Music
3:15				
3:30	New Friends of Music	Gene Autry's Melody Ranch	The Show of the Week	Beat the Band
3:45				
4pm	F. A. Young, talk	Tapestry of Life	The Bach Cantata Series	Professor Puzzlewit
4:15	Dots and Dashes			
4:30	Church Federation Vespers	The Gulf Screen Guild Theater	Shorty Baker Orchestra	The Fitch Bandwagon
4:45				

DAYTIME — WINTER, 1940

Monday-Friday

BLUE	CBS	MBS	NBC	
Oh, Mr. Dinwiddy	Hilltop House	Music	Agnes White, talk	1:30
Music	Stepmother	Book a Week	Meet Miss Julia	1:45
School News	By Kathleen Norris	John B. Hughes, news	Girl Alone	2pm
The Classic Hour	David Harum	The Johnson Family	Midstream	2:15
	It Happened in Hollywood	Music	Kitty Keene, Inc.	2:30
	Scattergood Baines		The Career of Alice Blair	2:45
	The Lanny Ross Show		Pictorial	3pm
	Music / Background in Living		Talk / Show Without a Name	3:15
Talk and Music	Tena and Tim	Talk and Music	Women's Magazine of the Air	3:30
Lil' Abner	European News			3:45
The Unclassic Hour	Fletcher Wiley, talk	Community Hall	Talk and Music / Easy Aces	4pm
		The Haven of Rest	Talk and Music / Mr. Keen, Tracer of Lost Persons	4:15
Talk and Music			Art Baker's Notebook	4:30
		Talk and Music		4:45

DAYTIME — WINTER, 1940

Saturday

	BLUE	CBS	MBS	NBC
8am	Forty-Plus Associates	News	Mirandy and Friends	Quartet
8:15	Music	Mr. Hamp Goes to Town	This Wonderful World	Smilin' Ed McDonnell, songs
8:30	The Unclassic Hour	Nancy Dixon, talk	Music	Hilda Hope, M. D.
8:45	The Federation of Churches	The Saturday Party	Mirandy's Garden Patch	
9am	The American Education Forum		Chet Ryk Orchestra	The Eastman School of Music
9:15				
9:30	The National Farm and Home Hour	Let's Pretend	Music	Call to Youth
9:45				County Medical Association Talks
10am		What Price America	Ed Fitzgerald and Company	Dance Orchestra
10:15				The Stamp Club
10:30	Dance Orchestra	The Town Crier	The University Life Forum	On the Job
10:45		Dog Friends		Lani McIntryre Orchestra
11am	The Metropolitan Opera	Columbia's Country Journal	Music	Public Affairs
11:15				
11:30		Melody		Music
11:45				
12pm		Music	News	Melody
12:15			Music	
12:30				Dol Brissett Orchestra
12:45				
1pm		Bull Session	Songs	Campus Capers
1:15			Horse Racing	
1:30		Music		Station Presents
1:45			Music	

DAYTIME — WINTER, 1940

Saturday

	BLUE	CBS	MBS	NBC
2pm	Dance Orchestra	Music	Sammy Kaye Orchestra	Sunset and Vine
2:15	Magic Waves			
2:30	The Classic Hour	Henry King Orchestra		Music
2:45				
3pm		News	Buckeye	Kaltenmeyer's Kindegarten
3:15		Songs		
3:30	The Nutshell Playhouse	Which Way to Lasting Peace	Songs	Religion in the News
3:45		Today in Europe	The Charioteers Quartet	Southwestern Serenade
4pm	Message of Israel	The People's Platform	Trojan Horses	Horse Racing
4:15			Cats and Jammers	Music
4:30	The Unclassic Hour	Sky Blazers	Music	Art for Your Sake
4:45				

EVENING — SPRING, 1940

Sunday

	BLUE	CBS	MBS	NBC
5pm	The Musical Comedy Revue	The Adventures of Ellery Queen	The American Forum of the Air	The Charlie McCarthy Show
5:15				
5:30	The Voice of Hawaii	So You Think You Know Music		One Man's Family
5:45				
6pm	Lifelong Planning	The Ford Sunday Evening Hour	The Old Fashioned Revival Hour	The Manhattan Merry-Go-Round
6:15				
6:30	Melody			The American Album of Familiar Music
6:45	The Colgate Sports Newsreel, Bill Stern			
7pm	The Passing Parade	I Was There	The Goodwill Hour	The Hour of Charm
7:15	The Chapel Quartet			
7:30	News	Postmaster Parley		Carefree Carnival
7:45	Music			
8pm	The Good Old Days	Dance Orchestra	The Answer Man	The Night Editor
8:15			Music	Irene Rich Dramas
8:30	Sweet and Low	The March of California	Lazy Rhapsody	The Jello Program, Jack Benny
8:45				
9pm	Shep Fields Orchestra	Ray Noble Orchestra	Peter Kent Orchestra	Walter Winchell's Jergens Journal
9:15			The Voice of Prophecy	The Parker Family
9:30	News	Take It or Leave It		I Want a Divorce
9:45	The University Explorer		Art Kassel Orchestra	
10pm	Phil-Harmonia	The Ten o'Clock Wire	Dance Orchestra	The Richfield Reporter
10:15		Conway Peters Orchestra		Bridge to Dreamland
10:30			Sterling Young Orchestra	
10:45				

EVENING — SPRING, 1940

Monday

BLUE	CBS	MBS	NBC	
Twilight Tales	Jack Owens, songs	News	Art Baker's Notebook (4:30PM)	5pm
Tom Mix and His Ralston Straight Shooters	The Dream Dealer	Shafter Parker, comment	Music	5:15
News	Talk	Jack Armstrong, the All-American Boy	Music	5:30
The Adventures of Pinocchio	News	Little Orphan Annie	The Voice of the World	5:45
The Green Hornet	The Lux Radio Theater	The Adventures of Superman	Dr. I. Q., the Mental Banker	6pm
		Dance Orchestra		6:15
Rochester Civic Orchestra		John B. Hughes, news	Alec Templeton Time	6:30
		Paging the Past		6:45
The Starlet Fame March	Guy Lombardo Orchestra	Raymond Gram Swing, news	The Carnation Contented Hour	7pm
		This is Magic		7:15
News	Blondie	The Lone Ranger	Sammy Kaye Orchestra	7:30
Jack Owens, songs				7:45
The Studio Dark Room	Amos 'n' Andy	Pull Over, Neighbor	Chesterfield Time	8pm
	The Lanny Ross Show		H. V. Kaltenborn, news	8:15
Little Ol' Hollywood	The Model Minstrels	Radio Charades	Music	8:30
		Music	Richard Himber Orchestra	8:45
True or False	Tune Up Time	News	Edgar Allen Poe Drama	9pm
		Music		9:15
News	Art Baker's Notebook	Fulton Lewis, Jr., news	Hawthorne House	9:30
Peter Kent Orchestra	The Camera Club	Bob Crosby Orchestra		9:45
Youth in the Toils	The Ten o'Clock Wire	Music	The Richfield Reporter	10pm
Phil-Harmonia	Sports		The Blue Moonlight	10:15
	Dance Orchestra	Who is the Latest	Dance Orchestra	10:30
		Zeke Manners		10:45

EVENING — SPRING, 1940

Tuesday

	BLUE	CBS	MBS	NBC
5pm	Bud Barton	Jack Owens, songs	News	The Aldrich Family
5:15	Tom Mix and His Ralston Straight Shooters	The Dream Dealer	Shafter Parker, comment	
5:30	News	The Court of Missing Hers	Jack Armstong, the All-American Boy	Pot o' Gold
5:45	Tunes		Little Orphan Annie	
6pm	Music	Second Husband	Meet the Stars	The Cavalcade of America
6:15				
6:30		Music	John B. Hughes, news	Fibber McGee and Molly
6:45			Paging the Past	
7pm	Information, Please	Moonlight Serenade	Raymond Gram Swing, news	The Pepsodent Show, Bob Hope
7:15		The Inglewood Park Concert	The Inside of Sports	
7:30	Minstrels		Ned Jordan, Secret Agent	Uncle Walter's Dog House
7:45		Sports		
8pm	Cecil Golly Orchestra	Amos 'n' Andy	Music	Chesterfield Time
8:15		Jimmy Fidler, gossip	The Laugh and Swing Club	H. V. Kaltenborn, news
8:30	The Aldrich Family	Big Town		Johnny Presents
8:45			Twilight	
9pm	Candlelight	We, the People	News	The Passing Parade
9:15			Don't You Believe It	Lee P. Payne news
9:30	News	The Answer Auction	Fulton Lewis, Jr., news	Battle of the Sexes
9:45	The University Explorer		Music	
10pm	Phil-Harmonia	The Ten o'Clock Wire	Chuck Foster Orchestra	The Richfield Reporter
10:15		Sports		Ho Hum
10:30		Dance Orchestra	What's the Latest	Peter Kent Orchestra
10:45			Jimmy Grier Orchestra	Ernie Hecksher Orchestra

EVENING — SPRING, 1940

Wednesday

BLUE	CBS	MBS	NBC	
Bud Barton	Jack Owens, songs	News	Chesterfield Time	5pm
Tom Mix and His Ralston Straight Shooters	The Dream Dealer	Shafter Parker, comment	Speaking of Glamour	5:15
News	Music	Jack Armstong, the All-American Boy	Songs	5:30
The Adventures of Pinocchio	News	Little Orphan Annie	The Voice of the World	5:45
The Green Hornet	The Texaco Star Theater	The Adventures of Superman	Meet Some People	6pm
		Public Affairs	Richard Himber Orchestra	6:15
The Word Hunters		John B. Hughes, news	The Hollywood Playhouse	6:30
		Paging the Past		6:45
Public Affairs	Moonlight Serenade	Raymond Gram Swing, news	Kay Kyser's College of Musical Knowledge	7pm
	This is Magic	The Chapel Quartet		7:15
News	Burns and Allen	The Lone Ranger		7:30
Serenade				7:45
Breezin' Along	Amos 'n' Andy	The Answer Man	Cabbages and Kings	8pm
	The Lanny Ross Show	Cootie Williams Orchestra	H. V. Kaltenborn, news	8:15
Quicksilver	Dr. Christian	Faith Music	Avalon Variety Time, Cliff Arquette	8:30
				8:45
With Frankie Masters	Ben Bernie, the Old Maestro	News	The Fred Allen Show	9pm
		Dance Orchestra		9:15
News	The Grouch Club	Fulton Lewis, Jr., news		9:30
The University Explorer		Jimmy Grier Orchestra		9:45
Phil-Harmonia	The Ten o'Clock Wire	Chuck Foster Orchestra	The Richfield Reporter	10pm
	Sports		Peter Kent Orchestra	10:15
	Public Affairs	What's the Latest	Al Goodman Orchestra	10:30
	Will Osborne Orchestra	Sterling Young Orchestra		10:45

EVENING — SPRING, 1940

Thursday

	BLUE	CBS	MBS	NBC
5pm	Twilight Tales	Jack Owens, songs	A Mutual Friend (4:45 PM)	Mr. District Attorney
5:15	Tom Mix and His Ralston Straight Shooters	The Dream Dealer	Shafter Parker, comment	
5:30	News and Views	Talk	Jack Armstong, the All-American Boy	General Facts
5:45		News	Little Orphan Annie	The Voice of the World
6pm	Rochester Philharmonic Orchestra	Major Bowes' Original Amateur Hour	Melody	Good News of 1940
6:15				
6:30	America's Town Meeting of the Air		John B. Hughes, news	Vallee Varieties
6:45			Paging the Past	
7pm		Moonlight Serenade	Raymond Gram Swing, news	The Kraft Music Hall, Bing Crosby
7:15		The Columbia Workshop	The Inside of Sports	
7:30	News		Henry Weber's Musical Revue	
7:45	Songs	Sports		
8pm	Mayor Bowron, comment	Amos 'n' Andy	Morton Gould Orchestra	Chesterfield Time
8:15	Outdoor Reporter	The Lanny Ross Show		H. V. Kaltenborn, news
8:30		The Ask-It Basket	Dance Orchestra	The Standard Symphony Hour
8:45				
9pm	Operatic Airs	Strange As It Seems	News	
9:15	Music		Don't You Believe It	
9:30	News	Opera	Fulton Lewis, Jr., news	I Love a Mystery
9:45	Peter Kent Orchestra		Music	
10pm	Phil-Harmonia	The Ten o'Clock Wire	Jimmy Grier Orchestra	The Richfield Reporter
10:15		Ted Fiorito Orchestra		Dance Orchestra
10:30		Will Osborne Orchestra	What's the Latest	Don Draper Orchestra
10:45		News	Sterling Young Orchestra	

EVENING — SPRING, 1940

Friday

BLUE	CBS	MBS	NBC	
Bud Barton	Jack Owens, songs	News	Music By Woodbury	5pm
Tom Mix and His Ralston Straight Shooters	The Dream Dealer	Shafter Parker, comment		5:15
News	Dances	Jack Armstong, the All-American Boy	Music	5:30
The Adventures of Pinocchio	Music	Little Orphan Annie	The Voice of the World	5:45
Paducah Plantation, Red Foley	Professor Quiz	The Adventures of Superman	Waltz Time	6pm
		Franda Oagen Orchestra		6:15
Claude Sweeten Orchestra	The First Nighter Program	John B. Hughes, news	What's My Name	6:30
		Paging the Past		6:45
What Would You Have Done	Grand Central Station	Raymond Gram Swing, news	The Don Ameche Variety Show	7pm
		The Voices of Yesterday		7:15
Glen Gray Orchestra	Believe It or Not	The Lone Ranger	The Quiz Court	7:30
				7:45
Les Brown Orchestra	Amos 'n' Andy	Story Drama	Chesterfield Time	8pm
	The Lanny Ross Show	Jimmy Grier Orchestra	H. V. Kaltenborn, news	8:15
Music	Johnny Presents Dramatized Short Stories	Public Affairs	Death Valley Days	8:30
		Music		8:45
This Amazing America	The Kate Smith Hour	News	Music	9pm
		Music	Lee P. Payne, news	9:15
News		Fulton Lewis, Jr., news	The University Explorer	9:30
Music		The Legion Fights	Donald Novis, songs	9:45
Phil-Harmonia	The Ten o'Clock Wire		The Richfield Reporter	10pm
	Sports		Dance Orchestra	10:15
	Will Osborne Orchestra			10:30
		Sterling Young Orchestra		10:45

EVENING — SPRING, 1940

Saturday

	BLUE	CBS	MBS	NBC
5pm	Al Goodman Orchestra	Console	Eddie Fitzpatrick Orchestra	Landmark's of Radio
5:15	European News	News		
5:30	The Radio Guild	Wayne King Orchestra	Hawaii Calls	Dance Orchestra
5:45				
6pm	Know Your Schools	Lud Gluskin Orchestra	The World's Fair Party	Youth vs. Age
6:15	Maurice Winnick Orchestra			
6:30	The March of Progress	Sports	John B. Hughes, news	Traffic Tribunal
6:45	Ricardo and His Caballeros	Saturday Night Serenade	Music	King's Cowboy Revue
7pm	NBC Symphony Orchestra		Tropical Serenade, Don Arres	The Camel Caravan
7:15		Public Affairs	The Inside of Sports	
7:30			The WPA Report	Music
7:45		Sports		
8pm		Sky Blazers	Imperial Intrigue	The National Barn Dancet
8:15				
8:30	Hall Orchestra	Gangbusters	Skinnay Ennis Orchestra	
8:45				
9pm	The Marriage Club	Your Hit Parade	News	Music
9:15			The Saturday Night Party	
9:30	News			Grand Ole Opry
9:45	Shep Fields Orchestra	Dance Orchestra		
10pm	Phil-Harmonia	By the Way		Ray Pearl Orchestra
10:15		Sports		
10:30		Dance Orchestra		Benny Goodman Orchestra
10:45				

DAYTIME — SPRING, 1940

Sunday

	BLUE	CBS	MBS	NBC
8am	News	The West Coast Church	The Comics Weekly Man	Melody
8:15	Melodic Moods			
8:30	The Book of Books	Major Bowes' Capitol Family	The Prophecy Choir	Music and American Youth
8:45	The Four Bells		The Canary Pet Shop	Dr. Casselbury, health
9am	The Radio City Music Hall			The Story of All of Us
9:15			Don Arres, songs	Dr. Casselbury, health
9:30		The Salt Lake Tabernable Choir	American Wildlife	On Your Job
9:45			Food for Thought	
10am	Garden Talk	The CBS Church of the Air	Piano Recital	Pilgrimage of Poetry
10:15	The Vass Family, songs		Romance of the Highways	Health Talk
10:30	Harry Reser Orchestra	Democracy in Action	Symphony Orchestra	From Hollywood Today
10:45				
11am	Great Plays	Salute to the Americas	Salute to the Americas	Salute to the Americas
11:15				
11:30		Music from Pittsburgh	Swing	The University of Chicago Round Table
11:45				
12pm	Mischa Mischakoff, violin	New York Philharmonic Orchestra	Melody	News
12:15	Foreign Policy Association Talks			Organ Recital
12:30	Nick Harris		The Haven of Rest	European News
12:45	Music			H. V. Kaltenborn, news
1pm	National Vespers		Nobody's Children	Glen Gray Orchestra
1:15				

DAYTIME — SPRING, 1940

Monday-Friday

BLUE	CBS	MBS	NBC	
Financial Services	Mary Foster, Editor's Daughter	Victor Lindlahr, health	The Johnny Murray Show	8am
Young Dr. Malone	News		News	8:15
The Unclassic Hour	Nancy Dixon, talk	Talk / Keep Fit	Against the Storm	8:30
News	Toast and Jam / My Children	Music / Mirandy's Garden Patch	The Guiding Light	8:45
The Old Rambler	Kate Smith Speaks	Talk and Music	The Career of Alice Blair	9am
Talk and Music	When a Girl Marries		Portia Faces Life	9:15
The National Farm and Home Hour	The Romance of Helen Trent	Music	The Bridge Club	9:30
	Our Gal Sunday	The Carters of Elm Street		9:45
	The Goldbergs	News	Music / The Heart of Julia Blake	10am
Between the Bookends	Life Can Be Beautiful	Norma Young, talk	Ben Bernie, the Old Maestro	10:15
Talk and Music	The Right to Happiness	Talk and Music	Songfellow	10:30
	Fletcher Wiley, talk / Mary Lee Taylor, cooking	Bachelor's Children	Dr. Kate	10:45
	Big Sister	Talk and Music	The Light of the World	11am
	Aunt Jenny's True Life Stories	Eddie Albright, organ	Arnold Grimm's Daughter	11:15
	Life Begins	Talk and Music	Valiant Lady	11:30
News	My Son and I		Hymns of All Churches / Betty Crocker, cooking	11:45
Orphans of Divorce	Society Girl	News	The Story of Mary Marlin	12pm
Amanda of Honeymoon Hill	News	Curtis Springer, health	Ma Perkins	12:15
John's Other Wife	The American School of the Air	Dance Orchestra	Pepper Young's Family	12:30
Just Plain Bill		Let's Play Bridge	Vic and Sade	12:45
Club Matinee, Garry Moore	Pretty Kitty Kelly	The National School of the Air	The Road of Life	1pm
	The Story of Myrt and Marge		Stella Dallas	1:15

DAYTIME — SPRING, 1940

Sunday

	BLUE	CBS	MBS	NBC
1:30	Look at Books	The Pursuit of Happiness	Henry Weber's Musical Revue	The World is Yours
1:45	The Chamber Music Society of Lower Basin Street			
2pm	Songs	Music	The Musical Steelmakers	Yvette Sings
2:15	You Are the Jury			Bob Becker's Dog Talks
2:30	Strings	The Adventures of Dr. Hunt	Music	Crossroads
2:45		Music	Memory Music	
3pm	The Catholic Hour	The Silver Theater	Rhythm	Gray Gordon Orchestra
3:15				
3:30	Hits and Bits	Gene Autry's Melody Ranch	The Show of the Week	Beat the Band
3:45				
4pm	European News	Wbat's on Your Mind	The Bach Cantata Series	Professor Puzzlewit
4:15				
4:30	Church Federation Vespers	The Gulf Screen Guild Theater	Ray Pearl Orchestra	The Fitch Bandwagon
4:45				

DAYTIME — SPRING, 1940

Monday-Friday

BLUE	CBS	MBS	NBC	
Talk and Music	Hilltop House	Music	Local Page	*1:30*
	Stepmother	Book a Week	Meet Miss Julia	*1:45*
School News	By Kathleen Norris	John B. Hughes, news	Girl Alone	*2pm*
The Classic Hour	My Children	Talk / The American Language	Midstream	*2:15*
	It Happened in Hollywood	The Johnson Family	Kitty Keene, Inc.	*2:30*
	Scattergood Baines	Talk and Music	The O'Neills	*2:45*
	Music		Pictorial	*3pm*
	Music / Background in Living		Talk	*3:15*
Talk and Music	Joyce Jordan, Girl Intern		Agnes White, talk	*3:30*
Rocky Gordan	The World Today	Talk / The Marriage Bureau	Women's Magazine of the Air	*3:45*
The Unclassic Hour	Fletcher Wiley, talk	Community Hall	Talk and Music / Easy Aces	*4pm*
		The Haven of Rest	Talk and Music / Mr. Keen, Tracer of Lost Persons	*4:15*
			Art Baker's Notebook	*4:30*
		A Mutual Friend		*4:45*

DAYTIME — SPRING, 1940

Saturday

	BLUE	CBS	MBS	NBC
8am	Forty-Plus Associates	News and Views	A Mutual Friend	Dance Orchestra
8:15	Music		This Wonderful World	Smilin' Ed McDonnell, songs
8:30	The Unclassic Hour	Nancy Dixon, talk	The US Army Band	Joseph Gallichio Orchestra
8:45	The Federation of Churches	Toast and Jam	Mirandy's Garden Patch	
9am	The American Education Forum		Public Affairs	Lincoln Highway
9:15		Columbia's Country Journal	Music	
9:30	The National Farm and Home Hour	Let's Pretend	Child Scrapbook	Call to Youth
9:45				County Medical Association Talks
10am		Quizaron	Ed Fitzgerald and Company	Gordon Benedict Orchestra
10:15				The Stamp Club
10:30	Ilka Chase Lunch	The Town Crier	The University Life Forum	On the Job
10:45		Dog Friends		Music
11am	Music	Americans at Work	Symphony Orchestra	Lani McIntyre Orchestra
11:15				Piano Recital
11:30		Horse Racing	Ted Fiorito Orchestra	
11:45				
12pm			News	News
12:15			Music	
12:30	Ricardo and His Caballeros	News and Views	Playmakers	Dol Brissett Orchestra
12:45				
1pm	Club Matinee, Garry Moore		Horse Racing	Campus Capers
1:15				
1:30		Buffalo Presents		A Boy, A Girl, and a Band
1:45				

DAYTIME — SPRING, 1940

Saturday

	BLUE	CBS	MBS	NBC
2pm	Magic Waves	Horse Racing	Sammy Kaye Orchestra	Dance Orchestra
2:15	Music			
2:30	The Classic Hour	The Human Adventure		Music
2:45				
3pm		News	Music	Kaltenmeyer's Kindegarten
3:15		Songs		
3:30		Which Way to Lasting Peace	Youth Drama	Religion in the News
3:45	The Nutshell Playhouse	The World of Today		Brisooe Joe, songs
4pm	Message of Israel	The People's Platform	Trojan Horses	Art for Your Sake
4:15			The Legion Aviation Roundup	
4:30	The Unclassic Hour	Music	Sinfonietta	Dance Orchestra
4:45				H. V. Kaltenborn, news

EVENING — SUMMER, 1940

Sunday

	BLUE	CBS	MBS	NBC
5pm	Church Federation Vespers	The Ford Summer Hour	The Old Fashioned Revival Hour	The Manhattan Merry-Go-Round
5:15				
5:30	Lifelong Planning			Organ Recital
5:45	Sports			
6pm	The Goodwill Hour	Art Baker's Notebook	The Symphonic Hour	The Hour of Charm
6:15		Songs		
6:30		Public Affairs		Carefree Carnival
6:45				
7pm	Rhythm	The Music Game	The Answer Man	The World is a Stage
7:15	Chansonette		Dance Orchestra	Irene Rich Dramas
7:30	Melody Time	Dance Orchestra	McFarland Twins Orchestra	When the Presses Roar
7:45				
8pm	Dance Orchestra	The Grant Park Concerts	Once Over Lightly	Walter Winchell's Jergens Journal
8:15			The Pastor's Study	The Parker Family
8:30	The Colgate Sports Newsreel, Bill Stern	Take It or Leave It	Command Performance	News
8:45	Joseph Jackson, books			General Fact
9pm	Dance Orchestra	Jan Garber Orchestra	News	The Night Editor
9:15	The University Explorer		The Voice of Prophecy	Dance Orchestra
9:30		Dance Orchestra		Carl Ravazza Orchestra
9:45	News	News	Dance Orchestra	
10pm	Phil-Harmonia	Dick Jurgens Orchestra	Gus Arnheim Orchestra	The Richfeld Reporter
10:15				Bridge to Dreamland
10:30		Henry Busse Orchestra	Eddy Howard Orchestra	
10:45				

EVENING — SUMMER, 1940

Monday

BLUE	CBS	MBS	NBC	
Twilight Tales	Forecast	News	Dr. I. Q., the Mental Banker	5pm
Tarzan, the Ape Man		Daily Comics		5:15
News		Shafter Parker, comment	The Voice of Firestone	5:30
Sports		Cheer Up, Gang		5:45
European News	Guy Lombardo Orchestra	Raymond Gram Swing, news	The Carnation Contented Hour	6pm
Music		The Johnson Family		6:15
The Green Hornet	Blondie	John B. Hughes, news	Burns and Allen	6:30
		News		6:45
Reading Adventures	Amos 'n' Andy	Paging the Past	Chesterfield Time	7pm
	The Lanny Ross Show	Trio	News	7:15
Washington Merry-Go-Round	The Model Minstrels	The Lone Ranger	Where and When	7:30
				7:45
The Passing Parade	What's on Your Mind	Pull Over, Neighbor	American Challenge	8pm
Jimmy Dorsey Orchestra				8:15
News	Lady Esther Serenade	The Laff 'n' Swing Club	Hawthorne House	8:30
Donald Novis, songs				8:45
Little Old Hollywood	Paul Sullivan, news	News	Classics	9pm
	Sports	Music		9:15
The Shadow of Fu Manchu	Dance Orchestra	Fulton Lewis, Jr., news	Dance Orchestra	9:30
News	Robert Garred, news	Dance Orchestra		9:45
Phil-Harmonia	Dick Jurgens Orchestra	David Diamond Orchestra	The Richfeld Reporter	10pm
			The Heart of Julia Blake	10:15
	The Camera Club	Ray Pearl Orchestra	The Bridge Club	10:30
	Peter Kent Orchestra		Music	10:45

EVENING — SUMMER, 1940

Tuesday

	BLUE	CBS	MBS	NBC
5pm	Esposition Band	Second Husband	News	Mexican Marimba Typica Band
5:15			Daily Comics	News
5:30	News	The Court of Missing Heirs	Shafter Parker, comment	Meredith Wilson's Musical Revue
5:45	Sports		The Blue Beetle	
6pm	European News	Moonlight Serenade	Raymond Gram Swing, news	Summer Pastime
6:15	Music	Public Affairs	The Johnson Family	
6:30	Monsieur Le Capitaine	War News	John B. Hughes, news	Uncle Walter's Dog House
6:45		Sports	The Court of the Moon	
7pm	Information, Please	Amos 'n' Andy	Paging the Past	Chesterfield Time
7:15		The Lanny Ross Show	The Inside of Sports	News
7:30	Cabbages and Kings	Dance Orchestra	Ned Jordan, Secret Agent	Johnny Presents
7:45	Music			
8pm	Easy Aces	We, the People	Meet the Stars	Musical Americana
8:15	Mr. Keen, Tracer of Lost Persons			
8:30	News	Professor Quiz	Stan Keller Orchestra	Battle of the Sexes
8:45	Charlie Barnet Orchestra		Twilight Tales	
9pm	Music	Paul Sullivan, news	News	The Passing Parade
9:15		Sports	Music	Music
9:30	The Shadow of Fu Manchu	Aguliar Orchestra	Fulton Lewis Jr., news	Rudolph Friml Orchestra
9:45	News	Robert Garred, news	Joe Sudy Orchestra	
10pm	Phil-Harmonia	Dick Jurgens Orchestra	Gus Arnheim Orchestra	The Richfield Reporter
10:15				Rudolph Friml Orchestra
10:30		Jan Garber Orchestra	Eddy Howard Orchestra	The Bridge Club
10:45				Music

EVENING — SUMMER, 1940

Wednesday

BLUE	CBS	MBS	NBC	
Government Reports	The Summer Show	News	Organ Recital	*5pm*
Tarzan, the Ape Man		Daily Comics		*5:15*
News	New York Philharmonic Orchestra	Shafter Parker, comment	Ricardo and His Caballeros	*5:30*
Sports		Cheer Up, Gang	Brazilian Symphony Orchestra	*5:45*
Music / Public Affairs	Moonlight Serenade	Raymond Gram Swing, news	Kay Kyser's College of Musical Knowledge	*6pm*
	News	The Johnson Family		*6:15*
	War News	John B. Hughes, news		*6:30*
	Sports	Melody		*6:45*
The Green Hornet	Amos 'n' Andy	The Answer Man	The Hollywood Playhouse	*7pm*
	The Lanny Ross Show	The Chapel Quartet		*7:15*
What Would You Have Done	Dr. Christian	The Lone Ranger	Paducah Plantation, Whitey Ford	*7:30*
				7:45
Easy Aces	Meet Mr. Meek	P. E. Gardner, religion	Abbott and Costello	*8pm*
Mr. Keen, Tracer of Lost Persons				*8:15*
News	Uncle Jim's Question Bee	Gus Arnheim Orchestra	Mr. District Attorney	*8:30*
Dance Orchestra				*8:45*
Music	Paul Sullivan, news	News	All Aboard	*9pm*
	Sports	Ray Pearl Orchestra		*9:15*
The Shadow of Fu Manchu	Public Affairs	Fulton Lewis Jr., news	The University Explorer	*9:30*
News	Robert Garred, news	Eddy Howard Orchestra	Irving Miller Orchestra	*9:45*
Phil-Harmonia	Dick Jurgens Orchestra	Blue Barron Orchestra	The Richfeld Reporter	*10pm*
			The Heart of Julia Blake	*10:15*
	Jan Garber Orchestra	Dance Orchestra	The Bridge Club	*10:30*
			Music	*10:45*

EVENING — SUMMER, 1940

Thursday

	BLUE	CBS	MBS	NBC
5pm	Twilight Tales	Major Bowes' Original Amateur Hour	News	The Kraft Music Hall, Bob Burns
5:15	Swing		Daily Comics	
5:30	News		Shafter Parker, comment	
5:45	Sports		The Blue Beetle	
6pm	European News	Moonlight Serenade	Raymond Gram Swing, news	Bob Crosby Orchestra
6:15	Music	Public Affairs	The Johnson Family	
6:30	Concert in Miniature	War News	John B. Hughes, news	Charles Hoag, talk
6:45		Sports	G-Men	Meet Some People
7pm	This, Our America	Amos 'n' Andy	Paging the Past	Chesterfield Time
7:15		The Lanny Ross Show	The Inside of Sports	News
7:30	Montreal Symphony Orchestra	The Ask-It Basket	Gabriel Heatter, news	Good News of 1940
7:45			Leo Reisman Orchestra	
8pm	Easy Aces	Strange as It Seems	California Melodies	The Aldrich Family
8:15	Mr. Keen, Tracer of Lost Persons			
8:30	News	Answer Auction	The Plantationaires	The Standard Symphony Hour
8:45	Outdoor Reporter			
9pm	The Studio Dark Room	Paul Sullivan, news	News	
9:15		Sports	Dance Orchestra	
9:30	The Shadow of Fu Manchu	Sam Rivers Orchestra	Fulton Lewis, Jr., news	Dress Rehearsal
9:45	News	Robert Garred, news	Dance Orchestra	
10pm	Phil-Harmonia	Dick Jurgens Orchestra	Gus Arnheim Orchestra	The Richfeld Reporter
10:15				Harpa Symphony Orchestra
10:30		Jan Garber Orchestra	Eddy Howard Orchestra	The Bridge Club
10:45				Music

EVENING — SUMMER, 1940

Friday

BLUE	CBS	MBS	NBC	
Twilight Tales	Music	News	Charles Dant Orchestra	5pm
Tarzan, the Ape Man		Daily Comics		5:15
News	Grand Central Station	Shafter Parker, comment	What's My Name	5:30
Sports		Cheer Up, Gang		5:45
European News	Public Affairs	Raymond Gram Swing, news	The Don Ameche Variety Show	6pm
The Dinah Shore Show		The Johnson Family		6:15
Renfrew of the Mounted	Al Pearce and His Gang	John B. Hughes, news	The Quiz Kids	6:30
		Music		6:45
Don Messner Orchestra	Amos 'n' Andy	Paging the Past	Chesterfield Time	7pm
	The Lanny Ross Show	The Voices of Yesterday	News	7:15
Music	Johnny Presents Dramatized Short Stories	The Lone Ranger	Show Boat	7:30
				7:45
Mayor Bowron, comment	Songs	The Golden Hour	The Quiz Court	8pm
Music	Man About Hollywood			8:15
News			Death Valley Days	8:30
Dance Orchestra	Dance Orchestra			8:45
Gray Gordon Orchestra	Paul Sullivan, news	News	Gray Gordon Orchestra	9pm
	Sports	Dance Orchestra		9:15
The Shadow of Fu Manchu	Henry King Orchestra	Fulton Lewis, Jr., news	Music By Woodbury	9:30
News	Robert Garred, news	Legion Fights	Dance Orchestra	9:45
Phil-Harmonia	Dick Jurgens Orchestra		The Richfeld Reporter	10pm
			The Heart of Julia Blake	10:15
	Jan Garber Orchestra		The Bridge Club	10:30
		Eddy Howard Orchestra	Rudolph Friml Orchestra	10:45

EVENING — SUMMER, 1940

Saturday

	BLUE	CBS	MBS	NBC
5pm	The Unclassic Hour (4:30PM)	Music	Hawaii Calls	Dance Orchestra
5:15				
5:30		Henry Busse Orchestra	Daily Comics	Grand Ole Party
5:45	Sports	Music	Music	
6pm	Music		The World's Fair Party	Uncle Ezra's Radio Station
6:15		Public Affairs		
6:30			John B. Hughes, news	Traffic Tribunal
6:45		Sports	In Chicago Tonight	King's Cowboy Revue
7pm	The Marriage Club	Sky Blazers		The National Barn Dance
7:15			The Inside of Sports	
7:30	The Music Mirror	New Voices of 1940	Gabriel Heatter, news	
7:45			Larry Clinton Orchestra	
8pm	Tune Out Time	Your Hit Parade	Buddy Maleville Orchestra	European News
8:15				Jimmy Dorsey Orchestra
8:30			Dance Orchestra	Sports
8:45		Ray Noble Orchestra		Gray Gordon Orchestra
9pm	Dance Orchestra	By the Way	News	Freddy Martin Orchestra
9:15		Sports	The Saturday Night Party	
9:30		Henry King Orchestra		Dance Orchestra
9:45		Ray Noble Orchestra		
10pm	Phil-Harmonia	Dick Jurgens Orchestra		Rudolph Friml Orchestra
10:15				
10:30		Jan Garber Orchestra		Eddy Duchin Orchestra
10:45				

DAYTIME — SUMMER, 1940

Sunday

	BLUE	CBS	MBS	NBC
8am	I Am An American	The West Coast Church	The Comics Weekly Man	Bonnie Stewart, songs
8:15				The Book of Books
8:30	Church	The Salt Lake Tabernacle Choir	The Prophecy Choir	Wings Over America
8:45			The Canary Pet Shop	
9am	Public Affairs	The CBS Church of the Air	P. E. Gardner, religion	Gray Gordon Orchestra
9:15	The Vass Family, songs		Don Arres, songs	Dr. Casselbury, health
9:30	Harry Reser Orchestra	The March of Games	Outdoor Wildlife	The Silver Strings
9:45			Food for Thought	
10am	Garden Talk	Architect Program	Music	Southwestern Serenade
10:15			Romance of the Highways	
10:30		News and Views	Music	The University of Chicago Round Table
10:45				
11am	Swing	New York Philharmonic Orchestra	Music	Charles Holland, songs
11:15				
11:30				Yvette Sings
11:45				H. V. Kaltenborn, news
12pm	National Vespers		News	Chautauqua Symphony Orchestra
12:15			Music	
12:30	Garden Talk	Invitation to Learning	Nobody's Children	
12:45	The Chamber Music Society of Lower Basin Street			
1pm	Nick Harris	World's Fair Vespers	Tommy Reynolds Orchestra	The World is Yours

DAYTIME — SUMMER, 1940

Monday-Friday

BLUE	CBS	MBS	NBC	
The Breakfast Club	Nancy Dixon, talk	Music / The Breakfast Club	The Woman in White	8am
	When a Girl Marries		The O'Neills	8:15
Words and Music	The Romance of Helen Trent		Music / The Johnny Murray Show	8:30
	Our Gal Sunday	The Carters of Elm Street	News	8:45
Talk / Beauty Council	The Goldbergs	Music	Music / Your Treat	9am
Between the Bookends	Life Can Be Beautiful	Roy L. Lauren, talk	Agnes White, talk	9:15
Jamboree	The Right to Happiness	Talk and Music	By Kathleen Norris	9:30
	Mary Lee Taylor, cooking / Short, Short Story		Dr. Kate	9:45
Our Half Hour	Big Sister		The Light of the World	10am
	Aunt Jenny's True Life Stories	Norma Young, talk	Arnold Grimm's Daughter	10:15
Views and Reviews	Talk		Valiant Lady	10:30
	My Son and I	Bachelor's Children	Hymns of All Churches / Betty Crocker, cooking	10:45
Orphans of Divorce	Society Girl	Friendly Neighbors	The Story of Mary Marlin	11am
Amanda of Honeymoon Hill	Talk and Music	Eddie Albright, organ	Ma Perkins	11:15
John's Other Wife		Music	Pepper Young's Family	11:30
Just Plain Bill	News		Vic and Sade	11:45
News	Pretty Kitty Kelly	News	The Road of Life	12pm
The Word Hunters	The Story of Myrt and Marge	Talk and Music	Stella Dallas	12:15
Club Matinee, Garry Moore	Hilltop House		Lorenzo Jones	12:30
	Stepmother		Portia Faces Life	12:45
The Classic Hour	By Kathleen Norris		Girl Alone	1pm

DAYTIME — SUMMER, 1940

Sunday

	BLUE	CBS	MBS	NBC
1:15	Bobby Byrne Orchestra			
1:30	Joseph Jackson, books	Flow Gently, Sweet Rhythm	Jack Teagarden Orchestra	Horace Heidt Orchestra
1:45	The Voice of Hawaii			
2pm	The Catholic Hour	Music	Tropical Serenade, Don Arres	Gray Gordon Orchestra
2:15				
2:30	Hits and Bits	Gene Autry's Melody Ranch	Tommy Thompson Orchestra	Beat the Band
2:45	You Are the Jury			
3pm	European News	World News Roundup	Rendezvous	Professor Puzzlewit
3:15				
3:30	The World's Fair Band	The Canadian Grenadiers	News	The Fitch Bandwagon
3:45			Music	
4pm	The Sunday Night Concert	Music	The American Forum of the Air	The Bishop and the Gargoyle
4:15				
4:30		Chuck Foster Orchestra		One Man's Family
4:45				

DAYTIME — SUMMER, 1940

Monday-Friday

BLUE	CBS	MBS	NBC	
	My Children		Kitty Keene, Inc.	1:15
	Catalina Fun Quiz	Community Hall	Midstream	1:30
	Scattergood Baines	Let's Play Bridge	The O'Neills	1:45
	Young Dr. Malone	John B. Hughes, news	True Life Dramas	2pm
	Music / Backgrounds in Living	Music / The Bookworm	Mine to Cherish	2:15
Against the Storm	Joyce Jordan, Girl Intern		The Career of Alice Blair	2:30
The Guiding Light	Kate Smith Speaks		Meet Miss Julia	2:45
The Unclassic Hour	Mary Foster, Editor's Daughter	Fulton Lewis, Jr., news	Talk and Music	3pm
	Talk	Talk and Music		3:15
		The Haven of Rest	Music / Black Velvet	3:30
	European News Roundup		H. V. Kaltenborn, news	3:45
Bud Barton	Fletcher Wiley, talk	Talk and Music	Music / The Bell Telephone Hour / The Roy Shield Revue / Gentleman Relax	4pm
Rocky Gordon				4:15
Music / Frank Watanabe and Honorable Archie			Music / Tums Treasure Chest	4:30
Malcolm Claire, children's stories	Robert Garred, news			4:45

DAYTIME — SUMMER, 1940

Saturday

	BLUE	CBS	MBS	NBC
8am	News	Nancy Dixon, songs	Dance Orchestra	Songfolk
8:15	The Breakfast Club	Music		Julio Oyanguren, guitar
8:30	News	Let's Pretend	British News	Call to Youth
8:45	The Federation of Churches		Music	
9am	Music	Keyboard Capers	Ricardo and His Caballeros	Lincoln Highway
9:15	Social Relations	Highways to Health		
9:30	Ilka Chase Lunch	Motor City Melodies	Dance Orchestra	Songfellow
9:45				County Medical Association Talks
10am	Our Half Hour	Columbia's Country Journal	This Might Be You	I Am an American
10:15			Music	On Your Job
10:30	The World's Fair Band	The Town Crier	Ray Noble Orchestra	Music
10:45		The Brush Creek Follies		
11am	The Chaparral Club	US Marine Band	Manhatters Orchestra	Matinee in Rhythm
11:15		Dog Friend	Alvino Rey Orchestra	
11:30	The National Music Camp	In Old Vienna		Paul La Valle Orchestra
11:45				The World's Fair Band
12pm	Club Matinee, Garry Moore	Bull Session	News	News
12:15			Buck Rogers of the 25th Century	Boy Scouts of the Air
12:30		Horse Racing		Cab Calloway Orchestra
12:45			Music	
1pm	The Classic Hour	Buffalo Presents	Songs of the Purple Sage	The Hollywood Bowl Preview
1:15			Music	Tommy Dorsey Orchestra
1:30		Nat Brandwynne Orchestra	Dance Orchestra	
1:45			Horse Racing	

DAYTIME — SUMMER, 1940

Saturday

	BLUE	CBS	MBS	NBC
2pm	So You Want a Job	Horse Racing		Horse Racing
2:15			Music	
2:30	Renfrew of the Mounted	Yella Pessi, harp	Youth Drama	Religion in the News
2:45		News		Sports
3pm	Message of Israel	The Gay Nineties Revue	Music	Kaltenmeyer's Kindegarten
3:15				
3:30	The Garden Club	Music	Buddy Maleville Orchestra	Eddy Duchin Orchestra
3:45	The Nutshell Playhouse	European News		H. V. Kaltenborn, news
4pm	The Radio Guild	Rumba	Dance Orchestra	Bobby Byrne Orchestra
4:15			George Sterney Orchestra	Gladys Swartout, songs
4:30	The Unclassic Hour	The Human Adventure	Music	The Listener's Playhouse
4:45				

EVENING — FALL, 1940

Sunday

	BLUE	CBS	MBS	NBC
5pm	Music	The People's Plaform	The American Forum of the Air	The Charlie McCarthy Show
5:15				
5:30	Sherlock Holmes	Public Affairs		One Man's Family
5:45			Dorothy Thompson, news	
6pm	Behind the Mike	The Ford Sunday Evening Hour	The Old Fashioned Revival Hour	The Manhattan Merry-Go-Round
6:15				
6:30	Joseph Jackson, books			The American Album of Familiar Music
6:45	Organ Recital			
7pm	The Goodwill Hour	Take It or Leave It	USC Hancock Ensemble	The Hour of Charm
7:15				
7:30		The Helen Hayes Theater	Music	Carefree Carnival
7:45			Wythe Williams, news	
8pm	Sports	Crime Doctor	The Answer Man	The Night Editor
8:15	The Chapel Quartet		Public Affairs	Irene Rich Dramas
8:30	Dance Orchestra	Music	In Chicago Tonight	The Jello Program, Jack Benny
8:45				
9pm	Public Affairs	The Gulf Screen Theater		Walter Winchell's Jergens Journal
9:15			The Voice of Prophecy	The Parker Family
9:30	News	What's On Your Mind		Sherlock Holmes
9:45	The University Explorer		The Hawaiians	
10pm	Phil-Harmonia	The Ten o'Clock Wire	Dance Orchestra	The Richfield Reporter
10:15		Air Views		Bridge to Dreamland
10:30		The Columbia Workshop	News	Inside the News
10:45			Jack Harris Orchestra	

EVENING — FALL, 1940

Monday

BLUE	CBS	MBS	NBC	
Twilight Tales	European News	News	The Bell Telephone Hour	5pm
Tarzan, the Ape Man	Talk	Daily Comics		5:15
News		Shafter Parker, comment	Public Affairs	5:30
Tom Mix and His Ralston Straight Shooters	News	Captain Midnight	Jack Armstong, the All-American Boy	5:45
Public Affairs	The Lux Radio Theater	Fulton Lewis, Jr., news	Dr. I. Q., the Mental Banker	6pm
		The Flying Football		6:15
Little Ol' Hollywood		John B. Hughes, news	The Show Boat	6:30
		Music		6:45
Public Affairs	Guy Lombardo Orchestra	Raymond Gram Swing, news	The Carnation Contented Hour	7pm
		Charade		7:15
News	Blondie	The Lone Ranger	Burns and Allen	7:30
Music				7:45
John Dockweller, news	Amos 'n' Andy	Pull Over, Neighbor	Chesterfield Time	8pm
The Passing Parade	The Lanny Ross Show		H. V. Kaltenborn, news	8:15
I Love a Mystery	The Model Minstrels	Double or Nothing	Where and When	8:30
				8:45
True or False	Those We Love	News	The American Challenge	9pm
		Public Affairs		9:15
News	Public Affairs	Boake Carter, news	Hawthorne House	9:30
Public Affairs	The Camera Club	Wake Up, America		9:45
Youth in the Toils	The Ten o'Clock Wire		The Richfield Reporter	10pm
Phil-Harmonia	Music		The Blue Moonlight	10:15
	Music Masterworks		Inside the News	10:30
		Music	The Bridge Club	10:45

EVENING — FALL, 1940

Tuesday

	BLUE	CBS	MBS	NBC
5pm	Twilight Tales	European News	News	General Fact
5:15	Music	Talk	Daily Comics	Jack Armstrong, the All-American Boy
5:30	News	The First Nighter Program	Shafter Parker, comment	Tums Treasure Chest
5:45	Tom Mix and His Ralston Straight Shooters		Captain Midnight	
6pm	Music	Public Affairs	Fulton Lewis, Jr., news	Music
6:15			The Flying Football	
6:30	The Bishop and the Gargoyle	Music	John B. Hughes, news	Fibber McGee and Molly
6:45			Talk	
7pm	Public Affairs	Moonlight Serenade	Raymond Gram Swing, news	The Pepsodent Show, Bob Hope
7:15		Public Affairs	The Inside of Sports	
7:30	Uncle Jim's Question Bee		Wythe Williams, news	Uncle Walter's Dog House
7:45		Sports	Music	
8pm	Information, Please	Amos 'n' Andy	The Two Cities Quiz	Chesterfield Time
8:15		The Lanny Ross Show		H. V. Kaltenborn, news
8:30	Ben Bernie, the Old Maestro	The Court of Missing Heirs	Sing with the Band	Johnny Presents
8:45				
9pm	Easy Aces	We, the People	News	The Passing Parade
9:15	Mr. Keen, Tracer of Lost Persons		Music	Manchester Boddy, news
9:30	News	All Around Town	Hal Kemp Orchestra	Battle of the Sexes
9:45	Frank Watanabe and Honorable Archie	Bob Crosby Orchestra		
10pm	The Five Edwards	The Ten o'Clock Wire	The Haven of Rest	The Richfield Reporter
10:15	Phil-Harmonia	Night Cap Yarns		Music
10:30		Music Masterworks	News	Inside the News
10:45			Jack Harris Orchestra	The Bridge Club

EVENING — FALL, 1940

Wednesday

BLUE	CBS	MBS	NBC	
Government Reports	European News	News	Chesterfield Time	5pm
Tarzan, the Ape Man	Talk	Daily Comics	Jack Armstong, the All-American Boy	5:15
News	Public Affairs	Shafter Parker, comment	Public Affairs	5:30
Tom Mix and His Ralston Straight Shooters	News	Captain Midnight	Strings	5:45
Public Affairs	Music	Fulton Lewis, Jr., news	Public Affairs	6pm
		The Flying Football	King's Cowboy Revue	6:15
Piano Recital	Public Affairs	John B. Hughes, news	The Cavalcade of America	6:30
		Cheer Up, Gang		6:45
Public Affairs	Moonlight Serenade	Raymond Gram Swing, news	Kay Kyser's College of Musical Knowledge	7pm
	Dorothy Thompson, news	Music		7:15
News	Public Affairs	The Lone Ranger		7:30
The Cavalcade of History				7:45
The Quiz Kids	Amos 'n' Andy	The Answer Man	The Hollywood Playhouse	8pm
	The Lanny Ross Show	Rhythm		8:15
Manhattan at Midnight	Dance Orchestra		Paducah Plantation, Red Foley	8:30
		The Chapel Quartet		8:45
Easy Aces	The Texaco Star Theater, Fred Allen	News	Time to Smile, Eddie Cantor	9pm
Mr. Keen, Tracer of Lost Persons		Public Affairs		9:15
News		Boake Carter, news	Mr. District Attorney	9:30
Frank Watanabe and Honorable Archie		Hal Kemp Orchestra		9:45
Phil-Harmonia	The Ten o'Clock Wire	The Haven of Rest	The Richfield Reporter	10pm
	Organ Recital		Public Affairs	10:15
	Music Masterworks	News	Inside the News	10:30
		Sports	The Bridge Club	10:45

EVENING — FALL, 1940

Thursday

	BLUE	CBS	MBS	NBC
5pm	Pot o' Gold	European News	News	Strings
5:15		Talk	Daily Comics	Jack Armstong, the All-American Boy
5:30	News	Public Affairs	Shafter Parker, comment	The Aldrich Family
5:45	Tom Mix and His Ralston Straight Shooters	News	Captain Midnight	
6pm	Singing and Swinging	Major Bowes' Original Amateur Hour	Fulton Lewis, Jr., news	The Kraft Music Hall, Bing Crosby
6:15			Arthur Mann, news	
6:30	Music		John B. Hughes, news	
6:45	Mayor Bowron, comment		The Forum	
7pm	Vallee Varieties	Moonlight Serenade	Gabriel Heatter, news	Bob Crosby Orchestra
7:15		Public Affairs	The Inside of Sports	
7:30	News		Wythe Williams, news	Musical Americana
7:45	Public Affairs	Sports	The Two Cities Quiz	
8pm	The School Kids Quiz	Amos 'n' Andy	The Standard Symphony Hour	Chesterfield Time
8:15		The Lanny Ross Show		H. V. Kaltenborn, news
8:30	Fame and Fortune	The Ask-It Basket		Maxwell House Coffee Time, Brice and Morgan
8:45				
9pm	Easy Aces	Strange As It Seems	News	The Quiz Court
9:15	Mr. Keen, Tracer of Lost Persons		Music	
9:30	News	Music	Film Preview	When the Presses Roar
9:45	Public Affairs	Public Affairs	Music	
10pm	Phil-Harmonia	The Ten o'Clock Wire	The Haven of Rest	The Richfield Reporter
10:15		Sports		Dance Orchestra
10:30		Music Masterworks	News	Inside the News
10:45			Jack Harris Orchestra	The Bridge Club

EVENING — FALL, 1940

Friday

BLUE	CBS	MBS	NBC	
Twilight Tales	European News	News	Friendly Counselor	5pm
Tarzan, the Ape Man	Talk	Daily Comics	Jack Armstong, the All-American Boy	5:15
News	Public Affairs	Shafter Parker, comment	Music	5:30
Tom Mix and His Ralston Straight Shooters	News	Captain Midnight		5:45
Public Affairs	The Texas Rangers	Fulton Lewis, Jr., news	Public Affairs	6pm
Jack Owens, songs	Public Affairs	The Flying Football		6:15
John B. Kennedy, news		John B. Hughes, news	Everyman's Theater	6:30
Time Out		Public Affairs		6:45
Madison Square Garden Boxiing	Believe It or Not	Raymond Gram Swing, news	Wings of Destiny	7pm
		The Voices of Yesterday		7:15
News	Al Pearce and His Gang	The Lone Ranger	Alec Templeton Time	7:30
Public Affairs				7:45
Public Affairs	Amos 'n' Andy	The Two Cities Quiz	Chesterfield Time	8pm
	The Lanny Ross Show		H. V. Kaltenborn, news	8:15
Music	Johnny Presents Dramatized Short Stories	I Want a Divorce	Death Valley Days	8:30
Public Affairs				8:45
Gangbusters	The Kate Smith Hour	News	The University Explorer	9pm
		Public Affairs	Manchester Boddy, news	9:15
News		Boake Carter, news	Public Affairs	9:30
Public Affairs		Public Affairs		9:45
Phil-Harmonia	The Ten o'Clock Wire	The Haven of Rest	The Richfield Reporter	10pm
	Sports		Public Affairs	10:15
	Music Masterworks	News	Inside the News	10:30
		Jack Harris Orchestra	The Bridge Club	10:45

EVENING — FALL, 1940

Saturday

	BLUE	CBS	MBS	NBC
5pm	Music	European News	Listen To	Freddy Martin Orchestra
5:15		Music	Daily Comics	
5:30	The Parade of Hits	Wayne King Orchestra	Football Scores	Traffic Tribunal
5:45	Sports		Public Affairs	Public Affairs
6pm	Music	Kids' Quizaroo	The Marines Tell It to You	The National Barn Dance
6:15	Public Affairs			
6:30	John B. Kennedy, news	Public Affairs	John B. Hughes, news	
6:45	Ricardo and His Caballeros		Music	
7pm	NBC Symphony Orchestra		Gabriel Heatter, news	Uncle Ezra's Radio Station
7:15			The Inside of Sports	
7:30		By the Way	Lew Loyal Orchestra	Grand Ole Opry
7:45		Sports		
8pm	Music	The Marriage Club	Music	Truth or Consequences
8:15				
8:30	Public Affairs	Film Preview	California Melodies	The Knickerbocker Playhouse
8:45		Public Affairs		
9pm	Tune Out Time	Your Hit Parade	News	Public Affairs
9:15			Sterling Young Orchestra	Music
9:30			Boake Carter, news	
9:45	Public Affairs	Public Affairs	Hal Kemp Orchestra	
10pm	Phil-Harmonia	The Ten o' Clock Wire	The Haven of Rest	The Richfield Reporter
10:15		Sports		Eddie Mallory Orchestra
10:30		Henry Busse Orchestra	News	Johnny Richards Orchestra
10:45			Jack Harris Orchestra	

DAYTIME — FALL, 1940

Sunday

	BLUE	CBS	MBS	NBC
8am	Songs	The West Coast Church	The Comics Weekly Man	Bonnie Stewart, songs
8:15				The Book of Books
8:30	The Three Men Tune	Major Bowes' Capitol Family	The Prophecy Choir	Words and Music
8:45	Betty and the Escorts		The Canary Pet Shop	
9am	The Radio City Music Hall			Dr. Casselbury, health
9:15			Don Arres, songs	Guitar Recital
9:30		The Salt Lake Tabernable Choir	The Sing a Song of Safety Club	Wings Over America
9:45			Food for Thought	
10am	Swing	The CBS Church of the Air	Strings	I Am an American
10:15			Romance of the Highways	Health Talk
10:30		Public Affairs	Benny Light, songs	On Your Job
10:45		What, No Architect		
11am		Public Affairs	Public Affairs	American Pilgrimage
11:15				
11:30		News	Nobody's Children	The University of Chicago Round Table
11:45	Ahead of the Headllines	Music		
12pm	Great Plays	New York Philharmonic Orchestra	News	That's Amazing
12:15			The Haven of Rest	Public Affairs
12:30				H. V. Kaltenborn, news
12:45				Bob Becker's Dog Talks
1pm	Garden Talk		Peter Quill	National Vespers
1:15	The Three Cheers			

DAYTIME — FALL, 1940

Monday-Friday

BLUE	CBS	MBS	NBC	
The Breakfast Club	Music	Good Morning, Neighbor / The Breakfast Club	The Johnny Murray Show	*8am*
	News		Against the Storm	*8:15*
News	The Goldbergs	News	The Road of Life	*8:30*
The Musical Clock	By Kathleen Norris	Foreign News	News	*8:45*
Beauty Council	Kate Smith Speaks	Victor Lindlahr, health	Your Treat	*9am*
	When a Girl Marries	The Family Bible	The O'Neills	*9:15*
News	The Romance of Helen Trent	Talk / Let's Play Bridge	Mine to Cherish / The Heart of Julia Blake	*9:30*
Between the Bookends	Our Gal Sunday	Keep Fit	The Bridge Club	*9:45*
Jamboree	Life Can Be Beautiful	News	News	*10am*
	The Woman in White	Talk and Music / I'll Never Forget	Talk	*10:15*
Views and Reviews	The Right to Happiness	The Johnson Family	By Kathleen Norris	*10:30*
	Mary Lee Taylor, cooking / Short, Short Story	Bachelor's Children	Dr. Kate	*10:45*
Our Half Hour	Big Sister	Friendly Neighbors	Hymns of the World All Churches / Betty Crocker, cooking	*11am*
	Aunt Jenny's True Life Stories	Ruth Hauser, songs	Arnold Grimm's Daughter	*11:15*
Music / Family Doctor	Talk	Talk and Music	Valiant Lady	*11:30*
News	My Son and I		The Light of the World	*11:45*
Orphans of Divorce	Martha Webster	News	The Story of Mary Marlin	*12pm*
Amanda of Honeymoon Hill	The KNX Playhouse	Music	Ma Perkins	*12:15*
John's Other Wife	Kate Hopkins, Angel of Mercy		Pepper Young's Family	*12:30*
Just Plain Bill	News		Vic and Sade	*12:45*
Mother of Mine	Portia Faces Life	The National School of the Air	Mary Noble, Backstage Wife	*1pm*
Club Matinee, Garry Moore	The Story of Myrt and Marge		Stella Dallas	*1:15*

DAYTIME — FALL, 1940

Sunday

	BLUE	CBS	MBS	NBC
1:30	Look at Books	Invitation to Learning	Sinfoniietta	The World is Yours
1:45	Tempos			
2pm	Nick Harris	Design for Happiness	The Musical Steelmakers	The Metropolitan Opera Auditions
2:15	Henry King Orchestra			The Three Cheers
2:30	Behind the Mike	Editorially Speaking	Music Memories	Your Dream Has Come True
2:45		Talk		
3pm	The Catholic Hour	The Silver Theater	The Marines Tell It to You	Music
3:15				
3:30	New Friends of Music	Gene Autry's Melody Ranch	The Show of the Week	Beat the Band
3:45				
4pm	The Dinning Sisters, songs	News of the World	The Gospel Tabernacle	Professor Puzzlewit
4:15	European News			
4:30	Speak Up, America	The Adventures of Dr. Hunt	Berlin News	The Fitch Bandwagon
4:45		Mark Strand Orchestra		

DAYTIME — FALL, 1940

Monday-Friday

BLUE	CBS	MBS	NBC	
	Hilltop House	Talk	Lorenzo Jones	1:30
	Stepmother		Young Widder Brown	1:45
School News	The American School of the Air	John B. Hughes, news	Girl Alone	2pm
The Classic Hour		Talk	Lone Journey	2:15
	Talk	Community Hall	The Guiding Light	2:30
	Scattergood Baines	Talk and Music	Life Can Be Beautiful	2:45
The Unclassic Hour	Young Dr. Malone		Talk and Music	3pm
	Background in Living			3:15
	Joyce Jordan, M. D.		The Career of Alice Blair	3:30
	Kitty Keene, Inc.		Meet Miss Julia	3:45
	Second Wife	Paging the Past	Talk and Music	4pm
Set Sail	We, the Abbotts	Talk and Music		4:15
Bud Barton	Music		Music	4:30
Talk / The Adventures of Superman	Talk		Fleetwood Lawton, news	4:45

DAYTIME — FALL, 1940

Saturday

	BLUE	CBS	MBS	NBC
8am	The Breakfast Club	The Town Crier	A Mutual Friend	Songs
8:15		News	Foreign News	The Federation of Women's Clubs
8:30	News	Music	The US Army Band	News
8:45	The Federation of Churches			Smilin' Ed McConnell, songs
9am	The American Education Forum	Columbia's Country Journal	Willard Alexander Orchestra	Lincoln Highway
9:15				
9:30	News	Music	Play Bridge	The Heart of Juiie Blake
9:45	Forty-Plus Associates		The Air Cadet Quiz	County Medical Association Talks
10am	Uncle Dan's Quiz	The Saturday Party		On the Job
10:15			Talk	The Stamp Club
10:30	Ilka Chase Lunch		Music	Public Affairs
10:45		Sports	Sports	
11am	Sports			Sports
11:15				
11:30				
11:45				
12pm				
12:15				
12:30				
12:45				
1pm				
1:15				
1:30		Quartet		
1:45				

DAYTIME — FALL, 1940

Saturday

	BLUE	CBS	MBS	NBC
2pm	The Classic Hour	Buffalo Presents	Listen To	Music
2:15			News	
2:30		Sports	Horse Racing	Jimmy Dorsey Orchestra
2:45				
3pm	Cecil Golly Orchestra			Sports
3:15				
3:30	The Listener's Playhouse		Youth Drama	Religion in the News
3:45				Abe Lyman Orchestra
4pm	Message of Israel		Music	
4:15			The Charioteers Quartet	European News
4:30	Horse Racing		Music	Songs
4:45	Music			H. V. Kaltenborn, news

LISTINGS FOR 1941

EVENING — WINTER, 1941

Sunday

	BLUE	CBS	MBS	NBC
5pm	Church Federation Vespers	Calling All Cars	The American Forum of the Air	The Charlie McCarthy Show
5:15				
5:30	Sherlock Holmes	Spelling Beeliner		One Man's Family
5:45			Dorothy Thompson, news	
6pm	Records	The Ford Sunday Evening Hour	The Old Fashioned Revival Hour	The Manhattan Merry-Go-Round
6:15				
6:30	Joseph Jackson, books			The American Album of Familiar Music
6:45	The Colgate Sports Newsreel, Bill Stern			
7pm	The Goodwill Hour	Take It or Leave It	USC Hancock Ensemble	The Hour of Charm
7:15				
7:30		The Helen Hayes Theater	Music	Carefree Carnival
7:45			Wythe Williams, news	
8pm	The Chapel Quartet	Crime Doctor	Freddy Martin Orchestra	The Night Editor
8:15	Dance Orchestra			Irene Rich Dramas
8:30	Johnny Long Orchestra	Smarty Party	Chicago Symphony Orchestra	The Jello Program, Jack Benny
8:45				
9pm	The University Explorer	The Hollywood Showcase	News	Walter Winchell's Jergens Journal
9:15	News		The Sons of the Pioneers	The Parker Family
9:30	Serenade to Loveliness	The Gulf Screen Theater	The Voice of Prophecy	Sherlock Holmes
9:45				
10pm	Phil-Harmonia	The Ten o'Clock Wire	The Sunday Playhouse	The Richfield Reporter
10:15		Air Views		Bridge to Dreamland
10:30		Songs	The Hawaiians	Inside the News
10:45			Jack Harris Orchestra	

EVENING — WINTER, 1941

Monday

BLUE	CBS	MBS	NBC	
Twilight Tales	European News	News	The Bell Telephone Hour	5pm
Waltzes	Talk	Daily Comics		5:15
News		Shafter Parker, comment	The Hurlburt Field Band	5:30
Tom Mix and His Ralston Straight Shooters	News	Captain Midnight	Jack Armstong, the All-American Boy	5:45
You're in the Army Now	The Lux Radio Theater	Fulton Lewis, Jr., news	Dr. I. Q., the Mental Banker	6pm
		The Johnson Family		6:15
The Chamber Music Society of Lower Basin Street		John B. Hughes, news	The Show Boat	6:30
		Art Linkletter, comment		6:45
Story Dramas	Guy Lombardo Orchestra	Raymond Gram Swing, news	The Carnation Contented Hour	7pm
Bob Hannon, songs		Something to Talk About		7:15
News	Blondie	The Lone Ranger	Burns and Allen	7:30
Music				7:45
Marshall Orchestra	Amos 'n' Andy	In Chicago Tonight	Chesterfield Time	8pm
The Passing Parade	The Lanny Ross Show		H. V. Kaltenborn, news	8:15
I Love a Mystery	Woody Guthrie Orchestra	Double or Nothing	Point Sublime	8:30
				8:45
Interlude	Those We Love	Glenn Hardy, news	The American Challenge	9pm
		Songs		9:15
News	Dance Orchestra	Boake Carter, news	Hawthorne House	9:30
Music	News	Wake Up, America		9:45
Youth in the Toils	The Ten o'Clock Wire		The Richfield Reporter	10pm
Phil-Harmonia	Night Cap Yarns		Frazier Hunt, news	10:15
	Music Masterworks		Inside the News	10:30
		Music	Music By Woodbury	10:45

EVENING — WINTER, 1941

Tuesday

	BLUE	CBS	MBS	NBC
5pm	Talk	European News	News	Interlude
5:15		Talk	Daily Comics	Jack Armstrong, the All-American Boy
5:30	News	The First Nighter Program	Shafter Parker, comment	Tums Treasure Chest
5:45	Tom Mix and His Ralston Straight Shooters		Captain Midnight	
6pm	Clancy Orchestra	Second Husband	Fulton Lewis, Jr., news	Tuesday at Six
6:15			Talk	
6:30	Inner Sanctum Mysteries	Professor Quiz	John B. Hughes, news	Fibber McGee and Molly
6:45			The Affairs of State	
7pm	Story Dramas	Moonlight Serenade	Raymond Gram Swing, news	The Pepsodent Show, Bob Hope
7:15	Gordon Jenkins Orchestra	The Inglewood Park Concert	The Inside of Sports	
7:30	Uncle Jim's Question Bee		Wythe Williams, news	Uncle Walter's Dog House
7:45		News	Music	
8pm	Grand Central Station	Amos 'n' Andy	The Clinic Forum	Chesterfield Time
8:15		The Lanny Ross Show		H. V. Kaltenborn, news
8:30	Ben Bernie, the Old Maestro	The Court of Missing Heirs	Sing with the Band	Johnny Presents
8:45				
9pm	Easy Aces	We, the People	Glenn Hardy, news	The World's a Stage
9:15	Mr. Keen, Tracer of Lost Persons		Songs	Dance Orchestra
9:30	News	All Around Town	Freddy Martin Orchestra	Battle of the Sexes
9:45	Old and New			
10pm	The Five Edwards	The Ten o'Clock Wire	The Haven of Rest	The Richfield Reporter
10:15	Phil-Harmonia	Night Cap Yarns		Music
10:30			News	Inside the News
10:45			Jack Harris Orchestra	Nottingham Symphony Orchestra

EVENING — WINTER, 1941

Wednesday

BLUE	CBS	MBS	NBC	
Uncle Dan's Quiz	European News	News	Chesterfield Time	5pm
Tom Mix and His Ralston Straight Shooters	Talk	Daily Comics	Jack Armstong, the All-American Boy	5:15
Manhattan at Midnight	Philharmonic Talk	Shafter Parker, comment	Charles Dant Orchestra	5:30
	Robert Garred, news	Captain Midnight		5:45
The Roy Shields Revue	Don't Be Personal	Fulton Lewis, Jr., news	Freddy Martin Orchestra	6pm
	Songs	Public Affairs	King's Cowboy Revue	6:15
Spin and Win	Big Town	John B. Hughes, news	The Cavalcade of America	6:30
		The Answer Man		6:45
Story Dramas	Moonlight Serenade	Gabriel Heatter, news	Kay Kyser's College of Musical Knowledge	7pm
	Music	The Chapel Quartet		7:15
News	Meet Mr. Meek	The Lone Ranger		7:30
The Cavalcade of History				7:45
The Quiz Kids	Amos 'n' Andy	The Show of the Week	Tony Martin, songs	8pm
	The Lanny Ross Show		How Did You Meet	8:15
Tommy Tucker Orchestra	Dr. Christian	Music	Paducah Plantation, Red Foley	8:30
				8:45
Easy Aces	The Texaco Star Theater, Fred Allen	Glenn Hardy, news	Time to Smile, Eddie Cantor	9pm
Mr. Keen, Tracer of Lost Persons		Songs		9:15
News		Freddy Martin Orchestra	Mr. District Attorney	9:30
The Music Revue				9:45
Phil-Harmonia	The Ten o'Clock Wire	Ted Dale Orchestra	The Richfield Reporter	10pm
	Night Cap Yarns		Frazier Hunt, news	10:15
	Music Masterworks	Boake Carter, news	Inside the News	10:30
		Jack Harris Orchestra	Dance Orchestra	10:45

EVENING — WINTER, 1941

Thursday

	BLUE	CBS	MBS	NBC
5pm	Pot o' Gold	European News	News	Strings
5:15		Talk	Daily Comics	Jack Armstrong, the All-American Boy
5:30	News	Music	Shafter Parker, comment	The Aldrich Family
5:45	Tom Mix and His Ralston Straight Shooters	Robert Garred, news	Captain Midnight	
6pm	Rochester Philharmonic Orchestra	Major Bowes' Original Amateur Hour	Fulton Lewis, Jr., news	The Kraft Music Hall, Bing Crosby
6:15			Public Affairs	
6:30	Music		John B. Hughes, news	
6:45	Mayor Bowron, comment		The Affairs of State	
7pm	Vallee Varieties	Moonlight Serenade	Gabriiel Heatter, news	Xavier Cugat Orchestra
7:15		What's on Your Mind	The Inside of Sports	
7:30	Ahead of the Headlines		Wythe Williams, news	The American Challenge
7:45	Cabbages and Kings	Sports	Art Linkletter, comment	
8pm	The School Kids Quiz	Amos 'n' Andy	The Standard Symphony Hour	Chesterfield Time
8:15		The Lanny Ross Show		H. V. Kaltenborn, news
8:30	Fame and Fortune	The Ask-It Basket		Maxwell House Coffee Time, Brice and Morgan
8:45				
9pm	Easy Aces	City Desk	Glenn Hardy, news	The Quiz Court
9:15	Mr. Keen, Tracer of Lost Persons		Songs	
9:30	News	Jerry Wald Orchestra	Freddy Martin Orchestra	When the Presses Roar
9:45	Bonaldi Sings			
10pm	Phil-Harmonia	The Ten o'Clock Wire	The Haven of Rest	The Richfield Reporter
10:15		Night Cap Yarns		Chuck Foster Orchestra
10:30		Music Masterworks	News	Inside the News
10:45			Jack Harris Orchestra	Dance Orchestra

EVENING — WINTER, 1941

Friday

BLUE	CBS	MBS	NBC	
Twilight Tales	European News	News	Organ Recital	5pm
Government Reports	Talk	Daily Comics	Jack Armstong, the All-American Boy	5:15
News		Shafter Parker, comment	Infomation, Please	5:30
Tom Mix and His Ralston Straight Shooters	Robert Garred, news	Captain Midnight		5:45
Doctors at Work	Talk Your Way Out of This One	Fulton Lewis, Jr., news	Waltz Time	6pm
	Skipper Storm	The Johnson Family		6:15
Your Happy Birthday	The Campbell Playhouse	John B. Hughes, news	Everyman's Theater	6:30
		Art Linkletter, comment		6:45
Madison Square Garden Boxing	Public Affairs	Raymond Gram Swing, news	Wings of Destiny	7pm
		General Fact		7:15
News	Al Pearce and His Gang	The Lone Ranger	Alec Templeton Time	7:30
Music				7:45
The Army Show	Amos 'n' Andy	The Two Cities Quiz	Chesterfield Time	8pm
	The Lanny Ross Show		H. V. Kaltenborn, news	8:15
Treasure Hunt	Johnny Presents Dramatized Short Stories	I Want a Divorce	Death Valley Days	8:30
Camacho and Hart, songs				8:45
Gangbusters	The Kate Smith Hour	Glenn Hardy, news	Glen Gray Orchestra	9pm
		Songs		9:15
News		Freddy Martin Orchestra	Dance Orchestra	9:30
Music				9:45
Phil-Harmonia	The Ten o'Clock Wire	Dance Orchestra	The Richfield Reporter	10pm
	Night Cap Yarns		Frazier Hunt, news	10:15
	Music Masterworks	News	Inside the News	10:30
		Jack Harris Orchestra	Dance Orchestra	10:45

EVENING — WINTER, 1941

Saturday

	BLUE	CBS	MBS	NBC
5pm	The Garden Club	European News	Dr. Matthews, religion	Dance Orchestra
5:15		Sports		Traffic Tribunal
5:30	The Bishop and the Gargoyle	Wayne King Orchestra	Freddy Martin Orchestra	Music
5:45				
6pm	The Song of Your Life	Kids' Quizaroo	Innocent Bystander	The National Barn Dance
6:15			Billiard Meet	
6:30	NBC Symphony Orchestra	The Fact Finder	John B. Hughes, news	
6:45		Saturday Night Serenade	The Answer Man	
7pm			Gabriel Heatter, news	Uncle Ezra's Radio Station
7:15		Public Affairs	The Inside of Sports	
7:30		By the Way	Dance Orchestra	Grand Ole Opry
7:45		News		
8pm	Music	The Marriage Club	Hawaii Calls	Truth or Consequences
8:15				
8:30	Tune Out Time	Film Preview	California Melodies	The Knickerbocker Playhouse
8:45		Guy Lombardo Orchestra		
9pm		Your Hit Parade	Glenn Hardy, news	Glen Gray Orchestra
9:15			Songs	The Sports Forum
9:30	Unlimited Horizons		Freddy Martin Orchestra	Russ Morgan Orchestra
9:45		Behind the Headlines		
10pm	Phil-Harmonia	The Ten o' Clock Wire	Dance Orchestra	The Richfield Reporter
10:15		Music		Ben Bernie, the Old Maestro
10:30		Dance Orchestra	Boake Carter, news	Dance Orchestra
10:45			Jack Harris Orchestra	

DAYTIME — WINTER, 1941

Sunday

	BLUE	CBS	MBS	NBC
8am	Songs	The West Coast Church	The Comics Weekly Man	Rhapsody of the Rockies
8:15	Dance Orchestra			The Book of Books
8:30	Sweet Land of Liberty	Major Bowes' Capitol Family	The Faith Builder	Music and American Youth
8:45				
9am	Nick Harris		Strings	Music
9:15	I Am an American		The Prophecy Choir	
9:30	Wings Over America	The Salt Lake Tabernable Choir	P. E. Gardner, religion	The Radio City Music Hall
9:45			Food for Thought	
10am	Swing	The CBS Church of the Air	Strings	
10:15			Romance of the Highways	
10:30		Music	Sunday Songs	On Your Job
10:45		What, No Architect	The Canary Pet Shop	
11am	American Pilgrimage	Music	Swing	Health Talk
11:15	Foreign Policy Association Talks			Strings
11:30	Music	News		The University of Chicago Round Table
11:45		Music		
12pm	Great Plays	New York Philharmonic Orchestra	News	Fantastic Fact
12:15			Midnight Mission	H. V. Kaltenborn, news
12:30				The Customs Corner
12:45				Bob Becker's Dog Talks
1pm	Garden Talk		Peter Quill	National Vespers
1:15	Look at Books			

DAYTIME — WINTER, 1941

Monday-Friday

BLUE	CBS	MBS	NBC	
The Breakfast Club	The Music Express	Good Morning, Neighbor / The Haven of Rest	The Johnny Murray Show	*8am*
	Nancy Dixon, talk		Against the Storm	*8:15*
News	The Goldbergs	News	The Road of Life	*8:30*
Robert L. Johnson, talk	By Kathleen Norris	Music / Foreign News	News	*8:45*
Talk	Kate Smith Speaks	The Family Bible	Your Treat / Words and Music	*9am*
Music	When a Girl Marries	Talk and Music		*9:15*
Homer Griffith, sports	The Romance of Helen Trent		The Voice of Experience / The Heart of Julia Blake	*9:30*
News	Our Gal Sunday	Keep Fit	The Bridge Club	*9:45*
I Love Linda Dale	Life Can Be Beautiful	News	News	*10am*
Between the Bookends	The Woman in White	Talk and Music	Talk	*10:15*
Talk and Music	The Right to Happiness	The Johnson Family	The Wife Saver	*10:30*
	Music / Mary Lee Taylor, cooking	Bachelor's Children	Dr. Kate	*10:45*
Our Half Hour	Big Sister	Friendly Neighbors	Hymns of All Churches / Betty Crocker, cooking	*11am*
	Aunt Jenny's True Life Stories	Songs / The Clinic Forum	Arnold Grimm's Daughter	*11:15*
Music / Family Doctor	Talk	Victor Lindlahr, health	Valiant Lady	*11:30*
News	Home of the Brave	Talk	The Light of the World	*11:45*
Orphans of Divorce	Martha Webster	News	The Story of Mary Marlin	*12pm*
Amanda of Honeymoon Hill	The Song Treasury	Talk	Ma Perkins	*12:15*
John's Other Wife	Kate Hopkins, Angel of Mercy	Music	Pepper Young's Family	*12:30*
Just Plain Bill	Woman of Courage		Vic and Sade	*12:45*
Mother of Mine	Portia Faces Life	Talk and Music	Mary Noble, Backstage Wife	*1pm*
Club Matinee, Garry Moore	The Story of Myrt and Marge		Stella Dallas	*1:15*

DAYTIME — WINTER, 1941

Sunday

	BLUE	CBS	MBS	NBC
1:30	America's Town Meeting on the Air	The Pause That Refreshes	The Lutheran Hour	Art Pageant
1:45				
2pm		Design for Happiness	The Musical Steelmakers	The Metropolitan Opera Auditions
2:15				
2:30	Hidden Stars	Editorially Speaking	Music Memories	Your Dream Has Come True
2:45		Talk		
3pm	The Catholic Hour	The Silver Theater	The Chicago Theater of the Air	Music
3:15				Rhythms
3:30	New Friends of Music	Gene Autry's Melody Ranch		Beat the Band
3:45				
4pm	European News	News of the World	The Wallenstein Concert	Professor Puzzlewit
4:15				
4:30	News for the Americas	I Disagree	Soldier Talent	The Fitch Bandwagon
4:45	Music		Songs	

DAYTIME — WINTER, 1941

Monday-Friday

BLUE	CBS	MBS	NBC	
	Hilltop House	Talk	Lorenzo Jones	1:30
Music	Stepmother		Young Widder Brown	1:45
School News	The American School of the Air	John B. Hughes, news	Girl Alone	2pm
The Classic Hour		Talk	Lone Journey	2:15
	News	Trojan Horses / Community Hall	The Guiding Light	2:30
	Scattergood Baines	Let's Play Bridge	Life Can Be Beautiful	2:45
	Young Dr. Malone	Talk and Music	Talk and Music	3pm
The Singing Story Lady	Background in Living			3:15
Jamboree	Joyce Jordan, M. D.			3:30
	Talk / The Citadel			3:45
Music / Vaughn de Leath, songs	Second Wife	Fulton Lewis, Jr., news		4pm
King Arthur, Jr.	We, the Abbotts	Talk and Music		4:15
Bud Barton	Music		Music	4:30
Talk / The Adventures of Superman	Talk		Fleetwood Lawton, news	4:45

DAYTIME — WINTER, 1941

Saturday

	BLUE	CBS	MBS	NBC
8am	The Breakfast Club	The Town Crier	News	The Musical Clock
8:15		News	Foreign News	The Federation of Women's Clubs
8:30	News	Cincinatti Conservatory Recitals	The US Army Band	News
8:45	Robert L. Johnson, talk			Smilin' Ed McConnell, songs
9am	The American Education Forum	Columbia's Country Journal	Willard Alexander Orchestra	Lincoln Highway
9:15				
9:30	Forty-Plus Associates	The Saturday Party	Scrapbook Stories	The Heart of Juiie Blake
9:45	News		Music	County Medical Association Talks
10am	The School Harmonica Band	Let's Pretend		On the Job
10:15	Music		Food for Thought	The Stamp Club
10:30	Ilka Chase Lunch	No Politics	The Air Cadet Quiz	Manhatters Orchestra
10:45				The US Army Band
11am	The Metropolitan Opera	The Brush Creek Follies	Music	
11:15				Know Your Schools
11:30		Public Affairs	Senator Wagner, comment	Music
11:45				On the Job
12pm		Music	News	Gordon Jenkins Orchestra
12:15			The Choristers	
12:30		Public Affairs	Alvino Rey Orchestra	Saturday Soiree
12:45				
1pm		Matinee	Horse Racing	Campus Capers
1:15				
1:30	Music			A Boy, A Girl and a Band
1:45			Piano Recital	

DAYTIME — WINTER, 1941

Saturday

	BLUE	CBS	MBS	NBC
2pm	The Classic Hour	News of the Americas	Public Affairs	The World is Yours
2:15		Buffalo Presents		
2:30			Dr. Miebelson, health talk	Music
2:45		News		
3pm	Naomi Reynolds, songs	Report to the Nation	Sagmaster Comments	Charlie Spivak Orchestra
3:15	Know Your Schools		Pappy and His Boys	
3:30	The Vass Family, songs	News		Religion in the News
3:45	Edward Tomlinson, news	Music		Glen Gray Orchestra
4pm	Message of Israel	The People's Plafform	The First Offender	Horse Racing
4:15				
4:30	Little Ol' Hollywood	The Gay Nineties Revue	Music	Songs
4:45				H. V. Kaltenborn, news

EVENING — SPRING, 1941

Sunday

	BLUE	CBS	MBS	NBC
5pm	Church Federation Vespers	The Columbia Workshop	The American Forum of the Air	The Charlie McCarthy Show
5:15				
5:30	Marimba Band	Spelling Beeliner		One Man's Family
5:45	Public Affairs		Rabbi Magnin, religion	
6pm	Ricardo and His Caballeros	The Ford Sunday Evening Hour	The Old Fashioned Revival Hour	The Manhattan Merry-Go-Round
6:15	The Chapel Quartet			
6:30	Joseph Jackson, books			The American Album of Familiar Music
6:45	The Colgate Sports Newsreel, Bill Stern			
7pm	The Goodwill Hour	Take It or Leave It	Gabriel Heatter, news	The Hour of Charm
7:15			Music	
7:30		The Helen Hayes Theater		Carefree Carnival
7:45				
8pm	Inner Sanctum Mysteries	Crime Doctor		The Night Editor
8:15				Irene Rich Dramas
8:30	The Star Spangled Theater	Smarty Party	USC Hancock Ensemble	The Jello Program, Jack Benny
8:45				
9pm	The University Explorer	Raymond Scott Orchestra	News	Walter Winchell's Jergens Journal
9:15	News		The Voice of Prophecy	The Parker Family
9:30	Richard Himber Orchestra	Don't Be Personal		When the Presses Roar
9:45			Freddy Martin Orchestra	
10pm	Phil-Harmonia	The Ten o'Clock Wire	Jack Teagarden Orchestra	The Richfield Reporter
10:15		Air Views		Bridge to Dreamland
10:30		Songs	Ted Fiorito Orchestra	Inside the News
10:45				

EVENING — SPRING, 1941

Monday

BLUE	CBS	MBS	NBC	
Twilight Tales	European News	News	The Bell Telephone Hour	5pm
Film Commentator	Talk	Daily Comics		5:15
Drama Behind the News		Shafter Parker, comment	Organ Recital	5:30
Tom Mix and His Ralston Straight Shooters	News	Captain Midnight	Jack Armstong, the All-American Boy	5:45
News	The Lux Radio Theater	Little Orphan Annie	Dr. I. Q., the Mental Banker	6pm
Bud Barton		Fulton Lewis, Jr., news		6:15
The Chamber Music Society of Lower Basin Street		John B. Hughes, news	The Show Boat	6:30
		Art Linkletter, comment		6:45
Frazier Hunt, news	Guy Lombardo Orchestra	Raymond Gram Swing, news	The Carnation Contented Hour	7pm
Music		Something to Talk About		7:15
	Blondie	The Lone Ranger	The Cavalcade of America	7:30
				7:45
	Amos 'n' Andy	The Amazing Mr. Smith	Chesterfield Time	8pm
	The Lanny Ross Show		H. V. Kaltenborn, news	8:15
I Love a Mystery	The Gay Nineties Revue	Double or Nothing	Point Sublime	8:30
				8:45
Claude Sweeten Orchestra	Those We Love	Glenn Hardy, news	Ted Cook, sports	9pm
		Dance Orchestra	Music	9:15
News	What's On Your Mind	The Shadow	Hawthorne House	9:30
Ricardo and His Caballeros				9:45
Phil-Harmonia	The Ten o'Clock Wire	Jack Teagarden Orchestra	The Richfield Reporter	10pm
	Night Cap Yarns	Laws and Lawyers	Music Travelogues	10:15
	Music Masterworks	News	Inside the News	10:30
		Dance Orchestra	Music By Woodbury	10:45

EVENING — SPRING, 1941

Tuesday

	BLUE	CBS	MBS	NBC
5pm	Speaking of Glamour	European News	News	Music
5:15		Talk	Daily Comics	Jack Armstrong, the All-American Boy
5:30	Drama Behind the News	The First Nighter Program	Shafter Parker, comment	Tums Treasure Chest
5:45	Tom Mix and His Ralston Straight Shooters		Captain Midnight	
6pm	News	Second Husband	Little Orphan Annie	Latitude Zero
6:15	Bud Barton		Fulton Lewis, Jr., news	
6:30	Unlimited Horizons	Invitation to Learning	John B. Hughes, news	Fibber McGee and Molly
6:45			The Affairs of State	
7pm	Public Affairs	Moonlight Serenade	Raymond Gram Swing, news	The Pepsodent Show, Bob Hope
7:15		The Inglewood Park Concert	The Inside of Sports	
7:30	Uncle Jim's Question Bee		Wythe Williams, news	Uncle Walter's Dog House
7:45		News	Strollin' Tom	
8pm	Grand Central Station	Amos 'n' Andy	Morton Gould Orchestra	Chesterfield Time
8:15		The Lanny Ross Show		H. V. Kaltenborn, news
8:30	Ben Bernie, the Old Maestro	The Court of Missing Heirs	The Laugh and Swing Club	Johnny Presents
8:45				
9pm	Easy Aces	We, the People	Glenn Hardy, news	The World's a Stage
9:15	Dance Orchestra		Music	Dance Orchestra
9:30	News	The Hollywood Showcase	The Clinic Forum	Battle of the Sexes
9:45	Claude Sweeten Orchestra			
10pm	The Five Edwards	The Ten o'Clock Wire	The Haven of Rest	The Richfield Reporter
10:15	Phil-Harmonia	Night Cap Yarns		Chuck Foster Orchestra
10:30		Music Masterworks	News	Inside the News
10:45			Dance Orchestra	Nottingham Symphony Orchestra

EVENING — SPRING, 1941

Wednesday

BLUE	CBS	MBS	NBC	
Lee Sweetland, news	European News	News	Chesterfield Time	5pm
Tom Mix and His Ralston Straight Shooters	Talk	Daily Comics	Jack Armstong, the All-American Boy	5:15
Manhattan at Midnight	Philharmonic Talk	Shafter Parker, comment	Music	5:30
	Robert Garred, news	Captain Midnight		5:45
News	Music	Little Orphan Annie	Freddy Martin Orchestra	6pm
Bud Barton	Bill Henry, news	Fulton Lewis, Jr., news		6:15
Spin and Win	Big Town	John B. Hughes, news	Charlie Dant Orchestra	6:30
		The Round Towner		6:45
Author's Playhouse	Moonlight Serenade	Gabriel Heatter, news	Kay Kyser's College of Musical Knowledge	7pm
	All Around Town	The Chapel Quartet		7:15
News	Meet Mr. Meek	The Lone Ranger		7:30
Hits and Bits				7:45
The Quiz Kids	Amos 'n' Andy	In Chicago Tonight	Tony Martin, songs	8pm
	The Lanny Ross Show		How Did You Meet	8:15
General Fact	Dr. Christian	Barrel of Fun, Charlie Ruggles	Paducah Plantation, Red Foley	8:30
Today's Frontiers				8:45
Easy Aces	The Texaco Star Theater, Fred Allen	Glenn Hardy, news	Time to Smile, Eddie Cantor	9pm
Dance Orchestra		Dance Orchestra		9:15
News		Music	Mr. District Attorney	9:30
National Defense				9:45
Phil-Harmonia	The Ten o'Clock Wire	Freddy Martin Orchestra	The Richfield Reporter	10pm
	Night Cap Yarns		Chuck Foster Orchestra	10:15
	Music Masterworks	News	Inside the News	10:30
		Tommy Marvin Orchestra	Enric Madriguera Orchestra	10:45

EVENING — SPRING, 1941

Thursday

	BLUE	CBS	MBS	NBC
5pm	Pot o' Gold	European News	News	Lee Sweetland, news
5:15		Talk	Daily Comics	Jack Armstrong, the All-American Boy
5:30	Drama Behind the News	Music	Shafter Parker, comment	The Aldrich Family
5:45	Tom Mix and His Ralston Straight Shooters	Robert Garred, news	Captain Midnight	
6pm	News	Major Bowes' Original Amateur Hour	Little Orphan Annie	The Kraft Music Hall, Bing Crosby
6:15	Bud Barton		Fulton Lewis, Jr., news	
6:30	Music		John B. Hughes, news	
6:45	Mayor Bowron, comment		The Affairs of State	
7pm	Vallee Varieties	Moonlight Serenade	Berlin News	The Cugat Rumba Revue
7:15		Professor Quiz	The Inside of Sports	
7:30	Ahead of the Headlines		Wythe Williams, news	The American Challenge
7:45	Cabbages and Kings	Elmer Davis, news	Art Linkletter, comment	
8pm	The School Kids Quiz	Amos 'n' Andy	The Standard Symphony Hour	Chesterfield Time
8:15		The Lanny Ross Show		H. V. Kaltenborn, news
8:30	Public Affairs	Spotlight		Maxwell House Coffee Time, Brice and Morgan
8:45				
9pm	Easy Aces	City Desk	Glenn Hardy, news	The Quiz Court
9:15	Dance Orchestra		Roundup Time	
9:30	News	Answer Auction		Tommy Riggs and Betty Lou
9:45	Bonaldi Sings		Music	
10pm	Phil-Harmonia	The Ten o'Clock Wire	The Haven of Rest	The Richfield Reporter
10:15		Night Cap Yarns		Chuck Foster Orchestra
10:30		Music Masterworks	News	Inside the News
10:45			Dance Orchestra	Music By Woodbury

EVENING — SPRING, 1941

Friday

BLUE	CBS	MBS	NBC	
Twilight Tales	European News	News	Organ Recital	5pm
Film Commentator	Talk	Daily Comics	Jack Armstong, the All-American Boy	5:15
Drama Behind the News		Shafter Parker, comment	Infomation, Please	5:30
Tom Mix and His Ralston Straight Shooters	Robert Garred, news	Captain Midnight		5:45
News	Music	Little Orphan Annie	Waltz Time	6pm
Bud Barton	Bill Henry, news	Fulton Lewis, Jr., news		6:15
Your Happy Birthday	The Campbell Playhouse	John B. Hughes, news	Rhyme and Rhythm	6:30
		Art Linkletter, comment		6:45
Madison Square Garden Boxiing	Hollywood Premiere	Raymond Gram Swing, news	Wings of Destiny	7pm
		Strollin' Tom		7:15
News	Al Pearce and His Gang	The Lone Ranger	Alec Templeton Time	7:30
Music				7:45
Blue Barron Orchestra	Amos 'n' Andy	The Two Cities Quiz	Chesterfield Time	8pm
	The Lanny Ross Show		H. V. Kaltenborn, news	8:15
The New Army Game, Ben Bernie	Great Moments from Great Plays	I Want a Divorce	Death Valley Days	8:30
				8:45
Music	The Kate Smith Hour	Glenn Hardy, news	Ted Cook, sports	9pm
		Dance Orchestra	Dance Orchestra	9:15
News		Freddy Martin Orchestra	This Was My Inspiration	9:30
Postal Oddities				9:45
Phil-Harmonia	The Ten o'Clock Wire	Ray Noble Orchestra	The Richfield Reporter	10pm
	Night Cap Yarns		Chuck Foster Orchestra	10:15
	Music Masterworks	News	Inside the News	10:30
		Stan Keller Orchestra	Dance Orchestra	10:45

EVENING — SPRING, 1941

Saturday

	BLUE	CBS	MBS	NBC
5pm	The Garden Club	All Around Town (4:45 PM)	Dr. Matthews, religion	Oriental News
5:15	Government Reports	The March of California		Traffic Tribunal
5:30	The Bishop and the Gargoyle	Sports	Hawaii Calls	Organ Recital
5:45		News		
6pm	Doctors at Work	Kids' Quizaroo	Innocent Bystander	The National Barn Dance
6:15			Batavia News	
6:30	NBC Symphony Orchestra	By the Way	John B. Hughes, news	
6:45		Saturday Night Serenade	Contact	
7pm			Gabriel Heatter, news	Uncle Ezra's Radio Station
7:15		Parade	The Inside of Sports	
7:30			Seaside Shindig	Grand Ole Opry
7:45		News		
8pm	Dance Orchestra	The Marriage Club		Truth or Consequences
8:15				
8:30	Tune Out Time	Duffy's Tavern	California Melodies	The Knickerbocker Playhouse
8:45				
9pm		Your Hit Parade	Glenn Hardy, news	The Sports Forum
9:15			The Round Towner	Dance Orchestra
9:30	Enric Madriguera Orchestra		Freddy Martin Orchestra	
9:45		Music		
10pm	Phil-Harmonia	The Ten o' Clock Wire	Ray Noble Orchestra	The Richfield Reporter
10:15		Here's the Story		Dance Orchestra
10:30		Dance Orchestra	Fiesta Time	
10:45				

DAYTIME — SPRING, 1941

Sunday

	BLUE	CBS	MBS	NBC
8am	Songs	The West Coast Church	The Comics Weekly Man	Rhapsody of the Rockies
8:15	Red Cross Defense Program			The Book of Books
8:30	Sweet Land of Liberty	Major Bowes' Capitol Family	Sky Pilot	Music and American Youth
8:45				
9am	Nick Harris		P. E. Gardner, religion	Music
9:15	I Am an American		Songs	
9:30	Art Pageant	The Salt Lake Tabernacle Choir	The Haven of Rest	The Radio City Music Hall
9:45				
10am	Stan Kaye Orchestra	The CBS Church of the Air	News	
10:15			Romance of the Highways	
10:30		Music	Sunday Songs	On Your Job
10:45	Layman's Views of the News			
11am	American Pilgrimage	The Free Company	Swing	Health Talk
11:15	Foreign Policy Association Talks			Concert Petite
11:30	Music	The World Today		The University of Chicago Round Table
11:45	Dr. Casselbury, health			
12pm	Great Plays	New York Philharmonic Orchestra	News	Lavender and Old Lace
12:15			Music	H. V. Kaltenborn, news
12:30				The Customs Corner
12:45				Bob Becker's Dog Talks
1pm	Garden Talk		The Americas Speak	National Vespers
1:15	Look at Books			

DAYTIME — SPRING, 1941

Monday-Friday

BLUE	CBS	MBS	NBC	
The Breakfast Club	Music / Treat Time, Buddy Clark	Good Morning, Neighbor / The Haven of Rest	The Johnny Murray Show	*8am*
	Nancy Dixon, talk		Against the Storm	*8:15*
News	The Goldbergs	News	The Road of Life	*8:30*
Robert L. Johnson, talk	Hymns of All Churches / Betty Crocker, cooking	Music / Foreign News	David Harum	*8:45*
Talk	Kate Smith Speaks	Music	The Bridge Club	*9am*
Betty Randall, songs	When a Girl Marries	Talk and Music	News	*9:15*
Homer Griffith, sports	The Romance of Helen Trent		The Voice of Experience / The Heart of Julia Blake	*9:30*
Music	Our Gal Sunday	Top of the World	Midstream	*9:45*
The Munros	Life Can Be Beautiful	News	Talk	*10am*
Between the Bookends	The Woman in White	Talk	News	*10:15*
The Wife Saver	The Right to Happiness	Helen Holden, Government Girl	Talk and Music	*10:30*
Talk and Music	Music / Mary Lee Taylor, cooking	I'lll Find My Way	Dr. Kate	*10:45*
Our Half Hour	Big Sister	Friendly Neighbors	The Light of the World	*11am*
	Aunt Jenny's True Life Stories	Talk / The National School of the Air	The Mystery Man	*11:15*
Music / Family Doctor	Talk	Victor Lindlahr, health / The School of the Air	Valiant Lady	*11:30*
News	Home of the Brave		Arnold Grimm's Daughter	*11:45*
Orphans of Divorce	Martha Webster	News	The Story of Mary Marlin	*12pm*
Amanda of Honeymoon Hill	The Song Treasury	The Homemaker's Club	Ma Perkins	*12:15*
John's Other Wife	Kate Hopkins, Angel of Mercy		Pepper Young's Family	*12:30*
Just Plain Bill	Woman of Courage	Edith Adams' Future	Vic and Sade	*12:45*
Mother of Mine	Portia Faces Life	We Are Always Young	Mary Noble, Backstage Wife	*1pm*
Club Matinee, Garry Moore	The Story of Myrt and Marge	The Confessions of Corsair	Stella Dallas	*1:15*

DAYTIME — SPRING, 1941

Sunday

	BLUE	CBS	MBS	NBC
1:30	America's Town Meeting on the Air	The Pause That Refreshes	The Lutheran Hour	Music
1:45				
2pm			The Musical Steelmakers	Joe and Mabel
2:15		Music		
2:30	Spell-O-Win	What, No Architect	Music Memories	Your Dream Has Come True
2:45		Talk		
3pm	The Catholic Hour	The Silver Theater	The Lutheran Hour	Frazier Hunt, news
3:15				Serenade
3:30	Frank Black Presents	Gene Autry's Melody Ranch	Bulldog Drummond	What's Your Idea
3:45				
4pm	European News	Dear Mom (3:55PM)	Notebook	Professor Puzzlewit
4:15		Headlines and Bylines		
4:30	News for the Americas	Music	News	The Fitch Bandwagon
4:45	Music		Wythe Williams, news	

DAYTIME — SPRING, 1941

Monday-Friday

BLUE	CBS	MBS	NBC	
	Bess Johnson	The Johnson Family	Lorenzo Jones	1:30
Music	Stepmother	The Bookworm	Young Widder Brown	1:45
School News	The American School of the Air	John B. Hughes, news	Girl Alone	2pm
The Classic Hour		The Twig is Bent	Lone Journey Light	2:15
	News	Music / Community Hall	The Guiding Light	2:30
	Scattergood Baines	Let's Play Bridge	Life Can Be Beautiful	2:45
	Young Dr. Malone	Talk and Music	Talk and Music	3pm
	Background in Living		What's Doing Ladies	3:15
Talk / The Unclassic Hour	Joyce Jordan, M. D.		News	3:30
	Music		Gasoline Alley	3:45
The Singing Story Lady	The Second Mrs. Burton	Fulton Lewis, Jr., news	Talk	4pm
Music / Mr. Keen, Tracer of Lost Persons	We, the Abbotts	Here's Morgan		4:15
News	Music	Music		4:30
Talk / The Adventures of Superman	Talk		Fleetwood Lawton, news	4:45

DAYTIME — SPRING, 1941

Saturday

	BLUE	CBS	MBS	NBC
8am	The Breakfast Club	The Town Crier	Organ Recital	The Bright Idea Club
8:15		Talk	Foreign News	The Federation of Women's Clubs
8:30	The Federation of Churches	Will Roland Orchestra	The US Army Band	News
8:45	Robert L. Johnson, talk			Music
9am	The American Education Forum	Columbia's Country Journal	Garden Plots	Lincoln Highway
9:15				
9:30	Call to Youth	The Merry-Go-Round	Scrapbook Stories	The Heart of Juiie Blake
9:45	News	Jobs in National Defense	Music	Music
10am	Forty-Plus Associates	Let's Pretend	News	News
10:15	Music		Food for Thought	County Medical Association Talks
10:30	Ilka Chase Lunch	No Politics	Helen Holden, Government Girl	Manhatters Orchestra
10:45			I'll Find My Way	The US Army Band
11am	Indigo	The Brush Creek Follies	Music	On the Job
11:15				Know Your Schools
11:30		The Voice of Broadway	The Air Cadet Quiz	Gordon Jenkins Orchestra
11:45	News	Of Men and Books		
12pm	Music	Music	News	Music
12:15			The Choristers	News
12:30	America's Music		New World Diplomacy	Music
12:45		News		
1pm	Club Matinee, Garry Moore	Horse Racing	Legion News	Campus Capers
1:15			Alvino Rey Orchestra	
1:30		Invitation to Learning		A Boy, A Girl and a Band
1:45			Music	

DAYTIME — SPRING, 1941

Saturday

	BLUE	CBS	MBS	NBC
2pm	The Classic Hour	News of the Americas	Youth Drama	The World is Yours
2:15		F, O. B. Detroit		
2:30			The University Life Forum	Music
2:45		News		
3pm	Naomi Reynolds, songs	Report to the Nation	Ted Van de Veer, news	Claude Thornhill Orchestra
3:15	Know Your Schools		Pappy and His Boys	
3:30	The Vass Family, songs	News	Music	Religion in the News
3:45	Edward Tomlinson, news	Music		Sports
4pm	Message of Israel	The People's Plafform	The First Offender	Defense for America
4:15				
4:30	Little Ol' Hollywood	Music	Freddy Martin Orchestra	Songs
4:45		All Around Town		H. V. Kaltenborn, news

EVENING — SUMMER, 1941

Sunday

	BLUE	CBS	MBS	NBC
5pm	Songs	The Ford Summer Hour	The Old Fashioned Revival Hour	The Manhattan Merry-Go-Round
5:15				
5:30	Joseph Jackson, books			The American Album of Familiar Music
5:45	The Colgate Sports Newsreel, Bill Stern			
6pm	The Goodwill Hour	Take It or Leave It	Nobody's Children	The Hour of Charm
6:15				
6:30		The Columbia Workshop	Frank Blair, news	Ted Cook, sports
6:45			Music	Music
7pm	Inner Sanctum Mysteries	Crime Doctor	Gabriel Heatter, news	News
7:15			Britain Speaks	Irene Rich Dramas
7:30	Captain Quiz	Answer Auction	Dance Orchestra	Reg'lar Fellers
7:45			Jan Garber Orchestra	
8pm	Serenade	Music	The Golden Hour	Walter Winchell's Jergens Journal
8:15				The Parker Family
8:30	Organ Recital	Don't Be Personal		Carefree Carnival
8:45	Abe Lyman Orchestra			
9pm	Hal Saunders Orchestra	I Was There	Glenn Hardy, news	The Night Editor
9:15			The Voice of Prophecy	Cabbages and Kings
9:30	Woody Herman Orchestra	By the Way		When the Presses Roar
9:45		The Adventures of Cosmo Jones	Jimmie Lunceford Orchestra	
10pm	Phil-Harmonia	Hal Grayson Orchestra	Dance Orchestra	The Richfeld Reporter
10:15				Bridge to Dreamland
10:30		Songs	Paradise Isle	Inside the News
10:45				Bridge to Dreamland

EVENING — SUMMER, 1941

Monday

BLUE	CBS	MBS	NBC	
Twilight Tales	Forecast	News	Dr. I. Q., the Mental Banker	5pm
News		Captain Danger		5:15
Drama Behind the News		Shafter Parker, comment	Mr. Pertwee	5:30
Sports		Russell Bennett's Notebook		5:45
Gordon Jenkins Orchestra	Guy Lombardo Orchestra	Raymond Gram Swing, news	The Carnation Contented Hour	6pm
		Imperial Time, Mary Small		6:15
Boxing Bouts	Blondie	John B. Hughes, news	The Cavalcade of America	6:30
		They Say Today		6:45
Bob Strong Orchestra	Amos 'n' Andy	Gabriel Heatter, news	Chesterfield Time	7pm
	The Lanny Ross Show	Dance Orchestra	Lum and Abner	7:15
The World's Best Drama	The Gay Nineties Revue	The Lone Ranger	People vs. Supermind	7:30
				7:45
True or False	What's on Your Mind	Music	Film Commentator	8pm
			News	8:15
News	The Grant Park Concerts	Double or Nothing	Point Sublime	8:30
Sidestreet Vignettes				8:45
The Actor's Workshop	Paul Sullivan, news	Glenn Hardy, news	Hawthorne House	9pm
	Who, What, Where, Why	War Letters		9:15
News		Fulton Lewis, Jr., news	Pick a Tune	9:30
Music	Songs	Columns on Parade		9:45
The Chamber Music Society of Lower Basin Street	Hal Grayson Orchestra	David Diamond Orchestra	The Richfeld Reporter	10pm
			The Blue Moonlight	10:15
Phil-Harmonia	Music Masterworks	News	Inside the News	10:30
		Dance Orchestra	Woody Herman Orchestra	10:45

EVENING — SUMMER, 1941

Tuesday

	BLUE	CBS	MBS	NBC
5pm	Music	Second Husband	News	Speaking of Glamour
5:15	News		Captain Danger	News
5:30	Drama Behind the News	The Lewisohn Stadium Concerts	Shafter Parker, comment	Hap Hazard
5:45	Sports		Music	
6pm	The Grant Park Concert	Moonlight Serenade	Raymond Gram Swing, news	A Date with Judy
6:15		Public Affairs	Twilight	
6:30	Democracy Council		John B. Hughes, news	College Humor, Marlin Hurt
6:45	Story Drama	Music	Your Defense Reporter	
7pm	Bringng Up Father	Amos 'n' Andy	Gabriel Heatter, news	Chesterfield Time
7:15		The Lanny Ross Show	The Inside of Sports	Lum and Abner
7:30	Information, Please	The Court of Missing Heirs	Wythe Williams, news	Johnny Presents
7:45			Jan Garber Orchestra	
8pm	Easy Aces	We, the People	Barrel of Fun, Charlie Ruggles	The Adventures of the Thin Man
8:15	Songs			
8:30	News	The Hollywood Showcase	The Shadow	Battle of the Sexes
8:45	Sidestreet Vignetttes			
9pm	Music	Paul Sullivan, news	Glenn Hardy, news	Freddy Ebener Orchestra
9:15		Songs	War Letters	Manchester Boddy, news
9:30	News	By the Way	Fulton Lewis, Jr., news	Carl Ravazza Orchestra
9:45	Music	Elmo Tanner Orchestra	The Clinic Forum	
10pm	Phil-Harmonia	Hal Grayson Orchestra		The Richfield Reporter
10:15			The Haven of Rest	Woody Herman Orchestra
10:30		Music Masterworks	News	Inside the News
10:45			Freddy Martin Orchestra	Chuck Foster Orchestra

EVENING — SUMMER, 1941

Wednesday

BLUE	CBS	MBS	NBC	
The Chapel Quartet	The Treasury Hour	News	Charlie Dant Orchestra	5pm
News		London News		5:15
Drama Behind the News		Shafter Parker, comment	Music	5:30
Sports		Music		5:45
Author's Playhouse	Moonlight Serenade	Raymond Gram Swing, news	Kay Kyser's College of Musical Knowledge	6pm
	Public Affairs	Danger is My Business		6:15
Ray Kinney Orchestra	All Around Town	John B. Hughes, news		6:30
News	News	They Say Today		6:45
The Quiz Kids	Amos 'n' Andy	Gabriel Heatter, news	Music	7pm
	The Lanny Ross Show	Music	News	7:15
Manhattan at Midnight	Dr. Christian	The Lone Ranger	Paducah Plantation, Red Foley	7:30
				7:45
Easy Aces	Grand Central Station	Music	Quizzer Baseball	8pm
Public Affairs				8:15
News	Parade	The Great Gunns	Mr. District Attorney	8:30
Sidestreet Vignettes				8:45
Music	Paul Sullivan, news	Glenn Hardy, news	Chesterfield Time	9pm
	All Aboard	War Letters	Howard and Shelton	9:15
News		Fulton Lewis, Jr., news	The Five Edwards	9:30
Dance Orchestra	Songs	Columns on Parade		9:45
Phil-Harmonia	Hal Grayson Orchestra	Freddy Martin Orchestra	The Richfeld Reporter	10pm
			Songs	10:15
	Music Masterworks	News	Inside the News	10:30
		Henry King Orchestra	Woody Herman Orchestra	10:45

EVENING — SUMMER, 1941

Thursday

	BLUE	CBS	MBS	NBC
5pm	Music	Major Bowes' Original Amateur Hour	News	The Kraft Music Hall, Bob Burns
5:15	News		Music	
5:30	Drama Behind the News		Shafter Parker, comment	
5:45	Sports		The Blue Beetle	
6pm	Vallee Varieties	Moonlight Serenade	Raymond Gram Swing, news	The Cugat Rumba Revue
6:15		Professor Quiz	Twilight Tales	
6:30	Captain Quiz		John B. Hughes, news	Good Neighbors
6:45	News	Organ Recital	Music	
7pm	Dance Orchestra	Amos 'n' Andy	Art Jarrett Orchestra	Chesterfield Time
7:15		The Lanny Ross Show	The Inside of Sports	Lum and Abner
7:30	Howard and Shelton	The Marriage Club	Wythe Williams, news	Music
7:45	Mayor Bowron, comment		Public Affairs	
8pm	Easy Aces	Smarty Party	The Standard Symphony Hour	Bob Chester Orchestra
8:15	Industry News			
8:30	News	Death Valley Days		Tommy Riggs and Betty Lou
8:45	Sidestreet Vignettes			
9pm	Dance Orchestra	Paul Sullivan, news	Glenn Hardy, news	The Quiz Court
9:15		Songs	War Letters	
9:30	News	By the Way	Fulton Lewis, Jr., news	Music
9:45	Music	Music	Dance Orchestra	
10pm	Phil-Harmonia	Hal Grayson Orchestra	The Haven of Rest	The Richfeld Reporter
10:15				Woody Herman Orchestra
10:30		Music Masterworks	News	Inside the News
10:45			Freddy Martin Orchestra	Alan Stoker Orchestra

EVENING — SUMMER, 1941

Friday

BLUE	CBS	MBS	NBC	
Twilight Tales	Boulevard Interviews	News	Waltz Time	5pm
News	Music	Captain Danger		5:15
Drama Behind the News	Hollywood Premiere	Shafter Parker, comment	Uncle Walter's Dog House	5:30
Sports		Music		5:45
Music	Penthouse Party	Raymond Gram Swing, news	Wings of Destiny	6pm
		Twilight Tales		6:15
	The Symphonettes	John B. Hughes, news	Calling All Camps	6:30
News	News	They Say Today		6:45
Your Happy Birthday	Amos 'n' Andy	Gabriel Heatter, news	Chesterfield Time	7pm
	The Lanny Ross Show	Dance Orchestra	Lum and Abner	7:15
Ben Bernie, the Old Maestro	Great Moments from Great Plays	The Lone Ranger	Death Valley Days	7:30
				7:45
Grandpappy and His Pals	Claudia and David	The Two Cities Quiz	News	8pm
			Howard and Shelton	8:15
News	Jimmy Fidler, gossip		Woody Herman Orchestra	8:30
Sidestreet Vignettes	Here's a Clue			8:45
Dance Orchestra	Paul Sullivan, news	Glenn Hardy, news	Sports	9pm
	Songs	War Letters	Manchester Boddy, news	9:15
News	By the Way	Fulton Lewis, Jr., news	The Weekly Spectator	9:30
Postal Oddities	Dance Orchestra	Columns on Parade	Dance Orchestra	9:45
Phil-Harmonia	Hal Grayson Orchestra	Freddy Martin Orchestra	The Richfeld Reporter	10pm
			Chuck Foster Orchestra	10:15
	Music Masterworks	News	Inside the News	10:30
		Henry King Orchestra	Music	10:45

EVENING — SUMMER, 1941

Saturday

	BLUE	CBS	MBS	NBC
5pm	Piano Recital	Dance Orchestra	Dr. Mathews, religion	The National Barn Dance
5:15	Sports			
5:30	Music	Music	Music	
5:45		Saturday Night Serenade		
6pm	NBC Summer Symphony		The Chigagoland Concert Hour	Grand Ole Opry
6:15		Parade		
6:30				The Grant Park Concerts
6:45		Sports		Martha Tilton, songs
7pm	This is Judy Jones	Spotlight	Gabriel Heatter, news	Truth or Consequences
7:15			The Inside of Sports	
7:30	Spin and Win	City Desk	Music	Bob Chester Orchestra
7:45				
8pm	The Bishop and the Gargoyle	Your Hit Parade	Dance Orchestra	Carl Ravazza Orchestra
8:15				
8:30	Tune Out Time			Horace Heidt Orchestra
8:45		News		
9pm		Here's the Story	Glenn Hardy, news	Giant Fires of History
9:15		Dance Orchestra	Art Linkletter, comment	Music
9:30	News	By the Way	Dance Orchestra	Woody Herman Orchestra
9:45	Music	Baron Elliott Orchestra		
10pm	Phil-Harmonia	Hal Grayson Orchestra	Freddy Martin Orchestra	The Richfield Reporter
10:15				Lud Gluskin Orchestra
10:30		Songs	Dance Orchestra	Dance Orchestra
10:45				

DAYTIME — SUMMER, 1941

Sunday

	BLUE	CBS	MBS	NBC
8am	Rex Maupin Orchestra	The West Coast Church	The Comics Weekly Man	Emma Otero, songs
8:15	I Am An American			
8:30	The Radio City Music Hall	The Salt Lake Tabernacle Choir	Sky Pilot	Down South
8:45				
9am		The CBS Church of the Air	P. E. Gardner, religion	News
9:15				Music
9:30	Layman's Views of the News	You Decide	The Voice of Prophecy	Charles Dant Orchestra
9:45	The Garden Club		George Fisher, gossip	
10am	Hidden History	Invitation to Learning	News	Upton Close, news
10:15	Foreign Policy Association Talks		Romance of the Highways	Music
10:30	Tapestry Musicale	Music	The Canary Pet Shop	The University of Chicago Round Table
10:45			Music	
11am	African Trek	New York Philharmonic Orchestra	Swing	Concert Petite
11:15				H. V. Kaltenborn, news
11:30	Weekend Cruise			Sammy Kaye's Sunday Serenade
11:45				
12pm	National Vespers	Music	News	Chautauqua Symphony Orchestra
12:15		News	Music	
12:30	Afternoon Stars	The Spirit of '41	Young People's Church	
12:45				Dr. Casselbury, health
1pm	Music	Young Ideas	Dance Orchestra	Joe and Mabel
1:15	Dr. Casselbury, health			

DAYTIME — SUMMER, 1941

Monday-Friday

BLUE	CBS	MBS	NBC	
The Breakfast Club	Kate Smith Speaks	The Haven of Rest / The Breakfast Club	Sam Hayes, news	*8am*
	When a Girl Marries		Meet the Missus / The Johnny Murray Show	*8:15*
News	The Romance of Helen Trent	News	Talk and Music	*8:30*
Robert L. Johnson, talk	Our Gal Sunday	Talk	News	*8:45*
Talk / Beauty Council	Life Can Be Beautiful	John B. Hughes, news	Talk	*9am*
Between the Bookends	The Woman in White	The Breakfast Club	Bess Johnson	*9:15*
Here's to the Ladies	The Right to Happiness	Front Page Farrell	The Story of Ellen Randolph	*9:30*
Prescott Presents	Rita Murray, news	I'll Find My Way	Dr. Kate	*9:45*
Talk	Big Sister	Glenn Hardy, news	The Light of the World	*10am*
	Aunt Jenny's True Life Stories	Music	The Mystery Man	*10:15*
The Munros	You're the Expert	Norma Young, talk	Valiant Lady	*10:30*
Midstream	Kate Hopkins, Angel of Mercy		Arnold Grimm's Daughter	*10:45*
Orphans of Divorce	The Man I Married	Talk / The Clinic Forum	Against the Storm	*11am*
Amanda of Honeymoon Hill	Songs		Ma Perkins	*11:15*
John's Other Wife	News	Music	The Guiding Light	*11:30*
Just Plain Bill	Woman of Courage		Vic and Sade	*11:45*
Club Matinee, Garry Moore	Your Neighbor	News	Mary Noble, Backstage Wife	*12pm*
	The Story of Myrt and Marge	The Homemaker's Club	Stella Dallas	*12:15*
	The KNX Bandstand		Lorenzo Jones	*12:30*
	Stepmother	Talk and Music	Young Widder Brown	*12:45*
The Classic Hour	Hymns of All Churches / Betty Crocker, cooking	The Johnson Family	Home of the Brave	*1pm*
	The Road of Life	The Confessions of Corsair	Portia Faces Life	*1:15*

DAYTIME — SUMMER, 1941

Sunday

	BLUE	CBS	MBS	NBC
1:30	Rhythms By Ricardo	Public Affairs	USC Hancock Ensemble	News
1:45		Ted Husing, sports		Look at Books
2pm	The Catholic Hour	Music	America Preferred	The National Music Camp
2:15				
2:30	Music	Gene Autry's Melody Ranch	Egypt - Moscow News	Dr. I. Q., Jr.
2:45	Edward Tomlinson, news		Batavia News	
3pm	European News	Dear, Mom (2:55 PM)	The Lutheran Hour	Professor Puzzlewit
3:15		Talk		
3:30	Drew Pearson, news	World News Tonight	Dance Orchestra	The Fitch Bandwagon
3:45				
4pm	The Star Spangled Theater	The Pause That Refreshes	The American Forum of the Air	What's My Name
4:15				
4:30	Church Federation Vespers	Spelling Beeliner		One Man's Family
4:45			Music	

DAYTIME — SUMMER, 1941

Monday-Friday

BLUE	CBS	MBS	NBC	
	The O'Neills	We Are Always Young	We, the Abbotts	1:30
	Catalina Fun Quiz	Edith Adams' Future	The Story of Mary Marlin	1:45
Talk and Music	News	Helen Holden, Government Girl	Pepper Young's Family	2pm
What's Doing Ladies	Music / Background in Living	The Twig is Bent	Lone Journey	2:15
Buck Private and His Girl	Joyce Jordan, Girl Intern	John B. Hughes, news	Music / The Hollywood News Girl	2:30
Wings on Watch	Talk	Let's Play Bridge	Jack Owens, songs / The Heart of Julia Blake	2:45
Talk and Music	The Second Mrs. Burton	Talk and Music	News	3pm
Talk / Mr. Keen, Tracer of Lost Persons	Young Dr. Malone	Here's Morgan	Talk	3:15
The Unclassic Hour	News	Talk and Music	What's Doing Ladies	3:30
	Talk		H. V. Kaltenborn, news	3:45
News	European News Roundup	Fulton Lewis, Jr., news	Talk / The Bell Telephone Hour	4pm
Talk and Music	Fletcher Wiley, talk	Talk and Music		4:15
The Singing Story Lady	Music / Treat Time, Buddy Clark	Talk and Music / Ned Jordan, Secret Agent	Talk and Music / Tums Treasure Chest	4:30
Bud Barton	Robert Garred, news			4:45

DAYTIME — SUMMER, 1941

Saturday

	BLUE	CBS	MBS	NBC
8am	The Breakfast Club	Top of the Morning (7:45AM)	Dance Orchestra	Sam Hayes, news
8:15		The Town Crier		Meet the Missus
8:30	News	The Little Show	News	Call to Youth
8:45	Robert L. Johnson, talk		Music	News
9am	The Federation of Churches	Let's Pretend		Lincoln Highway
9:15	Forty-Plus Associates			
9:30	Cleveland Calling	Stars Over Hollywood	Garden Plots	America, the Free
9:45			I'll Find My Way	
10am	Johnny Long Orchestra	Report to the Nation	News	County Medical Association Talks
10:15			Food for Thought	On Your Job
10:30	Kenney Orchestra	The Voice of Broadway	Duffy Orchestra	The Bright Idea Club
10:45		Of Men and Books		
11am	What's Doing Ladies	Columbia's Country Journal	The Kentucky Mountains	Nature Sketches
11:15	Nick Harris			Patti Chapin, songs
11:30		Vera Brodsky, piano	Music	Music
11:45				
12pm	Club Matinee, Garry Moore	Calling Pan-America	News	News
12:15			Woman's West Coast Golf	What's Doing Ladies
12:30		Horse Racing	Horse Racing	A Boy, A Girl and a Band
12:45		The Symphonettes	Music	
1pm	News	Matinee	Legion News	The World is Yours
1:15	The Classic Hour		America Sings	
1:30			We're Always Young	Recital Period
1:45			Edith Adams' Future	Public Affairs

DAYTIME — SUMMER, 1941

Saturday

	BLUE	CBS	MBS	NBC
2pm		Proudly We Hail	Helen Holden, Government Girl	Traffic Tribunal
2:15	Naomi Reynolds, songs		The Arlington Classic	
2:30	Songs	Elmer Davis, news	Freddy Martin Orchestra	The Art of Living
2:45	Edward Tomlinson, news	News		Sports
3pm	Message of Israel	The People's Platform	Youth Drama	Defense for America
3:15				
3:30	Little Ol' Hollywood	The Hall of Song	Stan Kenton Orchestra	The Aristocrats Trio
3:45				H. V. Kaltenborn, news
4pm	Boy Meets Band	European News	The Green Hornet	Latitude Zero
4:15		Songs		
4:30	Woody Herman Orchestra	Hollywood and Vine	Hawaii Calls	Stories of American Liberties
4:45		Sports		

EVENING — FALL, 1941

Sunday

	BLUE	CBS	MBS	NBC
5pm	Blue Echoes	The Columbia Workshop	The American Forum of the Air	The Charlie McCarthy Show
5:15				
5:30	Music	Spelling Beeliner		One Man's Family
5:45	Drew Pearson, news		Music	
6pm	Grandpappy and His Pals	The Ford Sunday Evening Hour	The Old Fashioned Revival Hour	The Manhattan Merry-Go-Round
6:15				
6:30	Joseph Jackson, books			The American Album of Familiar Music
6:45	Piano Quartet			
7pm	The Goodwill Hour	Take It or Leave It	Gabriel Heatter, news	The Hour of Charm
7:15			Rabbi Magnin, religion	
7:30		The Helen Hayes Theater	The Moon Hangs Low	Sherlock Holmes
7:45				
8pm	Inner Sanctum Mysteries	Crime Doctor	USC Hancock Ensemble	Carefree Carnival
8:15				
8:30	The Jello Program, Jack Benny	I Was There	Answering You	News
8:45				The Chapel Quartet
9pm	Irene Rich Dramas	All Aboard	News	Walter Winchell's Jergens Journal
9:15	Over Our Coffee Cups		The Voice of Prophecy	The Parker Family
9:30	News	What's It All About		Cabbages and Kings
9:45	The University Explorer		Clyde McCoy Orchestra	Manchester Boddy, news
10pm	Music	The Gulf Screen Theater	Paradise Isle	The Richfield Reporter
10:15				Bridge to Dreamland
10:30		Report to the Nation	News	Inside the News
10:45	Paul Whiteman Orchestra		Ted Weems Orchestra	Rodriguez and Sutherland, news

EVENING — FALL, 1941

Monday

BLUE	CBS	MBS	NBC	
Twilight Tales	Talk (4:45 PM)	News	Don Winslow of the Navy	5pm
News	Lone Journey	Shafter Parker, comment	The Bridge Club	5:15
World News	By the Way	Captain Midnight	Music	5:30
Tom Mix and His Ralston Straight Shooters	Robert Garred, news	Jack Armstrong, the All-American Boy	News	5:45
Richard Brooks, news	The Lux Radio Theater	Gabriel Heatter, news	Dr. I. Q., the Mental Banker	6pm
Sports		Your Defense Reporter		6:15
The Best of the Week		John B. Hughes, news	That Brewster Boy	6:30
		Sports		6:45
The Monday Merry-Go-Round	The Orson Welles Theater	Raymond Gram Swing, news	The Carnation Contented Hour	7pm
		The KHJ Club		7:15
Tropic Tunes	Blondie	The Lone Ranger	The Cavalcade of America	7:30
News				7:45
The Flying Football	Amos 'n' Andy	The Amazing Mr. Smith	Chesterfield Time	8pm
Don't You Believe It	The Lanny Ross Show		Lum and Abner	8:15
I Love a Mystery	The Gay Nineties Revue	Double or Nothing	The Voice of Firestone	8:30
				8:45
True or False	Vox Pop	Glenn Hardy, news	The Bell Telephone Hour	9pm
		Cal Tinney, news		9:15
News	The Hollywood Showcase	Fulton Lewis, Jr., news	Hawthorne House	9:30
Music		News		9:45
Paul Whiteman Orchestra	The Ten o'Clock Wire	The Editor Speaks	The Richfield Reporter	10pm
	The World Today	Ted Weems Orchestra	Nothing But Praise	10:15
Carl Ravazza Orchestra	Music Masterworks	News	Inside the News	10:30
		The Lamplighter	Rodriguez and Sutherland, news	10:45

EVENING — FALL, 1941

Tuesday

	BLUE	CBS	MBS	NBC
5pm	The Passing Parade	Talk (4:45 PM)	News	Don Winslow of the Navy
5:15	News	Lone Journey	Shafter Parker, comment	News
5:30	World News	Talk	Captain Midnight	Tums Treasure Chest
5:45	Tom Mix and His Ralston Straight Shooters	News	Jack Armstong, the All-American Boy	
6pm	Richard Brooks, news	Second Husband	Gabriel Heatter, news	Burns and Allen
6:15	Sports		Public Affairs	
6:30	NBC Symphony Orchestra	Who, What, Where, Why	John B. Hughes, news	Fibber McGee and Molly
6:45			Sports	
7pm		Moonlight Serenade	Raymond Gram Swing, news	The Pepsodent Show, Bob Hope
7:15		The Inglewood Park Concert	The Inside of Sports	
7:30	The Treasury Hour		Music	The Raleigh Cigarette Program, Red Skelton
7:45		By the Way		
8pm		Amos 'n' Andy	Headlines and Bylines	Chesterfield Time
8:15		The Lanny Ross Show		Lum and Abner
8:30	Information, Please	The Court of Missing Heirs	The Shadow	Johnny Presents
8:45				
9pm	Easy Aces	We, the People	Glenn Hardy, news	The Adventures of the Thin Man
9:15	Listener's Lookout		Music	
9:30	News	The Bob Burns Show	Fulton Lewis, Jr., news	Battle of the Sexes
9:45	Mal Hallett Orchestra		The Clinic Forum	
10pm	Dance Orchestra	The Ten o'Clock Wire		The Richfield Reporter
10:15		The World Today	Ted Weems Orchestra	Nothing But Praise
10:30		Music Masterworks	News	Inside the News
10:45			Ray Noble Orchestra	Rodriguez and Sutherland, news

EVENING — FALL, 1941

Wednesday

BLUE	CBS	MBS	NBC	
Layman's Views of the News	Talk (4:45PM)	News	Don Winslow of the Navy	5pm
News	Lone Journey	Shafter Parker, comment	The Bridge Club	5:15
Captain Quiz	By the Way	Captain Midnight	Jack Owens, songs	5:30
Tom Mix and His Ralston Straight Shooters	Robert Garred, news	Jack Armstong, the All-American Boy	News	5:45
Richard Brooks, news	Talk	Gabriel Heatter, news	Chesterfield Time	6pm
Sports	Pigskin Preview	London News	Film Commentator	6:15
Penthouse Party	Big Town	John B. Hughes, news	Manchester Boddy, news	6:30
		Sports	News	6:45
The American Melody Hour	Moonlight Serenade	Raymond Gram Swing, news	Kay Kyser's College of Musical Knowledge	7pm
	Music	Danger is My Business		7:15
Ahead of the Headlines	Romance of the Ranchos	The Lone Ranger		7:30
News				7:45
The Quiz Kids	Amos 'n' Andy	The Green Hornet	Point Sublime	8pm
	The Lanny Ross Show			8:15
Manhattan at Midnight	Dr. Christian	Music	Paducah Plantation, Red Foley	8:30
				8:45
Easy Aces	The Texaco Star Theater, Fred Allen	Glenn Hardy, news	Time to Smile, Eddie Cantor	9pm
Army Camp News		Cal Tinney, news		9:15
Mayor Bowron, comment		Fulton Lewis, Jr., news	Mr. District Attorney	9:30
Music		Dance Orchestra		9:45
The Chamber Music Society of Lower Basin Street	The Ten o'Clock Wire	Larry Noble Orchestra	The Richfield Reporter	10pm
	The World Today	FM Swing	Nothing But Praise	10:15
Music	Music Masterworks	News	Inside the News	10:30
Hal Saunders Orchestra		Larry Noble Orchestra	The Blue Moonlight	10:45

EVENING — FALL, 1941

Thursday

	BLUE	CBS	MBS	NBC
5pm	The Passing Parade	Talk (4:45 PM)	News	Don Winslow of the Navy
5:15	News	Lone Journey	Shafter Parker, comment	News
5:30	World News	Talk	Captain Midnight	The KFI Playhouse
5:45	Tom Mix and His Ralston Straight Shooters	Robert Garred, news	Jack Armstrong, the All-American Boy	
6pm	Richard Brooks, news	Major Bowes' Original Amateur Hour	Gabriel Heatter, news	The Kraft Music Hall, Bing Crosby
6:15	Sports		Berlin News	
6:30	Mayor Bowron, comment		John B. Hughes, news	
6:45	Intermezzo		Sports	
7pm	Vallee Varieties	Moonlight Serenade	Raymond Gram Swing, news	The Cugat Rumba Revue
7:15		By the Way	The Inside of Sports	
7:30	Hillman and Clapper, news	Whodunit	Jimmy Fidler, gossip	The Tums Show, Frank Fay
7:45	News		Dance Orchestra	
8pm	The March of Time	Amos 'n' Andy	The Standard Symphony Hour	Chesterfield Time
8:15		The Lanny Ross Show		Lum and Abner
8:30	Saunders of the Circle X	Maudie's Diary		Maxwell House Coffee Time, Brice and Morgan
8:45				
9pm	Easy Aces	Duffy's Tavern	Glenn Hardy, news	The Aldrich Family
9:15	Camp Roberts		FM Swing	
9:30	News	Death Valley Days	Fulton Lewis, Jr., news	Tommy Riggs and Betty Lou
9:45	Music		News	
10pm	America's Town Meeting of the Air	The Ten o'Clock Wire	The Haven of Rest	The Richfield Reporter
10:15		The World Today		Irene Rich Dramas
10:30		Music Masterworks	News	Inside the News
10:45			Dance Orchestra	The University Explorer

EVENING — FALL, 1941

Friday

BLUE	CBS	MBS	NBC	
Twilight Tales	Talk (4:45 PM)	News	Don Winslow of the Navy	5pm
News	Lone Journey	Shafter Parker, comment	News	5:15
World News	By the Way	Captain Midnight	Calling All Camps	5:30
Tom Mix and His Ralston Straight Shooters	Robert Garred, news	Jack Armstrong, the All-American Boy		5:45
Richard Brooks, news	What's On Your Mind	Gabriel Heatter, news	Waltz Time	6pm
Sports		Ted Weems Orchestra		6:15
Michael and Kitty	The First Nighter Program	Three Ring Time	Uncle Walter's Dog House	6:30
				6:45
Rochester Civic Orchestra	Hollywood Premiere	Raymond Gram Swing, news	Wings of Destiny	7pm
		Sports		7:15
Jack Owens, songs	Al Pearce and His Gang	The Lone Ranger	Grand Central Station	7:30
				7:45
The Flying Football	Amos 'n' Andy	The Two Cities Quiz	Chesterfield Time	8pm
	The Lanny Ross Show		Lum and Abner	8:15
Gangbusters	The Phillip Morris Playhouse	The Rookies	Don't Be Personal	8:30
				8:45
Pigskin Party	The Kate Smith Hour	Music	The Quiz Court	9pm
		Press Conference		9:15
Music		Fulton Lewis, Jr., news	When the Presses Roar	9:30
		Music		9:45
The Hollywood Fights	The Ten o'Clock Wire	Ray Noble Orchestra	The Richfield Reporter	10pm
	The World Today	FM Swing	Nothing But Praise	10:15
	Music Masterworks	News	Inside the News	10:30
		Ray Noble Orchestra	Rodriguez and Sutherland, news	10:45

EVENING — FALL, 1941

Saturday

	BLUE	CBS	MBS	NBC
5pm	Dance Orchestra	Short Story	The Hawaiians	On the Scouting Trail
5:15			Envoys	
5:30	Little Ol' Hollywood	Hollywood and Vine	America Preferred	Traffic Tribunal
5:45		News		News
6pm	Message of Israel	Hi Neighbor	Sinfonietta	The National Barn Dance
6:15				
6:30	NBC Symphony Orchestra	Smarty Party	News	
6:45		Saturday Night Serenade	Sports	
7pm	Hemisphere Revue		John B. Hughes, news	The Colgate Sports Newsreel, Bill Stern
7:15		Public Affairs	The Inside of Sports	News
7:30	Naomi Reynolds, songs	Parade	America Preferred	Grand Ole Opry
7:45				
8pm	The Bishop and the Gargoyle	Guy Lombardo Orchestra	Ray Noble Orchestra	Truth or Consequences
8:15				
8:30	Spin and Win	Hobby Lobby	California Melodies	The Knickerbocker Playhouse
8:45				
9pm	Postal Oddities	Your Hit Parade	Glenn Hardy, news	Tune Out Time
9:15	Paul Whiteman Orchestra		FM Swing	
9:30	Music		Cootie Williams Orchestra	
9:45		Music	News	
10pm	Two Round Jamboree	The Ten o' Clock Wire	The Chicago Theater of the Air	The Richfield Reporter
10:15		Music		The Los Angeles County Band
10:30		The People's Platform		
10:45				Sports Scripts

DAYTIME — FALL, 1941

Sunday

	BLUE	CBS	MBS	NBC
8am	Songs	The West Coast Church	The Comics Weekly Man	Music
8:15	Hidden History			
8:30	Fiesta	Music	Dr. Johnson, religion	News
8:45				Sunday Down South
9am	The Garden Club	Columbia's Country Journal	P. E. Gardner, religion	Football Second Guessers
9:15	I Am an American			
9:30	The Radio City Music Hall	The Salt Lake Tabernable Choir	Foreign News	Emma Otero, songs
9:45			Songs	
10am		The CBS Church of the Air	News	Upton Close, news
10:15			Romance of the Highways	The Silver Strings
10:30	Speaking of Glamour	News	The Canary Pet Shop	The World is Yours
10:45	Layman's Views of the News	Captain Quiz	Swing	
11am	Wake Up, America	The Spirit of '41		Health Talk
11:15				Concert Petite
11:30		The World Today		The University of Chicago Round Table
11:45			George Fisher, gossip	
12pm	Nick Harris	New York Philharmonic Orchestra	News	Music
12:15			Music	H. V. Kaltenborn, news
12:30	Dr. Casselbury, health		The Disney Parade	Captain Quiz
12:45	Music		Football Preview	News
1pm	National Vespers		The Lutheran Hour	Look at Books
1:15		The Four Clubmen		Tony Wons' Scrapbook

DAYTIME — FALL, 1941

Monday-Friday

BLUE	CBS	MBS	NBC	
The Breakfast Club	Treat Time, Buddy Clark / Rita Murray, songs	The Breakfast Club	The Johnny Murray Show	*8am*
Captain Quiz	Your Neighbor		Talk / The KFI Bandstand	*8:15*
News	Hymns of All Churches / Betty Crocker, cooking	News	News	*8:30*
Robert L. Johnson, talk	Stories America Loves	The Twig is Bent	David Harum	*8:45*
Betty Randall, songs	Kate Smith Speaks	John B. Hughes, news	What's Doing Ladies	*9am*
	Big Sister	Norma Young, talk	Talk	*9:15*
Here's to the Ladies	The Romance of Helen Trent		Jackpot	*9:30*
Sketch Henderson	Our Gal Sunday	We're Always Young	The Road of Life	*9:45*
Music Mysteries	Life Can Be Beautiful	Glenn Hardy, news	Talk	*10am*
News / Family Doctor	The Woman in White	Helen Holden, Government Girl	Bess Johnson	*10:15*
The Breakfast Club	The Right to Happiness	Front Page Farrell	Bachelor's Children	*10:30*
	Music / Mary Lee Taylor, cooking	I'lll Find My Way	Dr. Kate	*10:45*
Prescott Presents	Bright Horizon	Victor Lindlahr, health / The Clinic Forum	The Light of the World	*11am*
	Aunt Jenny's True Life Stories	Music	The Mystery Man	*11:15*
Into the Light	Talk	Talk and Music / The National School of the Air	Valiant Lady	*11:30*
Midstream	Kate Hopkins, Angel of Mercy		Arnold Grimm's Daughter	*11:45*
Orphans of Divorce	The Man I Married	News	The Farm Reporter	*12pm*
Amanda of Honeymoon Hill	Knox Manning, news	The Homemaker's Club	Ma Perkins	*12:15*
John's Other Wife	Music		The Guiding Light	*12:30*
Just Plain Bill	Woman of Courage	The Music Shop	Vic and Sade	*12:45*
News	Stepmother	The Bookworm	Mary Noble, Backstage Wife	*1pm*
Dearest Mother	The Story of Myrt and Marge	Music	Stella Dallas	*1:15*

DAYTIME — FALL, 1941

Sunday

	BLUE	CBS	MBS	NBC
1:30	Behind the Mike	The Pause That Refreshes	Young People's Church	String Symphony
1:45				
2pm	News	The Prudential Family Hour	Blue Barron Orchestra	The Metropolitan Opera Auditions
2:15	Music			
2:30	The Musical Steelmakers		America Singing	The Nickels Family of Five
2:45		William L. Shirer, news		
3pm	The Catholic Hour	The Silver Theater	The Haven of Rest	Professor Puzzlewit
3:15				
3:30	Church Federation Vespers	Gene Autry's Melody Ranch	Bulldog Drummond	The Great Gildersleeve
3:45				
4pm	Edward Tomlinson, news	Dear Mom (3:55PM)	Public Affairs	The Jelllo Program, Jack Benny
4:15		Public Affairs		
4:30	Captain Flagg and Sergeant Quirt	Tailspin Tommy	Nobody's Children	The Fitch Bandwagon
4:45				

DAYTIME — FALL, 1941

Monday-Friday

BLUE	CBS	MBS	NBC	
Club Matinee, Garry Moore	Talk and Music	The Johnson Family	Lorenzo Jones	1:30
		The Music Depriciation Hour	Young Widder Brown	1:45
The Classic Hour	The KNX Playhouse		When a Girl Marries	2pm
	The Road of Life	Talk	Portia Faces Life	2:15
	The O'Neills		We, the Abbotts	2:30
	The Ben Bernie War Worker's Program	Let's Play Bridge	The Story of Mary Marlin	2:45
Between the Bookends	Joyce Jordan, M. D.	Music / The Haven of Rest	Pepper Young's Family	3pm
Bud Barton	Music / Backgrounds iin Living		Lone Journey	3:15
The Unclassic Hour	Music	Talk and Music	Against the Storm	3:30
	Nancy Dixon, talk		News	3:45
News	The Second Mrs. Burton	Fulton Lewis, Jr., news	Talk	4pm
Talk / Mr. Keen, Tracer of Lost Persons	Young Dr. Malone	Here's Morgan		4:15
What's Doing Ladies	News	Casey Jones	Talk and Music	4:30
Talk / The Adventures of Superman	Talk	Little Orphan Annie		4:45

DAYTIME — FALL, 1941

Saturday

	BLUE	CBS	MBS	NBC
8am	The Breakfast Club	Top of the Morning	Lest We Forget	Organ Recital
8:15				The KFI Bandstand
8:30	News	The Town Crier	The US Army Band	News
8:45	Robert L. Johnson, talk	National Hillbilly Champions	Community Hall	On Your Job
9am	The Federation of Churches	The Armstrong Theater of Today	Dr. Matthews, religion	What's Doing Ladies
9:15	Howard Ropa, songs			Consumer Time
9:30	Forty-Plus Associates	Stars Over Hollywood	Garden Plots	Call to Youth
9:45			Food for Thought	County Medical Association Talks
10am	Church Women	Let's Pretend	News	Lincoln Highway
10:15	What's Doing Ladies		Helen Holden, Government Girl	
10:30	Music	The Voice of Broadway	Music	Amerca, the Free
10:45	Sports	Sports	Sports	
11am				Sports
11:15				
11:30				
11:45				
12pm				
12:15				
12:30				
12:45				
1pm				
1:15				
1:30				Music
1:45				

DAYTIME — FALL, 1941

Saturday

	BLUE	CBS	MBS	NBC
2pm	The Classic Hour			Stories of American Liberities
2:15				
2:30				Music
2:45				
3pm	Sports	Calling Pan-America		
3:15				
3:30		News		Religion in the News
3:45		Europeon News		The Board of Education Forums
4pm		The Pigskin Jamboree		Defense for America
4:15				
4:30				Music
4:45	Sports Roundup			H. V. Kaltenborn, news

LISTINGS FOR 1942

EVENING — WINTER, 1942

Sunday

	BLUE	CBS	MBS	NBC
5pm	Listen, America	The Columbia Workshop	The American Forum of the Air	The Charlie McCarthy Show
5:15				
5:30	Captain Quiz	Spelling Beeliner		One Man's Family
5:45	Drew Pearson, news		Music	
6pm	Grandpappy and His Pals	The Ford Sunday Evening Hour	The Old Fashioned Revival Hour	The Manhattan Merry-Go-Round
6:15				
6:30	Joseph Jackson, books			The American Album of Familiar Music
6:45	Songs By Dinah Shore			
7pm	The Goodwill Hour	Take It or Leave It	San Quentin on the Air	The Hour of Charm
7:15			Lieutenent Healy, comment	
7:30		The Helen Hayes Theater	Keep 'Em Rolling	Sherlock Holmes
7:45				
8pm	Inner Sanctum Mysteries	Crime Doctor	USC Hancock Ensemble	The Great Gildersleeve
8:15				
8:30	The Jello Program, Jack Benny	I Was There	Nobody's Children	News
8:45				The Chapel Quartet
9pm	Irene Rich Dramas	The Holllywood Playhouse	News	Walter Winchell's Jergens Journal
9:15	Over Our Coffee Cups		The Voice of Prophecy	The Parker Family
9:30	News	What's It All About		Carefree Carnival
9:45	Charm and Social Grace		Dr. Polyzoides, health	
10pm	Music	The Gulf Screen Theater	Americas Speak	The Richfield Reporter
10:15				Bridge to Dreamland
10:30	Tommy Dorsey Orchestra	Lud Gluskin Orchestra	Miles Davis Orchestra	Inside the News
10:45				Bridge to Dreamland

EVENING — WINTER, 1942

Monday

BLUE	CBS	MBS	NBC	
Twilight Tales	Talk (4:45PM)	News	Don Winslow of the Navy	5pm
News	Lone Journey	Little Orphan Annie	The Bridge Club	5:15
World News	By the Way	Captain Midnight	Music	5:30
Tom Mix and His Ralston Straight Shooters	Robert Garred, news	Jack Armstong, the All-American Boy	News	5:45
Choices and Voices	The Lux Radio Theater	Gabriel Heatter, news	Dr. I. Q., the Mental Banker	6pm
Sports		News		6:15
Claude Sweeten Orchestra		The Editor Speaks	That Brewster Boy	6:30
		Music		6:45
The Monday Merry-Go-Round	The Orson Welles Theater	Raymond Gram Swing, news	The Carnation Contented Hour	7pm
		Spotlight Bands		7:15
Tropic Tunes	Blondie	The Lone Ranger	The Cavalcade of America	7:30
News				7:45
The Herbert Marshall Show	Amos 'n' Andy	This, Our America	Chesterfield Time	8pm
	The Lanny Ross Show	Russell Bennett's Notebook	Lum and Abner	8:15
I Love a Mystery	The Gay Nineties Revue	Double or Nothing	The Voice of Firestone	8:30
				8:45
True or False	Vox Pop	Glenn Hardy, news	The Bell Telephone Hour	9pm
		Cal Tinney, news		9:15
News	The Hollywood Showcase	Fulton Lewis, Jr., news	Hawthorne House	9:30
Rodriguez and Sutherland, news		The Jerry Wayne Show		9:45
Phil Harris Orchestra	The Ten o'Clock Wire	Newsreel	The Richfield Reporter	10pm
	The World Today		Manchester Boddy, news	10:15
Tommy Dorsey Orchestra	Music Masterworks		Inside the News	10:30
			Stoker Orchestra	10:45

EVENING — WINTER, 1942

Tuesday

	BLUE	CBS	MBS	NBC
5pm	Music	Talk (4:45pm)	News	Don Winslow of the Navy
5:15	News	Lone Journey	Little Orphan Annie	News
5:30	World News	Talk	Captain Midnight	Tums Treasure Chest
5:45	Tom Mix and His Ralston Straight Shooters	News	Jack Armstrong, the All-American Boy	
6pm	Adventures in Hollywood	Second Husband	Gabriel Heatter, news	Burns and Allen
6:15	Sports		News	
6:30	NBC Symphony Orchestra	Report to the Nation	Morton Gould Orchestra	Fibber McGee and Molly
6:45				
7pm		Moonlight Serenade	Raymond Gram Swing, news	The Pepsodent Show, Bob Hope
7:15		The Inglewood Park Concert	Spotlight Bands	
7:30	Ricardo Tanturi Orchestra		London News	The Raleigh Cigarette Program, Red Skelton
7:45		Public Affairs	The Inside of Sports	
8pm	News	Amos 'n' Andy	What's My Name	Chesterfield Time
8:15	Captain Quiz	The Lanny Ross Show		Lum and Abner
8:30	Information, Please	The Court of Missing Heirs	The Shadow	Johnny Presents
8:45				
9pm	Easy Aces	We, the People	Glenn Hardy, news	The Adventures of the Thin Man
9:15	Don't You Believe It		The Story Teller	
9:30	News	The Bob Burns Show	Fulton Lewis, Jr., news	Battle of the Sexes
9:45	Rodriguez and Sutherland, news		The Jerry Wayne Show	
10pm	The Cugat Rumba Revue	The Ten o'Clock Wire	Newsreel	The Richfield Reporter
10:15		The World Today		Income Tax
10:30	Tommy Dorsey Orchestra	Music Masterworks		Inside the News
10:45				Dance Orchestra

EVENING — WINTER, 1942

Wednesday

BLUE	CBS	MBS	NBC	
Layman's Views of the News	Talk (4:45 PM)	News	Don Winslow of the Navy	5pm
News	Lone Journey	Little Orphan Annie	The Bridge Club	5:15
Captain Quiz	By the Way	Captain Midnight	Claude Sweeten Orchestra	5:30
Tom Mix and His Ralston Straight Shooters	Robert Garred, news	Jack Armstrong, the All-American Boy	News	5:45
Adventures in Hollywood	Romance of the Ranchos	Gabriel Heatter, news	Chesterfield Time	6pm
Sports		News	News	6:15
Music	Music	Music	The Quiz Court	6:30
				6:45
The American Melody Hour	Moonlight Serenade	Raymond Gram Swing, news	Kay Kyser's College of Musical Knowledge	7pm
	Great Moments in Music	Spotlight Bands		7:15
Ahead of the Headlines		The Lone Ranger		7:30
News	Mark Hawley, news			7:45
The Quiz Kids	Amos 'n' Andy	The Chicago Theater of the Air	Point Sublime	8pm
	The Lanny Ross Show			8:15
Manhattan at Midnight	Dr. Christian		Paducah Plantation, Red Foley	8:30
				8:45
Easy Aces	The Texaco Star Theater, Fred Allen	Glenn Hardy, news	Time to Smile, Eddie Cantor	9pm
Army Camp News		Cal Tinney, news		9:15
News		Fulton Lewis, Jr., news	Mr. District Attorney	9:30
Rodriguez and Sutherland, news		The Jerry Wayne Show		9:45
The Chamber Music Society of Lower Basin Street	The Ten o'Clock Wire	Newsreel	The Richfield Reporter	10pm
	The World Today		Manchester Boddy, news	10:15
Tommy Dorsey Orchestra	Music Masterworks		Inside the News	10:30
			Dance Orchestra	10:45

EVENING — WINTER, 1942

Thursday

	BLUE	CBS	MBS	NBC
5pm	Alvin Wilder, news	Talk (4:45PM)	News	Don Winslow of the Navy
5:15	News	Lone Journey	Little Orphan Annie	News
5:30	World News	By the Way	Captain Midnight	Ricardo and His Caballeros
5:45	Tom Mix and His Ralston Straight Shooters	Robert Garred, news	Jack Armstrong, the All-American Boy	
6pm	Adventures in Hollywood	Major Bowes' Original Amateur Hour	Gabriel Heatter, news	The Kraft Music Hall, Bing Crosby
6:15	Sports		News	
6:30	Mayor Bowron, comment	Big Town	Public Affairs	
6:45	Jack Owens, songs			
7pm	Vallee Varieties	Moonlight Serenade	Raymond Gram Swing, news	Al Pearce and His Gang
7:15		The First Line of Defense	Spotlight Bands	
7:30	Captain Quiz		Your Defense Reporter	The Tums Show, Frank Fay
7:45	News	Public Affairs	The Inside of Sports	
8pm	The March of Time	Amos 'n' Andy	The Standard Symphony Hour	Chesterfield Time
8:15		The Lanny Ross Show		Lum and Abner
8:30	Saunders of the Circle X	Maudie's Diary		Maxwell House Coffee Time, Brice and Morgan
8:45				
9pm	Easy Aces	Duffy's Tavern	Glenn Hardy, news	The Aldrich Family
9:15	Sports		The Story Teller	
9:30	News	Death Valley Days	Fulton Lewis, Jr., news	The Adventures of Ellery Queen
9:45	Rodriguez and Sutherland, news		Music	
10pm	America's Town Meeting of the Air	The Ten o'Clock Wire	Newsreel	The Richfield Reporter
10:15		The World Today		Irene Rich Dramas
10:30		Music Masterworks		Inside the News
10:45				Nothing But Praise

EVENING — WINTER, 1942

Friday

BLUE	CBS	MBS	NBC	
Twilight Tales	Talk (4:45pm)	News	Don Winslow of the Navy	5pm
News	Lone Journey	Little Orphan Annie	News	5:15
World News	By the Way	Captain Midnight	Music	5:30
Tom Mix and His Ralston Straight Shooters	Robert Garred, news	Jack Armstong, the All-American Boy	Weekend Dialing	5:45
Adventures in Holllywood	What's On Your Mind	Gabriel Heatter, news	Waltz Time	6pm
Sports		News		6:15
Michael Piper, Private Detective	The First Nighter Program	America Preferred	Uncle Walter's Dog House	6:30
				6:45
Elsa Maxwell's Party Line	The Ransom Sherman Show	Raymond Gram Swing, news	Wings of Destiny	7pm
Edward Tomlinson, news		Spotlight Bands		7:15
Jack Owens, songs	How'm I Doing	The Lone Ranger	Grand Central Station	7:30
				7:45
Music	Amos 'n' Andy	The Two Cities Quiz	Chesterfield Time	8pm
Don't You Believe It	The Lanny Ross Show		Lum and Abner	8:15
Gangbusters	The Phillip Morris Playhouse	Music	Weekly	8:30
				8:45
Three Ring Time, Milton Berle	The Kate Smith Hour	Glenn Hardy, news	Whodunit	9pm
		Cal Tinney, news		9:15
News		Fulton Lewis, Jr., news	When the Presses Roar	9:30
Rodriguez and Sutherland, news		Ray Noble Orchestra		9:45
The Hollywood Fights	The Ten o'Clock Wire	Newsreel	The Richfield Reporter	10pm
	The World Today		Manchester Boddy, news	10:15
Tommy Dorsey Orchestra	Music Masterworks		Inside the News	10:30
			Nothing But Praise	10:45

EVENING — WINTER, 1942

Saturday

	BLUE	CBS	MBS	NBC
5pm	Wilde Orchestra	Short Story	News	On the Scouting Trail
5:15		Organ Recital	Public Affairs	
5:30	The Green Hornet	News Review	Music	Traffic Tribunal
5:45		News		News
6pm	NBC Symphony Orchestra	Who, What, Where, When		The National Barn Dance
6:15				
6:30		Here's the Story	Sinfonietta	
6:45		Saturday Night Serenade		
7pm	Believe It or Not		John B. Hughes, news	The Colgate Sports Newsreel, Bill Stern
7:15		News	Spotlight Bands	News
7:30	Music	Hi Neighbor		Grand Ole Opry
7:45			The Inside of Sports	
8pm	Paul Whiteman Orchestra	Guy Lombardo Orchestra	Ray Noble Orchestra	Music
8:15	The University Exploorer			
8:30	Spin and Win	Hobby Lobby	The Clinic Forum	The Knickerbocker Playhouse
8:45				
9pm	Music	Your Hit Parade	Glenn Hardy, news	Truth or Consequences
9:15	Postal Oddities		Songs	
9:30	The Edwards Family			The Best of the Week
9:45		By the Way	Dance Orchestra	
10pm	Dance Orchestra	The Ten o' Clock Wire	Newsreel	The Richfield Reporter
10:15		Songs		Wilde Orchestra
10:30	Tommy Dorsey Orchestra	Public Affairs		Unlimited Horizons
10:45				

DAYTIME — WINTER, 1942

Sunday

	BLUE	CBS	MBS	NBC
8am	Songs	The West Coast Church	The Comics Weekly Man	Via Villa (7:45AM)
8:15	Music			Serenade
8:30	Fiesta	Invitation to Learning	Songs	Youth and Music
8:45			The Voice of Prophecy	
9am	The Garden Club	Syncopated Piece	P. E. Gardner, religion	Sunday Down South
9:15	I Am an American			Health Talk
9:30	The Radio City Music Hall	The Salt Lake Tabernable Choir	Foreign News	Emma Otero, songs
9:45			Songs	
10am		The CBS Church of the Air	News	Upton Close, news
10:15			Romance of the Highways	The Silver Strings
10:30	Speaking of Glamour	News	The Canary Pet Shop	The World is Yours
10:45	Cinema Review	Music	Music	
11am	Great Plays	The Spirit of '42		Music
11:15				Concert Petite
11:30		The World Today		The University of Chicago Round Table
11:45			George Fisher, gossip	
12pm	Wake Up, America	New York Philharmonic Orchestra	News	Bob Becker's Dog Talks
12:15			Far East News	H. V. Kaltenborn, news
12:30			Children's Chapel	News
12:45	Laymen's Views of the News			Look at Books
1pm	National Vespers		The Lutheran Hour	The University Explorer
1:15		The Four Clubmen		Tony Wons' Scrapbook

DAYTIME — WINTER, 1942

Monday-Friday

BLUE	CBS	MBS	NBC	
The Musical Clock	Treat Time, Buddy Clark / Rita Murray, songs	The Breakfast Club	The Johnny Murray Show	8am
The Breakfast Club	Your Neighbor		Talk and Music	8:15
News	Hymns of All Churches / Betty Crocker, cooking	News	News	8:30
Robert L. Johnson, talk	Stories America Loves	The Twig is Bent	David Harum	8:45
The Breakfast Club	Kate Smith Speaks	John B. Hughes, news	What's Doing Ladies	9am
	Big Sister	Victor Lindlahr, health	Talk	9:15
Here's to the Ladies	The Romance of Helen Trent	Norma Young, talk	News	9:30
News	Our Gal Sunday		The Road of Life	9:45
Vance and Lily, songs / Family Doctor	Life Can Be Beautiful	Glenn Hardy, news	Talk	10am
The Breakfast Club	The Woman in White	Helen Holden, Government Girl	Bess Johnson	10:15
	Vic and Sade	Front Page Farrell	Bachelor's Children	10:30
War News	Music / Mary Lee Taylor, cooking	Talk	Dr. Kate	10:45
Music	Bright Horizon	Cedric Foster, news / The Clinic Forum	The Light of the World	11am
	Aunt Jenny's True Life Stories	Music	The Mystery Man	11:15
Into the Light	Talk	Talk and Music / The National School of the Air	Valiant Lady	11:30
News	Kate Hopkins, Angel of Mercy		Arnold Grimm's Daughter	11:45
Orphans of Divorce	The Man I Married	News	The Farm Reporter	12pm
Amanda of Honeymoon Hill	Knox Manning, news	The Homemaker's Club	Ma Perkins	12:15
John's Other Wife	Music		Pepper Young's Family	12:30
Just Plain Bill	Woman of Courage	The Bookworm	Vic and Sade	12:45
Music / The Street Singer	Stepmother	Music	Mary Noble, Backstage Wife	1pm
Club Matinee, Garry Moore	The Story of Myrt and Marge		Stella Dallas	1:15

DAYTIME — WINTER, 1942

Sunday

	BLUE	CBS	MBS	NBC
1:30	Music	The Pause That Refreshes	Young People's Church	Music
1:45				
2pm	Waltzes and Fashions	The Prudential Family Hour	I Hear America Singing	The Metropolitan Opera Auditions
2:15	Nick Harris		The Disney Parade	
2:30	The Musical Steelmakers		Ned Jordan, Secret Agent	The Nickels Family of Family
2:45		William L. Shirer, news		
3pm	The Catholic Hour	The Silver Theater	Confessions	Professor Puzzlewit
3:15				
3:30	Church Federation Vespers	Gene Autry's Melody Ranch	Bulldog Drummond	News
3:45				Cabbages and Kings
4pm	Edward Tomlinson, news		The Fact Finders	The Jello Program, Jack Benny
4:15		Public Affairs	Rabbi Magnin, religion	
4:30	Captain Flagg and Sergeant Quirt	Dance Orchestra	In His Steps	The Fitch Bandwagon
4:45				

DAYTIME — WINTER, 1942

Monday-Friday

BLUE	CBS	MBS	NBC	
	The American School of the Air	The Johnson Family	Lorenzo Jones	1:30
		Boake Carter, news	Young Widder Brown	1:45
The Classic Hour	The KNX Playhouse	The Dime-Dance Parade	When a Girl Marries	2pm
	The Road of Life	I'll Find My Way	Portia Faces Life	2:15
	The O'Neills	News	We, The Abbots	2:30
	Scattergood Baines	Let's Play Bridge	The Story of Mary Marlin	2:45
Between the Bookends	Joyce Jordan, M. D.	Music / The Haven of Rest	The Right to Happiness	3pm
What's Doing Ladies	Talk and Music		Lone Journey	3:15
The Unclassic Hour	Music / The Voice of Broadway	Talk and Music	Against the Storm	3:30
	Nancy Dixon, talk		Guess a Tune	3:45
News	The Second Mrs. Burton	Fulton Lewis, Jr., news	Talk	4pm
Talk / Mr. Keen, Tracer of Lost Persons	Young Dr. Malone	South American Conference		4:15
Talk and Music	News	Talk and Music	Music	4:30
The Adventures of Superman	Talk	Shafter Parker, comment		4:45

DAYTIME — WINTER, 1942

Saturday

	BLUE	CBS	MBS	NBC
8am	The Musical Clock	Top of the Morning	BBC News	Agricultural Talk
8:15	The Breakfast Club			Minstrels
8:30	News	Let's Pretend	News	America, the Free
8:45	Robert L. Johnson, talk		The US Army Band	
9am	The Breakfast Club	The Armstrong Theater of Today	Music	What's Doing Ladies
9:15	The Federation of Churches		Songs	Consumer Time
9:30	Forty-Plus Associates	Stars Over Hollywood	Music	News
9:45			Food for Thought	County Medical Association Talks
10am	The Board of Education	The US Army Band	News	Lincoln Highway
10:15	Music	The Town Crier	Chet Mauthe Orchestra	
10:30	Dr. Casselberry, health	Adventures in Science		Youth to Call
10:45	War News	The Golden Gate Quartet		On Your Job
11am	The Metropolitan Opera	Of Men and Books	Hollywood Juniors	The US Marine Band
11:15				
11:30		The Brush Creek Follies		Whatcha Know, Joe
11:45				
12pm		Columbia's Country Journal	News	The Farm Reporter
12:15			Music	
12:30		News	The Playmakers	Music
12:45		Detroit Musicale		The US Army Band
1pm		Matinee	Horse Racing	News
1:15				Whimsey
1:30				Air Youth of America
1:45				Songs

DAYTIME — WINTER, 1942

Saturday

	BLUE	CBS	MBS	NBC
2pm		Cleveland Symphony Orchestra	Sunset Serenade	Stories of American Liberities
2:15				
2:30	Music			Music
2:45				
3pm		Calling Pan-America	Anchors Aweigh	The US Marine Band
3:15	What's Doing Ladies			Music
3:30	Songs	News	The News Parade	Religion in the News
3:45	Edward Tomlinson, news	The World Today		Pleasantville Follks
4pm	Message of Israel	The People's Platform	Dr. Matthews, religion	The War This Week
4:15				
4:30	Little Ol' Hollywood	The KNX Music Festival	Music	Music
4:45				H. V. Kaltenborn, news

EVENING — SPRING, 1942

Sunday

	BLUE	CBS	MBS	NBC
5pm	The Daughters of Uncle Sam, Mary Small	World News Tonight	The American Forum of the Air	The Charlie McCarthy Show
5:15				
5:30	News	William Winter, news		One Man's Family
5:45	Drew Pearson, news	News	Music	
6pm	Music	The Texaco Star Theater, Fred Allen	The Old Fashioned Revival Hour	The Manhattan Merry-Go-Round
6:15				
6:30	Talk Over the News			The American Album of Familiar Music
6:45	Songs By Dinah Shore			
7pm	The Goodwill Hour	Take It or Leave It	San Quentin on the Air	The Hour of Charm
7:15				
7:30		The Inglewood Park Concert	Keep 'Em Rolling	Walter Winchell's Jergens Journal
7:45		Al Goodman Orchestra		The Parker Family
8pm	Inner Sanctum Mysteries	Crime Doctor	USC Hancock Ensemble	The Great Gildersleeve
8:15				
8:30	The Jello Program, Jack Benny	Romance of the Ranchos	Nobody's Children	News
8:45				The Chapel Quartet
9pm	Grandpappy and His Pals	What's On Your Mind	News	Carefree Carnival
9:15	Over Our Coffee Cups		The Voice of Prophecy	
9:30	News	William Winter, news		Cabbages and Kings
9:45	The University Explorer		Dr. Polyzoides, health	Irene Rich Dramas
10pm	Sonny Dunham Orchestra	The Gulf Screen Theater	Americas Speak	The Richfield Reporter
10:15	Bridge to Dreamland			Music
10:30		They Live Forever	Ted Weems Orchestra	Inside the News
10:45				Music

EVENING — SPRING, 1942

Monday

BLUE	CBS	MBS	NBC	
Twilight Tales	Talk (4:45 PM)	News	Don Winslow of the Navy	5pm
News	Music	Little Orphan Annie	The Bridge Club	5:15
World News	Harry W. Flannery, news	Captain Midnight	Richard Crooks, songs	5:30
Jack Owens, songs	Robert Garred, news	Jack Armstrong, the All-American Boy	News	5:45
Film Commentator	The Lux Radio Theater	Gabriel Heatter, news	Music	6pm
News		News	News	6:15
For America We Sing		Spotlight Bands	Dr. I. Q., the Mental Banker	6:30
		Public Affairs		6:45
Music	Lady Esther Serenade	John Gunther, news	The Carnation Contented Hour	7pm
		Toast to Our Allies		7:15
Jimmy Fidler, gossip	Blondie	The Lone Ranger	The Cavalcade of America	7:30
News				7:45
Music	Amos 'n' Andy	This, Our America	Chesterfield Time	8pm
Irene Rich Dramas	The Lanny Ross Show		Lum and Abner	8:15
I Love a Mystery	The Gay Nineties Revue	Double or Nothing	Hawthorne House	8:30
				8:45
News	I Was There	Glenn Hardy, news	The Bell Telephone Hour	9pm
Talk Over the News		Cal Tinney, news		9:15
The Hollywood Spotlight	The Hollywood Showcase	Fulton Lewis, Jr., news	Claude Sweeten Orchestra	9:30
Rodriguez and Sutherland, news		Hank Keene and His Gang		9:45
Wilde Orchestra	The Ten o'Clock Wire	Newsreel	The Richfield Reporter	10pm
	Lud Gluskin Orchestra		Manchester Boddy, news	10:15
Sonny Dunham Orchestra	Music Masterworks		Inside the News	10:30
			Stoker Orchestra	10:45

EVENING — SPRING, 1942

Tuesday

	BLUE	CBS	MBS	NBC
5pm	Alvin Wilder, news	Talk (4:45PM)	News	Don Winslow of the Navy
5:15	News	The Home Front	Little Orphan Annie	Music
5:30	World News	Harry W. Flannery, news	Captain Midnight	Tums Treasure Chest
5:45	Jack Owens, songs	News	Jack Armstong, the All-American Boy	
6pm	Jimmy Starr, gossip	The American Melody Hour	Gabriel Heatter, news	Burns and Allen
6:15	News		News	
6:30	NBC Symphony Orchestra	Report to the Nation	Spotlight Bands	Fibber McGee and Molly
6:45			Australian News	
7pm		Music	John B. Hughes, news	The Pepsodent Show, Bob Hope
7:15			Ned Jordan, Secret Agent	
7:30	Red Ryder			The Raleigh Cigarette Program, Red Skelton
7:45		Frazier Hunt, news	The Inside of Sports	
8pm	Three Ring Time, Milton Berle	Amos 'n' Andy	What's My Name	Chesterfield Time
8:15		The Lanny Ross Show		Lum and Abner
8:30	Information, Please	The Court of Missing Heirs	The Shadow	Johnny Presents
8:45				
9pm	Easy Aces	We, the People	Glenn Hardy, news	The Adventures of the Thin Man
9:15	Talk Over the News		The Story Teller	
9:30	The Hollywood Spotlight	The Bob Burns Show	Fulton Lewis, Jr., news	Battle of the Sexes
9:45	Rodriguez and Sutherland, news		Joe Reichman Orchestra	
10pm	The Cugat Rumba Revue	The Ten o'Clock Wire	Newsreel	The Richfield Reporter
10:15		Music		Sports
10:30	Sonny Dunham Orchestra	Music Masterworks		Inside the News
10:45				Harry Owens Orchestra

EVENING — SPRING, 1942

Wednesday

BLUE	CBS	MBS	NBC	
Alvin Wilder, news	Talk (4:45pm)	News	Don Winslow of the Navy	5pm
News	The Home Front	Little Orphan Annie	The Bridge Club	5:15
World News	Harry W. Flannery, news	Captain Midnight	Service Program	5:30
Jack Owens, songs	Robert Garred, news	Jack Armstong, the All-American Boy	Bill Henry, news	5:45
Jimmy Starr, gossip	Junior Miss	Gabriel Heatter, news	Chesterfield Time	6pm
News		News	Gordon Jenkins Orchestra	6:15
Cab Calloway's Quizzicale	The Ransom Sherman Show	Spotlight Bands	Mr. District Attorney	6:30
		Australian News		6:45
Three-Thirds of the Nation	Moonlight Serenade	John B. Hughes, news	Kay Kyser's College of Musical Knowledge	7pm
	Great Moments in Music	Toast to the Allies		7:15
Music		The Lone Ranger		7:30
News	Mark Hawley, news			7:45
The Quiz Kids	Amos 'n' Andy	Wings Over the Coast	Point Sublime	8pm
	The Lanny Ross Show			8:15
Manhattan at Midnight	Dr. Christian	Tune Up, America	Uncle Walter's Dog House	8:30
				8:45
Easy Aces	That Brewster Boy	Glenn Hardy, news	The Quiz Court	9pm
Talk Over the News		Cal Tinney, news		9:15
The Hollywood Spotlight	Wiliam Winter, news	Fulton Lewis, Jr., news	Chesterfield Time	9:30
Rodriguez and Sutherland, news	Dance Orchestra	Hank Keene and His Gang	Mel Powell Orchestra	9:45
The Chamber Music Society of Lower Basin Street	The Ten o'Clock Wire	Newsreel	The Richfield Reporter	10pm
	Music		Manchester Boddy, news	10:15
Sonny Dunham Orchestra	Music Masterworks		Inside the News	10:30
			Dance Orchestra	10:45

EVENING — SPRING, 1942

Thursday

	BLUE	CBS	MBS	NBC
5pm	Alvin Wilder, news	Talk (4:45 PM)	News	Don Winslow of the Navy
5:15	News	The Home Front	Little Orphan Annie	News
5:30	World News	Harry W. Flannery, news	Captain Midnight	Paging John Doe
5:45	Jack Owens, songs	Robert Garred, news	Jack Armstrong, the All-American Boy	Bill Henry, news
6pm	Film Commentator	Major Bowes' Original Amateur Hour	Gabriel Heatter, news	The Kraft Music Hall, Bing Crosby
6:15	News		News	
6:30	Mayor Bowron, comment	Big Town	Spotlight Bands	
6:45	Claude Sweeten Orchestra		Toast to the Allies	
7pm	Vallee Varieties	Moonlight Serenade	John Gunther, news	Al Pearce and His Gang
7:15		The First Line of Defense	The Secret Legion	
7:30	Red Ryder			The Tums Show, Frank Fay
7:45		Frazier Hunt, news	The Inside of Sports	
8pm	Dorothy Thompson, news	Amos 'n' Andy	The Standard Symphony Hour	Chesterfield Time
8:15	News	The Lanny Ross Show		Lum and Abner
8:30	Your Blind Date	Death Valley Days		Maxwell House Coffee Time, Brice and Morgan
8:45				
9pm	News	Music	Glenn Hardy, news	The Aldrich Family
9:15	Talk Over the News	What Are We Fighiing For	The Story Teller	
9:30	The Hollywood Spotlight	Maudie's Diary	Fulton Lewis, Jr., news	The Adventures of Ellery Queen
9:45	Rodriguez and Sutherland, news		Dance Orchestra	
10pm	America's Town Meeting of the Air	The Ten o'Clock Wire	Newsreel	The Richfield Reporter
10:15		Music		Sports
10:30		Music Masterworks		Inside the News
10:45				Ricardo Tanturi Orchestra

EVENING — SPRING, 1942

Friday

BLUE	CBS	MBS	NBC	
Twilight Tales	Talk (4:45 PM)	News	Don Winslow of the Navy	5pm
News	Music	Little Orphan Annie	News	5:15
World News	Harry W. Flannery, news	Captain Midnight	Paging John Doe	5:30
Jack Owens, songs	Robert Garred, news	Jack Armstrong, the All-American Boy	Bill Henry, news	5:45
The March of Time	Lud Gluskin Orchestra	Gabriel Heatter, news	Waltz Time	6pm
		News		6:15
Film Commentator	The First Nighter Program	Spotlight Bands	Paducah Plantation, Red Foley	6:30
News		Public Affairs		6:45
Elsa Maxwell's Party Line	Moonlight Serenade	Cedric Foster, news	People Are Funny	7pm
The First Piano Quartet	Music	Toast to the Allies		7:15
Mitchell Ayres Orchestra	How'm I Doin'	The Lone Ranger	Grand Central Station	7:30
				7:45
The Herbert Marshall Show	Amos 'n' Andy	Buddy Johnson Orchestra	Chesterfield Time	8pm
	The Lanny Ross Show	Music	Lum and Abner	8:15
Celebrity Theater	The Phillip Morris Playhouse	Songs	Whodunit	8:30
				8:45
News	The Kate Smith Hour	Glenn Hardy, news	Dark Fantasy	9pm
Talk Over the News		Cal Tinney, news		9:15
The Hollywood Spotlight		Fulton Lewis, Jr., news	When the Presses Roar	9:30
Rodriguez and Sutherland, news		Hank Keene and His Gang		9:45
The Hollywood Fights	The Ten o'Clock Wire	Newsreel	The Richfield Reporter	10pm
	Music		Manchester Boddy, news	10:15
	Music Masterworks		Inside the News	10:30
			Nothing But Praise	10:45

EVENING — SPRING, 1942

Saturday

	BLUE	CBS	MBS	NBC
5pm	The Green Hornet	Short Story	News	On the Scouting Trail
5:15			Serenade	
5:30	SWOP Night	News Review	The Chicago Concert	Traffic Tribunal
5:45		News		Bill Henry, news
6pm	The Call of the West	Look Who's Here		The National Barn Dance
6:15			News	
6:30	News	Here's the Story	Spotlight Bands	
6:45	Rochester Civic Orchestra	Saturday Night Serenade		
7pm	Tune Out Time		John B. Hughes, news	The Colgate Sports Newsreel, Bill Stern
7:15		Music	Spotlight Bands	Labor for Victory
7:30	Red Ryder			Grand Ole Opry
7:45		Frazier Hunt, news	The Inside of Sports	
8pm	News	Guy Lombardo Orchestra	California Melodies	Truth or Consequences
8:15	Postal Oddities			
8:30	The A. B. C. D. News	Hobby Lobby	The Clinic Forum	Abie's Irish Rose
8:45				
9pm	Believe It or Not	Your Hit Parade	Glenn Hardy, news	Music
9:15			Songs	
9:30	Film Commentator			The Richfield Reporter
9:45	This is War	This is War	This is War	This is War
10pm				
10:15	Yerba Buena Orchestra	News	Newsreel	The University Explorer
10:30	Sonny Dunham Orchestra	Lud Gluskin Orchestra		The Best of the Week
10:45				

DAYTIME — SPRING, 1942

Sunday

	BLUE	CBS	MBS	NBC
8am	News	The West Coast Church	The Comics Weekly Man	News
8:15	Dialing Today			The Book of Books
8:30	Nick Harris	Invitation to Learning	The Junior Army Hour	Youth and Music
8:45			The Voice of Prophecy	
9am	The Garden Club	Syncopated Piece	The Detroit Bible Class	Freedom's People
9:15	The First Piano Quartet			
9:30	The Radio City Music Hall	The Salt Lake Tabernable Choir	Far East News	
9:45				
10am		The CBS Church of the Air	News	News
10:15			Romance of the Highways	Music
10:30	Captain Quiz	News	The Canary Pet Shop	The World is Yours
10:45	Speaking of Glamour	Music	Music	
11am	The Blue Theater	The Spirit of '42	The Little Show	Sammy Kaye's Sunday Serenade
11:15			Music	News
11:30	Today's Song	The Columbia Workshop		The University of Chicago Round Table
11:45			George Fisher, gossip	
12pm	Wake Up, America	New York Philharmonic Orchestra	News	Bob Becker's Dog Talks
12:15			Music	H. V. Kaltenborn, news
12:30			The University Glee Club	The Army Hour
12:45			Alvin Wilder, news	
1pm	National Vespers		The Lutheran Hour	

DAYTIME — SPRING, 1942

Monday-Friday

BLUE	CBS	MBS	NBC	
The Musical Clock	Songs / Rita Murray, songs	The Breakfast Club	The Johnny Murray Show	8am
The Breakfast Club	Brushcreek Way		Inside Stories / The Musical Clock	8:15
News	Valiant Way	News	News	8:30
Robert L. Johnson, talk	Stories America Loves	Miss Meade's Children	David Harum	8:45
The Breakfast Club	Kate Smith Speaks	John B. Hughes, news	Bess Johnson	9am
	Big Sister	Victor Lindlahr, health	Bachelor's Children	9:15
Here's to the Ladies	The Romance of Helen Trent	Norma Young, talk	News	9:30
	Our Gal Sunday		What's Doing Ladies	9:45
H. R. Baukage, news	Life Can Be Beautiful	Glenn Hardy, news	Talk	10am
Second Husband	The Woman in White	I'll Find My Way	Music	10:15
Amanda of Honeymoon Hill	Vic and Sade	Women Today	Talk	10:30
John's Other Wife	Music / Mary Lee Taylor, cooking	Your Date with Don Norman	Dr. Kate	10:45
Just Plain Bill	Bright Horizon	Cedric Foster, news / The Clinic Forum	The Light of the World	11am
Between the Bookends / Family Doctor	Aunt Jenny's True Life Stories	Music	Arnold Grimm's Daughter	11:15
Chaplain Jim, USA	We Love and Learn	Talk and Music / The National School of the Air	The Guiding Light	11:30
News	The Goldbergs		Hymns of All Churches / Betty Crocker, cooking	11:45
Prescott Presents	The Man I Married	News	The Farm Reporter	12pm
	Knox Manning, news	The Homemaker's Club	Ma Perkins	12:15
Men of the Sea	Joyce Jordan, M. D.		Pepper Young's Family	12:30
Music / The Southernaires Quartet	Woman of Courage	Music	The Right to Happiness	12:45
Music / The Street Singer	Stepmother	Mutual Calling	Mary Noble, Backstage Wife	1pm

DAYTIME — SPRING, 1942

Sunday

	BLUE	CBS	MBS	NBC
1:15				
1:30	Nothing But the Truth	The Pause That Refreshes	Young People's Church	News
1:45				Look at Books
2pm	Waltzes and Fashions	The Prudential Family Hour	I Hear America Singing	Ports of the Pacific
2:15	Music			
2:30	The Musical Steelmakers		The Halls of Montezuma	Plays for Americans
2:45		William L. Shirer, news		
3pm	The Catholic Hour	The Silver Theater	This is War	Professor Puzzlewit
3:15				
3:30	Church Federation Vespers	Gene Autry's Melody Ranch	Mystery Hall	Serenade
3:45				Upton Close, news
4pm	Edward Tomlinson, news		The Fact Finders	The Jello Program, Jack Benny
4:15		Public Affairs	Rabbi Magnin, religion	
4:30	Alias John Freedom	What's It All About	In His Steps	The Fitch Bandwagon
4:45				

DAYTIME — SPRING, 1942

Monday-Friday

BLUE	CBS	MBS	NBC	
Club Matinee, Garry Moore	The Story of Myrt and Marge		Stella Dallas	1:15
	The American School of the Air	Music	Lorenzo Jones	1:30
			Young Widder Brown	1:45
Music	William Winter, news	The Dime-Dance Parade	When a Girl Marries	2pm
	The Road of Life	In the Future	Portia Faces Life	2:15
The Classic Hour	Nancy Dixon, talk	News	The Andersons	2:30
	Scattergood Baines	The Bookworm	Lone Journey	2:45
	Music	B. S. Bercovici, news	Vic and Sade	3pm
	Music / The Voice of Broadway	Music	Bud Barton	3:15
What's Doing Ladies	Songs	Talk and Music	Against the Storm	3:30
News	The World Today		News	3:45
Music / Easy Aces	The Second Mrs. Burton	Fulton Lewis, Jr., news	Talk	4pm
Talk / Mr. Keen, Tracer of Lost Persons	Young Dr. Malone	The Johnson Family		4:15
Hillman and Linley, news	News	Talk and Music	Talk and Music	4:30
Talk and Music	Talk			4:45

DAYTIME — SPRING, 1942

Saturday

	BLUE	CBS	MBS	NBC
8am	The Musical Clock	Music	Music	On Your Job
8:15	The Breakfast Club	God's Country, Burl Ives	Australian News	The Musical Clock
8:30	News	Let's Pretend	News	News
8:45	Robert L. Johnson, talk		The US Army Band	Songs
9am	The Breakfast Club	The Armstrong Theater of Today	Sinfonietta	What's Doing Ladies
9:15	The Federation of Churches			Consumer Time
9:30	Music	Stars Over Hollywood	Music	Ilka Chase Entertains
9:45	Naomi Reynolds, songs		Food for Thought	
10am	Dr. Casselberry, health	The US Army Band	News	Lincoln Highway
10:15	Vincent Lopez Orchestra	The Town Crier	US Coast Guard Band	
10:30	The Parents Forum	Home Front Action	Public Affairs	America, the Free
10:45	Books That Live	The Treasury Star Parade		
11am	Music	Of Men and Books	Woody Herman Orchestra	Music
11:15				
11:30	Songs	The Brush Creek Follies	Carmen Cavallero Orchestra	
11:45	News			
12pm	Royal Canadian Air Force Band	Columbia's Country Journal	News	The Farm Reporter
12:15			Land of the Free	Horse Racing
12:30	Horse Racing	Detroit Musicale	University Music	
12:45				News
1pm	Club Matinee, Garry Moore	Matinee	Horse Racing	Down Mexico Way
1:15				
1:30				Air Youth of America
1:45				County Medical Association Talks

DAYTIME — SPRING, 1942

Saturday

	BLUE	CBS	MBS	NBC
2pm	The US Army Band	Strings	Sunset Serenade	
2:15	Music	Music		
2:30				Ricardo and His Caballeros
2:45			Charlie Spivak Orchestra	News
3pm		Navy Recruiting Program	Anchors Aweigh	Music
3:15		Calling Pan-America		Music
3:30	What's Doing Ladies	The Four Clubmen	Fighting Tools	Religion in the News
3:45	Edward Tomlinson, news	The World Today		The Three Suns
4pm	The Little Blue Playhouse	The People's Platform	Dr. Matthews, religion	Noah Webster Says
4:15		Farming for Victory		
4:30	Message of Israel	Tillie the Toiler	Confidentially Yours	Wings Over the West
4:45			The Treasury Star Parade	H. V. Kaltenborn, news

EVENING — SUMMER, 1942

Sunday

	BLUE	CBS	MBS	NBC
5pm	Music	World News Tonight	The American Forum of the Air	Star Spangled Vaudeville, Walter O'Keefe
5:15	The Mills Brothers, songs			
5:30	We Cover the Battlefront	William Winter, news		One Man's Family
5:45	Drew Pearson, news	News	Music	
6pm	Remember	Mischa the Magnificent	The Old Fashioned Revival Hour	The Manhattan Merry-Go-Round
6:15				
6:30	Inner Sanctum Mysteries	The Texaco Star Theater, Jane Froman		The American Album of Familiar Music
6:45				
7pm	The Goodwill Hour	Take It or Leave It	John B. Hughes, news	The Hour of Charm
7:15			Wings Over the West Coast	
7:30		The Inglewood Park Concert	This is Our Enemy	Claire Booth Luce, talk
7:45		Al Goodman Orchestra		The Parker Family
8pm	Earl Godwin, news	Crime Doctor	Dance Orchestra	News
8:15	Jimmy Fidler, gossip			The Chapel Quartet
8:30	The Quiz Kids	Music	Answering You	The Remarkable Miss Tuttle
8:45				
9pm	Grandpappy and His Pals	William Winter, news	News	The Army Hour
9:15		The Nature of the Enemy	The Voice of Prophecy	
9:30	News			
9:45	Ray Noble Orchestra	What's It All About	Dr. Polyzoides, health	
10pm	Music		Henry King Orchestra	The Richfield Reporter
10:15	Bridge to Dreamland	Ted Fiorito Orchestra		Songs
10:30		Report to the Nation	Cab Calloway Orchestra	Inside the News
10:45				Music

EVENING — SUMMER, 1942

Monday

BLUE	CBS	MBS	NBC	
Twilight Tales	Vox Pop	News	H. V. Kaltenborn, news	5pm
The Victory March		Industrial Engineernig	News	5:15
News	Harry W. Flannery, news	Bulldog Drummond	Vivian Della Chiesa, songs	5:30
Sports	Robert Garred, news		News	5:45
Edwin Franko Goldman Band	The Victory Theater	Gabriel Heatter, news	Public Affairs	6pm
News		News	Songs	6:15
Songs		The Better Half	Dr. I. Q., the Mental Banker	6:30
				6:45
Your Blind Date	Lady Esther Serenade	Raymond Gram Swing, news	The Carnation Contented Hour	7pm
		Hank Keene and His Gang		7:15
Lightning Jim	Vaughn Monroe Orchestra	The Lone Ranger	The Cavalcade of America	7:30
				7:45
Roy Porter, news	Amos 'n' Andy	This, Our America	Chesterfield Time	8pm
Lum and Abner	Music		John W. Vandercook, news	8:15
Music	The Gay Nineties Revue	Double or Nothing	Hawthorne House	8:30
				8:45
News	I Was There	Glenn Hardy, news	The Bell Telephone Hour	9pm
Hillman and Linley, news		Cal Tinney, news		9:15
The Hollywood Spotlight	The Hollywood Showcase	Jan Savitt Orchestra	Unlimited Horizons	9:30
Rodriguez and Sutherland, news		Fulton Lewis, Jr., news		9:45
The National Radio Forum	The Ten o'Clock Wire	Henry Busse Orchestra	The Richfield Reporter	10pm
	Ted Fiorito Orchestra		Stoker Orchestra	10:15
Songs	Les Brown Orchestra	Matty Malneck Orchestra	Inside the News	10:30
			Stoker Orchestra	10:45

EVENING — SUMMER, 1942

Tuesday

	BLUE	CBS	MBS	NBC
5pm	Claude Sweeten Orchestra	Music	News	H. V. Kaltenborn, news
5:15	Alvin Wilder, news	The Home Front	Johnny Richards Orchestra	Music
5:30	News	Harry W. Flannery, news	Ned Jordan, Secret Agent	Tums Treasure Chest
5:45	Sports	News		
6pm	The Green Hornet	The American Melody Hour	Gabriel Heatter, news	Battle of the Sexes
6:15			News	
6:30	Mystery Program	Cheers from the Camps	Jamboree	Meredith Willson's Musical Revue
6:45				
7pm	Counterspy		John B. Hughes, news	A Date with Judy
7:15			The Johnson Family	
7:30	Red Ryder	Music	Morton Gould Orchestra	Tommy Dorsey's Variety Program
7:45		Frazier Hunt, news		
8pm	Roy Porter, news	Amos 'n' Andy	What's My Name	Chesterfield Time
8:15	Lum and Abner	Moonlight Serenade		John W. Vandercook, news
8:30	Information, Please	The Court of Missing Heirs	The Shadow	Johnny Presents
8:45				
9pm	News	Music	Glenn Hardy, news	The Adventures of the Thin Man
9:15	Hillman and Linley, news		Cab Calloway Orchestra	
9:30	The Hollywood Spotlight		John B. Hughes, news	Cabbages and Kings
9:45	Rodriguez and Sutherland, news		Fulton Lewis, Jr., news	Roy Shields Orchestra
10pm	Sing for Dough	The Ten o'Clock Wire	Henry King Orchestra	The Richfield Reporter
10:15		Ted Fiorito Orchestra		Organ Recital
10:30	Freddy Martin Orchestra	Les Brown Orchestra	Dance Orchestra	Inside the News
10:45				Harry Owens Orchestra

EVENING — SUMMER, 1942

Wednesday

BLUE	CBS	MBS	NBC	
Music	The New Old Gold Program, Nelson Eddy	News	H. V. Kaltenborn, news	5pm
The Victory March		Anaylsis of Propaganda	News	5:15
News	Harry W. Flannery, news	The Canadian Band	Interlude	5:30
Sports	Robert Garred, news		Bill Henry, news	5:45
You Can't Do Business with Hitler	Junior Miss	Gabriel Heatter, news	Those We Love	6pm
News		News		6:15
Edwin Franko Goldman Band	Suspense	Pass in Review	Mr. District Attorney	6:30
				6:45
The Garry Moore Variety Show / The Danny Thomas Show	Great Moments in Music	John B. Hughes, news	Kay Kyser's College of Musical Knowledge	7pm
		Hank Keene and His Gang		7:15
Lightning Jim	The Twenty Second Letter	The Lone Ranger		7:30
				7:45
Earl Godwin, news	Amos 'n' Andy	The Coast Quiz	Point Sublime	8pm
Lum and Abner	Moonlight Serenade			8:15
Manhattan at Midnight	Dr. Christian	Tune Up, America	Freddy Martin Orchestra	8:30
				8:45
News	William Winter, comment	Glenn Hardy, news	The Quiz Court	9pm
Hillman and Linley, news		Cal Tinney, news		9:15
The Hollywood Spotlight	Wilbur Hatch Orchestra	Henry King Orchestra	Claude Sweeten Orchestra	9:30
Rodriguez and Sutherland, news		Fulton Lewis, Jr., news	Civilian Defense	9:45
The Chamber Music Society of Lower Basin Street	The Ten o'Clock Wire	Cab Calloway Orchestra	The Richfield Reporter	10pm
	Ted Fiorito Orchestra		Organ Recital	10:15
Freddy Martin Orchestra	Les Brown Orchestra	Wilde Orchestra	Inside the News	10:30
			Harry Owens Orchestra	10:45

EVENING — SUMMER, 1942

Thursday

	BLUE	CBS	MBS	NBC
5pm	Claude Sweeten Orchestra	Thirty Minutes to Play	Sinfonietta	John Gunther, news
5:15	Alvin Wilder, news			News
5:30	News	Harry W. Flannery, news	It Pays to Be Ignorant	Paging John Doe
5:45	Sports	Robert Garred, news		Bill Henry, news
6pm	Let's Be Neighbors	Major Bowes' Original Amateur Hour	Gabriel Heatter, news	The Kraft Music Hall, Mary Martin
6:15	News		News	
6:30	Mayor Bowron, comment	Music	Jamboree	
6:45	Keyboard Capers			
7pm	Vallee Varieties	The First Line of Defense	Raymond Gram Swing, news	How'm I Doin'
7:15			Hank Keene and His Gang	
7:30	Red Ryder	Music	Americans at Ramparts	The March of Time
7:45		Frazier Hunt, news		
8pm	Earl Godwin, news	Amos 'n' Andy	The Standard Symphony Hour	Chesterfield Time
8:15	Lum and Abner	Moonlight Serenade		John W. Vandercook, news
8:30	Major Hoople	Death Valley Days		Post Toastiies Time, Frank Morgan
8:45				
9pm	News	United We Sing	Glenn Hardy, news	Have You Heard
9:15	Hillman and Linley, news	What Are We Fighiing For	Jan Savitt Orchestra	
9:30	The Hollywood Spotlight	Maudie's Diary	John B. Hughes, news	Music
9:45	Rodriguez and Sutherland, news		Fulton Lewis, Jr., news	
10pm	America's Town Meeting of the Air	The Ten o'Clock Wire	Henry Busse Orchestra	The Richfield Reporter
10:15		Ted Fiorito Orchestra		Organ Recital
10:30		Les Brown Orchestra		Inside the News
10:45				Karl Kalash Orchestra

EVENING — SUMMER, 1942

Friday

BLUE	CBS	MBS	NBC	
Twilight Tales	Music	News	H. V. Kaltenborn, news	*5pm*
The Victory March	The Home Front	Analysis of Propaganda	News	*5:15*
News	Harry W. Flannery, news	Songs for Marching Men	Paging John Doe	*5:30*
Sports	Robert Garred, news		Bill Henry, news	*5:45*
The Treasury Star Parade	Music	Gabriel Heatter, news	Waltz Time	*6pm*
News		News		*6:15*
In Person, Dinah Shore	That Brewster Boy	The Secret Legion	Paducah Plantation, Red Foley	*6:30*
Music				*6:45*
Meet Your Navy	The Camel Comedy Caravan, Herb Shriner	Songs	People Are Funny	*7pm*
				7:15
Lightning Jim		The Lone Ranger	The Skippy Hollywood Theater	*7:30*
				7:45
Earl Godwin, news	Amos 'n' Andy	At Your Service, Men	Chesterfield Time	*8pm*
Outdoor Reporter	Irene Rich Dramas		John W. Vandercook, news	*8:15*
Gangbusters	The Phillip Morris Playhouse	San Quentin on the Air	Songs	*8:30*
				8:45
News	Ray Kinney Orchestra	Glenn Hardy, news	Tent Show Tonite	*9pm*
Hillman and Linley, news		Cal Tinney, news		*9:15*
The Hollywood Spotlight	Raffles, the Amateur Cracksman	Public Affairs	Claude Sweeten Orchestra	*9:30*
Rodriguez and Sutherland, news		Fulton Lewis, Jr., news		*9:45*
The Hollywood Fights	The Ten o'Clock Wire	Bob Crosby Orchestra	The Richfield Reporter	*10pm*
	Ted Fiorito Orchestra		Organ Recital	*10:15*
	Les Brown Orchestra	Jan Savitt Orchestra	Inside the News	*10:30*
			Music	*10:45*

EVENING — SUMMER, 1942

Saturday

	BLUE	CBS	MBS	NBC
5pm	The Little Blue Playhouse	Soldiers With Wings	News	News
5:15			The Treasury Star Parade	
5:30	SWOP Night	News Analyst	California Melodies	Traffic Tribunal
5:45		News		Bill Henry, news
6pm	NBC Summer Symphony	The USO Program	America Loves a Melody	The National Barn Dance
6:15				
6:30		George Fisher, gossip		The Grant Park Concerts
6:45	James G. McDonald, news	Saturday Night Serenade		
7pm	Tune Out Time		John B. Hughes, news	The Colgate Sports Newsreel, Bill Stern
7:15		Here's the Story	Tropical Serenade, Don Arres	Labor for Victory
7:30	Red Ryder	Music		Grand Ole Opry
7:45		Frazier Hunt, news	The G-Man Story	
8pm	Earl Godwin, news	News	The American Eagles Club	News
8:15	Gibbs and Finney, General Delivery	Claude Thornhill Orchestra		Story Dramas
8:30	Cab Calloway's Quizzicale	Dick Jurgens Orchestra	The Clinic Forum	Hospitality Time
8:45				
9pm	Believe It or Not	Your Hit Parade	Glenn Hardy, news	Music
9:15			Jan Savitt Orchestra	
9:30	News	Reggie Childs Orchestra	Henry Busse Orchestra	
9:45	Ray Noble Orchestra	The Whistler		
10pm	Music		Henry King Orchestra	The Richfield Reporter
10:15		Ted Fiorito Orchestra		Dance Orchestra
10:30	Freddy Martin Orchestra	Les Brown Orchestra	Bob Crosby Orchestra	Henry Owens Orchestra
10:45				

DAYTIME — SUMMER, 1942

Sunday

	BLUE	CBS	MBS	NBC
8am	News	The West Coast Church	The Comics Weekly Man	Rhapsodies of the Rockies
8:15	Horace Heidt Orchestra			The Book of Books
8:30		Invitation to Learning	The Junior Army Hour	Highlights of the Weeks' News
8:45			The Voice of Prophecy	Commando Mary
9am	The Garden Club	Music	The Detroit Bible Class	Sunday Down South
9:15	The First Piano Quartet	Woman Power		Your Physical Well Being
9:30	The Radio City Music Hall	The Salt Lake Tabernable Choir	The Sing a Song of Safety Club	Songs
9:45			Letter to My Son	
10am		The CBS Church of the Air	News	People
10:15			Romance of the Highways	Health Talk
10:30	Nick Harris	Green Valley, USA	The Little Show	Music
10:45	Speaking of Glamour		Music	
11am	News	The Spirit of '42	The Pilgrim Hour	Sammy Kaye's Sunday Serenade
11:15	Music			Alvin Wilder, news
11:30		St. Louis Municipal Opera		The University of Chicago Round Table
11:45				
12pm		Columbia Symphony Orchestra	Broadway News	Music
12:15	Wake Up, America		Music	Upton Close, news
12:30				The Army Hour
12:45				
1pm	National Vespers		Baseball Roundup	
1:15			Theme and Variations	

DAYTIME — SUMMER, 1942

Monday-Friday

BLUE	CBS	MBS	NBC	
Between the Lines	Music / The Treasury Star Parade	The Breakfast Club / The Haven of Rest	The Johnny Murray Show	8am
The Breakfast Club	The Melody Express		Talk / The Musical Clock	8:15
News	Valiant Way	News	News	8:30
Robert L. Johnson, talk	Stories America Loves	Miss Meade's Children	David Harum	8:45
The Breakfast Club	Kate Smith Speaks	Boake Carter, news	Bess Johnson	9am
Helen Hiett, news	Big Sister	Music	Bachelor's Children	9:15
The Breakfast Club	The Romance of Helen Trent	Norma Young, talk	Talk	9:30
	Our Gal Sunday		What's Doing Ladies	9:45
H. R. Baukage, news	Life Can Be Beautiful	Glenn Hardy, news	Talk / The Bridge Club	10am
Second Husband	The Woman in White	Talk and Music	News	10:15
Amanda of Honeymoon Hill	Vic and Sade	Women Today	Betty and Bob	10:30
John's Other Wife	Mary Lee Taylor, cooking / Galen Drake, talk	I'll Find My Way	Dr. Kate	10:45
Just Plain Bill	Bright Horizon	Australian News / The Clinic Forum	The Light of the World	11am
Between the Bookends / Family Doctor	Aunt Jenny's True Life Stories	Music	Lonely Women	11:15
Chaplain Jim, USA	We Love and Learn	Talk and Music	The Guiding Light	11:30
News	The Goldbergs		Hymns of All Churches / Betty Crocker, cooking	11:45
Prescott Presents	Music	Broadway News	The Farm Reporter	12pm
	Knox Manning, news	The Homemaker's Club	Ma Perkins	12:15
10-2-4 Ranch / The Novelty Revue	Joyce Jordan, M. D.		Pepper Young's Family	12:30
Talk and Music	Music	Talk and Music	The Right to Happiness	12:45
Club Matinee, Garry Moore		Bill's Wax Shop	Mary Noble, Backstage Wife	1pm
	Sam Hayes, news	Baseball Roundup	Stella Dallas	1:15

DAYTIME — SUMMER, 1942

Sunday

	BLUE	CBS	MBS	NBC
1:30	The Army-Navy Game	The Pause That Refreshes	Young People's Church	News
1:45				Look at Books
2pm	Waltzes and Fashions	The Prudential Family Hour	I Hear America Singing	Dear Adolf
2:15	Music			
2:30	Alias John Freedom		The Halls of Montezuma	The Music of the Americas
2:45		William L. Shirer, news		
3pm	The Catholic Hour	Edward R. Murrow, news	Wythe Williams, news	We Cover the Battlefront
3:15		Songs	Overseas News	
3:30	Church Federation Vespers	Gene Autry's Melody Ranch	Nobody's Children	The Victory Parade
3:45				
4pm	Tommy Dorsey's Variety Show	Music	Dance Orchestra	How Do You Do It
4:15		The Laugh Club, Lou Holtz		Fleetwood Lawton, news
4:30	The Inevitable Mr. Sand	Harry James Orchestra	Stars and Stripes in Britian	The Fitch Bandwagon
4:45				

DAYTIME — SUMMER, 1942

Monday-Friday

BLUE	CBS	MBS	NBC	
	Talk	Horse Racing	Lorenzo Jones	1:30
			Young Widder Brown	1:45
Talk and Music	Music	Talk and Music	When a Girl Marries	2pm
			Portia Faces Life	2:15
The Classic Hour	William Winter, news	News	Talk	2:30
	The Ben Bernie War Worker's Program	The Bookworm	Lone Journey	2:45
	Talk and Music	B. S. Bercovici, news	The Road of Life	3pm
	Postcard to You / The Voice of Broadway	Baseball Roundup	Vic and Sade	3:15
What's Doing Ladies	Songs	Talk and Music	Against the Storm	3:30
Music	The World Today	Jan Savitt Orchestra	News	3:45
Music / Easy Aces	The Second Mrs. Burton	Fulton Lewis, Jr., news	Talk	4pm
Talk / Mr. Keen, Tracer of Lost Persons	Young Dr. Malone	Nancy Dixon, talk		4:15
Hillman and Linley, news	News	Bob Crosby Orchestra	Music / The Victory March	4:30
The Sea Hound	Talk		Bud Barton	4:45

DAYTIME — SUMMER, 1942

Saturday

	BLUE	CBS	MBS	NBC
8am	Between the Lines	Music	The Haven of Rest	The Musical Clock
8:15	The Breakfast Club	God's Country, Burl Ives		What's Doing Ladies
8:30	News	Let's Pretend	News	America, the Free
8:45	Robert L. Johnson, talk		The US Army Band	
9am	The Breakfast Club	The Armstrong Theater of Today	The Army-Navy House Party	Don Goddard, news
9:15	The Federation of Churches			Consumer Time
9:30	Music	Stars Over Hollywood	The Red Cross Program	Ilka Chase Entertains
9:45	Dr. Casselberry, health		Food for Thought	
10am	Vincent Lopez Orchestra	Columbia's Country Journal	News	Whatcha Know Joe
10:15			US Coast Guard Band	
10:30	County Medical Association Talks	Home Front Action	Music	All Out for Victory
10:45	Songs	The Treasury Star Parade		John W. Vandercook, news
11am	Listen, America	Of Men and Books	Australian News	The US Marine Band
11:15				
11:30	Young Dr. Hickory	The US Army Band	The National School on the Air	On Your Job
11:45	News	The Town Crier	John Duffy Orchestra	Music
12pm	Royal Canadian Air Force Band	Youth on Parade	News	The Farm Reporter
12:15			Arts Festival	Charles Dant Orchestra
12:30	Interlude	Detroit Musicale	Music	Neighborhood Call
12:45				News
1pm	Club Matinee, Garry Moore	Hello from Hawaii		Down Mexico Way
1:15			Baseball Roundup	
1:30		Horse Racing	Music	Smarty Party
1:45				

DAYTIME — SUMMER, 1942

Saturday

	BLUE	CBS	MBS	NBC
2pm	Music	Matinee	Jimmy Dorsey's Salute to the Navy	Music
2:15				
2:30				The Three Suns
2:45				News
3pm		Songs	Anchors Aweigh	Horse Racing
3:15		Calling Pan-America		The US Army Band
3:30	What's Doing Ladies		Hawaii Calls	The Art of Living
3:45	Edward Tomlinson, news	The World Today		The Hollywood Bowl Preview
4pm	Message of Israel	The People's Platform	Music	Noah Webster Says
4:15				
4:30	Freddy Martin Orchestra	Tillie the Toiler	Bob Crosby Orchestra	Take a Flyer
4:45				Donald Novis, songs

EVENING — FALL, 1942

Sunday

	BLUE	CBS	MBS	NBC
5pm	Man Your Battle Stations	Commandos	The American Forum of the Air	The Charlie McCarthy Show
5:15	Pan-American Rhythm			
5:30		William Winter, news		One Man's Family
5:45	Drew Pearson, news	Dick Joy, news	Gabriel Heatter, news	
6pm	The Quiz Kids	The Radio Reader's Digest	The Old Fashioned Revival Hour	The Manhattan Merry-Go-Round
6:15				
6:30	Inner Sanctum Mysteries	The Texaco Star Theater, Fred Allen		The American Album of Familiar Music
6:45				
7pm	The Goodwill Hour	Take It or Leave It	John B. Hughes, news	The Hour of Charm
7:15			News	
7:30		Melodies America Loves	This is Our Enemy	Walter Winchell's Jergens Journal
7:45				The Parker Family
8pm	Earl Godwin, news	Crime Doctor	The Army War Show	The Great Gildersleeve
8:15	Jimmy Fidler, gossip	Ned Calmer, news (8:25pm)		
8:30	Music	Music	Wings Over the West Coast	News
8:45				Cabbages and Kings
9pm	Grandpappy and His Pals	William Winter, news	Glenn Hardy, news	The Standard Symphony Hour
9:15		The Whistler	The Voice of Prophecy	
9:30	News			
9:45	Music	Les Hite Orchestra	Music	The Chapel Quartet
10pm	The University Explorer	The Ten o'Clock Wire	Charlie Holmes Orchestra	The Richfield Reporter
10:15	Dorothy Thompson, news	Matty Malneck Orchestra		Betty Martin, news
10:30	Bridge to Dreamland	What's It All About	Erskine Hawkins Orchestra	Inside the News
10:45				When Evening Comes

EVENING — FALL, 1942

Monday

BLUE	CBS	MBS	NBC	
Don Winslow of the Navy	Army Recruiting Program	Broadway News	H. V. Kaltenborn, news	5pm
News		The Johnson Family	News	5:15
Jack Armstrong, the All-American Boy	Harry W. Flannery, news	Music	The Voice of Firestone	5:30
Captain Midnight	Truman Bradley, news	Strollin' Tom		5:45
Counterspy	The Lux Radio Theater	Gabriel Heatter, news	Music	6pm
		News	News	6:15
Spotlight Bands		Curtain, America	Dr. I. Q., the Mental Banker	6:30
The Gracie Fields Show (6:55PM)				6:45
Raymond Gram Swing, news	The Lady Esther Screen Guild Theater	Raymond Clapper, news	The Carnation Contented Hour	7pm
Alias John Freedom		Music		7:15
	Blondie	The Lone Ranger	Lands of the Free	7:30
A Man and His Music				7:45
Earl Godwin, news	Amos 'n' Andy	This, Our America	Chesterfield Time	8pm
Lum and Abner	Elizabeth Bemis, news		John W. Vandercook, news	8:15
Eyewitness News	The Gay Nineties Revue	Double or Nothing	The Cavalcade of America	8:30
News				8:45
True or False	I Was There	Glenn Hardy, news	The Bell Telephone Hour	9pm
		Cal Tinney, news		9:15
Erskine Johnson, gossip	Vox Pop	John B. Hughes, news	Hawthorne House	9:30
News		Fulton Lewis Jr., news		9:45
The University Explorer	The Ten o'Clock Wire	Ray McKinley Orchestra	The Richfield Reporter	10pm
Major Hoople	Dance Orchestra	Paul Schubert, news	Manchester Boddy, news	10:15
	Jimmy Dorsey Orchestra	The Symphonette	Inside the News	10:30
Joseph James, songs			Carl Kalash Orchestra	10:45

EVENING — FALL, 1942

Tuesday

	BLUE	CBS	MBS	NBC
5pm	Don Winslow of the Navy	Jay Burnett, news	Broadway News	H. V. Kaltenborn, news
5:15	News	George Fisher, gossip	The Johnson Family	News
5:30	Jack Armstrong, The All-American Boy	Harry W. Flannery, news	The Federal Ace	Don Vining, news
5:45	Captain Midnight	Truman Bradley, news		By the Way
6pm	Hop Harrigan	Burns and Allen	Gabriel Heatter, news	Battle of the Sexes
6:15	Homicide O'Kane		News	
6:30	Spotlight Bands	Suspense	Jamboree	Fibber McGee and Molly
6:45	The Gracie Fields Show (6:55PM)			
7pm	Raymond Gram Swing, news	Public Affairs	John B. Hughes, news	The Pepsodent Show, Bob Hope
7:15	News		Public Affairs	
7:30	Red Ryder	Time Out for Melody		The Raleigh Cigarette Program, Red Skelton
7:45				
8pm	Earl Godwin, news	Amos 'n' Andy	The Pay Day Quiz	Chesterfield Time
8:15	Lum and Abner	Chesterfield Time		John W. Vandercook, news
8:30	Information, Please	Lights Out	The Shadow	The Purple Heart Show, Ginny Simms
8:45				
9pm	News	Duffy's Tavern	Glenn Hardy, news	The Adventures of the Thin Man
9:15	Rodriguez and Sutherland, news		Music	
9:30	Erskine Johnson, gossip	The American Melody Hour	The Rumor Busters	Tums Treasure Chest
9:45	News		Fulton Lewis Jr., news	
10pm	This Nation at War	The Ten o'Clock Wire	Johnny Holmes Orchestra	The Richfield Reporter
10:15		The Changing Tide	Paul Schubert, news	Public Affairs
10:30	Freddy Martin Orchestra	Jimmy Dorsey Orchestra	The Symphonette	Inside the News
10:45				Carl Kalash Orchestra

EVENING — FALL, 1942

Wednesday

BLUE	CBS	MBS	NBC	
Don Winslow of the Navy	The New Old Gold Program, Nelson Eddy	Broadway News	H. V. Kaltenborn, news	5pm
News		The Johnson Family	News	5:15
Jack Armstrong, The All-American Boy	Harry W. Flannery, news	The True Story Theater of the Air	Manchester Boddy, news	5:30
Captain Midnight	Truman Bradley, news		By the Way	5:45
Hop Harrigan	The Bob Burns Show	Gabriel Heatter, news	Time to Smile, Eddie Cantor	6pm
Homicide O'Kane		News		6:15
Spotlight Bands	The Mayor of the Town	Colonial Melody	Mr. District Attorney	6:30
The Gracie Fields Show (6:55 PM)				6:45
Raymond Gram Swing, news	Great Moments in Music	John B. Hughes, news	Kay Kyser's College of Musical Knowledge	7pm
A Man and His Music		Ray Kassel Orchestra		7:15
The Chamber Music Society of Lower Basin Street	The Man Behind the Gun	The Lone Ranger		7:30
				7:45
Earl Godwin, news	Amos 'n' Andy	The Cresta Blanca Carnival	Point Sublime	8pm
Lum and Abner	Chesterfield Time			8:15
Manhattan at Midnight	Dr. Christian		Tommy Dorsey's Variety Show	8:30
		Music		8:45
News	William Winter, news	Glenn Hardy, news	The Quiz Court	9pm
Rodriguez and Sutherland, news	Raffles, the Amateur Cracksman	Cal Tinney, news		9:15
Erskine Johnson, gossip		John B. Hughes, news	The Hollywood Theater	9:30
News	Music	Fulton Lewis Jr., news		9:45
The National Radio Forum	The Ten o'Clock Wire	Public Affairs	The Richfield Reporter	10pm
	Music	Paul Schubert, news	Starlight Souvenirs	10:15
Freddy Martin Orchestra	Jimmy Dorsey Orchestra	The Symphonette	Inside the News	10:30
			Carl Kalash Orchestra	10:45

EVENING — FALL, 1942

Thursday

	BLUE	CBS	MBS	NBC
5pm	Don Winslow of the Navy	Jay Burnett, news	Broadway News	H. V. Kaltenborn, news
5:15	News	George Fisher, gossip	The Johnson Family	News
5:30	Jack Armstrong, the All-American Boy	Harry W. Flannery, news	It Pays to Be Ignorant	Paging John Doe
5:45	Captain Midnight	Truman Bradley, news		By the Way
6pm	Hop Harrigan	Major Bowes' Original Amateur Hour	Gabriel Heatter, news	The Kraft Music Hall, Bing Crosby
6:15	Homicide O'Kane		News	
6:30	Spotlight Bands	Stage Door Canteen	Jamboree	
6:45	The Gracie Fields Show (6:55PM)			
7pm	Raymond Gram Swing, news	The First Line of Defense	Raymond Clapper, news	Abbott and Costello
7:15	News		News	
7:30	Red Ryder	CBS Dance Orchestra	The Cisco Kid	The March of Time
7:45		Frazier Hunt, news		
8pm	Earl Godwin, news	Amos 'n' Andy	The Bombardier Quiz	Chesterfield Time
8:15	Lum and Abner	Chesterfield Time		The Night Editor
8:30	Sing for Dough	Death Valley Days	This is the Hour	Maxwell House Coffee Time, Fanny Brice
8:45				
9pm	News	Music	Glenn Hardy, news	The Aldrich Family
9:15	Rodriguez and Sutherland, news	Soldiers in Mufti	Public Affairs	
9:30	Erskine Johnson, gossip	The Hollywood Showcase	The Rumor Busters	The Adventures of Ellery Queen
9:45	News		Fulton Lewis Jr., news	
10pm	America's Town Meeting of the Air	The Ten o'Clock Wire	Music	The Richfield Reporter
10:15		The Changing Tide	Paul Schubert, news	The Chapel Quartet
10:30		Jimmy Dorsey Orchestra	The Symphonette	Inside the News
10:45				Carl Kalash Orchestra

EVENING — FALL, 1942

Friday

BLUE	CBS	MBS	NBC	
Don Winslow of the Navy	Jay Burnett, news	Broadway News	H. V. Kaltenborn, news	5pm
Twilight Tales	America's Home Front	The Johnson Family	News	5:15
Jack Armstrong, the All-American Boy	Harry W. Flannery, news	The Community Chest	Paging John Doe	5:30
Captain Midnight	News	Strollin' Tom	By the Way	5:45
Hop Harrigan	CBS Dance Orchestra	Gabriel Heatter, news	Waltz Time	6pm
Homicide O'Kane	Leon Henderson, news	News		6:15
Spotlight Bands	That Brewster Boy	The Quiz of Two Cities	Paducah Plantation, Red Foley	6:30
The Gracie Fields Show (6:55PM)				6:45
Meet Your Navy	The Camel Caravan, Herb Shriner	John B. Hughes, news	People Are Funny	7pm
		Public Affairs		7:15
Vallee Varieties		The Lone Ranger	Tommy Riggs and Betty Lou	7:30
				7:45
Earl Godwin, news	Amos 'n' Andy	Memory Lane	Chesterfield Time	8pm
In Person, Dinah Shore	Elizabeth Bemis, news		John W. Vandercook, news	8:15
Gangbusters	The Phillip Morris Playhouse	Music	Whodunit	8:30
				8:45
News	The Kate Smith Hour	Glenn Hardy, news	Public Affairs	9pm
Rodriguez and Sutherland, news		Cal Tinney, news		9:15
Erskine Johnson, gossip		John B. Hughes, news	Uncle Sam Presents	9:30
News		Fulton Lewis Jr., news		9:45
The Legion Stadium Fights	The Ten o'Clock Wire	Public Affairs	The Richfield Reporter	10pm
	Music	Paul Schubert, news	Civilian Defense	10:15
	Jimmy Dorsey Orchestra	The Symphonette	Inside the News	10:30
			Carl Kalash Orchestra	10:45

EVENING — FALL, 1942

Saturday

	BLUE	CBS	MBS	NBC
5pm	News	Talk	News	News
5:15	Sports	Songs	Musical Matinee	Sports
5:30	The Little Blue Playhouse	Harry W. Flannery, news	California Meloldies	Traffic Tribunal
5:45		News		Paul Martin Orchestra
6pm	Hop Harrigan	Sports	Murder Clinic	The National Barn Dance
6:15	Sports	Lud Gluskin Orchestra		
6:30	Spotlight Bands		The Secret Legion	Can You Top This
6:45	News (6:55 PM)	Saturday Night Serenade		
7pm	The Green Hornet		John B. Hughes, news	The Colgate Sports Newsreel, Bill Stern
7:15		Here's the Story	Saturday Night Bondwagon	Campana Serenade, Dick Powell
7:30	Red Ryder	Accent on Rhythm		Grand Ole Opry
7:45		Frazier Hunt, news	Dance Orchestra	
8pm	Earl Godwin, news	Victory Belles	The American Eagle Club	Truth or Consequences
8:15	The Treasury Star Parade			
8:30	Dance Orchestra	Hobby Lobby	Flying Feet	Abie's Irish Rose
8:45		Dick Joy, news (8:55 PM)		
9pm	The Prescott Variety Show	Your Hit Parade	Glenn Hardy, news	News
9:15			Music / Public Affairs	The Radio Canteen
9:30	Men, Machines and Victory			
9:45	News	Don't You Believe It		The Community Chest
10pm	The Danny Thomas Show	The Ten o'Clock Wire	Dance Orchestra	The Richfield Reporter
10:15		Les Hite Orchestra	Charlie Holmes Orchestra	Music
10:30	Freddy Martin Orchestra	Jimmy Dorsey Orchestra	McFarland Twins Orchestra	Postal Oddities
10:45				Carl Kalash Orchestra

DAYTIME — FALL, 1942

Sunday

	BLUE	CBS	MBS	NBC
8am	The Sunday Morning Revue	The West Coast Church	The Funny Paper Man	Rhapsodies of the Rockies
8:15				The Book of Books
8:30		Invitation to Learning	The Radio Chapel	Highlights of the Week's News
8:45				The Dinning Sisters, songs
9am	News	Quincy Howe, news	The Detroit Bible Class	Hospitality Time
9:15	The Garden Club	Woman Power		Your Physical Well Being
9:30	The Music Hour	The Salt Lake Tabernacle Choir	Walter Compton, news	Christian Endeavors
9:45			America at War	
10am		The CBS Church of the Air	Glenn Hardy, news	Robert St. John, news
10:15			Romance of the Highways	Labor for Victory
10:30	The Radio News Weekly	Music	Public Affairs	The Fact Finders
10:45	Nick Harris		The Canary Pet Shop	Modern Music
11am	News	Those We Love	The Pilgrim Hour	Serenade
11:15	Sammy Kaye's Sunday Serenade			Alvin Wilder, news
11:30		World News Today		The University of Chicago Round Table
11:45	News			
12pm	John W. Vandercook, news	New York Philharmonic Orchestra	Broadway News	News
12:15	Wake Up, America		Music	Upton Close, news
12:30			The Children's Chapel	The Army Hour
12:45				
1pm	National Vespers		The Lutheran Hour	
1:15				

DAYTIME — FALL, 1942

Monday-Friday

BLUE	CBS	MBS	NBC	
Between the Lines	The Treasury Star Parade / The Four Clubmen	The Breakfast Club	The Johnny Murray Show	8am
Sideshow	The Melody Express		Betty and Bob	8:15
	Valiant Lady		News	8:30
The Breakfast Club	Stories America Loves	Victor Lindlahr, health	David Harum	8:45
	Kate Smith Speaks	Boake Carter, news	The O'Neills	9am
	Big Sister	Women Today	What's Doing	9:15
	The Romance of Helen Trent	Norma Young, talk	Ted Steele Orchestra	9:30
	Our Gal Sunday		For Women Only	9:45
H. R. Baukhage, news	Life Can Be Beautiful	Glenn Hardy, news	The Bridge Club / The Standard School Broadcast /	10am
The Gospel Singer	Ma Perkins	I'll Find My Way	Mirandy's Garden Patch	10:15
The Benny Walker Show	Vic and Sade	Women Today	Agnes White	10:30
	The Goldbergs	Palmer House Orchestra	Dr. Kate	10:45
Songs	Young Dr. Malone	Music	The Light of the World	11am
Between the Bookends	Aunt Jenny's True Life Stories	The Market Place	Lonely Women	11:15
Sideshow	We Love and Learn	The Eddie Albright Show	The Guiding Light	11:30
News	Music		Betty Crocker, cooking / Hymns of All Churches	11:45
Prescott Presents	Dave Lane, news	Broadway News	The Farm Reporter	12pm
	Bob Anderson, news	The Homemaker's Club	Ma Perkins	12:15
10-2-4 Ranch / The Novelty Revue	Joyce Jordan, MD		Pepper Young's Family	12:30
Lt. Canady Reports	Bachelor's Children		The Right to Happiness	12:45
Club Matinee, Garry Moore	Galen Drake, talk	Bill's Wax Shop	Mary Noble, Backstage Wife	1pm
	Arthur Godfrey, songs	Sweet and Sentimental	Stella Dallas	1:15

DAYTIME — FALL, 1942

Sunday

	BLUE	CBS	MBS	NBC
1:30	Musical Memories	The Pause That Refreshes	The Young People's Church	Soldiers of the Press
1:45	Music By Bach			Look at Books
2pm	African Trek	The Prudential Family Hour	Hawaii Calls	NBC Symphony Orchestra
2:15	The Latest Word (2:25PM)			
2:30	The Musical Steelmakers		Bulldog Drummond	Britain to America
2:45		William L. Shirer, news		
3pm	We Believe	Edward R. Murrow, news	The First Nighter Program	The Catholic Hour
3:15		Irene Rich Dramas		
3:30	Church Federation Vespers	Gene Autry's Melody Ranch	Anchors Aweigh	Reports from the Battlefield
3:45				The News Makers
4pm	Stars from the Blue	Public Affairs	Nobody's Children	The Grape Nuts Program, Jack Benny
4:15		Time Out for Laughs		
4:30	The Inevitable Mr. Sand	United We Sing	Stars and Stripes in Britain	The Fitch Bandwagon
4:45				

DAYTIME — FALL, 1942

Monday-Friday

BLUE	CBS	MBS	NBC	
	The American School of the Air		Lorenzo Jones	1:30
			Young Widder Brown	1:45
Music	The Victory Front	Music / The Don Lee Newsreel Theater	When a Girl Marries	2pm
	Music		Portia Faces Life	2:15
The Classic Hour	William Winter, news		Just Plain Bill	2:30
	The Ben Bernie War Workers' Program		Front Page Farrell	2:45
	Matinee Musicale	Philip Keyne Gordon, news	Lone Journey	3pm
	Action on the Home Front	Music	The Road of Life	3:15
What's Doing Ladies	Music / The Squibb Golden Treasury of Song		Vic and Sade	3:30
Stringtime	The World Today	Bill Hay's Bible Readings	Against the Storm	3:45
Music / Scramble / You Can't Do Business With Hitler	The Second Mrs. Burton	Fulton Lewis Jr., news	Art Baker's Notebook	4pm
The Four Keys	Sam Hayes, news	Nancy Dixon, home talk		4:15
News	Talk / Music / The American Melody Hour /	Music	News	4:30
Music/ Land, Sea, and Air	Easy Aces / Mr. Keen, Tracer of Lost Persons	Judy and Jane	The Story of Mary Marlin	4:45

DAYTIME — FALL, 1942

Saturday

	BLUE	CBS	MBS	NBC
8am	Between the Lines	The Delta Rhythm Boys	The Haven of Rest	The Musical Clock
8:15	The Breakfast Club	God's Country, Burl Ives		What's Doing
8:30	News	Let's Pretend		Coast Guard on Parade
8:45	Robert L. Johnson, talk		The Junior Army	
9am		The Armstrong Theater of Today	The Army-Navy House Party	News
9:15				Consumer Time
9:30		Stars Over Hollywood	Music	What'cha Know Joe
9:45			Food for Thought	
10pm	Dr. Casselbury, health	Columbia's Country Journal	Glenn Hardy, news	Pan-American Holiday
10:15	Freedom on the Land Forever		The Coast Guard Program	
10:30	County Medical Association Talks	Civilian Defense	Alvino Rey Orchestra	All Out for Victory
10:45	The Victory Twins	Sports		News
11am	Fantasy in Melody		Sports	Matinee in Rhythm
11:15				On the Job
11:30	Little Doctor Hickory			The US Marine Band
11:45	News			News
12pm	Sports			Sports
12:15				
12:30				
12:45				
1pm				
1:15				
1:30				
1:45				

DAYTIME — FALL, 1942

Saturday

	BLUE	CBS	MBS	NBC
2pm				Music
2:15				
2:30				The Three Suns
2:45				Alex Drier, news
3pm				Joseph Gallichio Orchestra
3:15				Army Recruiting Program
3:30				Religion in the News
3:45				Salon Orchestra
4pm				Public Affairs
4:15				
4:30		Songs		Music of the Americas
4:45				Upton Close, news

LISTINGS FOR 1943

EVENING — WINTER, 1943

Sunday

	BLUE	CBS	MBS	NBC
5pm	Songs	Hello, Americans	The American Forum of the Air	The Charlie McCarthy Show
5:15	The Four Keys			
5:30	Edward Tomlinson, news	William Winter, news		One Man's Family
5:45	Drew Pearson, news	Dick Joy, news	Gabriel Heatter, news	
6pm	News	The Radio Reader's Digest	The Old Fashioned Revival Hour	The Manhattan Merry-Go-Round
6:15	Soldiers of the Press			
6:30	Inner Sanctum Mysteries	The Texaco Star Theater, Fred Allen		The American Album of Familiar Music
6:45				
7pm	The Goodwill Hour	Take It or Leave It	John B. Hughes, news	The Hour of Charm
7:15			Rabbi Magnin, religion	
7:30		Melodies America Loves	This is Our Enemy	Walter Winchell's Jergens Journal
7:45				The Parker Family
8pm	Earl Godwin, news	Crime Doctor	Hancock Ensemble	The Great Gildersleeve
8:15	Jimmy Fidler, gossip	Ned Calmer, news (8:25PM)		
8:30	The Quiz Kids	The Whistler	Wings Over the West Coast	The Standard Symphony Hour
8:45				
9pm	Captain Quiz	William Winter, news	Glenn Hardy, news	
9:15	Freddy Martin Orchestra	News	The Voice of Prophecy	
9:30	News	Winner Takes All		Cabbages and Kings
9:45	The Chapel Quartet	Music	Dr. Polyzoides, health	Songs
10pm	The University Explorer	The Ten o'Clock Wire	News	The Richfield Reporter
10:15	Uncle Sam Melody	Dance Orchestra	Music	Betty Martin, news
10:30		What's It All About		Inside the News
10:45				When Evening Comes

EVENING — WINTER, 1943

Monday

BLUE	CBS	MBS	NBC	
Terry and the Pirates	The Treasury Star Parade	John B. Hughes, news	H. V. Kaltenborn, news	5pm
Twilight Tales	Dance Orchestra	The Adventures of Superman	News	5:15
Jack Armstrong, the All-American Boy	Harry W. Flannery, news	Norman Nesbitt, talk	The Voice of Firestone	5:30
Captain Midnight	Truman Bradley, news	Strollin' Tom		5:45
Hop Harrigan	The Lux Radio Theater	Gabriel Heatter, news	Eyes Aloft	6pm
Colonel Stoopnagle		News		6:15
Spotlight Bands		Bulldog Drummond	Dr. I. Q., the Mental Banker	6:30
War News (6:55PM)				6:45
Raymond Gram Swing, news	The Lady Esther Screen Guild Theater	Raymond Clapper, news	The Carnation Contented Hour	7pm
Talk		News		7:15
Music	Blondie	The Lone Ranger	Furlough Fun	7:30
Eyewitness News				7:45
Earl Godwin, news	Amos 'n' Andy	Just Five Lines	Chesterfield Time	8pm
Lum and Abner	Orson Welles, comment		John W. Vandercook, news	8:15
Counterspy	The Gay Nineties Revue	Double or Nothing	The Cavalcade of America	8:30
				8:45
The Chamber Music Society of Lower Basin Street	Quiz Court	Glenn Hardy, news	The Bell Telephone Hour	9pm
		Cal Tinney, news		9:15
Erskine Johnson, gossip	Vox Pop	John B. Hughes, news	Hawthorne House	9:30
News		Fulton Lewis Jr., news		9:45
The University Explorer	The Ten o'Clock Wire	Bob Mosley Orchestra	The Richfield Reporter	10pm
Major Hoople	Paul Le Baron Orchestra	Paul Schubert, news	Manchester Boddy, news	10:15
	Tommy Dorsey Orchestra	The Symphonette	Inside the News	10:30
Joseph James, songs			Stoker Orchestra	10:45

EVENING — WINTER, 1943

Tuesday

	BLUE	CBS	MBS	NBC
5pm	Terry and the Pirates	Jay Burnett, news	John B. Hughes, news	H. V. Kaltenborn, news
5:15	Alvin Wilder, news	George Fisher, gossip	The Adventures of Superman	News
5:30	Jack Armstrong, The All-American Boy	Harry W. Flannery, news	Norman Nesbitt, talk	Tums Treasure Chest
5:45	Captain Midnight	Truman Bradley, news	Singing Sam, the Barbasol Man	
6pm	Hop Harrigan	Burns and Allen	Gabriel Heatter, news	Battle of the Sexes
6:15	Colonel Stoopnagle		News	
6:30	Spotlight Bands	Suspense	Dark Destiny	Fibber McGee and Molly
6:45	War News (6:55PM)			
7pm	Raymond Gram Swing, news	Only Yesterday	John B. Hughes, news	The Pepsodent Show, Bob Hope
7:15	Public Affairs		Music	
7:30	Red Ryder	Face Facts	Anchors Aweigh	The Raleigh Cigarette Program, Red Skelton
7:45		Frazier Hunt, news		
8pm	Earl Godwin, news	Amos 'n' Andy	The Pay Day Quiz	Chesterfield Time
8:15	Lum and Abner	Chesterfield Time		John W. Vandercook, news
8:30	Information, Please	Lights Out	Sinfonietta	The Purple Heart Show, Ginny Simms
8:45				
9pm	Duffy's Tavern	The Colgate Program, Al Jolson	Glenn Hardy, news	Mr. and Mrs. North
9:15			Busy Money	
9:30	Erskine Johnson, gossip	The Hollywood Showcase	Music	Public Affairs
9:45	News		Fulton Lewis Jr., news	
10pm	This Nation at War	The Ten o'Clock Wire	Noble Sissel Orchestra	The Richfield Reporter
10:15		Paul Le Baron Orchestra	Paul Schubert, news	Merchant Marines
10:30	Music	Tommy Dorsey Orchestra	The Symphonette	Inside the News
10:45	Freddy Martin Orchestra			Carl Kalash Orchestra

EVENING — WINTER, 1943

Wednesday

BLUE	CBS	MBS	NBC	
Terry and the Pirates	The New Old Gold Program, Nelson Eddy	John B. Hughes, news	H. V. Kaltenborn, news	5pm
Alvin Wilder, news		The Adventures of Superman	News	5:15
Jack Armstrong, The All-American Boy	Harry W. Flannery, news	Norman Nesbitt, talk	Music	5:30
Captain Midnight	Truman Bradley, news	Strollin' Tom	Bill Henry, news	5:45
Hop Harrigan	The Mayor of the Town	Gabriel Heatter, news	Time to Smile, Eddie Cantor	6pm
Colonel Stoopnagle		News		6:15
Spotlight Bands	Good Listening	Colonial Melody	Mr. District Attorney	6:30
War News (6:55PM)				6:45
Raymond Gram Swing, news	Great Moments in Music	John B. Hughes, news	Kay Kyser's College of Musical Knowledge	7pm
Talk		Art Kassel Orchestra		7:15
Mayor Bowron, comment	The Man Behind the Gun	The Lone Ranger		7:30
Music				7:45
Earl Godwin, news	Amos 'n' Andy	The Cresta Blanca Carnival	Chesterfield Time	8pm
Lum and Abner	Chesterfield Time		John W. Vandercook, news	8:15
Manhattan at Midnight	Dr. Christian		Tommy Dorsey's Variety Show	8:30
		Bob Mosley Orchestra		8:45
Alias John Freedom	Sammy Kaye Orchestra	Glenn Hardy, news	Point Sublime	9pm
		Cal Tinney, news		9:15
Erskine Johnson, gossip		John B. Hughes, news	The Skippy Hollywood Theater	9:30
News		Fulton Lewis Jr., news		9:45
The National Radio Forum	The Ten o'Clock Wire	Jack McLean Orchestra	The Richfield Reporter	10pm
	Al Donahue Orchestra	Paul Schubert, news	Music	10:15
Freddy Martin Orchestra	Tommy Dorsey Orchestra	The Symphonette	Inside the News	10:30
			George Olsen Orchestra	10:45

EVENING — WINTER, 1943

Thursday

	BLUE	CBS	MBS	NBC
5pm	Terry and the Pirates	Jay Burnett, news	John B. Hughes, news	Manchester Boddy, news
5:15	Alvin Wilder, news	George Fisher, gossip	The Adventures of Superman	News
5:30	Jack Armstrong, the All-American Boy	Harry W. Flannery, news	Norman Nesbitt, talk	Paging John Doe
5:45	Captain Midnight	Truman Bradley, news	Singin' Sam, the Barbasol Man	Bill Henry, news
6pm	Hop Harrigan	Major Bowes' Original Amateur Hour	Gabriel Heatter, news	The Kraft Music Hall, Bing Crosby
6:15	Colonel Stoopnagle		News	
6:30	Spotlight Bands	Stage Door Canteen	Curtain, America	The Bob Burns Show
6:45	War News (6:55PM)			
7pm	Raymond Gram Swing, news	The First Line of Defense	Raymond Clapper, news	Abbott and Costello
7:15	Talk		News	
7:30	Red Ryder	Matter of Fact	Songs	The March of Time
7:45		Frazier Hunt, news		
8pm	Earl Godwin, news	Amos 'n' Andy	The Chicago Theater of the Air	Chesterfield Time
8:15	Lum and Abner	Chesterfield Time		The Night Editor
8:30	Wings to Victory	Death Valley Days		Maxwell House Coffee Time, Brice and Morgan
8:45				
9pm	The Green Hornet	Meet Corliss Archer	Glenn Hardy, news	The Aldrich Family
9:15			Busy Money	
9:30	Erskine Johnson, gossip	William Winter, news	The Rumor Busters	The Adventures of Ellery Queen
9:45	News	Public Affairs	Fulton Lewis Jr., news	
10pm	America's Town Meeting of the Air	The Ten o'Clock Wire	Dance Orchestra	The Richfield Reporter
10:15		Paul Le Baron Orchestra	Paul Schubert, news	Letter from Home
10:30		Tommy Dorsey Orchestra	The Symphonette	Inside the News
10:45				George Olsen Orchestra

EVENING — WINTER, 1943

Friday

BLUE	CBS	MBS	NBC	
Terry and the Pirates	Jay Burnett, news	John B. Hughes, news	Manchester Boddy, news	5pm
Twilight Tales	Organ Recital	The Adventures of Superman	News	5:15
Jack Armstrong, the All-American Boy	Harry W. Flannery, news	Norman Nesbitt, talk	Paging John Doe	5:30
Captain Midnight	News	Strollin' Tom	Bill Henry, news	5:45
Hop Harrigan	CBS Dance Orchestra	Gabriel Heatter, news	Waltz Time	6pm
News	Leon Henderson, news	News		6:15
Spotlight Bands	That Brewster Boy	The Quiz of Two Cities	People Are Funny	6:30
War News (6:55 PM)				6:45
John Gunther, news	The Camel Caravan, Herb Shriner	John B. Hughes, news	Tommy Riggs and Betty Lou	7pm
Talk		Art Kassel Orchestra		7:15
Scramble		The Lone Ranger	Hello, No America	7:30
				7:45
Earl Godwin, news	Amos 'n' Andy	Salute to the States	Chesterfield Time	8pm
In Person, Dinah Shore	Our Secret Weapon		John W. Vandercook, news	8:15
Gangbusters	The Phillip Morris Playhouse	Music	Road to Danger	8:30
				8:45
Meet Your Navy	The Kate Smith Hour	Glenn Hardy, news	Vallee Varieties	9pm
		Cal Tinney, news		9:15
Erskine Johnson, gossip		John B. Hughes, news	Uncle Sam Presents	9:30
News	Quiz Quotient (9:55 PM)	Fulton Lewis Jr., news		9:45
The Legion Stadium Fights	The Ten o'Clock Wire	Bob Mosley Orchestra	The Richfield Reporter	10pm
	Dance Orchestra	Paul Schubert, news	Civilian Defense	10:15
	Tommy Dorsey Orchestra	The Symphonette	Inside the News	10:30
			George Olsen Orchestra	10:45

EVENING — WINTER, 1943

Saturday

	BLUE	CBS	MBS	NBC
5pm	The Little Blue Playhouse (4:45PM)	Music	News	The Boy Scouts
5:15	Boston Symphony Orchestra		Musical Matinee	
5:30		Harry W. Flannery, news	This is the Hour	Traffic Tribunal
5:45		News		Music
6pm		Victory Bells	Murder Clinic	The National Barn Dance
6:15	Edward Tomlinson, news			
6:30	Spotlight Bands	The Changing Tide	The Secret Legion	Can You Top This
6:45	Hero Week (6:55PM)	Saturday Night Serenade		
7pm	John Gunther, news		John B. Hughes, news	The Colgate Sports Newsreel, Bill Stern
7:15	Music	Soldiers With Wings	Saturday Night Bondwagon	Campana Serenade, Dick Powell
7:30	Red Ryder	Accent on Rhythm		Grand Ole Opry
7:45		Frazier Hunt, news	Music	
8pm	Earl Godwin, news	Music	The Halls of Montezuma	Truth or Consequences
8:15	Music			
8:30	News	Hobby Lobby	The Clinic Forum	Abie's Irish Rose
8:45	Men, Machines, and Victory	Dick Joy, news (8:55PM)		
9pm	Over Here	Your Hit Parade	Glenn Hardy, news	News
9:15			Music	The Treasury Star Parade
9:30				The Story Editor
9:45		Don't You Believe It		
10pm	Bridge to Dreamland	The Ten o'Clock Wire		The Richfield Reporter
10:15		Dance Orchestra		Music
10:30	Freddy Martin Orchestra	Tommy Dorsey Orchestra	Jack McLean Orchestra	George Olsen Orchestra
10:45				

DAYTIME — WINTER, 1943

Sunday

	BLUE	CBS	MBS	NBC
8am	Soldiers Production	The West Coast Church	The Wesley Radio League	The Treasury Star Parade
8:15				The Book of Books
8:30	African Trek	Invitation to Learning	Aunt Ge Ge and Uncle Ge	Highlights of the Week's News
8:45				Songs
9am	News	Quincy Howe, news	The Detroit Bible Class	
9:15	The Garden Club	Woman Power		
9:30	The Music Hour	The Salt Lake Tabernacle Choir	The Sing-A-Song of Safety Club	That They Might Live
9:45			America at War	
10am		The CBS Church of the Air	Glenn Hardy, news	People
10:15			Romance of the Highways	Labor for Victory
10:30	Toast to Health	Music	The Canary Pet Shop	The Fact Finders
10:45	Nick Harris			Modern Music
11am	News	Those We Love	The Pilgrim Hour	The University of Chicago Round Table
11:15	Newsweekly			Alvin Wilder, news
11:30	Music	World News Today		The Westinghouse Program, John C. Thomas
11:45	John W. Vandercook, news			
12pm	Music	New York Philharmonic Orchestra	Broadway News	News
12:15	Wake Up, America		Music	Upton Close, news
12:30			The Children's Chapel	The Army Hour
12:45				
1pm	National Vespers		The Lutheran Hour	
1:15				
1:30	Musical Memories	The Pause That Refreshes	The Young People's Church	News
1:45	Music By Bach			NBC Symphony Orchestra

DAYTIME — WINTER, 1943

Monday-Friday

BLUE	CBS	MBS	NBC	
Between the Lines	Music	The Breakfast Club	The Johnny Murray Show	8am
The Breakfast Club	The Melody Express		Betty and Bob	8:15
News	Kitty Foyle		News	8:30
Women Make the News	Aunt Jenny's True Life Stories	Victor Lindlahr, health	David Harum	8:45
The Breakfast Club	Kate Smith Speaks	Boake Carter, news	The O'Neills	9am
	Big Sister	Time Out	Music	9:15
	The Romance of Helen Trent	Norma Young, talk	What's Doing	9:30
	Our Gal Sunday		For Women Only	9:45
H. R. Baukhage, news	Life Can Be Beautiful	Glenn Hardy, news	The Bridge Club / The Standard School Broadcast /	10am
Music	Ma Perkins	Garden Talk	Talk	10:15
Bill's Beanery	Vic and Sade	Strictly Personal	Agnes White	10:30
	The Goldbergs	Keyboards	Dr. Kate	10:45
Speaking of Glamour	Young Dr. Malone	Music / The Treasury Star Parade	The Light of the World	11am
The Mystery Chef	Joyce Jordan, MD	Know Your Navy	Lonely Women	11:15
Sideshow	We Love and Learn	Talk	The Guiding Light	11:30
News	Music	Music	Betty Crocker, cooking / Hymns of All Churches	11:45
The Three R's		Broadway News	The Farm Reporter	12pm
	News	Talk	Ma Perkins	12:15
News	William Winter, news		Pepper Young's Family	12:30
Land, Sea, and Air	Bachelor's Children		The Right to Happiness	12:45
Club Matinee, Garry Moore	Galen Drake, talk		Mary Noble, Backstage Wife	1pm
	News		Stella Dallas	1:15
	The American School of the Air	Music	Lorenzo Jones	1:30
			Young Widder Brown	1:45

DAYTIME — WINTER, 1943

Sunday

	BLUE	CBS	MBS	NBC
2pm	Grandpappy and His Pals	The Prudential Family Hour	College Choirs	
2:15			Upton Close, news	
2:30			The Shadow	
2:45		William L. Shirer, news		
3pm	The Catholic Hour	Edward R. Murrow, news	The First Nighter Program	We Believe
3:15		Irene Rich Dramas		
3:30	The Metropolitan Opera Auditions	Gene Autry's Melody Ranch	Music	Reports from the Battlefield
3:45				The News Makers
4pm	Church Federation Vespers	Commandos	Nobody's Children	The Grape Nuts Program, Jack Benny
4:15				
4:30	Music / Public Affairs	Bill Hay, talk	Stars and Stripes in Britain	The Fitch Bandwagon
4:45		Tommy Dorsey Orchestra		

DAYTIME — WINTER, 1943

Monday-Friday

BLUE	CBS	MBS	NBC	
Music	The Victory Front	Music / The Don Lee Newsreel Theater	When a Girl Marries	2pm
	Music		Portia Faces Life	2:15
The Classic Hour			Just Plain Bill	2:30
	The Ben Bernie War Workers' Program		Front Page Farrell	2:45
	William Winter, news	Philip Keyne Gordon, news	Lone Journey	3pm
	Action on the Home Front	Music	The Road of Life	3:15
What's Doing Ladies	Music	News	Vic and Sade	3:30
Between the Bookends	The World Today	Bill Hay's Bible Readings	Snow Village Sketches	3:45
Talk	The Second Mrs. Burton	Fulton Lewis Jr., news	The Story of Mary Marlin	4pm
	Sam Hayes, news	The Johnson Family	News	4:15
News	Talk / Music / The American Melody Hour /	Music	Talk	4:30
The Sea Hound	Easy Aces / Mr. Keen, Tracer of Lost Persons	Judy and Jane		4:45

DAYTIME — WINTER, 1943

Saturday

	BLUE	CBS	MBS	NBC
8am	Between the Lines	The Delta Rhythm Boys	The Haven of Rest	The Musical Clock
8:15	The Breakfast Club	God's Country, Burl Ives		What's Doing
8:30	News	Let's Pretend		Coast Guard on Parade
8:45	Smile in the Morning		The Junior Army	
9am	The Breakfast Club	The Armstrong Theater of Today	The Army-Navy House Party	News
9:15	The Miniature Workshop Hour			Consumer Time
9:30	The Breakfast Club	Stars Over Hollywood	Music	Music
9:45			Food for Thought	Neighborhood Call
10am	Music	Columbia's Country Journal	Glenn Hardy, news	What'cha Know Joe
10:15	Freedom on the Land Forever		The Coast Guard Program	
10:30	County Medical Association Talks	Youth on Parade	Music	On Your Job
10:45	The Victory Twins	Dave Cheskin Orchestra		The People's War
11am	The Metropolitan Opera	Of Men and Books	The Family News Room	Frank Black Orchestra
11:15				
11:30		The Spirit of '43	Music	
11:45				The PTA Congress
12pm		Detroit Musicale	Broadway News	The Farm Reporter
12:15			Music	Music
12:30		Hello from Hawaii	The Shady Valley Folks	
12:45				News
1pm		Report from Washington	Music	Matinee
1:15		Report from London		
1:30		Calling Pan-America	Horse Racing	Music of the Americas
1:45				

DAYTIME — WINTER, 1943

Saturday

	BLUE	CBS	MBS	NBC
2pm		Cleveland Symphony Orchestra	US Navy Bulletin	Doctors at War
2:15				
2:30	Music			The Three Suns
2:45	The Country Editor			Music
3pm	Music	Civilian Defense	I Hear America Singing	Dance Orchestra
3:15		An American in Russia /	Sports	Army Recruiting Program
3:30	Message of Israel	Guy Lombardo Orchestra	Hawaii Calls	Religion in the News
3:45		The World Today		Enjoy Yourself
4pm	Music	The People's Platform	Music	Noah Webster Says
4:15	Freddy Martin Orchestra			
4:30		Del Courtney Orchestra		Music of the Americas
4:45	The Little Blue Playhouse			America Looks Ahead

EVENING — SPRING, 1943

Sunday

	BLUE	CBS	MBS	NBC
5pm	The Cathoilc Hour	Meet Corliss Archer	The American Forum of the Air	The Charlie McCarthy Show
5:15				
5:30	Melody Lane	William Winter, news		One Man's Family
5:45	Drew Pearson, news	Dick Joy, news	Gabriel Heatter, news	
6pm	News	The Radio Reader's Digest	The Old Fashioned Revival Hour	The Manhattan Merry-Go-Round
6:15	Soldiers of the Press			
6:30	Inner Sanctum Mysteries	The Texaco Star Theater, Fred Allen		The American Album of Familiar Music
6:45				
7pm	The Goodwill Hour	Take It or Leave It	John B. Hughes, news	The Hour of Charm
7:15			Rabbi Magnin, religion	
7:30		The Man Behind the Gun	Music	Walter Winchell's Jergens Journal
7:45			Bobby Hooky	The Chamber Music Society of Lower Basin Street
8pm	Earl Godwin, news	Crime Doctor	Hancock Ensemble	The Great Gildersleeve
8:15	Jimmy Fidler, gossip	Ned Calmer, news (8:25PM)		
8:30	The Quiz Kids	The Ken Murray Show	Wings Over the West Coast	The Standard Symphony Hour
8:45				
9pm	Dorothy Thompson, news	William Winter, news	Glenn Hardy, news	
9:15	Captain Quiz	News	The Voice of Prophecy	
9:30	News	The Whistler		Cabbages and Kings
9:45	Russ Morgan Orchestra		Henry King Orchestra	The Chapel Quartet
10pm	The University Explorer	The Ten o'Clock Wire	News	The Richfield Reporter
10:15	Uncle Sam Melody	Paul Le Baron Orchestra	The Old Fashioned Revival Hour	The Red Cross March
10:30		Glen Gray Orchestra		Inside the News
10:45				When Evening Comes

EVENING — SPRING, 1943

Monday

BLUE	CBS	MBS	NBC	
Terry and the Pirates	Uncle Sam	John B. Hughes, news	H. V. Kaltenborn, news	5pm
Twilight Tales	Music	The Adventures of Superman	News	5:15
Jack Armstrong, the All-American Boy	Harry W. Flannery, news	Strollin' Tom	The Voice of Firestone	5:30
Captain Midnight	Truman Bradley, news	Norman Nesbitt, talk		5:45
Hop Harrigan	The Lux Radio Theater	Gabriel Heatter, news	Eyes Aloft	6pm
Colonel Stoopnagle		Faces and Places		6:15
Spotlight Bands		Flying High	Dr. I. Q., the Mental Banker	6:30
War News (6:55PM)				6:45
Raymond Gram Swing, news	The Lady Esther Screen Guild Theater	Raymond Clapper, news	The Carnation Contented Hour	7pm
The Gracie Fields Show		The Round Towner		7:15
Information, Please	Blondie	The Lone Ranger	Alec Templeton Time	7:30
				7:45
Earl Godwin, news	I Love a Mystery	San Quentin on the Air	Chesterfield Time	8pm
Lum and Abner	Ceiling Unlimited		John W. Vandercook, news	8:15
Counterspy	The Gay Nineties Revue	Double or Nothing	The Cavalcade of America	8:30
				8:45
True or False	John B. Kennedy, news	Glenn Hardy, news	The Bell Telephone Hour	9pm
	95 Minutes on Broadway	Cal Tinney, news		9:15
Erskine Johnson, gossip	Vox Pop	General Barrows, comment	Hawthorne House	9:30
News		Fulton Lewis Jr., news		9:45
The University Explorer	The Ten o'Clock Wire	Dr. Polyzoides, health	The Richfield Reporter	10pm
The Second War Loan	Raffles, the Amateur Cracksman	Paul Schubert, news	Manchester Boddy, news	10:15
Classics	Overseas Songs	The Symphonette	Inside the News	10:30
	Glenn Miller Orchestra		Music	10:45

EVENING — SPRING, 1943

Tuesday

	BLUE	CBS	MBS	NBC
5pm	Terry and the Pirates	Jay Burnett, news	John B. Hughes, news	H. V. Kaltenborn, news
5:15	Alvin Wilder, news	Organ Recital	The Adventures of Superman	News
5:30	Jack Armstrong, The All-American Boy	Harry W. Flannery, news	Norman Nesbitt, talk	Tums Treasure Chest
5:45	Captain Midnight	Truman Bradley, news	Singing Sam, the Barbasol Man	
6pm	Hop Harrigan	Burns and Allen	Gabriel Heatter, news	Battle of the Sexes
6:15	Victor Borge, piano		Faces and Places	
6:30	Spotlight Bands	Suspense	This is Our Enemy	Fibber McGee and Molly
6:45	War News (6:55PM)			
7pm	Raymond Gram Swing, news	The Inglewood Park Concert	John B. Hughes, news	The Pepsodent Show, Bob Hope
7:15	Public Affairs		Bulldog Drummond	
7:30	Red Ryder	Face Facts		The Raleigh Cigarette Program, Red Skelton
7:45		Frazier Hunt, news	The Citrus Front	
8pm	Earl Godwin, news	I Love a Mystery	The Pay Day Quiz	Chesterfield Time
8:15	Lum and Abner	Chesterfield Time		John W. Vandercook, news
8:30	Duffy's Tavern	Light's Out	Pass in Review	The Purple Heart Show, Ginny Simms
8:45				
9pm	Homicide O'Kane	The Colgate Program, Al Jolson	Glenn Hardy, news	Mr. and Mrs. North
9:15			Busy Money	
9:30	Erskine Johnson, gossip	Edwin C. Hill, news	General Barrows, comment	The Roy Shields Revue
9:45	News	Quiz Quotient	Fulton Lewis Jr., news	Interlude
10pm	Music	The Ten o'Clock Wire	Louis Armstrong Orchestra	The Richfield Reporter
10:15		Music	Paul Schubert, news	Songs
10:30	Harry Owens Orchestra	Overseas Songs	The Symphonette	Inside the News
10:45		Glen Gray Orchestra		Organ Recital

EVENING — SPRING, 1943

Wednesday

BLUE	CBS	MBS	NBC	
Terry and the Pirates	The New Old Gold Program, Nelson Eddy	John B. Hughes, news	H. V. Kaltenborn, news	5pm
Alvin Wilder, news		The Adventures of Superman	News	5:15
Jack Armstrong, The All-American Boy	Harry W. Flannery, news	Music	Paging John Doe	5:30
Captain Midnight	Truman Bradley, news	Norman Nesbitt, talk	Bill Henry, news	5:45
Hop Harrigan	The Mayor of the Town	Gabriel Heatter, news	Time to Smile, Eddie Cantor	6pm
Victor Borge, piano		Faces and Places		6:15
Spotlight Bands	The Milton Berle Show	Soldiers With Wings	Mr. District Attorney	6:30
War News (6:55PM)				6:45
Raymond Gram Swing, news	Great Moments in Music	John B. Hughes, news	Kay Kyser's College of Musical Knowledge	7pm
The Gracie Fields Show		The Round Towner		7:15
Music	The Cresta Blanca Carnival	The Lone Ranger		7:30
Talk				7:45
Earl Godwin, news	I Love a Mystery	California Melodies	Chesterfield Time	8pm
Lum and Abner	Chesterfield Time		Fleetwood Lawton, news	8:15
Manhattan at Midnight	Dr. Christian	Guy Lombardo Orchestra	Tommy Dorsey's Variety Show	8:30
		News		8:45
Alias John Freedom	Sammy Kaye Orchestra	Glenn Hardy, news	Point Sublime	9pm
		Cal Tinney, news		9:15
Erskine Johnson, gossip	William Winter, news	General Barrows, comment	The Skippy Hollywood Theater	9:30
News	Tony Hatch Orchestra	Fulton Lewis Jr., news		9:45
Dance Orchestra	The Ten o'Clock Wire	Dr. Polyzoides, health	The Richfield Reporter	10pm
	Raffes, the Amateur Cracksman	Paul Schubert, news	Music	10:15
Classics	Overseas Songs	The Symphonette	Inside the News	10:30
	Glen Gray Orchestra		George Olsen Orchestra	10:45

EVENING — SPRING, 1943

Thursday

	BLUE	CBS	MBS	NBC
5pm	Terry and the Pirates	Jay Burnett, news	John B. Hughes, news	Manchester Boddy, news
5:15	Alvin Wilder, news	Organ Recital	The Adventures of Superman	News
5:30	Jack Armstrong, the All-American Boy	Harry W. Flannery, news	Norman Nesbitt, talk	Paging John Doe
5:45	Captain Midnight	Truman Bradley, news	Singin' Sam, the Barbasol Man	Bill Henry, news
6pm	Hop Harrigan	Major Bowes' Original Amateur Hour	Gabriel Heatter, news	The Kraft Music Hall, Bing Crosby
6:15	Victor Borge, piano		Faces and Places	
6:30	Spotlight Bands	Stage Door Canteen	Songs	The Bob Burns Show
6:45	War News (6:55pm)			
7pm	Raymond Gram Swing, news	The First Line of Defense	Raymond Clapper, news	The Durante - Moore Show
7:15	The Gracie Fields Show		News	
7:30	Red Ryder	Face Facts	The Music Depreciation Hour	The March of Time
7:45		Frazier Hunt, news		
8pm	Earl Godwin, news	I Love a Mystery	The Chicago Theater of the Air	Chesterfield Time
8:15	Lum and Abner	Chesterfield Time		The Night Editor
8:30	Rodriguez and Sutherland, news	Death Valley Days		Maxwell House Coffee Time, Brice and Morgan
8:45	Music			
9pm	Wings to Victory	John B. Kennedy, news	Glenn Hardy, news	The Aldrich Family
9:15		The Victory Garden	Busy Money	
9:30	Erskine Johnson, gossip	The Ransom Sherman Show	General Barrows, comment	The Adventures of Ellery Queen
9:45	News		Fulton Lewis Jr., news	
10pm	America's Town Meeting of the Air	The Ten o'Clock Wire	Henry King Orchestra	The Richfield Reporter
10:15		Raffles, the Amateur Cracksman	Paul Schubert, news	Letter from Home
10:30		Overseas Songs	The Symphonette	Inside the News
10:45		Glen Gray Orchestra		George Olsen Orchestra

EVENING — SPRING, 1943

Friday

BLUE	CBS	MBS	NBC	
Terry and the Pirates	Jay Burnett, news	John B. Hughes, news	Manchester Boddy, news	5pm
Twilight Tales	Music	The Adventures of Superman	News	5:15
Jack Armstrong, the All-American Boy	Harry W. Flannery, news	Norman Nesbitt, talk	Music	5:30
Captain Midnight	News	Strollin' Tom	Bill Henry, news	5:45
Hop Harrigan	The Hollywood Showcase	Gabriel Heatter, news	Waltz Time	6pm
News		Faces and Places		6:15
Spotlight Bands	That Brewster Boy	The Quiz of Two Cities	People Are Funny	6:30
War News (6:55PM)				6:45
Free Men Fighting	The Camel Caravan, Herb Shriner	Music	Tommy Riggs and Betty Lou	7pm
The Gracie Fields Show				7:15
Music		The Lone Ranger	Hello, No America	7:30
Elmer Davis, news	Elmer Davis, news			7:45
Earl Godwin, news	I Love a Mystery	Music	Chesterfield Time	8pm
In Person, Dinah Shore	Our Secret Weapon		John W. Vandercook, news	8:15
Gangbusters	The Phillip Morris Playhouse		Your All-Time Hit Parade	8:30
		Remember		8:45
Meet Your Navy	The Kate Smith Hour	Glenn Hardy, news	Furlough Fun	9pm
		Cal Tinney, news		9:15
Erskine Johnson, gossip		General Barrows, comment	Vallee Varieties	9:30
News		Fulton Lewis Jr., news		9:45
The Legion Stadium Fights	The Ten o'Clock Wire	Music	The Richfield Reporter	10pm
	Raffles, the Amateur Cracksman	Paul Schubert, news	Elmer Davis, news	10:15
	Glen Gray Orchestra	The Symphonette	Inside the News	10:30
			George Olsen Orchestra	10:45

EVENING — SPRING, 1943

Saturday

	BLUE	CBS	MBS	NBC
5pm	William Parker, news	Cosmo Jones	News	The Boy Scouts
5:15	Boston Symphony Orchestra		The Songspinners	
5:30		Harry W. Flannery, news	Norman Nesbitt, talk	Traffic Tribunal
5:45		News	Music	The Red Cross March
6pm		Victory Belles	The Cisco Kid	The National Barn Dance
6:15	Edward Tomlinson, news			
6:30	Spotlight Bands	The Rudy Vallee Show	Upton Close, news	Can You Top This
6:45	Here America (6:55PM)	Saturday Night Serenade	The Berries	
7pm	The Green Hornet		John B. Hughes, news	The Colgate Sports Newsreel, Bill Stern
7:15		Pabst Blue Ribbon Town, Groucho Marx	Saturday Night Bondwagon	Freddy Martin Orchestra
7:30	Red Ryder			Grand Ole Opry
7:45		Frazier Hunt, news	The Treasury Star Parade	
8pm	Earl Godwin, news	Thanks to the Yanks	This is the Hour	Truth or Consequences
8:15	Newsweekly			
8:30	The People's Lobby	Hobby Lobby	The Clinic Forum	Abie's Irish Rose
8:45		Dick Joy, news (8:55PM)		
9pm	The Sol Lewis Show	Your Hit Parade	Glenn Hardy, news	News
9:15			Dance Orchestra	The Treasury Star Parade
9:30	The Falcon			The Mystery of the Month
9:45		Don't You Believe It	Joe Hite Orchestra	
10pm	Wings Over the World	The Ten o'Clock Wire	Freddie Slack Orchestra	The Richfield Reporter
10:15		Benny Carter Orchestra	Henry King Orchestra	Music
10:30	Harry Owens Orchestra	Glen Gray Orchestra	Jack McLean Orchestra	
10:45				

DAYTIME — SPRING, 1943

Sunday

	BLUE	CBS	MBS	NBC
8am	Soldiers Production	The West Coast Church	The Wesley Radio League	The Treasury Star Parade
8:15				The Book of Books
8:30	African Trek	Invitation to Learning	Aunt Ge Ge and Uncle Ge	Highlights of the Week's News
8:45				Al Williams, sports
9am	News	Transatlantic Call	The Detroit Bible Class	News
9:15	Speaking of Glamour	Woman Power		Songs
9:30	The Music Hour	The Salt Lake Tabernacle Choir	The Treasury Star Parade	That They Might Live
9:45			America at War	
10am		The Opportunity Hour	Glenn Hardy, news	News
10:15			Romance of the Highways	Labor for Victory
10:30	Toast to Health		Music	Rupert Hughes, news
10:45				Alvin Wilder, news
11am	News	Those We Love	The Pilgrim Hour	The University of Chicago Round Table
11:15	Newsweekly			
11:30	Music	World News Today		The Westinghouse Program, John C. Thomas
11:45	John W. Vandercook, news			
12pm	Music	New York Philharmonic Orchestra	Broadway News	News
12:15	Wake Up, America		Music	Upton Close, news
12:30			What Happened This Week	The Army Hour
12:45				
1pm	National Vespers		The Lutheran Hour	
1:15				
1:30	What Happened This Week	The Pause That Refreshes	Young People's Church	News
1:45	Music By Bach			

DAYTIME — SPRING, 1943

Monday-Friday

BLUE	CBS	MBS	NBC	
Between the Lines	Music	Cheer Up, Gang	The Johnny Murray Show	8am
News	The Melody Express		Music	8:15
The Breakfast Club	Kitty Foyle	News	News	8:30
	Aunt Jenny's True Life Stories	Victor Lindlahr, health	David Harum	8:45
Women Make the News	Kate Smith Speaks	Boake Carter, news	The O'Neills	9am
News	Big Sister	Time Out	Music	9:15
The Breakfast Club	The Romance of Helen Trent	Norma Young, talk	What's Doing Ladies	9:30
	Our Gal Sunday		For Women Only	9:45
H. R. Baukhage, news	Life Can Be Beautiful	Glenn Hardy, news	Music and Talk / The Standard School Broadcast /	10am
Music	Ma Perkins	Garden Talk	Peter de Lima's Closeups	10:15
	Vic and Sade	Strictly Personal	Art Baker's Notebook	10:30
	The Goldbergs	Talk	Dr. Kate	10:45
The Gospel Singer	Young Dr. Malone	Music / The Treasury Star Parade	The Light of the World	11am
The Mystery Chef	Joyce Jordan, MD	Music	Lonely Women	11:15
Sideshow	We Love and Learn	Calling	The Guiding Light	11:30
News	Music	Music	Betty Crocker, cooking / Hymns of All Churches	11:45
The Coke Club, Morton Downey	Crummit and Sanderson	Broadway News	The Farm Reporter	12pm
Music	News	Talk	Ma Perkins	12:15
	William Winter, news		Pepper Young's Family	12:30
Between the Bookends	Bachelor's Children		The Right to Happiness	12:45
The Blue Newsroom Review	Music Questions	Bill's Wax Shop	Mary Noble, Backstage Wife	1pm
	Music	Music	Stella Dallas	1:15
	The American School of the Air	Nobody's Children	Lorenzo Jones	1:30
			Young Widder Brown	1:45

DAYTIME — SPRING, 1943

Sunday

	BLUE	CBS	MBS	NBC
2pm	Grandpappy and His Pals	The Prudential Family Hour	Music	NBC Symphony Orchestra
2:15				
2:30			Bulldog Drummond	
2:45		William L. Shirer, news		
3pm		Edward R. Murrow, news	The First Nighter Program	News
3:15		Irene Rich Dramas		Fiesta Time
3:30	Free World Theater	Gene Autry's Melody Ranch	Upton Close, news	Reports from the Battlefield
3:45			Cosmopolitan	The News Makers
4pm	Church Federation Vespers	Commandos	Nobody's Children	The Grape Nuts Program, Jack Benny
4:15				
4:30	Music	Bill Hay, talk	Stars and Stripes in Britain	The Fitch Bandwagon
4:45		Glen Gray Orchestra		

DAYTIME — SPRING, 1943

Monday-Friday

BLUE	CBS	MBS	NBC	
What's Doing Ladies	The Victory Front	Music / The Don Lee Newsreel Theater	When a Girl Marries	2pm
	Music		Portia Faces Life	2:15
Music			Just Plain Bill	2:30
	Keep Home Fires Burning		Front Page Farrell	2:45
Burritt and Wheeler, talk	William Winter, news	Philip Keyne Gordon, news	Lone Journey	3pm
The Living God / Land, Sea, and Air	Music	Music	The Road of Life	3:15
Pat Bishop, talk		News	Vic and Sade	3:30
What's Doing Ladies	The World Today	Bill Hay's Bible Reading	Snow Village Sketches	3:45
My True Story	Hello from Hollywood	Fulton Lewis Jr., news	The Story of Mary Marlin	4pm
	Sam Hayes, news	Judy and Jane	News	4:15
News	Music / The American Melody Hour /	The Johnson Family	Talk	4:30
Music / Captain Jack	Easy Aces / Mr. Keen, Tracer of Lost Persons	Highway Patrol		4:45

DAYTIME — SPRING, 1943

Saturday

	BLUE	CBS	MBS	NBC
8am	Between the Lines	Let's Pretend	The Haven of Rest	The Musical Clock
8:15	News			Organ Recital
8:30	The Breakfast Club	Fashions in Rations, Billie Burke		Coast Guard on Parade
8:45			The Junior Army	Vegetables for Victory
9am		The Armstrong Theater of Today	Dr. Matthews, religion	News
9:15				Consumer Time
9:30		Stars Over Hollywood	The Lamplighter	Music
9:45			Food for Thought	Neighborhood Call
10am		Music	Glenn Hardy, news	Werner Janssen, news
10:15	News	The Treasury Star Parade	National Family Week	Music
10:30	Intermezzo	Youth on Parade	Alvino Rey Orchestra	On the Job
10:45	County Medical Association Talks	Music		The People's War
11am	The Metropolitan Opera	Columbia's Country Journal	The Family Newsroom	The Roy Shields Revue
11:15			Music	
11:30		The Spirit of '43	Calling	
11:45				PTA and Congress
12pm		Of Men and Books	News	The Farm Reporter
12:15			Music	Air Force News
12:30		William Winter, news	The Shady Valley Folks	News
12:45		Organ Recital		
1pm		Washington Report	Elmer Davis, news	Musical Matinee
1:15		London Report	The E Award	Horse Racing
1:30		Calling Pan-America		Music
1:45			Horse Racing	

DAYTIME — SPRING, 1943

Saturday

	BLUE	CBS	MBS	NBC
2pm		Cleveland Orchestra	US Navy Bulletin	Doctors at War
2:15				
2:30	Music			Music
2:45	Men, Machines, and Victory			
3pm	Our Nation at War	Civilian Defense	America Singing	
3:15		The People's Platform		Army Recruiting Program
3:30	Message of Israel		Hawaii Calls	Religion in the News
3:45		Tucker Voices		Public Affairs
4pm	Music	Report to the Nation	The American Eagle Club	
4:15				
4:30		The Treasury Star Parade	The Halls of Montezuma	Noah Webster Says
4:45		Music		

EVENING — SUMMER, 1943

Sunday

	BLUE	CBS	MBS	NBC
5pm	The Cathoilc Hour	Bill Hay, talk	A. L. Alexander's Mediation Board	Paul Whiteman Presents
5:15		Stan Kenton Orchestra		
5:30	Washington Inside and Out	William Winter, news		One Man's Family
5:45	Drew Pearson, news	Dick Joy, news	Gabriel Heatter, news	
6pm	Walter Winchell's Jergans Journal	The Radio Reader's Digest	The Old Fashioned Revival Hour	The Manhattan Merry-Go-Round
6:15	The Chamber Music Society of Lower Basin Street			
6:30		The Texaco Star Theater, James Melton		The American Album of Familiar Music
6:45	Jimmy Fidler, gossip			
7pm	The Goodwill Hour	Take It or Leave It	John B. Hughes, news	The Hour of Charm
7:15			The Songspinners	
7:30		Willam L. Shirer, news	The Round Towner	Bob Crosby Orchestra
7:45		Music	Bobby Hooky	
8pm	Earl Godwin, news	Crime Doctor	USC Hancock Ensemble	The Great Gildersleeve
8:15	News	Ned Calmer, news (8:25 PM)		
8:30	The Quiz Kids	Calling America	Wings Over the West Coast	The Standard Symphony Hour
8:45				
9pm	Inner Sanctum Mysteries	Talk	Glenn Hardy, news	
9:15		News	The Voice of Prophecy	
9:30	News	The Skippy Hollywood Theater		The Joe E. Brown Show
9:45	Captain Quiz		Joseph Reichman Orchestra	
10pm	The University Explorer	The Ten o'Clock Wire	The Old Fashioned Revival Hour	The Richfield Reporter
10:15	Uncle Sam Melody	Alvino Rey Orchestra		The Chapel Quartet
10:30		Stan Kenton Orchestra		Inside the News
10:45				When Evening Comes

EVENING — SUMMER, 1943

Monday

BLUE	CBS	MBS	NBC	
Dick Tracy	Songs	John B. Hughes, news	Talk	5pm
Twilight Tales	News	The Adventures of Superman	News	5:15
Jack Armstrong, the All-American Boy	Harry W. Flannery, news	Charles W. Hamp, news	The Voice of Firestone	5:30
News	Truman Bradley, news	Norman Nesbitt, talk		5:45
Hop Harrigan	The Lux Radio Theater	Gabriel Heatter, news	Eyes Aloft	6pm
Today in History		Faces and Places		6:15
Spotlight Bands		The Return of Nick Carter	Dr. I. Q., the Mental Banker	6:30
War News (6:55PM)				6:45
Raymond Gram Swing, news	The Lady Esther Screen Guild Theater	Paul Sullivan, news	The Carnation Contented Hour	7pm
News		News		7:15
Alec Templeton, piano	Blondie	The Lone Ranger	Vacation Serenade	7:30
The Romance of Industry				7:45
Earl Godwin, news	I Love a Mystery	Bulldog Drummond	Chesterfield Time	8pm
Lum and Abner	James Hilton, news		Fleetwood Lawton, news	8:15
Counterspy	The Gay Nineties Revue	Double or Nothing	The Cavalcade of America	8:30
				8:45
The Adventures of Nero Wolfe	I Was There	Glenn Hardy, news	The Bell Telephone Hour	9pm
		Cal Tinney, news		9:15
Erskine Johnson, gossip	Vox Pop	General Barrows, comment	Hawthorne House	9:30
News		Fulton Lewis Jr., news		9:45
The University Explorer	The Ten o'Clock Wire	Dr. Polyzoides, health	The Richfield Reporter	10pm
The 10-2-4 Ranch	The Charming Tide	Paul Schubert, news	Manchester Boddy, news	10:15
Classics	Overseas Songs	The Symphonette	Inside the News	10:30
	Glenn Miller Orchestra		H. V. Kaltenborn, news	10:45

EVENING — SUMMER, 1943

Tuesday

	BLUE	CBS	MBS	NBC
5pm	Dick Tracy	Songs	John B. Hughes, news	News
5:15	Alvin Wilder, news	Organ Music	The Adventures of Superman	
5:30	Jack Armstrong, The All-American Boy	Harry W. Flannery, news	Variety	Tums Treasure Chest
5:45	News	Truman Bradley, news	Norman Nesbitt, talk	
6pm	Hop Harrigan	Colonel Stoopnagle	Gabriel Heatter, news	Battle of the Sexes
6:15	Today in History		Faces and Places	
6:30	Spotlight Bands	Report to the Nation	The Cisco Kid	The Passing Parade
6:45	War News (6:55 PM)			
7pm	Raymond Gram Swing, news	The Park Concert	John B. Hughes, news	Johnny Mercer's Music Shop
7:15	News		News	
7:30	Red Ryder	Piano Music		Beat the Band
7:45		John B. Kennedy, news	The Citrus Front	
8pm	Earl Godwin, news	I Love a Mystery	The Pay Day Quiz	Chesterfield Time
8:15	Lum and Abner	Chesterfield Time		Fleetwood Lawton, news
8:30	Noah Webster Says	Lights Out	The Storyteller	The Purple Heart Show, Ginny Simms
8:45			Music	
9pm	Soldiers of the Press	The Colgate Program, Judy Canova	Glenn Hardy, news	Salute to Youth
9:15	What's in the Song		Busy Money	
9:30	Erskine Johnson, gossip	Edwin C. Hill, news	General Barrows, comment	The Roy Shields Revue
9:45	News	Music	Fulton Lewis Jr., news	
10pm	Music	The Ten o'Clock Wire	News	The Richfield Reporter
10:15		Music	Paul Schubert, news	Music
10:30	Classics	Overseas Songs	The Symphonette	Inside the News
10:45		Stan Kenton Orchestra		Organ Recital

EVENING — SUMMER, 1943

Wednesday

BLUE	CBS	MBS	NBC	
Dick Tracy	Songs	John B. Hughes, news	Talk	5pm
Alvin Wilder, news		The Adventures of Superman	News	5:15
Jack Armstrong, The All-American Boy	Harry W. Flannery, news	Charles W. Hamp, news	Paging John Doe	5:30
News	Truman Bradley, news	Norman Nesbitt, talk	Bill Henry, news	5:45
Hop Harrigan	The Inglewood Park Concert	Gabriel Heatter, news	A Date with Judy	6pm
Today in History		Faces and Places		6:15
Spotlight Bands	The Jack Carson Show	Soldiers With Wings	Mr. District Attorney	6:30
War News (6:55PM)				6:45
Raymond Gram Swing, news	Great Moments in Music	John B. Hughes, news	Kay Kyser's College of Musical Knowledge	7pm
News		News		7:15
Alec Templeton, piano	The Cresta Blanca Carnival	The Lone Ranger		7:30
Talk				7:45
Earl Godwin, news	I Love a Mystery	Take a Card	Chesterfield Time	8pm
Lum and Abner	Chesterfield Time		Fleetwood Lawton, news	8:15
Manhattan at Midnight	Dr. Christian	Sherlock Holmes	Tommy Dorsey's Variety Show	8:30
		News		8:45
Alias John Freedom	Sammy Kaye Orchestra	Glenn Hardy, news	Point Sublime	9pm
		Cal Tinney, news		9:15
Erskine Johnson, gossip	The Mayor of the Town	General Barrows, comment	Scramby Amby	9:30
News		Fulton Lewis Jr., news		9:45
Music	The Ten o'Clock Wire	Dr. Polyzoides, health	The Richfield Reporter	10pm
Freddy Martin Orchestra	The Changing Tide	Paul Schubert, news	The Enemy Within	10:15
The National Radio Forum	Overseas Songs	The Symphonette	Inside the News	10:30
	Stan Kenton Orchestra		H. V. Kaltenborn, news	10:45

EVENING — SUMMER, 1943

Thursday

	BLUE	CBS	MBS	NBC
5pm	Dick Tracy	Songs	John B. Hughes, news	Music
5:15	Alvin Wilder, news		The Adventures of Superman	News
5:30	Jack Armstrong, the All-American Boy	Harry W. Flannery, news		Music
5:45	News	Truman Bradley, news	Norman Nesbitt, talk	Bill Henry, news
6pm	Hop Harrigan	Major Bowes' Original Amateur Hour	Gabriel Heatter, news	The Kraft Music Hall, Bing Crosby
6:15	Today in History		Faces and Places	
6:30	Spotlight Bands	Stage Door Canteen	Music	That's Life, Fred Brady
6:45	War News (6:55pm)			
7pm	Raymond Gram Swing, news	The First Line of Defense	Raymond Clapper, news	The Durante - Moore Show
7:15	News		News	
7:30	Red Ryder	What Do You Think	The Better Half	Hello
7:45		John B. Kennedy, news		Music
8pm	Earl Godwin, news	I Love a Mystery	Music	Chesterfield Time
8:15	Lum and Abner	Chesterfield Time		The Night Editor
8:30	Music	Death Valley Days	News	Battle Stations
8:45			Variety	
9pm	Wings to Victory	The Roma Wine Show, Charlie Ruggles	Glenn Hardy, news	Blind Date
9:15			Busy Money	
9:30	Erskine Johnson, gossip	Quiz Quotient	General Barrows, comment	The Adventures of Ellery Queen
9:45	News	Music	Fulton Lewis Jr., news	
10pm	America's Town Meeting of the Air	The Ten o'Clock Wire	Music	The Richfield Reporter
10:15		The Third Clue	Paul Schubert, news	Manchester Boddy, news
10:30		Overseas Songs	The Symphonette	Inside the News
10:45		Stan Kenton Orchestra		Harry Owens Orchestra

EVENING — SUMMER, 1943

Friday

BLUE	CBS	MBS	NBC	
Dick Tracy	Songs	John B. Hughes, news	Talk	5pm
Twilight Tales	Music	The Adventures of Superman	News	5:15
Jack Armstrong, the All-American Boy	Harry W. Flannery, news		Charles W. Hamp, news	5:30
News	News	Norman Nesbitt, talk	Bill Henry, news	5:45
Hop Harrigan	The Hollywood Showcase	Gabriel Heatter, news	Waltz Time	6pm
Today in History		Faces and Places		6:15
Spotlight Bands	That Brewster Boy	The Music Depreciation Hour	People Are Funny	6:30
War News (6:55PM)				6:45
Free Men Fighting	Thanks to the Yanks	John B. Hughes, news	Tommy Riggs and Betty Lou	7pm
News		News		7:15
Alec Templeton, piano		The Lone Ranger	The Colgate Sports Newsreel, Bill Stern	7:30
	Bill Henry, news		Music	7:45
Earl Godwin, news	I Love a Mystery	For Victory	Chesterfield Time	8pm
The Parker Family	Our Secret Weapon	Music	Fleetwood Lawton, news	8:15
Gangbusters	The Phillip Morris Playhouse	Variety	Your All-Time Hit Parade	8:30
		Remember		8:45
Meet Your Navy	The Whistler	Glenn Hardy, news	Furlough Fun	9pm
		Cal Tinney, news		9:15
Erskine Johnson, gossip	The Adventures of the Thin Man	General Barrows, comment	The Sealtest Village Store, Davis and Haley	9:30
News		Fulton Lewis Jr., news		9:45
The Legion Stadium Fights	The Ten o'Clock Wire	Music	The Richfield Reporter	10pm
	The Changing Tide	Paul Schubert, news	Husbands and Wives	10:15
	Stan Kenton Orchestra	The Symphonette	Inside the News	10:30
			H. V. Kaltenborn, news	10:45

EVENING — SUMMER, 1943

Saturday

	BLUE	CBS	MBS	NBC
5pm	War News (4:45PM)	The Birth Clinic	News	The Hollywood Open House
5:15	Boston Symphony Orchestra		Music	
5:30		Harry W. Flannery, news		Traffic Tribunal
5:45		News	Norman Nesbitt, talk	The Red Cross March
6pm		The Man Behind the Gun	The Chicago Theater of the Air	The National Barn Dance
6:15	Music			
6:30	Spotlight Bands	The Rudy Vallee Show		Can You Top This
6:45	Here, America (6:55PM)	Saturday Night Serenade		
7pm	The Green Hornet		John B. Hughes, news	The Million Dollar Band, Barry Wood
7:15		Pabst Blue Ribbon Town, Groucho Marx	Saturday Night Bondwagon	
7:30	Red Ryder			Grand Ole Opry
7:45		Eric Johnston, news	The Treasury Star Parade	
8pm	Earl Godwin, news	George Fielding Elliiot, comment	This is the Hour	Public Affairs
8:15	Music	Piano Recital		
8:30	Enough on Time	Hobby Lobby	The Clinic Forum	Smith Goes to Town
8:45		Dick Joy, news (8:55PM)		
9pm	Cowboy Music	Your Hit Parade	Glenn Hardy, news	News
9:15			Dance Orchestra	The Treasury Star Parade
9:30	The Falcon			The Mystery of the Month
9:45		Don't You Believe It		
10pm	Wings Over the World	The Ten o'Clock Wire	News	The Richfield Reporter
10:15		Alvino Rey Orchestra	Joe Reichmann Orchestra	Music
10:30	Freddy Martin Orchestra	Stan Kenton Orchestra	Jack McLean Orchestra	Harry Owens Orchestra
10:45				

DAYTIME — SUMMER, 1943

Sunday

	BLUE	CBS	MBS	NBC
8am	Soldiers Production	The West Coast Church	The Wesley Radio League	Rhapsody
8:15				The Book of Books
8:30	African Trek	Invitation to Learning	Aunt Ge Ge and Uncle Ge	Music
8:45				Highlights of the Week's News
9am	News	The Salt Lake Tabernacle Choir	The Detroit Bible Class	Talk
9:15	Speaking of Glamour			News
9:30	The Music Hour	Trans-Atlantic Call	Memo for Tomorrow	That They Might Live
9:45		Letters to My Son		
10am		The Opportunity Hour	Glenn Hardy, news	News
10:15			Romance of the Highways	Labor for Victory
10:30	Toast to Health		What Happened This Week	Rupert Hughes, news
10:45				Alvin Wilder, news
11am	News	Make Believe Ballroom Time	The Pilgrim Hour	The University of Chicago Round Table
11:15	Newsweekly			
11:30	Music	World News Today		The Westinghouse Program, John C. Thomas
11:45	John W. Vandercook,			
12pm	Music	New York Philharmonic Orchestra	Broadway News	Rationing Reports
12:15	News		Music	Upton Close, news
12:30	Hot Copy			The Army Hour
12:45				
1pm	National Vespers		The Lutheran Hour	
1:15				
1:30	Music	The Pause That Refreshes	Young People's Church	News

DAYTIME — SUMMER, 1943

Monday-Friday

BLUE	CBS	MBS	NBC	
Between the Lines	Music	Cheer Up, Gang	The Johnny Murray Show	*8am*
News	The Melody Express		Music	*8:15*
The Breakfast Club	Kitty Foyle	News	News	*8:30*
	Aunt Jenny's True Life Stories	Victor Lindlahr, health	David Harum	*8:45*
Women Make the News	Kate Smith Speaks	Boake Carter, news	The Open Door	*9am*
News	Big Sister	Time Out	The Story of Mary Marlin	*9:15*
The Breakfast Club	The Romance of Helen Trent	Norma Young, talk	Listen to This	*9:30*
	Our Gal Sunday		The Home Economist	*9:45*
H. R. Baukhage, news	Life Can Be Beautiful	Glenn Hardy, news	Music and Talk / The Standard School Broadcast /	*10am*
Jay Burnett, news	Ma Perkins	Garden Talk	Peter de Lima's Closeups	*10:15*
Andy and Virginia, talk	Vic and Sade	Music	Burritt and Wheeler, talk	*10:30*
Listen to This	The Goldbergs	The Lady of Charm	Art Baker's Notebook	*10:45*
The Gospel Singer	Young Dr. Malone	Dr. Talbot, health	The Guiding Light	*11am*
The Mystery Chef	Joyce Jordan, MD		Lonely Women	*11:15*
Roundup	We Love and Learn	Calling	The Light of the World	*11:30*
	Pepper Young's Family	The Rose Room	Betty Crocker, cooking / Hymns of All Churches	*11:45*
The Coke Club, Morton Downey	Crummit and Sanderson	Broadway News	The Farm Reporter	*12pm*
News	News	Talk	Ma Perkins	*12:15*
	William Winter, news		Pepper Young's Family	*12:30*
Between the Bookends	Bachelor's Children	The Shady Valley Folks	The Right to Happiness	*12:45*
The Blue Newsroom Review	Homefront Report	Bill's Wax Shop	Mary Noble, Backstage Wife	*1pm*
		Music	Stella Dallas	*1:15*
	Music		Lorenzo Jones	*1:30*

DAYTIME — SUMMER, 1943

Sunday

	BLUE	CBS	MBS	NBC
1:45	What Happened This Week			The Treasury Star Parade
2pm	This is Official	The Prudential Family Hour	Music	NBC Symphony Orchestra
2:15				
2:30	Sneak Preview		The US Navy Band	
2:45		Irene Rich Dramas		
3pm	Music	The Silver Theater	Murder Clinic	News
3:15				Fiesta Time
3:30		Gene Autry's Melody Ranch	Upton Close, news	Reports from the Battlefield
3:45	News		The Round Towner	The News Makers
4pm	Church Federation Vespers	The Jerry Lester Show	Nobody's Children	Those We Love
4:15				
4:30	Sammy Kaye's Sunday Serenade	The Question of the Week	Stars and Stripes in Britain	The Fitch Bandwagon
4:45		Woody Herman Orchestra		

DAYTIME — SUMMER, 1943

Monday-Friday

BLUE	CBS	MBS	NBC	
	Talk / Uncle Sam		Young Widder Brown	1:45
What's Doing Ladies	Raffles, the Amatuer Cracksman	Music / The Don Lee Newsreel Theater	When a Girl Marries	2pm
	Music		Portia Faces Life	2:15
Music			Just Plain Bill	2:30
	Keep Home Fires Burning		Front Page Farrell	2:45
News	Talk	Philip Keyne Gordon, news	The Dreft Star Playhouse	3pm
Music		Music	The Road of Life	3:15
The Blue Frolics	Music	News	Vic and Sade	3:30
	The World Today	Bill Hay's Bible Reading	Snow Village Sketches	3:45
My True Story	Hello from Hollywood	Fulton Lewis Jr., news	Dr. Kate	4pm
	Sam Hayes, news	Judy and Jane	News	4:15
News	Music / The American Melody Hour /	The Johnson Family	Talk	4:30
Music / Captain Jack	Easy Aces / Mr. Keen, Tracer of Lost Persons	Bill's Wax Shop	H. V. Kaltenborn, news	4:45

DAYTIME — SUMMER, 1943

Saturday

	BLUE	CBS	MBS	NBC
8am	Between the Lines	Let's Pretend	The Haven of Rest	Peter's Pidgeons
8:15	News			
8:30	Talley Time	Fashions in Rations, Billie Burke	News	Coast Guard on Parade
8:45			The Junior Army	Vegetables for Victory
9am	Smile in the Morning	The Armstrong Theater of Today	Dr. Matthews, religion	News
9:15	The Miniature Worship Hour			Consumer Time
9:30	The Breakfast Club	Stars Over Hollywood	Music	Music
9:45			Food for Thought	
10am		Music	Glenn Hardy, news	Uncle Sam
10:15	News	The Treasury Star Parade	Music	Music
10:30	The Week in Review	Youth on Parade	Victor Lopez Orchestra	On Your Job
10:45	County Medical Association Talks	Dave Cheskin Orchestra		War Telescope
11am	The Music Box	Columbia's Country Journal	Music	The Roy Shields Revue
11:15				
11:30	Tucker Topics	The Spirit of '43	Calling	Public Affairs
11:45				
12pm	Music	Of Men and Books	News	The Farm Reporter
12:15			The Lamplighter	The Air Force Band
12:30	George Hicks, news	William Winter, news	Music	News
12:45	Marshall Orchestra	Victory Gardens		Visiting Nurse
1pm		Report from London	The Salvation Army	Musical Matinee
1:15		Horse Racing	Horse Racing	Horse Racing
1:30		Calling Pan-America	Music	Music
1:45	News			

DAYTIME — SUMMER, 1943

Saturday

	BLUE	CBS	MBS	NBC
2pm	Horace Heidt's Saturday Revue	Ted Weems Maritime	US Navy Bulletin	Not for Glory
2:15				
2:30		Commandos		The Three Suns
2:45				Music
3pm	Our Nation at War	Civilian Defense	I Hear America Singing	
3:15		The People's Platform		Army Recruiting Program
3:30	Message of Israel		Hawaii Calls	The Art of Living
3:45		The World Today		Music
4pm	Men, Machines, and Victory	Meet Corliss Archer	The American Eagle Club	For This We Fight
4:15	Freddy Martin Orchestra			
4:30	News	Music	Music	Perpetual Motion
4:45	War News			

EVENING — FALL, 1943

Sunday

	ABC	CBS	MBS	NBC
5pm	National Vespers	Broadway Bandbox, Frank Sinatra	A. L. Alexander's Mediation Board	The Charlie McCarthy Show
5:15				
5:30	The Hero of the Week	William Winter, news		One Man's Family
5:45	Drew Pearson, news	Dick Joy, news	Gabriel Heatter, news	
6pm	Walter Winchell's Jergans Journal	The Radio Reader's Digest	Cleveland Symphony Orchestra	The Manhattan Merry-Go-Round
6:15	The Chamber Music Society of Lower Basin Street			
6:30		The Texaco Star Theater, James Melton		The American Album of Familiar Music
6:45	Jimmy Fidler, gossip			
7pm	The Gertrude Lawrence Show	Take It or Leave It	John B. Hughes, news	The Hour of Charm
7:15			News	
7:30	The Weird Circle	The Adventures of the Thin Man	Variety	Bob Crosby Orchestra
7:45			Bobby Hooky	
8pm	Earl Godwin, news	Lud Gluskin Orchestra	USC Hancock Ensemble	The Great Gildersleeve
8:15	That's a Good One	Ned Calmer, news (8:25PM)		
8:30	The Quiz Kids	Elsie Janis	Wings Over the West Coast	The Standard Symphony Hour
8:45				
9pm	Keepsakes, Dorothy Kirsten	The Storyteller	Glenn Hardy, news	
9:15		War News	Music	
9:30	T.B. Blakisten, talk	Point Sublime		The Skippy Hollywood Theater
9:45	Washington Inside and Out			
10pm	The Court of Public Opinion	The Ten o'Clock Wire	The Old Fashioned Revival Hour	The Richfield Reporter
10:15		The Whistler		The Chapel Quartet
10:30	Uncle Sam Melody			Inside the News
10:45		Dance Orchestra		Labor for Victory

EVENING — FALL, 1943

Monday

ABC	CBS	MBS	NBC	
Terry and the Pirates	Galen Drake, talk	John B. Hughes, news	The Voice of a Nation	5pm
Twilight Tales	The Rangers	The Adventures of Superman	News	5:15
Jack Armstrong, the All-American Boy	Harry W. Flannery, news	The Radio Tour	The Voice of Firestone	5:30
Captain Midnight	Truman Bradley, news	Norman Nesbitt, talk		5:45
News	The Lux Radio Theater	Gabriel Heatter, news	News	6pm
Today in History		The Gracie Fields Show	The Treasury Star Parade	6:15
Spotlight Bands		The Return of Nick Carter	Dr. I. Q., the Mental Banker	6:30
War News (6:55PM)				6:45
Raymond Gram Swing, news	The Lady Esther Screen Guild Theater	Paul Sullivan, news	The Carnation Contented Hour	7pm
News		News		7:15
Free Men Fighting	Blondie	The Lone Ranger	Information, Please	7:30
The Romance of Industry				7:45
Earl Godwin, news	I Love a Mystery	Sherlock Holmes	Chesterfield Time	8pm
Lum and Abner	Ed Sullivan Entertains		Fleetwood Lawton, news	8:15
Counterspy	The Gay Nineties Revue	Double or Nothing	The Cavalcade of America	8:30
				8:45
Blind Date	I Was There	Glenn Hardy, news	The Bell Telephone Hour	9pm
		Sam Balter, sports		9:15
Erskine Johnson, gossip	Vox Pop	General Barrows, comment	Hawthorne House	9:30
News		Fulton Lewis Jr., news		9:45
Music	The Ten o'Clock Wire	Dr. Polyzoides, health	The Richfield Reporter	10pm
The Mary Small Revue	John Burton, news	Paul Schubert, news	Manchester Boddy, news	10:15
	The Rangers	Alvino Rey Orchestra	Inside the News	10:30
Classics	Piano Recital		H. V. Kaltenborn, news	10:45

EVENING — FALL, 1943

Tuesday

	ABC	CBS	MBS	NBC
5pm	Terry and the Pirates	Galen Drake, talk	John B. Hughes, news	The Voice of a Nation
5:15	Alvin Wilder, news	The Rangers	The Adventures of Superman	News
5:30	Jack Armstrong, The All-American Boy	Harry W. Flannery, news	The Radio Tour	Tums Treasure Chest
5:45	Captain Midnight	Truman Bradley, news	Norman Nesbitt, talk	
6pm	News	Burns and Allen	Gabriel Heatter, news	The Molle' Mystery Theater
6:15	Today in History		The Gracie Fields Show	
6:30	Spotlight Bands	Report to the Nation	The American Forum of the Air	Fibber McGee and Molly
6:45	War News (6:55pm)			
7pm	Raymond Gram Swing, news	Suspense		The Pepsodent Show, Bob Hope
7:15	News		News	
7:30	Red Ryder	The Inglewood Park Concert	The Shadow	The Raleigh Cigarette Program, Red Skelton
7:45				
8pm	Earl Godwin, news	I Love a Mystery	The Pay Day Quiz	Chesterfield Time
8:15	Lum and Abner	Chesterfield Time		Fleetwood Lawton, news
8:30	Duffy's Tavern	Big Town	The Storyteller	The Purple Heart Show, Ginny Simms
8:45			Music	
9pm	Soldiers of the Press	The Colgate Program, Judy Canova	Glenn Hardy, news	Salute to Youth
9:15	What's in the Song		Rex Miller, news	
9:30	Erskine Johnson, gossip	Edwin C. Hill, news	Faces and Places	What is the World Fighting For
9:45	News	Deane Dickson, news	Fulton Lewis Jr., news	
10pm	Music	The Ten o'Clock Wire	News	The Richfield Reporter
10:15	Aircraft War Production Council	John Burton, news	Paul Schubert, news	Music
10:30	Opera Previews	The Rangers	Harrison Wood, news	Inside the News
10:45		Organ Recital	Music	Organ Recital

EVENING — FALL, 1943

Wednesday

ABC	CBS	MBS	NBC	
Terry and the Pirates	Galen Drake, talk	John B. Hughes, news	The Voice of a Nation	5pm
Alvin Wilder, news	The Rangers	The Adventures of Superman	News	5:15
Jack Armstrong, The All-American Boy	Harry W. Flannery, news	The Radio Tour	Alvin Wilder, news	5:30
Captain Midnight	Truman Bradley, news	Norman Nesbitt, talk	Bill Henry, news	5:45
The Bondwagon	The Opportunity	Gabriel Heatter, news	Time to Smile, Eddie Cantor	6pm
		The Gracie Fields Show		6:15
Spotlight Bands	The Jack Carson Show	Soldiers With Wings	Mr. District Attorney	6:30
War News (6:55PM)				6:45
Raymond Gram Swing, news	Great Moments in Music	John B. Hughes, news	Kay Kyser's College of Musical Knowledge	7pm
News		News		7:15
Free Men Fighting	The Cresta Blanca Carnival	The Lone Ranger		7:30
Mayor Bowron, comment				7:45
Earl Godwin, news	I Love a Mystery	Take a Card	Chesterfield Time	8pm
Lum and Abner	Chesterfield Time		Fleetwood Lawton, news	8:15
Battle of the Sexes	Dr. Christian	Bulldog Drummond	Tommy Dorsey's Variety Show	8:30
				8:45
This is My Country	Sammy Kaye Orchestra	Glenn Hardy, news	Mr. and Mrs. North	9pm
		Sam Balter, sports		9:15
Erskine Johnson, gossip	The Mayor of the Town	General Barrows, comment	Scramby Amby	9:30
News		Fulton Lewis Jr., news		9:45
Music	The Ten o'Clock Wire	Dr. Polyzoides, health	The Richfield Reporter	10pm
Freddy Martin Orchestra	John Burton, news	Paul Schubert, news	Navy Heroes	10:15
The National Radio Forum	The Rangers	Alvino Rey Orchestra	Inside the News	10:30
	Organ Recital		Music	10:45

EVENING — FALL, 1943

Thursday

	ABC	CBS	MBS	NBC
5pm	Terry and the Pirates	Galen Drake, talk	John B. Hughes, news	The Voice of a Nation
5:15	Alvin Wilder, news	The Rangers	The Adventures of Superman	News
5:30	Jack Armstrong, the All-American Boy	Harry W. Flannery, news	The Radio Tour	Alvin Wilder, news
5:45	Captain Midnight	Truman Bradley, news	Norman Nesbitt, talk	Bill Henry, news
6pm	News	Major Bowes' Original Amateur Hour	Gabriel Heatter, news	The Kraft Music Hall, Bing Crosby
6:15	Today in History		The Gracie Fields Show	
6:30	Spotlight Bands	The Birdseye Open House, Dinah Shore	You Tell Em' Club	The Bob Burns Show
6:45	War News (6:55PM)			
7pm	Raymond Gram Swing, news	The First Line of Defense	Raymond Clapper, news	Abbott and Costello
7:15	Frazier Hunt, news		Dale Carnegie, inspirational	
7:30	Red Ryder	Here's to Romance, Dick Haynes	San Quentin on the Air	The March of Time
7:45				
8pm	Earl Godwin, news	I Love a Mystery	Army Recruiting Program	Chesterfield Time
8:15	Lum and Abner	Chesterfield Time		The Night Editor
8:30	American Challenges	Death Valley Days	The Better Half	Maxwell House Coffee Time, Brice and Morgan
8:45				
9pm	Wings to Victory	The Roma Wine Show, Charlie Ruggles	Glenn Hardy, news	The Aldrich Famiily
9:15			Rex Miller, news	
9:30	Erskine Johnson, gossip	Dog Chats	Faces and Places	The Adventures of Ellery Queen
9:45	News	The Headline Builders	Fulton Lewis Jr., news	
10pm	America's Town Meeting of the Air	The Ten o'Clock Wire	Busy Money	The Richfield Reporter
10:15		John Burton, news	Paul Schubert, news	Manchester Boddy, news
10:30		The Rangers	Harrison Wood, news	Inside the News
10:45		Songs	Dance Orchestra	Prelude to Victory

EVENING — FALL, 1943

Friday

ABC	CBS	MBS	NBC	
Terry and the Pirates	Galen Drake, talk	John B. Hughes, news	The Voice of a Nation	5pm
Twilight Tales	The Rangers	The Adventures of Superman	News	5:15
Jack Armstrong, the All-American Boy	Harry W. Flannery, news	The Radio Tour	Alvin Wilder, news	5:30
Captain Midnight	News	Norman Nesbitt, talk	Bill Henry, news	5:45
News	The Hollywood Showcase	Gabriel Heatter, news	Waltz Time	6pm
Today in History		The Gracie Fields Show		6:15
Spotlight Bands	That Brewster Boy	The Music Depreciation Hour	People Are Funny	6:30
War News (6:55 PM)				6:45
Ray W. Smith, news	The Durante - Moore Show	Cedric Foster, news	Amos 'n' Andy	7pm
News		News		7:15
Free Men Fighting	Stage Door Canteen	The Lone Ranger	The Colgate Sports Newsreel, Bill Stern	7:30
Music			Music	7:45
Earl Godwin, news	I Love a Mystery	The Quiz of Two Cities	Chesterfield Time	8pm
The Parker Family	Date Line		Fleetwood Lawton, news	8:15
Gangbusters	The Phillip Morris Playhouse	What is the Name of that Song	Your All-Time Hit Parade	8:30
				8:45
Meet Your Navy	The Kate Smith Hour	Glenn Hardy, news	Furlough Fun	9pm
		Sam Balter, sports		9:15
Erskine Johnson, gossip		General Barrows, comment	The Sealtest Village Store, Davis and Haley	9:30
News		Fulton Lewis Jr., news		9:45
Freddy Martin Orchestra	The Ten o'Clock Wire	Dr. Polyzoides, health	The Richfield Reporter	10pm
	John Burton, news	Paul Schubert, news	Songs	10:15
Footballastics	The Rangers	Henry King Orchestra	Inside the News	10:30
	Organ Recital		Music	10:45

EVENING — FALL, 1943

Saturday

	ABC	CBS	MBS	NBC
5pm	William Parker, news	Henry Busse Orchestra	News	Music
5:15	Boston Symphony Orchestra		Sports	
5:30		Harry W. Flannery, news	Music	Traffic Tribunal
5:45		News	Norman Nesbitt, talk	News
6pm		Guest Star	The Chicago Theater of the Air	The National Barn Dance
6:15	Music	The Headline Builders		
6:30	Spotlight Bands	The Eleanor King Show		Can You Top This
6:45	War News (6:55PM)	Saturday Night Serenade		
7pm	The Green Hornet		John B. Hughes, news	The Million Dollar Band, Barry Wood
7:15		Pabst Blue Ribbon Town, Groucho Marx	Saturday Night Bondwagon	
7:30	Red Ryder			Grand Ole Opry
7:45		The Changing Tide	Music	
8pm	Earl Godwin, news	Thanks to the Yanks	California Melodies	Truth or Consequences
8:15	Edward Jorgenson, news			
8:30	Leon Henderson, news	Inner Sanctum Mysteries	The Clinic Forum	Abie's Irish Rose
8:45	Music	Dick Joy, news (8:55PM)		
9pm	Homocide O'Kane	Your Hit Parade	Glenn Hardy, news	Young Artist's Contest
9:15			News	
9:30	Army Service Forces		Faces and Places	
9:45		Don't You Believe It	The Lamplighter	Music
10pm	Bridge to Dreamland	The Ten o'Clock Wire	News	The Richfield Reporter
10:15		Mitchell Ayres Orchestra	Henry King Orchestra	The Unseen Enemy
10:30	Freddy Martin Orchestra	Music	Gus Arnheim Orchestra	George Olsen Orchestra
10:45				

DAYTIME — FALL, 1943

Sunday

	ABC	CBS	MBS	NBC
8am	Soldiers Production	The West Coast Church	The Wesley Radio League	Rhapsody
8:15				The Book of Books
8:30	The Hour of Faith	Invitation to Learning	The Voice of Prophecy	OK for Release
8:45				Waltzes America Loves
9am	News	The Salt Lake Tabernacle Choir	The Detroit Bible Class	Carveth Welles, news
9:15	Speaking of Glamour	Woman Power		Successful Gardening
9:30	The Music Hour	Transatlantic Call	Memo for Tomorrow	Music
9:45			Health News	
10am		The Merry Go Round	Glenn Hardy, news	
10:15			Romance of the Highways	Labor for Victory
10:30	Toast to Health		What Happened This Week	The University of Chicago Round Table
10:45				
11am	Newsweekly	Ceiling Unlimited	The Pilgrim Hour	Those We Love
11:15	This and That			
11:30	Music	World News Today		The Westinghouse Program, John C. Thomas
11:45	John W. Vandercook,			
12pm	Music	New York Philharmonic Orchestra	Broadway News	Rationing Reports
12:15			Music	Upton Close, news
12:30	Hot Copy		The Cavalcade of Medicine	The Army Hour
12:45				
1pm	Fun Valley, Al Pearce		The Lutheran Hour	
1:15				
1:30	The Master Radio Canaries	The Pause That Refreshes	Young People's Church	News Highlights

DAYTIME — FALL, 1943

Monday-Friday

ABC	CBS	MBS	NBC	
Between the Lines	Music	Dr. Talbot, health	The Johnny Murray Show	8am
News	The Melody Express		News	8:15
The Breakfast Club	Kitty Foyle	News	News	8:30
	Aunt Jenny's True Life Stories	Victor Lindlahr, health	David Harum	8:45
Women Make the News	Kate Smith Speaks	Boake Carter, news	The Open Door	9am
News	Big Sister	Time Out	A Woman of America	9:15
The Breakfast Club	The Romance of Helen Trent	The Sunny Side	The Gallant Heart	9:30
	Our Gal Sunday	A. P. Giannini, money	Betty and Bob	9:45
News	Life Can Be Beautiful	Glenn Hardy, news	Mirth and Madness, Jack Kirkwood	10am
Jay Burnett, news	Ma Perkins	Talk	Peter de Lima's Closeups	10:15
Sweet River	Bernadine Flynn, news	Points and Prices	Burritt and Wheeler, talk	10:30
The Gospel Singer	The Goldbergs	Music	Art Baker's Notebook	10:45
H. R. Baukhage, news	Young Dr. Malone	The Shady Valley Folks	The Guiding Light	11am
The Mystery Chef	Joyce Jordan, MD	The Humbard Family	Lonely Women	11:15
Roundup	We Love and Learn	Yours for a Song	The Light of the World	11:30
News	Linda's First Love	The Rose Room	Betty Crocker, cooking / Hymns of All Churches	11:45
The Coke Club, Morton Downey	Crummit and Sanderson	Broadway News	The Farm Reporter	12pm
News	News	Harrison Wood, news	Ma Perkins	12:15
Talk and Music	William Winter, news	Talk	Pepper Young's Family	12:30
Meet the Ladies	News		The Right to Happiness	12:45
Newsroom Review	Homefront Report	Music	Mary Noble, Backstage Wife	1pm
			Stella Dallas	1:15
	The Standard School of the Air		Lorenzo Jones	1:30

DAYTIME — FALL, 1943

Sunday

	ABC	CBS	MBS	NBC
1:45	What Happened This Week			News
2pm	Where Do We Stand	The Prudential Family Hour	The Fireside Party	NBC Symphony Orchestra
2:15				
2:30	The Musical Steelmakers		Music	
2:45		Irene Rich Dramas		
3pm	Sam Hayes, news	The Silver Theater	Foreign Assignment	The Catholic Hour
3:15	Wake Up America			
3:30		America in the Air	Upton Close, news	Reports from the Battlefield
3:45			The Round Towner	The News Makers
4pm	Church Federation Vespers	The Jerry Lester Show	The Old Fashioned Revival Hour	The Jello Program, Jack Benny
4:15				
4:30	Dorothy Thompson, news	We, the People		The Fitch Bandwagon
4:45	News and Views			

DAYTIME — FALL, 1943

Monday-Friday

ABC	CBS	MBS	NBC	
Rodriguez and Sutherland, news			Young Widder Brown	1:45
What's Doing Ladies	The Story of Mary Marlin	Music / The Don Lee Newsreel Theater	When a Girl Marries	2pm
	David's Almanac		Portia Faces Life	2:15
Ruth Wentworth, talk	News		Just Plain Bill	2:30
Between the Bookends	American Women		Front Page Farrell	2:45
News	Talk	Philip Keyne Gordon, news	The Dreft Star Playhouse	3pm
Talk		Music and Talk	The Road of Life	3:15
Ladies Be Seated	Music	News	Vic and Sade	3:30
	The World Today	Bill Hay's Bible Reading	Brave Tomorrow	3:45
My True Story	Hello from Hollywood	Fulton Lewis Jr., news	Dr. Kate	4pm
	Sam Hayes, news	Music	News	4:15
News	Open House / The American Melody Hour /	The Johnson Family	Talk	4:30
War News / Captain Jack	Easy Aces / Mr. Keen, Tracer of Lost Persons	News	H. V. Kaltenborn, news	4:45

DAYTIME — FALL, 1943

Saturday

	ABC	CBS	MBS	NBC
8am	Between the Lines	Let's Pretend	The Haven of Rest	Saturday Showdown
8:15	News			News
8:30	Talley Time	Fashions in Rations, Billie Burke	News	Coast Guard on Parade
8:45			The Junior Army	Vegetables for Victory
9am	Smile in the Morning	The Armstrong Theater of Today	Dr. Matthews, religion	News
9:15	The Miniature Worship Hour			Consumer Time
9:30	The Breakfast Club	Stars Over Hollywood	Hello, Mom	The Pet Parade
9:45				County Medical
10am		Campana Serenade, Dick Powell	Glenn Hardy, news	That They Might Live
10:15	News		Food for Thought	
10:30	Xavier Cugat Orchestra	Marilyn Pembrooke, talk	Victor Lopez Orchestra	On the Scouting Trail
10:45				
11am	The Week in Review	The Victory Gardener	Music	Music
11:15	News	Sports		Sports
11:30	Spelling Bee			
11:45	Sports			
12pm			News	
12:15			Sports	
12:30				
12:45				
1pm				
1:15				
1:30				
1:45				

DAYTIME — FALL, 1943

Saturday

	ABC	CBS	MBS	NBC
2pm		William Winter, news		Music
2:15	Horace Heidt's Saturday Revue	News		
2:30		Mother and Dad		Public Affairs
2:45				
3pm	Message of Israel	Civilian Defense		I Sustain the Wings
3:15		The People's Platform		
3:30	Our Nation at War			Curt Massey, songs
3:45		The World Today		Rupert Hughes, news
4pm	What's New	Meet Corliss Archer		For This We Fight
4:15				
4:30		Bill Hay, talk		Noah Webster Says
4:45				

LISTINGS FOR 1944

EVENING — WINTER, 1944

Sunday

	ABC	CBS	MBS	NBC
5pm	National Vespers	The Jerry Lester Show	A. L. Alexander's Mediation Board	The Charlie McCarthy Show
5:15				
5:30	Walter Duranty, news	William Winter, news		One Man's Family
5:45	Drew Pearson, news	Dick Joy, news	Gabriel Heatter, news	
6pm	Walter Winchell's Jergans Journal	The Radio Reader's Digest	Cleveland Symphony Orchestra	The Manhattan Merry-Go-Round
6:15	The Chamber Music Society of Lower Basin Street			
6:30		The Texaco Star Theater, Fred Allen		The American Album of Familiar Music
6:45	Jimmy Fidler, gossip			
7pm	The Gertrude Lawrence Show	Take It or Leave It	Cedric Foster, news	The Hour of Charm
7:15			The Goodwill Hour	
7:30	The Weird Circle	The Adventures of the Thin Man		Bob Crosby Orchestra
7:45				
8pm	Earl Godwin, news	Crime Doctor	Vaudeville Hotel	The Great Gildersleeve
8:15	Feature Section	Ned Calmer, news (8:25 PM)		
8:30	The Quiz Kids	Time to Come	The Jello Program, Jack Benny	The Standard Symphony Hour
8:45				
9pm	Deadline Dramas	I Was There	Glenn Hardy, news	
9:15			Rex Miller, news	
9:30	News	Sunday Salute	Wings Over the West Coast	The Skippy Hollywood Theater
9:45	Washington Inside and Out			
10pm	The Court of Public Opinion	The Ten o'Clock Wire	The Old Fashioned Revival Hour	The Richfield Reporter
10:15		The Changing Tide		The Chapel Quartet
10:30	Uncle Sam Melody	We Deliver the Goods		Inside the News
10:45		Les Brown Orchestra		Labor for Victory

EVENING — WINTER, 1944

Monday

ABC	CBS	MBS	NBC	
Terry and the Pirates	Galen Drake, talk	John B. Hughes, news	OK for Release	5pm
Twilight Tales	The Rangers	The Adventures of Superman	News	5:15
Jack Armstrong, the All-American Boy	Harry W. Flannery, news	World Front Page	The Voice of Firestone	5:30
Captain Midnight	Truman Bradley, news	Gordon Burke, news		5:45
Counterspy	The Lux Radio Theater	Gabriel Heatter, news	News and Views	6pm
		Believe It or Not		6:15
Spotlight Bands		Variety Musicale	Dr. I. Q., the Mental Banker	6:30
War News (6:55PM)				6:45
Raymond Gram Swing, news	The Lady Esther Screen Guild Theater	Paul Sullivan, news	The Carnation Contented Hour	7pm
Frazier Hunt, news		The People's Reporter		7:15
Horace Heidt for the Servicemen	Blondie	The Lone Ranger	Information, Please	7:30
				7:45
Earl Godwin, news	I Love a Mystery	Sherlock Holmes	Chesterfield Time	8pm
Lum and Abner	Ed Sullivan Entertains		Fleetwood Lawton, news	8:15
American Challenges	The Gay Nineties Revue	Point Sublime	The Cavalcade of America	8:30
				8:45
Blind Date	Suspense	Glenn Hardy, news	The Bell Telephone Hour	9pm
		Sam Balter, sports		9:15
Lowell Thomas, news	Vox Pop	General Barrows, comment	Hawthorne House	9:30
Feature Section		Fulton Lewis Jr., news		9:45
Erskine Johnson, gossip	The Ten o'Clock Wire	Dr. Polyzoides, health	The Richfield Reporter	10pm
The 10-2-4 Ranch	John Burton, news	Music	Manchester Boddy, news	10:15
A Boy, A Girl, and a Band	The Symphonette	Public Affairs	Inside the News	10:30
			The Voice of a Nation	10:45

EVENING — WINTER, 1944

Tuesday

	ABC	CBS	MBS	NBC
5pm	Terry and the Pirates	Galen Drake, talk	John B. Hughes, news	OK for Release
5:15	Alvin Wilder, news	The Rangers	The Adventures of Superman	News
5:30	Jack Armstrong, the All-American Boy	Dr. Sterling, health	World Front Page	Tums Treasure Chest
5:45	Captain Midnight	Truman Bradley, news	Gordon Burke, news	
6pm	News	Burns and Allen	Gabriel Heatter, news	The Molle' Mystery Theater
6:15	Today in History		Believe It or Not	
6:30	Spotlight Bands	Report to the Nation	The American Forum of the Air	Fibber McGee and Molly
6:45	War News (6:55PM)			
7pm	Raymond Gram Swing, news	Romance		The Pepsodent Show, Bob Hope
7:15	Frazier Hunt, news		The People's Reporter	
7:30	Red Ryder	The Inglewood Park Concert	The Shadow	The Raleigh Cigarette Program, Red Skelton
7:45				
8pm	Earl Godwin, news	I Love a Mystery	The Pay Day Quiz	Chesterfield Time
8:15	Lum and Abner	Chesterfield Time		Fleetwood Lawton, news
8:30	Duffy's Tavern	Big Town	Sinfonietta	The Purple Heart Show, Ginny Simms
8:45				
9pm	Soldiers of the Press	The Colgate Program, Judy Canova	Glenn Hardy, news	Everything for the Boys
9:15	Hoffman and Menendes, news		Rex Miller, news	
9:30	Lowell Thomas, news	Edwin C. Hill, news	Faces and Places	What is the World Fighting For
9:45	Feature Section	Deane Dickson, news	Fulton Lewis Jr., news	
10pm	Erskine Johnson, gossip	The Ten o'Clock Wire	Harrison Wood, news	The Richfield Reporter
10:15	Music	John Burton, news	Music	Music
10:30	Freddy Martin Orchestra	Congress Speaks		Inside the News
10:45		Organ Recital	The Education of Freedom	The Voice of a Nation

EVENING — WINTER, 1944

Wednesday

ABC	CBS	MBS	NBC	
Terry and the Pirates	Galen Drake, talk	John B. Hughes, news	OK for Release	5pm
Alvin Wilder, news	The Rangers	The Adventures of Superman	News	5:15
Jack Armstrong, the All-American Boy	Harry W. Flannery, news	World Front Page	Alvin Wilder, news	5:30
Captain Midnight	Truman Bradley, news	Gordon Burke, news	Bill Henry, news	5:45
News	Songs By Sinatra	Gabriel Heatter, news	Time to Smile, Eddie Cantor	6pm
Today in History		Believe It or Not		6:15
Spotlight Bands	The Jack Carson Show	Soldiers With Wings	Mr. District Attorney	6:30
War News (6:55pm)				6:45
Raymond Gram Swing, news	Great Moments in Music	John B. Hughes, news	Kay Kyser's College of Musical Knowledge	7pm
Frazier Hunt, news		The People's Reporter		7:15
Free Men Fighting	The Cresta Blanca Carnival	The Lone Ranger		7:30
Mayor Bowron, comment				7:45
Earl Godwin, news	I Love a Mystery	The Main Line	Chesterfield Time	8pm
Lum and Abner	Chesterfield Time		Fleetwood Lawton, news	8:15
Battle of the Sexes	Dr. Christian	Bulldog Drummond	Beat the Band	8:30
				8:45
Dunninger, the Mentalist	Sammy Kaye Orchestra	Glenn Hardy, news	Mr. and Mrs. North	9pm
		Sam Balter, sports		9:15
Lowell Thomas, news	Orson Welles Radio Almanac	General Barrows, comment	Scramby Amby	9:30
Feature Section		Fulton Lewis Jr., news		9:45
Erskine Johnson, gossip	The Ten o'Clock Wire	Dr. Polyzoides, health	The Richfield Reporter	10pm
Music	John Burton, news	Arch Ward, news	Income Tax	10:15
Freddy Martin Orchestra	The Symphonette	The Halls of Montezuma	Inside the News	10:30
			The Voice of a Nation	10:45

EVENING — WINTER, 1944

Thursday

	ABC	CBS	MBS	NBC
5pm	Terry and the Pirates	Galen Drake, talk	John B. Hughes, news	OK for Release
5:15	Alvin Wilder, news	The Rangers	The Adventures of Superman	News
5:30	Jack Armstrong, the All-American Boy	Harry W. Flannery, news	World Front Page	Alvin Wilder, news
5:45	Captain Midnight	Truman Bradley, news	Gordon Burke, news	Bill Henry, news
6pm	News	Major Bowes' Original Amateur Hour	Gabriel Heatter, news	The Kraft Music Hall, Bing Crosby
6:15	Today in History		Believe It or Not	
6:30	Spotlight Bands	The Birdseye Open House, Dinah Shore	The Song Hour	The Bob Burns Show
6:45	War News (6:55PM)			
7pm	Raymond Gram Swing, news	The First Line of Defense	Raymond Clapper, news	Abbott and Costello
7:15	Frazier Hunt, news		The People's Reporter	
7:30	Red Ryder	Here's to Romance, Dick Haynes	Public Affairs	The March of Time
7:45				
8pm	Earl Godwin, news	I Love a Mystery	Pick and Pat Time	Chesterfield Time
8:15	Lum and Abner	Chesterfield Time		The Night Editor
8:30	Star for a Night	Death Valley Days	The Human Adventure	Maxwell House Coffee Time, Brice and Morgan
8:45				
9pm	This is My Country	Hollywood Inn	Glenn Hardy, news	The Aldrich Famiily
9:15			Rex Miller, news	
9:30	Lowell Thomas, news	Dog Chats	Faces and Places	The Adventures of Ellery Queen
9:45	Feature Secton	Night Clubs for Victory	Fulton Lewis Jr., news	
10pm	Erskine Johnson, gossip	The Ten o'Clock Wire	A Date with Cugat	The Richfield Reporter
10:15	Music	John Burton, news		Songs
10:30	America's Town Meeting of the Air	News and Views	Music	Inside the News
10:45				The Voice of a Nation

EVENING — WINTER, 1944

Friday

ABC	CBS	MBS	NBC	
Terry and the Pirates	Galen Drake, talk	John B. Hughes, news	OK for Release	5pm
Twilight Tales	The Rangers	The Adventures of Superman	News	5:15
Jack Armstrong, the All-American Boy	Harry W. Flannery, news	World Front Page	Alvin Wilder, news	5:30
Captain Midnight	Truman Bradley, news	Gordon Burke, news	Bill Henry, news	5:45
News	The Hollywood Showcase	Gabriel Heatter, news	Waltz Time	6pm
Today in History		Believe It or Not		6:15
Spotlight Bands	That Brewster Boy	Double or Nothing	People Are Funny	6:30
War News (6:55PM)				6:45
Ray W. Smith, news	The Durante - Moore Show	Dale Carnegie, comment	Amos 'n' Andy	7pm
Frazier Hunt, news		The People's Reporter		7:15
Free Men Fighting	Stage Door Canteen	The Lone Ranger	The Colgate Sports Newsreel, Bill Stern	7:30
			Cabbages and Kings	7:45
Earl Godwin, news	I Love a Mystery	The Quiz of Two Cities	Chesterfield Time	8pm
The Parker Family	Music		Fleetwood Lawton, news	8:15
Gangbusters	The Phillip Morris Playhouse	What is the Name of that Song	Your All-Time Hit Parade	8:30
				8:45
Meet Your Navy	The Kate Smith Hour	Glenn Hardy, news	Furlough Fun	9pm
		Sam Balter, sports		9:15
Lowell Thomas, news		General Barrows, comment	The Sealtest Village Store, Davis and Haley	9:30
Feature Section		Fulton Lewis Jr., news		9:45
Erskine Johnson, gossip	The Ten o'Clock Wire	Freedom of Opportunity	The Richfield Reporter	10pm
Music	John Burton, news		Manchester Boddy, news	10:15
Your OPA	The Symphonette	Music	Inside the News	10:30
Freddy Martin Orchestra			The Voice of a Nation	10:45

EVENING — WINTER, 1944

Saturday

		ABC	CBS	MBS	NBC
5pm		William Parker, news	F. O. B. Detroit	News	Music
5:15		Serenade		Between the Lines	News
5:30		Boston Symphony Orchestra	Harry W. Flannery, news	Music	Traffic Tribunal
5:45			News	Gordon Burke, news	News
6pm			Meet Joe Public	The Chicago Theater of the Air	The National Barn Dance
6:15		Music			
6:30		Spotlight Bands	The Eleanor King Show		Can You Top This
6:45		War News (6:55PM)	Saturday Night Serenade		
7pm		Jobs for Heroes		John B. Hughes, news	The Million Dollar Band, Barry Wood
7:15			Pabst Blue Ribbon Town, Groucho Marx	Saturday Night Bondwagon	
7:30		Red Ryder			Grand Ole Opry
7:45			The Storyteller	Service Unlimited	
8pm		Earl Godwin, news	Thanks to the Yanks	California Melodies	Truth or Consequences
8:15		Danny Shane, news			
8:30		Leon Henderson, news	Inner Sanctum Mysteries	The Clinic Forum	Abie's Irish Rose
8:45		Grandpa's Day	Dick Joy, news (8:55PM)		
9pm		The Blue Playhouse	Your Hit Parade	Glenn Hardy, news	Young Artist's Contest
9:15				Music	
9:30		Army Service Forces		Faces and Places	
9:45			Don't You Believe It	Songs	Music
10pm		Wings to Victory	The Ten o'Clock Wire	Dr. Polyzoides, health	The Richfield Reporter
10:15			Mitchell Ayres Orchestra	The Victory Auction	The Unseen Enemy
10:30		Freddy Martin Orchestra	The Hollywood Barn Dance		Sammy Kaye Orchestra
10:45					

DAYTIME — WINTER, 1944

Sunday

	ABC	CBS	MBS	NBC
8am	War Job	The West Coast Church	The Wesley Radio League	Rhapsody
8:15				The Book of Books
8:30	The Hour of Faith	Invitation to Learning	The Voice of Prophecy	Waltzes America Loves
8:45				News
9am	News	The Salt Lake Tabernacle Choir	The Detroit Bible Class	Carveth Welles, news
9:15	The Master Radio Canaries	Woman Power		Successful Gardening
9:30	The Music Hour	Transatlantic Call	The Treasury Star Parade	Music
9:45			Health News	
10am	John B. Kennedy, news	The Merry Go Round	Glenn Hardy, news	
10:15	Captain Quiz		Romance of the Highways	
10:30	Toast to Health		Hookey Hall	The University of Chicago Round Table
10:45		Edward R. Murrow, news		
11am	Newsweekly	Ceiling Unlimited	The Pilgrim Hour	Those We Love
11:15	Behind the War News			
11:30	Music	World News Today		The Westinghouse Program, John C. Thomas
11:45	John W. Vandercook, news			
12pm	The Life of Riley	New York Philharmonic Orchestra	Broadway News	Rationing Reports
12:15			Music	Upton Close, news
12:30	Hot Copy		The Children's Chapel	The Army Hour
12:45				
1pm	Fun Valley, Al Pearce		The Lutheran Hour	
1:15				
1:30	The Metropolitan Opera Auditions	The Pause That Refreshes	The Abe Lincoln Story	News Highlights

DAYTIME — WINTER, 1944

Monday-Friday

ABC	CBS	MBS	NBC	
Between the Lines	Collins Calling	Dr. Talbot, health	The Johnny Murray Show	*8am*
News	The Melody Express		News	*8:15*
The Breakfast Club	Kitty Foyle	News	News	*8:30*
	Aunt Jenny's True Life Stories	Victor Lindlahr, health	David Harum	*8:45*
Women Make the News	Kate Smith Speaks	Boake Carter, news	The Gallant Heart	*9am*
News	Big Sister	Time Out	A Woman of America	*9:15*
The Breakfast Club	The Romance of Helen Trent	Music	Across the Threshold	*9:30*
	Our Gal Sunday		Betty and Bob	*9:45*
News	Life Can Be Beautiful	Glenn Hardy, news	Mirth and Madness, Jack Kirkwood	*10am*
Sweet River	Ma Perkins	Talk	Peter de Lima's Closeups	*10:15*
Jay Burnett, news	Bernadine Flynn, news	How Say I	Burritt and Wheeler, talk	*10:30*
Treasury Salute	The Goldbergs	Music	Art Baker's Notebook	*10:45*
H. R. Baukhage, news	Young Dr. Malone	The Changing World	The Guiding Light	*11am*
The Mystery Chef	Joyce Jordan, MD	Pan Americana	Today's Children	*11:15*
Roundup	We Love and Learn	The Rose Room	The Light of the World	*11:30*
News	Linda's First Love		Betty Crocker cooking / Hymns of All Churches	*11:45*
The Coke Club, Morton Downey	Neighbors, Irene Beasley	Broadway News	The Farm Reporter	*12pm*
News	The Open Door	Music	Ma Perkins	*12:15*
Talk and Music	William Winter, news	Talk	Pepper Young's Family	*12:30*
Music	News		The Right to Happiness	*12:45*
Sam Hayes, news	Broadway Matinee	Music	Mary Noble, Backstage Wife	*1pm*
News		Strollin' Tom	Stella Dallas	*1:15*
News and Views	The Standard School of the Air	Music	Lorenzo Jones	*1:30*

DAYTIME — WINTER, 1944

Sunday

	ABC	CBS	MBS	NBC
1:45				News
2pm	Where Do We Stand	The Prudential Family Hour	Shep Fields Orchestra	NBC Symphony Orchestra
2:15				
2:30	The Musical Steelmakers		Music	
2:45		Irene Rich Dramas		
3pm	The Radio Hall of Fame	The Silver Theater	The First Nighter Program	The Catholic Hour
3:15				
3:30		America in the Air	Upton Close, news	Reports from the Battlefield
3:45			The Round Towner	The News Makers
4pm	News	William L. Shirer, news	The Old Fashioned Revival Hour	The Jello Program, Jack Benny
4:15	Church Federation Vespers	Talk		
4:30	Sam Hayes, news	The Whistler		The Fitch Bandwagon
4:45	War News			

DAYTIME — WINTER, 1944

Monday-Friday

ABC	CBS	MBS	NBC	
Rodriguez and Sutherland, news			Young Widder Brown	1:45
What's Doing Ladies	The Story of Mary Marlin	News	When a Girl Marries	2pm
	Pot Luck	Music / The Don Lee Newsreel Theater	Portia Faces Life	2:15
Edward Jorgenson, news	News		Just Plain Bill	2:30
White Elephant	American Women		Front Page Farrell	2:45
News	Talk	Philip Keyne Gordon, news	The Dreft Star Playhouse	3pm
Talk		Music and Talk	The Road of Life	3:15
Ruth Wentworth, talk	Music	News	Vic and Sade	3:30
Ladies Be Seated	The World Today	Bill Hay's Bible Reading	Brave Tomorrow	3:45
My True Story	Music	Fulton Lewis Jr., news	Dr. Kate	4pm
	Sam Hayes, news	The Johnson Family	News	4:15
News	Open House / The American Melody Hour /	Music and Talk	Talk	4:30
War News / Captain Jack	Easy Aces / Mr. Keen, Tracer of Lost Persons		H. V. Kaltenborn, news	4:45

DAYTIME — WINTER, 1944

Saturday

	ABC	CBS	MBS	NBC
8am	Between the Lines	Let's Pretend	The Haven of Rest	Hook 'n' Ladder
8:15	News			
8:30	Talley Time	Fashions in Rations, Billie Burke	News	Lighted Windows
8:45			The Junior Army	
9am	Art Baker's Notebook	The Armstrong Theater of Today	Dr. Matthews, religion	News
9:15	The Miniature Worship Hour			Consumer Time
9:30	The Breakfast Club	Stars Over Hollywood	Hello, Mom	The Pet Parade
9:45				County Medical
10am		Campana Serenade, Dick Powell	Glenn Hardy, news	Here's to Youth
10:15	News		Music	
10:30	Music	Public Affairs		The Baxters
10:45	The Week in Review	Music		War Telescope
11am	The Metropolitan Opera	Mary Lee Taylor, cooking	Music	The Roy Shields Revue
11:15				
11:30		Calling Pan America	Calling	The Grantland Rice Story
11:45				
12pm		Columbia's Country Journey	News	The Farm Reporter
12:15			Music	Piano Recital
12:30		William Winter, news	House Party	On the Scouting Trail
12:45		Talk		
1pm		Report from Washington	Tenpin Topics	Rupert Hughes, news
1:15		Report from London	Horse Racing	The People's War
1:30		The Colonel		Doctors at War
1:45				

DAYTIME — WINTER, 1944

Saturday

	ABC	CBS	MBS	NBC
2pm		Meet Corliss Archer	US Navy Bulletin	Your America
2:15	Horace Heidt's Saturday Revue			
2:30		Mother and Dad	The American Eagle Club	Behind the Headlines
2:45				Public Affairs
3pm	The Korn Kobblers	News	College Choir	
3:15	The Storyland Theater	The People's Platform		I Sustain the Wings
3:30	Andy Russell, news			
3:45	War News	The World Today		Religious News
4pm	What's New	The Man Behind the Gun	The Return of Nick Carter	The Department of State
4:15				
4:30		Bill Hay, talk	Flying High	Noah Webster Says
4:45		Music		

EVENING — SPRING, 1944

Sunday

	ABC	CBS	MBS	NBC
5pm	National Vespers	The Star and the Story	A. L. Alexander's Mediation Board	The Charlie McCarthy Show
5:15				
5:30	Walter Duranty, news	William Winter, news		One Man's Family
5:45	Drew Pearson, news	Dick Joy, news	Gabriel Heatter, news	
6pm	Walter Winchell's Jergans Journal	The Radio Reader's Digest	Cleveland Symphony Orchestra	The Manhattan Merry-Go-Round
6:15	The Chamber Music Society of Lower Basin Street			
6:30		The Texaco Star Theater, Fred Allen		The American Album of Familiar Music
6:45	Jimmy Fidler, gossip			
7pm	The Green Hornet	Take It or Leave It	Cedric Foster, news	The Hour of Charm
7:15			The Goodwill Hour	
7:30	The Weird Circle	The Adventures of the Thin Man		Bob Crosby Orchestra
7:45				
8pm	The Village Chapel	Crime Doctor	California Melodies	The Great Gildersleeve
8:15	Feature Section	Ned Calmer, news (8:25pm)		
8:30	The Quiz Kids	Time to Come	The Jello Program, Jack Benny	The Standard Symphony Hour
8:45				
9pm	Deadline Dramas	I Was There	Glenn Hardy, news	
9:15			Rex Miller, news	
9:30	News	Builders of the West	The Human Adventure	The Skippy Hollywood Theater
9:45	Washington Inside and Out			
10pm	The Two Bells Theater	The Ten o'Clock Wire	The Old Fashioned Revival Hour	The Richfield Reporter
10:15		Talk		The Chapel Quartet
10:30	Uncle Sam Melody	We Deliver the Goods		Inside the News
10:45		Les Brown Orchestra		Labor for Victory

EVENING — SPRING, 1944

Monday

ABC	CBS	MBS	NBC	
Terry and the Pirates	Galen Drake, talk	Frolics (4:45 PM)	OK for Release	5pm
Dick Tracy	Music	The Adventures of Superman	Alvin Wilder, news	5:15
Jack Armstrong, the All-American Boy	Harry W. Flannery, news	World Front Page	The Voice of Firestone	5:30
Captain Midnight	Truman Bradley, news	Gordon Burke, news		5:45
News	The Lux Radio Theater	Gabriel Heatter, news	A Song is Born	6pm
Today in History		The Return of Nick Carter		6:15
Spotlight Bands		Army Air Forces	Information, Please	6:30
War News (6:55 PM)				6:45
Raymond Gram Swing, news	The Lady Esther Screen Guild Theater	Paul Sullivan, news	The Carnation Contented Hour	7pm
Top of the Evening		The People's Reporter		7:15
Horace Heidt for the Servicemen	Blondie	The Lone Ranger	Dr. I. Q., the Mental Banker	7:30
				7:45
Earl Godwin, news	I Love a Mystery	Sherlock Holmes	Chesterfield Time	8pm
Lum and Abner	Ed Sullivan Entertains		Fleetwood Lawton, news	8:15
Counterspy	The Gay Nineties Revue	Point Sublime	The Cavalcade of America	8:30
				8:45
Blind Date	Suspense	Glenn Hardy, news	The Bell Telephone Hour	9pm
		Cecil Brown, news		9:15
Lowell Thomas, news	Vox Pop	Fulton Lewis Jr., news	Hawthorne House	9:30
Feature Section		Public Affairs		9:45
Erskine Johnson, gossip	The Ten o'Clock Wire	Dr. Polyzoides, health	The Richfield Reporter	10pm
The 10-2-4 Ranch	William Winter, news	Dance Orchestra	Manchester Boddy, news	10:15
The Court of Public Opinion	The Symphonette	The Johnson Family	Inside the News	10:30
		Music	The Voice of a Nation	10:45

EVENING — SPRING, 1944

Tuesday

	ABC	CBS	MBS	NBC
5pm	Terry and the Pirates	Galen Drake, talk	John B. Hughes, news	OK for Release
5:15	Dick Tracy	Music	The Adventures of Superman	Alvin Wilder, news
5:30	Jack Armstrong, the All-American Boy	Gordon Burke, news	World Front Page	A Date with Judy
5:45	Captain Midnight	Truman Bradley, news	Gordon Burke, news	
6pm	News	Burns and Allen	Gabriel Heatter, news	The Molle' Mystery Theater
6:15	Today in History		The Return of Nick Carter	
6:30	Spotlight Bands	Report to the Nation	The American Forum of the Air	Fibber McGee and Molly
6:45	War News (6:55 PM)			
7pm	Raymond Gram Swing, news	Columbia Presents Corwin		The Pepsodent Show, Bob Hope
7:15	Top of the Evening		The People's Reporter	
7:30	Red Ryder	The Inglewood Park Concert	The Shadow	The Raleigh Cigarette Program, Red Skelton
7:45				
8pm	Earl Godwin, news	I Love a Mystery	The Pay Day Quiz	Chesterfield Time
8:15	Lum and Abner	The Passing Parade		Fleetwood Lawton, news
8:30	Duffy's Tavern	Big Town	Freedom of Opportunity	The Purple Heart Show, Ginny Simms
8:45				
9pm	Let Yourself Go, Milton Berle	The Colgate Program, Judy Canova	Glenn Hardy, news	Everything for the Boys
9:15			Rex Miller, news	
9:30	Lowell Thomas, news	Edwin C. Hill, news	Fulton Lewis Jr., news	Star Performance
9:45	Feature Section	Deane Dickson, news	Public Affairs	
10pm	Erskine Johnson, gossip	The Ten o'Clock Wire	Music	The Richfield Reporter
10:15	Music	William Winter, news	The Political Editor	Music
10:30	Creeps By Night	Congress Speaks	The Johnson Family	Inside the News
10:45		Songs	Music	The Voice of a Nation

EVENING — SPRING, 1944

Wednesday

ABC	CBS	MBS	NBC	
Terry and the Pirates	Galen Drake, talk	John B. Hughes, news	OK for Release	5pm
Dick Tracy	Music	The Adventures of Superman	News	5:15
Jack Armstrong, the All-American Boy	Harry W. Flannery, news	World Front Page	Alvin Wilder, news	5:30
Captain Midnight	Truman Bradley, news	Gordon Burke, news	Louis Lochner, news	5:45
News	Songs By Sinatra	Gabriel Heatter, news	Time to Smile, Eddie Cantor	6pm
Today in History		The Return of Nick Carter		6:15
Spotlight Bands	The Jack Carson Show	The First Nighter Program	Mr. District Attorney	6:30
War News (6:55pm)				6:45
Raymond Gram Swing, news	Great Moments in Music	John B. Hughes, news	Kay Kyser's College of Musical Knowledge	7pm
Top of the Evening		The People's Reporter		7:15
Soldiers With Wings	The Cresta Blanca Carnival	The Lone Ranger		7:30
				7:45
Earl Godwin, news	I Love a Mystery	The Main Line	Chesterfield Time	8pm
Lum and Abner	The Passing Parade		Fleetwood Lawton, news	8:15
My Best Girls	Dr. Christian	Bulldog Drummond	Beat the Band	8:30
				8:45
Dunninger, the Mentalist	The New Old Gold Program, Allan Jones	Glenn Hardy, news	Mr. and Mrs. North	9pm
		Cecil Brown, news		9:15
Lowell Thomas, news	Orson Welles Radio Almanac	Fulton Lewis Jr., new	Scramby Amby	9:30
Feature Section		Public Affairs		9:45
Erskine Johnson, gossip	The Ten o'Clock Wire	Dr. Polyzoides, health	The Richfield Reporter	10pm
Music	William Winter, news	Music	The Treasury Star Parade	10:15
Public Affairs	The Symphonette	The Johnson Family	Inside the News	10:30
Freddy Martin Orchestra		Music	The Voice of a Nation	10:45

EVENING — SPRING, 1944

Thursday

	ABC	CBS	MBS	NBC
5pm	Terry and the Pirates	Galen Drake, talk	John B. Hughes, news	OK for Release
5:15	Dick Tracy	Music	The Adventures of Superman	News
5:30	Jack Armstrong, the All-American Boy	Harry W. Flannery, news	World Front Page	Alvin Wilder, news
5:45	Captain Midnight	Truman Bradley, news	Gordon Burke, news	Louis Lochner, news
6pm	News	Major Bowes' Original Amateur Hour	Gabriel Heatter, news	The Kraft Music Hall, Bing Crosby
6:15	Today in History		The Return of Nick Carter	
6:30	Spotlight Bands	The Birdseye Open House, Dinah Shore	The Song Hour	The Bob Burns Show
6:45	War News (6:55PM)			
7pm	Raymond Gram Swing, news	The First Line of Defense	Raymond Clapper, news	Abbott and Costello
7:15	Top of the Evening		The People's Reporter	
7:30	Red Ryder	Here's to Romance, Dick Haynes	The Cisco Kid	The March of Time
7:45				
8pm	Earl Godwin, news	I Love a Mystery	Pick and Pat Time	Chesterfield Time
8:15	Lum and Abner	The Passing Parade		The Night Editor
8:30	This is My Country	Death Valley Days	A Date with Cugat	Maxwell House Coffee Time, Brice and Morgan
8:45				
9pm	The Joe E. Brown Show	Three of a Kind	Glenn Hardy, news	The Aldrich Familiy
9:15			Rex Miller, news	
9:30	Lowell Thomas, news	The Citizens Forum	Fulton Lewis Jr., news	The Adventures of Ellery Queen
9:45	Feature Secton		Public Affairs	
10pm	Erskine Johnson, gossip	The Ten o'Clock Wire	Wings Over the West Coast	The Richfield Reporter
10:15	Music	William Winter, news		Mayor Bowron, comment
10:30	America's Town Meeting of the Air	The Rangers	The Johnson Family	Inside the News
10:45		Organ Recital	Music	The Voice of a Nation

EVENING — SPRING, 1944

Friday

ABC	CBS	MBS	NBC	
Terry and the Pirates	Galen Drake, talk	John B. Hughes, news	OK for Release	5pm
Dick Tracy	Music	The Adventures of Superman	News	5:15
Jack Armstrong, the All-American Boy	Harry W. Flannery, news	World Front Page	Alvin Wilder, news	5:30
Captain Midnight	Truman Bradley, news	Gordon Burke, news	Louis Lochner, news	5:45
News	The Hollywood Showcase	Gabriel Heatter, news	Waltz Time	6pm
Today in History		The Return of Nick Carter		6:15
Spotlight Bands	That Brewster Boy	Double or Nothing	People Are Funny	6:30
War News (6:55PM)				6:45
Hoffman and Garretson, news	The Durante - Moore Show	Dale Carnegie, comment	Amos 'n' Andy	7pm
Top of the Evening		The People's Reporter		7:15
The Adventures of Nero Wolfe	Stage Door Canteen	The Lone Ranger	The Colgate Sports Newsreel, Bill Stern	7:30
			Cabbages and Kings	7:45
Earl Godwin, news	I Love a Mystery	The Quiz of Two Cities	Chesterfield Time	8pm
The Parker Family	The Press Club		Fleetwood Lawton, news	8:15
Gangbusters	The Phillip Morris Playhouse	What is the Name of that Song	Your All-Time Hit Parade	8:30
				8:45
Meet Your Navy	The Kate Smith Hour	Glenn Hardy, news	Furlough Fun	9pm
		Cecil Brown, news		9:15
Lowell Thomas, news		Fulton Lewis Jr., news	The Sealtest Village Store, Davis and Haley	9:30
Feature Section		Public Affairs		9:45
Erskine Johnson, gossip	The Ten o'Clock Wire	San Quentin on the Air	The Richfield Reporter	10pm
Music	William Winter, news		Manchester Boddy, news	10:15
Your OPA	The Symphonette	The Johnson Family	Inside the News	10:30
Freddy Martin Orchestra		Public Affairs	The Voice of a Nation	10:45

EVENING — SPRING, 1944

Saturday

	ABC	CBS	MBS	NBC
5pm	William Parker, news	Pabst Blue Ribbon Town, Groucho Marx	News	The Good Old Days
5:15	Serenade		Between the Lines	News
5:30	Boston Symphony Orchestra	Harry W. Flannery, news	Mark Twain	Traffic Tribunal
5:45		News	Gordon Burke, news	Louis Lochner, news
6pm		Mark Twain	The Chicago Theater of the Air	The National Barn Dance
6:15	Music	Public Affairs		
6:30	Spotlight Bands	The Eleanor King Show	London Column	Can You Top This
6:45		Saturday Night Serenade		
7pm			Jobs for Heroes	Palmolive Party, Barry Wood and Patsy Kelly
7:15	News	The Mayor of the Town		
7:30	Red Ryder		Hawaii Calls	Grand Ole Opry
7:45		The Storyteller		
8pm	Early American Dance Music	Thanks to the Yanks	Downbeat Derby	Truth or Consequences
8:15	Danny Shane, news			
8:30	Club of Good Cheer	Inner Sanctum Mysteries	The Clinic Forum	Abie's Irish Rose
8:45		Dick Joy, news (8:55PM)		
9pm	Ray W. Smith, news	Your Hit Parade	Glenn Hardy, news	Young Artist's Contest
9:15	News		Leo Diamond Orchestra	
9:30	Grandpa's Day		Organ Recital	
9:45	An Ounce of Prevention	Don't You Believe It	Songs	Music
10pm	News	The Ten o'Clock Wire	Dr. Polyzoides, health	The Richfield Reporter
10:15	Public Affairs	Music	Music	The Unseen Enemy
10:30	Freddy Martin Orchestra	The Hollywood Barn Dance	Gus Arnheim Orchestra	Dance Orchestra
10:45				

DAYTIME — SPRING, 1944

Sunday

	ABC	CBS	MBS	NBC
8am	War Job	The West Coast Church	The Wesley Radio League	Rhapsody
8:15				The Book of Books
8:30	The Hour of Faith	Invitation to Learning	The Voice of Prophecy	Waltzes America Loves
8:45				News
9am	News	The Salt Lake Tabernacle Choir	The Detroit Bible Class	Carveth Welles, news
9:15	The Master Radio Canaries	Woman Power		Public Affairs
9:30	The Music Hour	Transatlantic Call	Music	Music
9:45				
10am	John B. Kennedy, news	The Merry Go Round	Glenn Hardy, news	News and Views
10:15	Music		Commander Scott	Serenade
10:30	Toast to Health		Hookey Hall	The University of Chicago Round Table
10:45		Edward R. Murrow, news		
11am	Newsweekly	Ceiling Unlimited	The Pilgrim Hour	Those We Love
11:15	Behind the War News			
11:30	The Remember Hour	World News Today		The Westinghouse Program, John C. Thomas
11:45				
12pm	The Life of Riley	New York Philharmonic Orchestra	Broadway News	World News
12:15			Music	
12:30	Hot Copy		Quizvents	The Army Hour
12:45				
1pm	Fun Valley, Al Pearce		Wide Horizons	
1:15				
1:30	The World of Song	The Pause That Refreshes	The Abe Lincoln Story	News Highlights

DAYTIME — SPRING, 1944

Monday-Friday

ABC	CBS	MBS	NBC	
Between the Lines	The Mark Brenneman Show	Dr. Talbot, health	The Johnny Murray Show	8am
News	The Melody Express		T.B. Blackiston, news	8:15
The Breakfast Club	Kitty Foyle	News	News	8:30
	Aunt Jenny's True Life Stories	Victor Lindlahr, health	David Harum	8:45
Women Make the News	Kate Smith Speaks	Boake Carter, news	News	9am
News	Big Sister	Time Out	A Woman of America	9:15
The Breakfast Club	The Romance of Helen Trent	Music	Major Turner, comment	9:30
	Our Gal Sunday		Peter de Lima's Closeups	9:45
News	Life Can Be Beautiful	Glenn Hardy, news	Larry Smith, news	10am
Sweet River	Ma Perkins	The Jack Berch Show	Burritt and Wheeler, talk	10:15
My True Story	Bernadine Flynn, news	Luncheon with Lopez	Aunt Mary	10:30
	The Goldbergs		Art Baker's Notebook	10:45
H. R. Baukhage, news	Portia Faces Life	The Changing World	The Guiding Light	11am
The Mystery Chef	Joyce Jordan, MD	Music	Today's Children	11:15
Music	Young Dr. Malone		The Light of the World	11:30
News	Perry Mason	Around Town	Betty Crocker, cooking / Hymns of All Churches	11:45
The Coke Club, Morton Downey	The Story of Mary Marlin	Broadway News	The Farm Reporter	12pm
Hollywood Star Time	Neighbors, Irene Beasley	The Johnson Family	Ma Perkins	12:15
Talk and Music	Bright Horizon	Talk	Pepper Young's Family	12:30
Music	News		The Right to Happiness	12:45
Sam Hayes, news	Broadway Matinee		Mary Noble, Backstage Wife	1pm
News			Stella Dallas	1:15
News	The Standard School of the Air	Music	Lorenzo Jones	1:30

DAYTIME — SPRING, 1944

Sunday

	ABC	CBS	MBS	NBC
1:45				News
2pm	Mary Small's Revue	The Prudential Family Hour	Green Valley, USA	NBC Symphony Orchestra
2:15			Jimmy Dorsey Orchestra	
2:30	The Musical Steelmakers			
2:45		Irene Rich Dramas		
3pm	The Radio Hall of Fame	The Silver Theater	Roosty of the AAF	The Catholic Hour
3:15				
3:30		America in the Air	Upton Close, news	Mark Twain
3:45			Music	Reports from the Battlefield
4pm	News	William L. Shirer, news	The Old Fashioned Revival Hour	The Jello Program, Jack Benny
4:15	Church Federation Vespers	Letters from the Servicemen		
4:30	Sam Hayes, news	The Whistler		The Fitch Bandwagon
4:45	Dorothy Thompson, news			

DAYTIME — SPRING, 1944

Monday-Friday

ABC	CBS	MBS	NBC	
Rodriguez and Sutherland, news			Young Widder Brown	1:45
What's Doing Ladies	The Open Door	News	When a Girl Marries	2pm
	Pot Luck	Music / The Don Lee Newsreel Theater	We Love and Learn	2:15
Edward Jorgenson, news	News		Just Plain Bill	2:30
The Frances Scully Show	American Women	The Radio Tour	Front Page Farrell	2:45
News	Talk	Philip Keyne Gordon, news	The Dreft Star Playhouse	3pm
Talk		E. H. Wileman, news	The Road of Life	3:15
News and Views	Music	Talk	Vic and Sade	3:30
Jay Burnett, news	The World Today	Bill Hay's Bible Reading	Brave Tomorrow	3:45
News	Music	Fulton Lewis Jr., news	Dr. Kate	4pm
Ruth Wentworth, talk	Sam Hayes, news	Polly and Trudy, songs	News	4:15
Talk / Andy and Virginia, songs	Open House / The American Melody Hour /	Lullaby	Talk	4:30
Twilight Tales / Captain Jack	Easy Aces / Mr. Keen, Tracer of Lost Persons	Music / Frolics	H. V. Kaltenborn, news	4:45

DAYTIME — SPRING, 1944

Saturday

	ABC	CBS	MBS	NBC
8am	Between the Lines	Let's Pretend	The Haven of Rest	Hook 'n' Ladder
8:15	News			
8:30	Talley Time	Fashions in Rations, Billie Burke	News	Lighted Windows
8:45			The Junior Army	
9am	Art Baker's Notebook	The Armstrong Theater of Today	Dr. Matthews, religion	News
9:15	The Miniature Worship Hour			Consumer Time
9:30	The Breakfast Club	Stars Over Hollywood	Hello, Mom	The Pet Parade
9:45				County Medical
10am		Grand Central Station	Glenn Hardy, news	Here's to Youth
10:15	News		Health Talk	
10:30	Serenade	Music	Music	The Baxters
10:45	The Week in Review			War Telescope
11am	The Metropolitan Opera	Mary Lee Taylor, cooking	The Clinic Forum	Here Comes the Band
11:15				
11:30		Calling Pan America	Music	On the Scouting Trail
11:45			Service Unlimited	
12pm		Columbia's Country Journey	News	The Farm Reporter
12:15			Music	The Treasury Star Parade
12:30		Philadelphia Symphony Orchestra	Bundy's Carnival	Smilin' Ed's Buster Brown Gang
12:45				
1pm			Public Affairs	Horse Racing
1:15			Horse Racing	Rupert Hughes, news
1:30		The Colonel		Doctors at War
1:45			Music	

DAYTIME — SPRING, 1944

Saturday

	ABC	CBS	MBS	NBC
2pm		Meet Corliss Archer	US Navy Bulletin	Your America
2:15	Horace Heidt's Saturday Revue			
2:30		Mother and Dad	Tommy Dorsey Orchestra	Behind the Headlines
2:45				Public Affairs
3pm	Music	News	College Choir	
3:15	Hello Sweetheart, Nancy Martin	The People's Platform	Organ Recital	I Sustain the Wings
3:30	Bible Message			
3:45	Leon Henderson, news	The World Today		Religion in the News
4pm	The American Eagle Club	Victory F. O. B.	The American Eagle Club	The American Story
4:15	War News			
4:30	Music	Bill Hay, talk	Flying High	Now is the Time
4:45		Music		

EVENING — SUMMER, 1944

Sunday

	ABC	CBS	MBS	NBC
5pm	National Vespers	The Star and the Story	A. L. Alexander's Mediation Board	The Gracie Fields Show
5:15				
5:30	Walter Duranty, news	William Winter, news		One Man's Family
5:45	Drew Pearson, news	Dick Joy, news	Gabriel Heatter, news	
6pm	Walter Winchell's Jergans Journal	The Radio Reader's Digest	Leonidas Witherall	The Manhattan Merry-Go-Round
6:15	The Chamber Music Society of Lower Basin Street			
6:30		The Texaco Star Theater, James Melton	California Melodies	The American Album of Familiar Music
6:45	Jimmy Fidler, gossip			
7pm	The Life of Riley	Take It or Leave It	Cedric Foster, news	The Hour of Charm
7:15			The Goodwill Hour	
7:30	The Green Hornet	The Whistler		The Jackie Gleason - Les Tremayne Show
7:45				
8pm	The Village Chapel	Crime Doctor	Worship Music	News
8:15	Hoffman and Garretson, news	Ned Calmer, news (8:25PM)		Behind the Headlines
8:30	The Quiz Kids	Romance of the Ranchos	The Sky Riders	The Standard Symphony Hour
8:45				
9pm	Deadline Dramas	I Was There	Glenn Hardy, news	
9:15			Rex Miller, news	
9:30	News	The Adventures of Bill Lance	The Human Adventure	The Skippy Hollywood Theater
9:45	Washington Inside and Out			
10pm	The Two Bells Theater	The Ten o'Clock Wire	The Old Fashioned Revival Hour	The Richfield Reporter
10:15		Letters from the Servicemen		The Chapel Quartet
10:30	News	We Deliver the Goods		Inside the News
10:45	Feature Section			Treasury Salute

EVENING — SUMMER, 1944

Monday

ABC	CBS	MBS	NBC	
Terry and the Pirates	Galen Drake, talk	News	OK for Release	5pm
Dick Tracy	Music	The Adventures of Superman	Alvin Wilder, news	5:15
Jack Armstrong, the All-American Boy	Harry W. Flannery, news	Tom Mix and His Ralston Straight Shooters	The Voice of Firestone	5:30
The Korn Kobblers	Truman Bradley, news	Gordon Burke, news		5:45
News	The Mayor of the Town	Gabriel Heatter, news	A Song is Born	6pm
Peter de Lima, news		Screen Test		6:15
Spotlight Bands	The Man Called X	Army Air Forces	Vacation Serenade	6:30
War News (6:55PM)				6:45
Raymond Gram Swing, news	The Lady Esther Screen Guild Theater	Paul Sullivan, news	The Carnation Contented Hour	7pm
Ted Malone from England		Lowell Thomas, news		7:15
Horace Heidt for the Servicemen	Thanks to the Yanks	The Lone Ranger	Dr. I. Q., the Mental Banker	7:30
				7:45
Earl Godwin, news	I Love a Mystery	Sherlock Holmes	Johnny Mercer's Music Shop	8pm
Lum and Abner	Dateline		Fleetwood Lawton, news	8:15
Counterspy	The Gay Nineties Revue	Point Sublime	The Cavalcade of America	8:30
				8:45
Blind Date	Suspense	Glenn Hardy, news	The Bell Telephone Hour	9pm
		Cecil Brown, news		9:15
News	Vox Pop	Fulton Lewis Jr., news	Hawthorne House	9:30
News		The Return of Nick Carter		9:45
Erskine Johnson, gossip	The Ten o'Clock Wire	Music	The Richfield Reporter	10pm
The 10-2-4 Ranch	Harry W. Flannery, news		Manchester Boddy, news	10:15
The Court of Public Opinion	Sports Review	The Johnson Family	Inside the News	10:30
	Organ Recital	Music	Music	10:45

EVENING — SUMMER, 1944

Tuesday

	ABC	CBS	MBS	NBC
5pm	Terry and the Pirates	Galen Drake, talk	John B. Hughes, news	OK for Release
5:15	Dick Tracy	Music	The Adventures of Superman	Alvin Wilder, news
5:30	Jack Armstrong, the All-American Boy	Gordon Burke, news	Tom Mix and His Ralston Straight Shooters	A Date with Judy
5:45	The Korn Kobblers	Truman Bradley, news	Gordon Burke, news	
6pm	News	The Jack Pepper Show	Gabriel Heatter, news	The Molle' Mystery Theater
6:15	Peter de Lima, news		Screen Test	
6:30	Spotlight Bands	The Doctor Fights	The American Forum of the Air	Words at War
6:45	War News (6:55PM)			
7pm	Raymond Gram Swing, news	Columbia Presents Corwin		The Charlotte Greenwood Show
7:15	News		Lowell Thomas, news	
7:30	Red Ryder	The Inglewood Park Concert	The Shadow	The Raleigh Room, Hildegarde
7:45				
8pm	Earl Godwin, news	I Love a Mystery	The Pay Day Quiz	Johnny Mercer's Music Shop
8:15	Lum and Abner	The Passing Parade		Fleetwood Lawton, news
8:30	Nit-Wit Court	Big Town	Freedom of Opportunity	The Purple Heart Show, Ginny Simms
8:45				
9pm	Let Yourself Go, Milton Berle	Theater of Romance	Glenn Hardy, news	Everything for the Boys, Dick Haymes
9:15			Rex Miller, news	
9:30	News	Edwin C. Hill, news	Fulton Lewis Jr., news	The Adventures of Radio
9:45	Preview Parade	Life Tapestries	The Return of Nick Carter	
10pm	Erskine Johnson, gossip	The Ten o'Clock Wire	Music	The Richfield Reporter
10:15	Music	Harry W. Flannery, news		Music
10:30	Creeps By Night	Treasury Salute	The Johnson Family	Inside the News
10:45		Organ Recital	Music	Music

EVENING — SUMMER, 1944

Wednesday

ABC	CBS	MBS	NBC	
Terry and the Pirates	Galen Drake, talk	John B. Hughes, news	OK for Release	5pm
Dick Tracy	Music	The Adventures of Superman	News	5:15
Jack Armstrong, the All-American Boy	Harry W. Flannery, news	Tom Mix and His Ralston Straight Shooters	Alvin Wilder, news	5:30
The Korn Kobblers	Truman Bradley, news	Gordon Burke, news	Louis Lochner, news	5:45
News	The Jack Carson Show	Gabriel Heatter, news	The Alan Young Show	6pm
Peter de Lima, news		The Return of Nick Carter		6:15
Spotlight Bands	The Mildred Bailey Show	The First Nighter Program	Mr. District Attorney	6:30
War News (6:55pm)				6:45
Raymond Gram Swing, news	Great Moments in Music	John B. Hughes, news	Kay Kyser's College of Musical Knowledge	7pm
Ted Malone from London		Lowell Thomas, news		7:15
This is My Country	Report to the Nation	The Lone Ranger		7:30
				7:45
Earl Godwin, news	I Love a Mystery	The Main Line	Johnny Mercer's Music Shop	8pm
Lum and Abner	The Passing Parade		Fleetwood Lawton, news	8:15
My Best Girls	Dr. Christian	Bulldog Drummond	Beat the Band	8:30
				8:45
Dunninger, the Mentalist	The New Old Gold Program, Allan Jones	Glenn Hardy, news	Mr. and Mrs. North	9pm
		Cecil Brown, news		9:15
News	Orson Welles Radio Almanac	Fulton Lewis Jr., news	Scramby Amby	9:30
Preview Parade		Organ Recital		9:45
Erskine Johnson, gossip	The Ten o'Clock Wire	Music	The Richfield Reporter	10pm
Music	William Winter, news		KFEyewitness	10:15
Freddy Martin Orchestra	Sports Review	The Johnson Family	Inside the News	10:30
	Organ Recital	Music	Music	10:45

EVENING — SUMMER, 1944

Thursday

	ABC	CBS	MBS	NBC
5pm	Terry and the Pirates	Galen Drake, talk	John B. Hughes, news	OK for Release
5:15	Dick Tracy	Music	The Adventures of Superman	News
5:30	Jack Armstrong, the All-American Boy	Harry W. Flannery, news	Tom Mix and His Ralston Straight Shooters	Alvin Wilder, news
5:45	The Korn Kobblers	Truman Bradley, news	Gordon Burke, news	Louis Lochner, news
6pm	News	Major Bowes' Original Amateur Hour	Gabriel Heatter, news	The Kraft Music Hall, Bing Crosby
6:15	Peter de Lima, news		Screen Test	
6:30	Spotlight Bands	Meet Corliss Archer	Starlight Serenade	Charlie Chan
6:45	War News (6:55pm)			
7pm	Raymond Gram Swing, news	The First Line of Defense	Raymond Clapper, news	Harry Savoy Orchestra
7:15	News		Lowell Thomas, news	
7:30	Red Ryder	Here's to Romance, Dick Haynes	The Cisco Kid	By Request
7:45				
8pm	Earl Godwin, news	I Love a Mystery	Pick and Pat Time	Johnny Mercer's Music Shop
8:15	Lum and Abner	The Passing Parade		The Night Editor
8:30	Club of Good Cheer	Death Valley Days	A Date with Cugat	Those We Love
8:45				
9pm	The Joe E. Brown Show	Mystery Time	Glenn Hardy, news	News
9:15			Rex Miller, news	Music
9:30	News	The Citizen's Forum	Fulton Lewis Jr., news	The Adventures of Ellery Queen
9:45	News		The Return of Nick Carter	
10pm	Erskine Johnson, gossip	The Ten o'Clock Wire	Wings Over the West Coast	The Richfield Reporter
10:15	Music	Harry W. Flannery, news		Mayor Bowron, comment
10:30	America's Town Meeting of the Air	Riders of the Purple Sage	The Johnson Family	Inside the News
10:45		Organ Recital	Music	Music

EVENING — SUMMER, 1944

Friday

ABC	CBS	MBS	NBC	
Terry and the Pirates	Galen Drake, talk	John B. Hughes, news	OK for Release	5pm
Dick Tracy	Music	The Adventures of Superman	News	5:15
Jack Armstrong, the All-American Boy	Harry W. Flannery, news	Tom Mix and His Ralston Straight Shooters	Alvin Wilder, news	5:30
The Korn Kobblers	Truman Bradley, news	Gordon Burke, news	Louis Lochner, news	5:45
News	The Hollywood Showcase	Gabriel Heatter, news	Waltz Time	6pm
Peter de Lima, news		Screen Test		6:15
Spotlight Bands	That Brewster Boy	Double or Nothing	People Are Funny	6:30
War News (6:55 PM)				6:45
Earl Godwin, news	The Durante - Moore Show	Tiny Ruffner, comment	Boston Blackie	7pm
Ted Malone from London		Lowell Thomas, news		7:15
The Adventures of Nero Wolfe	Stage Door Canteen	The Lone Ranger	H. V. Kaltenborn, news	7:30
			Cabbages and Kings	7:45
Earl Godwin, news	I Love a Mystery	The Quiz of Two Cities	Johnny Mercer's Music Shop	8pm
The Parker Family	The Press Club		Fleetwood Lawton, news	8:15
Gangbusters	It Pays to Be Ignorant	What is the Name of that Song	The Adventures of the Thin Man	8:30
				8:45
Meet Your Navy	Maxwell House Coffee Time, Charlie Ruggles	Glenn Hardy, news	Furlough Fun	9pm
		Cecil Brown, news		9:15
News	Service to the Front	Fulton Lewis Jr., news	The Sealtest Village Store, Davis and Haley	9:30
Preview Parade		The Return of Nick Carter		9:45
Erskine Johnson, gossip	The Ten o'Clock Wire	San Quentin on the Air	The Richfield Reporter	10pm
The 10-2-4 Ranch	William Winter, news		Manchester Boddy, news	10:15
Your OPA	Sports Review	The Johnson Family	Inside the News	10:30
Freddy Martin Orchestra	Organ Recital	Music	Music	10:45

EVENING — SUMMER, 1944

Saturday

	ABC	CBS	MBS	NBC
5pm	William Parker, news	The Kenny Baker Program	News	The Good Old Days
5:15	News		Easy Listening	News
5:30	Boston Symphony Orchestra	Harry W. Flannery, news	Music	Traffic Tribunal
5:45		News	Gordon Burke, news	Louis Lochner, news
6pm		This is My Story	The Chicago Theater of the Air	The National Barn Dance
6:15				
6:30	Spotlight Bands	Ona Munson, comment	London Column	Can You Top This
6:45	War News (6:55 PM)	Saturday Night Serenade		
7pm	Guy Lombardo Orchestra		News and Views	Palmolive Party, Barry Wood and Patsy Kelly
7:15	News	Money on the Line		
7:30	Red Ryder		Music	Grand Ole Opry
7:45		The Storyteller		
8pm	Early American Dance Music	Job for Heroes	Downbeat Derby	News
8:15		Music		John W. Vandercook, news
8:30	Leland Stowe, news	Inner Sanctum Mysteries	The Clinic Forum	Abie's Irish Rose
8:45	News	Dick Joy, news (8:55 PM)		
9pm	Music	Your Hit Parade	Glenn Hardy, news	Young Artist's Contest
9:15			Leo Diamond Orchestra	
9:30	Grandpa's Day			
9:45	The Denny Shane Show	Don't You Believe It	Songs	Music
10pm	News	The Ten o'Clock Wire	Music	BBC Calling
10:15	Soldiers of the Press	Music		The Unseen Enemy
10:30	Freddy Martin Orchestra			News
10:45				Music

DAYTIME — SUMMER, 1944

Sunday

	ABC	CBS	MBS	NBC
8am	AAF Symphonic Flight	The West Coast Church	The Wesley Radio League	Rhapsody of the Rockies
8:15				The Book of Books
8:30	The Hour of Faith	News	The Voice of Prophecy	Waltzes America Loves
8:45		Music		News
9am	News	The Salt Lake Tabernacle Choir	The Detroit Bible Class	Carveth Welles, news
9:15	Treasury Salute	Woman Power		Successful Gardening
9:30	The Music Hour	Transatlantic Call	Music	Music
9:45				
10am	John B. Kennedy, news	The Merry Go Round	Glenn Hardy, news	News and Views
10:15	Ben Sweetland, stories		Commander Scott	
10:30	Sammy Kaye's Sunday Serenade		Hookey Hall	The University of Chicago Round Table
10:45		Edward R. Murrow, news		
11am	Newsweekly	Dangerously Yours	Music	Music
11:15	Behind the War News			
11:30	The Remember Hour	World News Today		The Lee Sweetland Show
11:45				
12pm	Listen, the Women	New York Philharmonic Orchestra	Broadway News	World News
12:15			Music	
12:30	Rex Maupin Orchestra		The Northwest Reviewing Stand	The Army Hour
12:45				
1pm	Fun Valley, Al Pearce		Music	
1:15				
1:30	The World of Song	The Pause That Refreshes	Roosty of the AAF	News Highlights

LISTINGS FOR 1944

DAYTIME — SUMMER, 1944

Monday-Friday

ABC	CBS	MBS	NBC	
Between the Lines	The Mark Brenneman Show	The Shady Valley Folks	The Johnny Murray Show	8am
News	Valiant Lady		T.B. Blackiston, news	8:15
The Breakfast Club	The Light of the World	News	News	8:30
	Aunt Jenny's True Life Stories	Victor Lindlahr, health	David Harum	8:45
Glamour Manor, Cliff Arquette	Kate Smith Speaks	Boake Carter, news	News	9am
	Big Sister	Time Out	Larry Smith, news	9:15
The Breakfast Club	The Romance of Helen Trent	Midland, USA	Major Turner, comment	9:30
	Our Gal Sunday	The Amazing Jennifer Logan	Music	9:45
News	Life Can Be Beautiful	Glenn Hardy, news	The Voice of a Nation	10am
Robert L. Johnson, news	Ma Perkins	The Jack Berch Show	Peter de Lima's Closeups	10:15
My True Story	Bernadine Flynn, news	Luncheon with Lopez	Aunt Mary	10:30
	The Goldbergs		Art Baker's Notebook	10:45
H. R. Baukhage, news	Portia Faces Life	Cedric Foster, news	The Guiding Light	11am
The Mystery Chef	Joyce Jordan, MD	Music	Today's Children	11:15
Music	Young Dr. Malone	Jane Cowl, talk	The Woman in White	11:30
News	Perry Mason	Around Town	Betty Crocker. cooking / Hymns of All Churches	11:45
The Coke Club, Morton Downey	The Story of Mary Marlin	Broadway News	The Farm Reporter	12pm
Hollywood Star Time	Neighbors, Irene Beasley	The Johnson Family	Ma Perkins	12:15
Talk and Music	Bright Horizon	Music	Pepper Young's Family	12:30
Music	Bachelor's Children		The Right to Happiness	12:45
World Wide Review	Broadway Matinee		Mary Noble, Backstage Wife	1pm
The Radio Parade			Stella Dallas	1:15
Times Views the News	The Music Library	Music	Lorenzo Jones	1:30

393

DAYTIME — SUMMER, 1944

Sunday

	ABC	CBS	MBS	NBC
1:45				Sam Balter, sports
2pm	Mary Small's Revue	The Prudential Family Hour	Green Valley, USA	NBC Symphony Orchestra
2:15			Jimmy Dorsey Orchestra	
2:30	Hot Copy			
2:45		Irene Rich Dramas		
3pm	The Philco Summer Hour	The Silver Theater	Quick as a Flash	The Catholic Hour
3:15				
3:30		America in the Air	Upton Close, news	News
3:45			Music	Reports from the Battlefield
4pm	News	Invasion News		Your All-Time Hit Parade
4:15	Church Federation Vespers			
4:30	Ray W. Smith, news	Nelson Pringle, news		The Fitch Bandwagon
4:45	What Happened This Week	Talk		

DAYTIME — SUMMER, 1944

Monday-Friday

ABC	CBS	MBS	NBC	
The Blue Newsroom Review			Young Widder Brown	1:45
What's Doing Ladies	Potluck Party	This Changing World	When a Girl Marries	2pm
	Music	Today on the Coast	We Love and Learn	2:15
Edward Jorgenson, news	News		Just Plain Bill	2:30
The Frances Scully Show	Wilderness Road	The Radio Tour	Front Page Farrell	2:45
News	Talk	Philip Keyne Gordon, news	The Road of Life	3pm
Music		Music	The Dreft Star Playhouse	3:15
Ruth Wentworth, talk	Music	Talk	Vic and Sade	3:30
Jay Burnett, news	The World Today	Bill Hay's Bible Reading	A Woman of America	3:45
News	Lady of the Press	Fulton Lewis Jr., news	Dr. Kate	4pm
General Junius Pierce, comment	Music	The Merry Moons	News	4:15
Talk / Andy and Virginia, songs	Open House / The American Melody Hour /	World Front Page	Talk	4:30
Twilight Tales / Captain Jack	Easy Aces / Mr. Keen, Tracer of Lost Persons	Frolics		4:45

DAYTIME — SUMMER, 1944

Saturday

	ABC	CBS	MBS	NBC
8am	Between the Lines	Let's Pretend	Rainbow House	The US Army Band
8:15	News			
8:30	Talley Time	Fashions in Rations, Billie Burke	News	Melody Round-Up
8:45			The Junior Army	
9am	Fannie Hurst Presents	The Armstrong Theater of Today	Dr. Matthews, religion	News
9:15	The Miniature Worship Hour			Consumer Time
9:30	The Breakfast Club	Stars Over Hollywood	Hello, Mom	News
9:45				County Medical
10am		Grand Central Station	Glenn Hardy, news	Here's to Youth
10:15	Collins Calling		Health Talk	Music
10:30	News	Music	Music	Indiana Indigo
10:45	The Week in Review			War Telescope
11am	Women in Blue	Mary Lee Taylor, cooking	The Clinic Forum	Here Comes the Band
11:15				
11:30	News	Calling Pan America	Music	The Grantland Rice Story
11:45	The Worship Hour		Service Unlimited	
12pm	News	Columbia's Country Journey	News	The Farm Reporter
12:15	Diamond Dramas		The Eagle Speaks	Minstrel Melodies
12:30	Music	The Visiting Hour	Music	Music
12:45				
1pm	Horace Heidt's Saturday Revue	The Colonel		Rupert Hughes, news
1:15		Horse Racing	Horse Racing	Horse Racing
1:30	On Stage Everybody			
1:45		Report from London		

DAYTIME — SUMMER, 1944

Saturday

	ABC	CBS	MBS	NBC
2pm	News	Casey, Press Photographer	News	Your America
2:15	Music		Navy Bulletin	
2:30		Mother and Dad	Music	Music
2:45	Hello Sweetheart, Nancy Martin			
3pm	The Summer Hour	Quincy Howe, news		Vegatables for Victory
3:15		The People's Platform	The Novelaires	I Sustain the Wings
3:30	Sports		Hawaii Calls	Curt Massey, songs
3:45		The World Today		The Art of Living
4pm	The American Eagle Club	Victory F. O. B.	The American Eagle Club	The American Story
4:15	War News			
4:30	Music	Wave Recruiting Program	Flying High	Noah Webster Says
4:45		Music		

EVENING — FALL, 1944

Sunday

	ABC	CBS	MBS	NBC
5pm	Music	News and Views	A. L. Alexander's Mediation Board	The Charlie McCarthy Show
5:15				
5:30	Monday Headlines	Sunset Inn		One Man's Family
5:45	Drew Pearson, news	Bob Trout, news (8:55PM)	Gabriel Heatter, news	
6pm	Walter Winchell's Jergens Journal	The Radio Reader's Digest	Steel Horizons	The Manhattan Merry-Go-Round
6:15	Hollywood Mystery Time			
6:30		The Texaco Star Theater, James Melton	Cedric Foster, news	The American Album of Familiar Music
6:45	Jimmy Fidler, gossip		The Columbus Boy's Choir	
7pm	The Life of Riley	Take It or Leave It	The Goodwill Hour	The Hour of Charm
7:15				
7:30	Keep Up With the World	The Baby Snooks Show		The Old Gold Comedy Theater of the Air
7:45				
8pm	The Greenfield Village Choir	Crime Doctor	California Melodies	The Great Gildersleeve
8:15	Dorothy Thompson, news	Songs (8:25PM)		
8:30	The Quiz Kids	Blondie	Tonight at Hoagy's	The Standard Symphony Hour
8:45				
9pm	The Green Hornet	The Adventures of Bill Lance	Glenn Hardy, news	
9:15			Rex Miller, news	
9:30	News	Romance of the Ranchos	The Human Adventure	The Lucky Strike Program, Jack Benny
9:45	Washington Inside and Out			
10pm	Soldiers of the Press	The Ten o'Clock Wire	Roosty of the AAF	The Richfield Reporter
10:15	The Blue Preview	Talk		The Chapel Quartet
10:30	News	We Deliver the Goods	News and Views	Inside the News
10:45	The Weekend Feature Section			Gems of Melody

EVENING — FALL, 1944

Monday

ABC	CBS	MBS	NBC	
Terry and the Pirates	Burritt and Wheeler, talk	Broadway News	OK for Release	5pm
Dick Tracy	Music	The Adventures of Superman	News	5:15
Jack Armstrong, the All-American Boy	Harry W. Flannery, news	Tom Mix and His Ralston Straightshooters	The Voice of Firestone	5:30
Captain Midnight	Truman Bradley, news	The Nightly News Wire		5:45
News	The Lux Radio Theater	Gabriel Heatter, news	A Song is Born	6pm
Peter de Lima, news		Screen Test		6:15
Spotlight Bands		Public Affairs	Information, Please	6:30
Short Story (6:55PM)				6:45
Raymond Gram Swing, news	The Lady Esther Screen Guild Theater	Henry Gladstone, news	The Carnation Contented Hour	7pm
Ted Malone from England		Lowell Thomas, news		7:15
Horace Heidt for the Servicemen	The Bob Hawk Show	The Lone Ranger	Dr. I. Q., the Mental Banker	7:30
				7:45
Earl Godwin, news	I Love A Mystery	Sherlock Holmes	The Chesterfield Music Shop	8pm
Lum and Abner	Hedda Hopper's Hollywood		Roy Maypole, news	8:15
Counterspy	The Gay Nineties Revue	Michael Shayne, Private Detective	The Cavalcade of America	8:30
				8:45
Blind Date	The Whistler	Glenn Hardy, news	The Bell Telephone Hour	9pm
		Cecil Brown, news		9:15
Rodriguez and Sutherland, news	Vox Pop	Fulton Lewis Jr., news	Noah Webster Says	9:30
War Chest		Sunny Skylar, songs		9:45
George Fisher, gossip	The Ten o'Clock Wire	The Right to Work	The Richfield Reporter	10pm
The 10-2-4 Ranch	John Cohee, news	Public Affairs	Manchester Boddy, news	10:15
Sam Balter, sports	The World's Most Honored Music	The Johnson Family	Inside the News	10:30
Music		Music	Medals in Music	10:45

EVENING — FALL, 1944

Tuesday

	ABC	CBS	MBS	NBC
5pm	Terry and the Pirates	Burritt and Wheeler, news	Broadway News	OK for Release
5:15	Dick Tracy	Music	The Adventures of Superman	News
5:30	Jack Armstrong, the All-American Boy	Harry W. Flannery, news	Tom Mix and His Ralston Straightshooters	A Date with Judy
5:45	Captain Midnight	Truman Bradley, news	The Nightly News Wire	
6pm	News	Burns and Allen	Gabriel Heatter, news	The Molle' Mystery Theater
6:15	Peter de Lima, news		Screen Test	
6:30	Spotlight Bands	This is My Best	The American Forum of the Air	Fibber McGee and Molly
6:45	Short Story (6:55PM)			
7pm	Raymond Gram Swing, news	Service to the Front		The Pepsodent Show, Bob Hope
7:15	Norman Nesbitt, talk		Lowell Thomas, news	
7:30	Let Yourself Go, Milton Berle	Melodies America Loves	Red Ryder	The Raleigh Room, Hildegarde
7:45				
8pm	Earl Godwin, news	I Love a Mystery	The Count of Monte Cristo	The Chesterfield Music Shop
8:15	Lum and Abner	The Passing Parade		Fleetwood Lawton, news
8:30	The Alan Young Show	Theater of Romance	Freedom of Opportunity	The Purple Heart Show, Ginny Simms
8:45				
9pm	Club Good Cheer	Big Town	Glenn Hardy, news	Everything for the Boys, Dick Haymes
9:15			Rex Miller, news	
9:30	Rodriguez and Sutherland, news	Edwin C. Hill, news	Fulton Lewis Jr., news	The Bullocks Show
9:45	Public Affairs	Tapestries of Life	Sunny Skylar, songs	
10pm	George Fisher, gossip	The Ten o'Clock Wire	Public Affairs	The Richfield Reporter
10:15	Music	John Cohee, news		Check Your Music
10:30	Sam Balter, sports	Congress Speaks	The Johnson Family	Inside the News
10:45	Music	Organ Recital	The Feeling is Mutual	Taylor Made Melodies

EVENING — FALL, 1944

Wednesday

ABC	CBS	MBS	NBC	
Terry and the Pirates	Burritt and Wheeler, news	Broadway News	OK for Release	5pm
Dick Tracy	Music	The Adventures of Superman	News	5:15
Jack Armstrong, the All-American Boy	Harry W. Flannery, news	Tom Mix and His Ralston Straightshooters	Alvin Wilder, news	5:30
Captain Midnight	Truman Bradley, news	The Nightly News Wire	Louis Lochner, news	5:45
News	Songs By Sinatra	Gabriel Heatter, news	Time to Smile, Eddie Cantor	6pm
Peter de Lima, news		The Return of Nick Carter		6:15
Spotlight Bands	Which is Which	The First Nighter Program	Mr. District Attorney	6:30
Short Story (6:55PM)				6:45
Raymond Gram Swing, news	Great Moments in Music	Sumner Welles, news	Kay Kyser's College of Musical Knowledge	7pm
Ted Malone from England		Lowell Thomas, news		7:15
Scramby Amby	The Electric Hour, Nelson Eddy	The Lone Ranger		7:30
			.	7:45
Earl Godwin, news	I Love a Mystery	The Main Line	The Chesterfield Music Shop	8pm
Lum and Abner	The Passing Parade		Fleetwood Lawton, news	8:15
My Best Girl	Dr. Christian	Bulldog Drummond	Carton of Cheer, Henny Youngman	8:30
	Wallace Sterling, news (8:55PM)			8:45
Dunninger, the Mentalist	The Jack Carson Show	Glenn Hardy, news	Mr. and Mrs. North	9pm
		Cecil Brown, news		9:15
Rodriguez and Sutherland, news	Money on the Line	Fulton Lewis Jr., news	Young Artist's Concert	9:30
The Two Bells Theater		Rupert Hughes, news		9:45
George Fisher, gossip	The Ten o'Clock Wire	Music	The Richfield Reporter	10pm
The 10-2-4 Ranch	John Cohee, news		KFEyewitness	10:15
Sam Balter, sports	Sports	The Johnson Family	Inside the News	10:30
What's New	Organ Recital	Dance Orchestra	Medals in Music	10:45

EVENING — FALL, 1944

Thursday

	ABC	CBS	MBS	NBC
5pm	Terry and the Pirates	Burritt and Wheeler, talk	Broadway News	OK for Release
5:15	Dick Tracy	Music	The Adventures of Superman	News
5:30	Jack Armstrong, the All-American Boy	Harry W. Flannery, news	Tom Mix and His Ralston Straightshooters	Alvin Wilder, news
5:45	Captain Midnight	Truman Bradley, news	The Nightly News Wire	Louis Lochner, news
6pm	News	Major Bowes' Original Amateur Hour	Gabriel Heatter, news	The Kraft Music Hall, Bing Crosby
6:15	Peter de Lima, news		Screen Test	
6:30	Spotlight Bands	Meet Corliss Archer	Starlight Serenade	The Bob Burns Show
6:45	Short Story (6:55PM)			
7pm	Raymond Gram Swing, news	The First Line of Defense	News	Abbott and Costello
7:15	Musical Portraits		Lowell Thomas, news	
7:30	The Side Show, Dave Elman	Here's to Romance, Martha Tilton	Red Ryder	The March of Time
7:45				
8pm	Earl Godwin, news	I Love a Mystery	Sammy Kaye Orchestra	The Chesterfield Music Shop
8:15	Lum and Abner	The Passing Parade		The Night Editor
8:30	Fred Waring Orchestra	Death Valley Sheriff	Stop That Villian	Maxwell House Coffee Time, Frank Morgan
8:45		Wallace Sterling, news (8:55PM)		
9pm	America's Town Meeting of the Air	Suspense	Glenn Hardy, news	The Birdseye Open House, Dinah Shore
9:15			Rex Miller, news	
9:30		The Citizen's Forum	Fulton Lewis Jr., news	The Adventures of Ellery Queen
9:45			Sunny Skylar, songs	
10pm	George Fisher, gossip	The Ten o'Clock Wire	Public Affairs	The Richfield Reporter
10:15	Music	John Cohee, news		Mayor Bowron, comment
10:30	Sam Balter, sports	Music	The Johnson Family	Inside the News
10:45	Your OPA	Organ Recital	Dance Orchestra	Taylor Made Melodies

EVENING — FALL, 1944

Friday

ABC	CBS	MBS	NBC	
Terry and the Pirates	Burritt and Wheerler, talk	Broadway News	OK for Release	5pm
Dick Tracy	Music	The Adventures of Superman	News	5:15
Jack Armstrong, the All-American Boy	Harry W. Flannery, news	Tom Mix and His Ralston Straightshooters	Alvin Wilder, news	5:30
Captain Midnight	Truman Bradley, news	The Nightly News Wire	Louis Lochner, news	5:45
News	Money on the Line	Gabriel Heatter, news	Waltz Time	6pm
Peter de Lima, news		Screen Test		6:15
Spotlight Bands	That Brewster Boy	Double or Nothing	People Are Funny	6:30
Short Story (6:55PM)				6:45
Earl Godwin, news	The Durante - Moore Show	Dale Carnegie, inspirational	Amos 'n' Andy	7pm
Ted Malone from England		Lowell Thomas, news		7:15
Happy Island	Stage Door Canteen	The Lone Ranger	The Colgate Sports Newsreel, Bill Stern	7:30
			Darlington Hoopes	7:45
Earl Godwin, news	I Love a Mystery	Madison Square Garden Boxing	The Chesterfield Music Shop	8pm
The Parker Family	The Press Club		Roy Maypole, news	8:15
Gangbusters	It Pays to Be Ignorant		Duffy's Tavern	8:30
				8:45
The Tom Breneman Show	The Aldrich Family	Glenn Hardy, news	Furlough Fun	9pm
		Cecil Brown, news		9:15
Rodriguez and Sutherland, news	The Adventures of the Thin Man	Fulton Lewis Jr., news	The Sealtest Villiage Store, Davis and Haley	9:30
The Two Bells Theater		Sunny Skylar, songs		9:45
George Fisher, gossip	The Ten o'Clock Wire	The San Francisco Opera	The Richfield Reporter	10pm
The 10-2-4 Ranch	John Cohee, news		Manchester Boddy, news	10:15
Sam Balter, sports	Sports		Inside the News	10:30
The Doctors Talk It Over	Organ Recital		Medals in Music	10:45

EVENING — FALL, 1944

Saturday

	ABC	CBS	MBS	NBC
5pm	News	The Kenny Baker Program	News	Traffic Tribunal
5:15	Music		Sports Scores	News
5:30	Boston Symphony Orchestra	Harry W. Flannery, news	Henry Morgenthau, comment	The Grid Review
5:45		Truman Bradley, news	The Nightly News Wire	Louis Lochner, news
6pm		This is My Story	The Chicago Theater of the Air	The National Barn Dance
6:15				
6:30	Spotlight Bands	That's a Good Idea	London Column	Can You Top This
6:45	News (6:55PM)	Saturday Night Serenade		
7pm	Guy Lombardo Orchestra		The Quiz of Two Cities	Palmolive Party, Barry Wood and Patsy Kelly
7:15		The Mayor of the Town		
7:30	The Man Called X		Red Ryder	Grand Ole Opry
7:45		The Story Teller		
8pm	Early American Dance Music	America in the Air	Downbeat Derby	Truth or Consequences
8:15				
8:30		Inner Sanctum Mysteries		Vallee Varieties
8:45	Leland Stowe, news	Bob Trout, news (8:55PM)		
9pm	Meet Your Navy	Your Hit Parade	Glenn Hardy, news	The Skippy Hollywood Theater
9:15			Dreamboat	
9:30	Soldiers with Wings		Vaughn Monroe Orchestra	News
9:45		Don't You Believe It	Songs of Good Cheer	This is My Country
10pm	News	The Ten o'Clock Wire	Music	BBC Calling
10:15	Music By Gill	Music		The Unseen Enemy
10:30		Henry Busse Orchestra	Results, Inc.	News
10:45	Harry Owens Orchestra			Music

DAYTIME — FALL, 1944

Sunday

	ABC	CBS	MBS	NBC
8am	AAF Symphonic Flight	The Blue Jacket Choir	The Wesley Radio League	The Eternal Light
8:15				
8:30	The Hour of Faith	Invitation to Learning	The Voice of Prophecy	Successful Gardening
8:45				News
9am	The Blue War Journal	The Salt Lake Tabernacle Choir	The Pilgrim Hour	The University of Chicago Round Table
9:15		Woman Power		
9:30	The Master Radio Canaries	Transatlantic Call	The Lutheran Hour	Stradivari Orchestra
9:45				
10pm	John B. Kennedy, news	The CBS Church of the Air	Glenn Hardy, news	Layman's Views of the News
10:15	George Hicks, news		Commander Scott	News
10:30	Sammy Kaye's Sunday Serenade	News	Hookey Hall	Music
10:45		Edward R. Murrow, news		
11am	WAC Salute	Matinee Theater	The Band Concert	Those We Love
11:15	Behind the War News			
11:30	The Remember Hour	World News Today	Morning Melodies	The Westinghouse Program, John C. Thomas
11:45			The Canary Pet Shop	
12pm	The Charlotte Greenwood Show	New York Philharmonic Orchestra	Broadway News	World's News Parade
12:15			Music	
12:30	Miss Hattie		Memory Music	The Army Hour
12:45				
1pm	Darts for Dough		Your America	
1:15				
1:30	The World of Song	The Pause That Refreshes	Name That Song	Peter de Lima, news

DAYTIME — FALL, 1944

Monday-Friday

ABC	CBS	MBS	NBC	
Between the Lines	The Mark Brenneman Show	The Shady Valley Folks	The Johnny Murray Show	8am
News	Valiant Lady		T. B. Blakiston, news	8:15
The Breakfast Club	The Light of the World	Frank Hemingway, news	News	8:30
	Aunt Jenny's Real Life Stories	Victor Lindlahr, health	David Harum	8:45
Glamor Manor, Cliff Arquette	Kate Smith Speaks	Boake Carter, news	Edward Jorgerson, news	9am
	Big Sister	Time Out	Larry Smith, news	9:15
Breakfast at Sardi's	The Romance of Helen Trent	Midland, USA	Magazine Page	9:30
	Our Gal Sunday	The Amazing Jennifer Logan	Ronnie Mansfield, songs	9:45
Tony Morse, news	Life Can Be Beautiful	Glenn Hardy, news	The Voice of a Nation	10am
The Jack Berch Show	Ma Perkins	Terry's House Party	Peter de Lima's Closeups	10:15
My True Story	Bernadine Flynn, news	Luncheon with Lopez	Aunt Mary	10:30
	The Goldbergs		Art Baker's Notebooks	10:45
H. R. Baukhage, news	Joyce Jordan, MD	Cedric Foster, news	The Guiding Light	11am
The Mystery Chef	Two on a Clue	The Owl Program	Today's Children	11:15
Musical Moments	Young Dr. Malone	Jane Cowl, talk	The Woman in White	11:30
News	Perry Mason		Betty Crocker, cooking / Hymns of All Churches	11:45
The Coke Club, Morton Downey	The Story of Mary Marlin	Broadway News	The Farm Reporter	12pm
Hollywood Star Time	Neighbors, Irene Beasley	The Johnson Family	Ma Perkins	12:15
Walter Kiernan, news	Bright Horizon	The Homemaker's Club	Pepper Young's Family	12:30
Memories in Melody	Bachelor's Children		The Right to Happiness	12:45
World Wide Review	This Changing World		Mary Noble, Backstage Wife	1pm
The Radio Parade	Bob Anderson, news	Human Horizons	Stella Dallas	1:15
Time Views the News	The American School of the Air	Public Affairs	Lorenzo Jones	1:30

DAYTIME — FALL, 1944

Sunday

	ABC	CBS	MBS	NBC
1:45				Sam Balter, sports
2pm	Mary Small's Revue	The Prudential Family Hour	You Can't Take It With You	NBC Symphony Orchestra
2:15				
2:30	Hot Copy		The Shadow	
2:45		William L. Shirer, news		
3pm	The Radio Hall of Fame	The Adventures of Ozzie and Harriet	Quick as a Flash	The Catholic Hour
3:15				
3:30		I Was There	Upton Close, news	News
3:45			Dick Brown, news	Report from the Battlefield
4pm	News	The Kate Smith Hour	Cleveland Symphony Orchestra	The Lucky Strike Program, Jack Benny
4:15	Church Federation Vespers			
4:30	National Vespers			The Fitch Bandwagon
4:45				

DAYTIME — FALL, 1944

Monday-Friday

ABC	CBS	MBS	NBC	
The Blue Newsroom Review	Afternoon Dance	The Handy Man	Young Widder Brown	1:45
What's Doing Ladies	Potlock Party	This Changing World	When a Girl Marries	2pm
	Music	Today on the Coast	Portia Faces Life	2:15
Behind the War News	Meet the Missus	Payroll Guarantee	Just Plain Bill	2:30
The Frances Scully Show		Radio Tour	Front Page Farrell	2:45
The Three o'Clock News	Burritt and Wheerler, talk	Philip Keyne Gordon, news	The Road of Life	3pm
Footlight Echoes		Sweet and Sentimental	The Dreft Star Playhouse	3:15
News	Talk / The Squibb Show	Nancy Young, talk	Rosemary	3:30
The Jay Burnett Show	The World Today	Bill Hay's Bible Readings	A Woman of America	3:45
Taylor Grant, news	Sandra Martin	Fulton Lewis Jr., news	Dr. Kate	4pm
General Junius Pierce, comment	Music	Real Stories from Real Life	News	4:15
Twilight Tales / Andy and Virginia, songs	Open House / The American Melody Hour /	The World's Front Page	Art Baker's Notebook	4:30
Hop Harrigan	Easy Aces / Mr. Keen, Tracer of Lost Persons	Public Affairs		4:45

DAYTIME — FALL, 1944

Saturday

	ABC	CBS	MBS	NBC
8am	The Breakfast Hour	Let's Pretend	Hubby's Hobby	K. C. Jamboree
8:15				
8:30		The Billie Burke Show	News	Melody Roundup
8:45			The Junior Army	
9am	Fannie Hurst Presents	The Armstrong Theater of Today	Hello, Mom	News
9:15				Consumer Time
9:30	Lois Long, shopping	Stars Over Hollywood	The Swap Shop	Alex Drier, news
9:45	Music			County Medical Association Talks
10am	News	Grand Central Station	Glenn Hardy, news	Adventure Ahead
10:15	Collins Calling		Health Talk	
10:30	What's Cooking	Report to the Nation	Luncheon with Lopez	Here's Babe Ruth
10:45				The War Telescope
11am	Horace Heidt's Saturday Revue	Mary Lee Taylor, cooking	The Clinic Forum	The Opportunity Theater
11:15				
11:30	News	Music		Spelling Bee
11:45	Sports	Sports	Service Unlimited	
12pm			Sports	The Farm Reporter
12:15				James Abee, news
12:30				Smilin' Ed's Buster Brown Gang
12:45				
1pm				Sports
1:15				
1:30				
1:45				

DAYTIME — FALL, 1944

Saturday

	ABC	CBS	MBS	NBC
2pm		Columbia Symphony Orchestra	News	Your America
2:15			Sports	
2:30				Rupert Hughes, news
2:45	Hello Sweetheart, Nancy Martin			Public Affairs
3pm	The Summer Hour	Music		Since Pearl Harbor
3:15		The People's Platform		I Sustain the Wings
3:30				Curt Massey, songs
3:45	It's Murder	The World Today		Religion in the News
4pm	News	Detroit Musicale		The World's Great Novels
4:15	The Hoosier Observer			
4:30	Curtain Calls	The Hollywood Barn Dance		On the Scouting Trail
4:45				

LISTINGS FOR 1945

EVENING — WINTER, 1945

Sunday

	ABC	CBS	MBS	NBC
5pm	General Junius Pierce, comment	American Rhapsody	A. L. Alexander's Mediation Board	The Charlie McCarthy Show
5:15	Footlight Favorites			
5:30	The Joe E. Brown Show	The Art Baker Show		One Man's Family
5:45		Ned Calmer, news (5:55PM)	Gabriel Heatter, news	
6pm	Walter Winchell's Jergens Journal	The Radio Reader's Digest	Steel Horizons	The Manhattan Merry-Go-Round
6:15	Hollywood Mystery Time			
6:30		The Texaco Star Theater, James Melton	Cedric Foster, news	The American Album of Familiar Music
6:45	Jimmy Fidler, gossip		Jerry Cooper, songs	
7pm	The Life of Riley	Take It or Leave It	Earl Wilson's Broadway Column	The Hour of Charm
7:15			Ramona and Her Minstels	
7:30	Keep Up With the World	The Baby Snooks Show	The Boy Choir	The Old Gold Comedy Theater of the Air
7:45			This Changing World	
8pm	The Greenfield Village Choir	Crime Doctor	The Music Depreciation Hour	The Great Gildersleeve
8:15	Music	Songs (8:55PM)		
8:30	The Quiz Kids	Blondie	Tonight at Hoagy's	The Standard Symphony Hour
8:45				
9pm	Sam Hayes, news	The Adventures of Bill Lance	Glenn Hardy, news	
9:15	Music of the Americas		Rex Miller, news	
9:30	Rodriguez and Sutherland, news	Romance of the Ranchos	The Human Adventure	The Lucky Strike Program, Jack Benny
9:45	Washington Inside and Out			
10pm	Soldiers of the Press	The Ten o'Clock Wire	Roosty of the AAF	The Richfield Reporter
10:15		Talk		The Chapel Quartet
10:30	News	We Deliver the Goods	Music	Inside the News
10:45	The Weekend Feature Section			News

EVENING — WINTER, 1945

Monday

ABC	CBS	MBS	NBC	
Terry and the Pirates	A Man Called Jordan	Sam Hayes, news	OK for Release	5pm
Dick Tracy	Through a Woman's Eyes	The Adventures of Superman	Alvin Wilder, news	5:15
Jack Armstrong, the All-American Boy	Harry W. Flannery, news	Tom Mix and His Ralston Straightshooters	The Voice of Firestone	5:30
Captain Midnight	Truman Bradley, news	The Nightly News Wire		5:45
Happy Island	The Lux Radio Theater	Gabriel Heatter, news	These Make History	6pm
		Real Stories from Real Life		6:15
Spotlight Bands		Music	Information, Please	6:30
Short Story (6:55pm)				6:45
Guy Lombardo Orchestra	The Lady Esther Screen Guild Theater	News	The Carnation Contented Hour	7pm
		Lowell Thomas, news		7:15
Horace Heidt for the Servicemen	The Bob Hawk Show	The Lone Ranger	Dr. I. Q., the Mental Banker	7:30
				7:45
Ted Malone from England	The Jack Kirkwood Show	Sherlock Holmes	The Chesterfield Supper Club	8pm
Lum and Abner	Heddy Hopper's Hollywood		Fleetwood Lawton, news	8:15
Earl Godwin, news	Burns and Allen	Michael Shayne, Private Detective	The Cavalcade of America	8:30
Peter de Lima, news	Wallace Sterling, news (8:55pm)			8:45
Blind Date	The Whistler	Glenn Hardy, news	The Bell Telephone Hour	9pm
		Cecil Brown, news		9:15
Rodriguez and Sutherland, news	Vox Pop	Mutual Musicale	Noah Webster Says	9:30
Feature Section				9:45
George Fisher, gossip	The Ten o'Clock Wire	Fulton Lewis Jr., news	The Richfield Reporter	10pm
Martha Mears, songs	John Cohee, news	News	Music	10:15
Sam Balter, sports	The World's Most Honored Music	The Johnson Family	Inside the News	10:30
What's New	Organ Recital	Music	The Voice of a Nation	10:45

EVENING — WINTER, 1945

Tuesday

	ABC	CBS	MBS	NBC
5pm	Terry and the Pirates	A Man Named Jordan	Sam Hayes, news	OK for Release
5:15	Dick Tracy	Through a Woman's Eyes	The Adventures of Superman	Alvin Wilder, news
5:30	Jack Armstrong, the All-American Boy	Harry W. Flannery, news	Tom Mix and His Ralston Straightshooters	A Date with Judy
5:45	Captain Midnight	Truman Bradley, news	The Nightly News Wire	
6pm	Earl Godwin, news	Inner Sanctum Mysteries	Gabriel Heatter, news	The Molle' Mystery Theater
6:15	Peter de Lima, news		Jimmy Fidler, gossip	
6:30	Spotlight Bands	This is My Best	The American Forum of the Air	Fibber McGee and Molly
6:45	Short Story (6:55PM)			
7pm	Listen, the Women	Service to the Front		The Pepsodent Show, Bob Hope
7:15			Lowell Thomas, news	
7:30	Hal McIntyre Orchestra	Money on the Line	Red Ryder	The Raleigh Room, Hildegarde
7:45				
8pm	Ted Malone from England	The Jack Kirkwood Show	The Count of Monte Cristo	The Chesterfield Supper Club
8:15	Lum and Abner	Music That Satisfies		Fleetwood Lawton, news
8:30	The Alan Young Show	Theater of Romance	The Mysterious Traveler	The Purple Heart Show, Ginny Simms
8:45		Wallace Sterling, news (8:55PM)		
9pm	The Gracie Fields Show	Big Town	Glenn Hardy, news	Everything for the Boys, Dick Haymes
9:15			Rex Miller, news	
9:30	Murder Will Out	Edwin C. Hill, news	The Roy Rogers Show	The Bullocks Show
9:45		Tapestries of Life		
10pm	George Fisher, gossip	The Ten o'Clock Wire	Fulton Lewis Jr., news	The Richfield Reporter
10:15	Music	John Cohee, news	News	Manchester Boddy, news
10:30	Sam Balter, sports	Congress Speaks	The Johnson Family	Inside the News
10:45	What's New	Behind the Scenes at CBS	Music	The Voice of a Nation

EVENING — WINTER, 1945

Wednesday

ABC	CBS	MBS	NBC	
Terry and the Pirates	A Man Named Jordan	Sam Hayes, news	OK for Release	5pm
Dick Tracy	Through a Woman's Eyes	The Adventures of Superman	News	5:15
Jack Armstrong, the All-American Boy	Harry W. Flannery, news	Tom Mix and His Ralston Straightshooters	Alvin Wilder, news	5:30
Captain Midnight	Truman Bradley, news	The Nightly News Wire	Louis Lochner, news	5:45
Earl Godwin, news	Songs By Sinatra	Gabriel Heatter, news	Time to Smile, Eddie Cantor	6pm
Peter de Lima, news		Real Stories from Real Life		6:15
Spotlight Bands	Which is Which	The Cisco Kid	Mr. District Attorney	6:30
Short Story (6:55pm)				6:45
The Ice Box Follies, Niles and Prindle	Great Moments in Music	Sumner Welles, news	Kay Kyser's College of Musical Knowledge	7pm
		Lowell Thomas, news		7:15
On Stage, Everybody	Let Yourself Go, Milton Berle	The Lone Ranger		7:30
				7:45
Ted Malone from England	The Jack Kirkwood Show	The Main Line	The Chesterfield Supper Club	8pm
Lum and Abner	Music That Satisfies		Fleetwood Lawton, news	8:15
Counterspy	Dr. Christian	Bulldog Drummond	Carton of Cheer, Henny Youngman	8:30
	Wallace Sterling, news (8:55pm)			8:45
The Weird Circle	The Jack Carson Show	Glenn Hardy, news	Mr. and Mrs. North	9pm
		Cecil Brown, news		9:15
Rodriguez and Sutherland, news	The Adventures of Ellery Queen	The Feeling is Mutual	Young Artist's Contest	9:30
The Two Bells Theater				9:45
George Fisher, gossip	The Ten o'Clock Wire	Fulton Lewis Jr., news	The Richfield Reporter	10pm
Martha Mears, songs	John Cohee, news	News	KFEyewitness	10:15
Sam Balter, sports	The World's Most Honored Music	The Johnson Family	Inside the News	10:30
What's New	Organ Recital	Music	The Voice of a Nation	10:45

EVENING — WINTER, 1945

Thursday

	ABC	CBS	MBS	NBC
5pm	Terry and the Pirates	A Man Named Jordan	Sam Hayes, news	OK for Release
5:15	Dick Tracy	Through a Woman's Eyes	The Adventures of Superman	Alvin Wilder, news
5:30	Jack Armstrong, the All-American Boy	Harry W. Flannery, news	Tom Mix and His Ralston Straightshooters	Major H. S. Turner, comment
5:45	Captain Midnight	Truman Bradley, news	The Nightly News Wire	Elmer Patterson, news
6pm	News and Views	Major Bowes' Original Amateur Hour	Gabriel Heatter, news	The Kraft Music Hall, Bing Crosby
6:15			Real Stories from Real Life	
6:30	Spotlight Bands	Meet Corliss Archer	The Treasure Hour of Song	The Bob Burns Show
6:45	Short Story (6:55PM)			
7pm	Fred Waring Orchestra	The First Line of Defense	News	Abbott and Costello
7:15			Lowell Thomas, news	
7:30	The March of Time	Here's to Romance, Martha Tilton	Red Ryder	The Rudy Vallee Show
7:45				
8pm	Earl Godwin, news	The Jack Kirkwood Show	Music	The Chesterfield Supper Club
8:15	Lum and Abner	Music That Satisfies		Fleetwood Lawton, news
8:30	America's Town Meeting of the Air	Death Valley Sheriff	Hercule Poirot	Maxwell House Coffee Time, Frank Morgan
8:45		Wallace Sterling, news (8:55PM)		
9pm		Suspense	Glenn Hardy, news	The Birdseye Open House, Dinah Shore
9:15			Rex Miller, news	
9:30	The Thrifty Theater of the Air	The Citizens Forum	Wings Over the Nation	The Saint
9:45				
10pm	George Fisher, gossip	The Ten o'Clock Wire	Fulton Lewis Jr., news	The Richfield Reporter
10:15	Music	John Cohee, news	News	Mayor Bowron, comment
10:30	Sam Balter, sports	Sports	The Johnson Family	Inside the News
10:45	Freddy Martin Orchestra	Organ Recital	Music	The Voice of a Nation

EVENING — WINTER, 1945

Friday

ABC	CBS	MBS	NBC	
Terry and the Pirates	A Man Named Jordan	Sam Hayes, news	OK for Release	5pm
Dick Tracy	Through a Woman's Eyes	The Adventures of Superman	News	5:15
Jack Armstrong, the All-American Boy	Harry W. Flannery, news	Tom Mix and His Ralston Straightshooters	Alvin Wilder, news	5:30
Captain Midnight	Truman Bradley, news	The Nightly News Wire	Elmer Patterson, news	5:45
Earl Godwin, news	Erskine Johnson's Hollywood	Gabriel Heatter, news	Waltz Time	6pm
Peter de Lima, news	Riders of the Purple Sage	Real Stories from Real Life		6:15
Spotlight Bands	That Brewster Boy	Double or Nothing	People Are Funny	6:30
Short Story (6:55PM)				6:45
Dance Orchestra	The Durante - Moore Show	Dale Carnegie, inspirational	Amos 'n' Andy	7pm
		Lowell Thomas, news		7:15
Rhumba Revue	Stage Door Canteen	The Lone Ranger	The Colgate Sports Newsreel, Bill Stern	7:30
			Cabbages and Kings	7:45
The Green Hornet	The Jack Kirkwood Show	Madison Square Garden Boxing	The Chesterfield Supper Club	8pm
	The Danny O'Neill Show		Fleetwood Lawton, news	8:15
Stars of the Future	It Pays to Be Ignorant		Duffy's Tavern	8:30
	Wallace Sterling, news (8:55PM)			8:45
The Tom Breneman Show	The Aldrich Family	Glenn Hardy, news	Furlough Fun	9pm
		Cecil Brown, news		9:15
Rodriguez and Sutherland, news	The Adventures of the Thin Man	Fulton Lewis Jr., news	The Sealtest Villiage Store, Davis and Haley	9:30
The Two Bells Theater		Sunny Skylar, songs		9:45
George Fisher, gossip	The Ten o'Clock Wire	Fulton Lewis Jr., news	The Richfield Reporter	10pm
Martha Mears, songs	John Cohee, news	News	The World and America	10:15
Sam Balter, sports	The World's Most Honored Music	The Johnson Family	Inside the News	10:30
What's New	Organ Recital	Songs to Remember	The Voice of a Nation	10:45

EVENING — WINTER, 1945

Saturday

	ABC	CBS	MBS	NBC
5pm	News	Pabst Blue Ribbon Time, Danny Kaye	News	Sports
5:15	What's New		Music	News
5:30	Boston Symphony Orchestra	Harry W. Flannery, news	Detroit Symphony Orchestra	Everybody's Favorite
5:45		Truman Bradley, news		Elmer Patterson, news
6pm		This is My Story	The Symphony of America	The National Barn Dance
6:15				
6:30	Spotlight Bands	That's a Good Idea	News	Can You Top This
6:45	Quick Quiz (6:55 PM)	Saturday Night Serenade	The Red Cross Report	
7pm	The Andy Russell Show		The Quiz of Two Cities	The Judy Canova Show
7:15		The Mayor of the Town		
7:30	A Man Called X		Red Ryder	Grand Ole Opry
7:45		The Story Teller		
8pm	Early American Dance Music	America in the Air	The Chicago Theater of the Air	Truth or Consequences
8:15				
8:30	Leland Stowe, news	The FBI in Peace and War		Gaslight Gaieties
8:45	News	Bob Trout, news (8:55 PM)		
9pm	Meet Your Navy	Your Hit Parade	Glenn Hardy, news	The Skippy Hollywood Theater
9:15			Dreamboat	
9:30	Soldiers with Wings		Music	News
9:45		Don't You Believe It	Songs of Good Cheer	This is My Country
10pm	News	The Ten o'Clock Wire	Music	Sick's Star Final
10:15	Income Tax	The Hollywood Barn Dance		The Unseen Enemy
10:30	Freddy Martin Orchestra			BBC Calling
10:45		Talk		News

DAYTIME — WINTER, 1945

Sunday

	ABC	CBS	MBS	NBC
8am	AAF Symphonic Flight	The Blue Jacket Choir	The Wesley Radio League	The Eternal Light
8:15				
8:30	The Hour of Faith	Invitation to Learning	The Voice of Prophecy	Successful Gardening
8:45				News
9am	The Blue Network War Journal	The Salt Lake Tabernacle Choir	The Pilgrim Hour	The University of Chicago Round Table
9:15		Woman Power		
9:30	News	Transatlantic Call	The Lutheran Hour	Stradivari Orchestra
9:45	The Master Radio Canaries			
10am	John B. Kennedy, news	The CBS Church of the Air	Glenn Hardy, news	Layman's Views of the News
10:15	George Hicks, news		Commander Scott	Collins Calling
10:30	Sammy Kaye's Sunday Serenade	News	Hookey Hall	Musical Milestones
10:45		Edward R. Murrow, news		Modern Music
11am	News	Matinee Theater	The Band Concert	Those We Love
11:15	Behind the War News			
11:30	The Remember Hour	World News Today	Bill Cunningham, news	The Westinghouse Program, John C. Thomas
11:45			The Canary Pet Shop	
12pm	The Charlotte Greenwood Show	New York Philharmonic Orchestra	Broadway News	World's News Parade
12:15			The Home Town Parade of States	
12:30	Miss Hattie		Memory Music	The Army Hour
12:45				
1pm	Darts for Dough		Your America	
1:15				
1:30	The Eight to the Bar Ranch, Andrew Sisters	The Electric Hour, Nelson Eddy	Name That Song	Peter de Lima, news

DAYTIME — WINTER, 1945

Monday-Friday

ABC	CBS	MBS	NBC	
The Breakfast Club	The Mark Brenneman Show	Arthur Gaeth, news	The Johnny Murray Show	8am
	Valiant Lady	The Korn Kobblers	Between the Lines	8:15
	The Light of the World	The Quiz Wizard / Take It Easy Time	The Homemakers	8:30
	Aunt Jenny's Real Life Stories	Music	David Harum	8:45
Glamor Manor, Cliff Arquette	Kate Smith Speaks	William Lang, news	Edward Jorgerson, news	9am
	Big Sister	The Coke Club, Morton Downey	Larry Smith, news	9:15
Breakfast at Sardi's	The Romance of Helen Trent	Time Out	News	9:30
	Our Gal Sunday	Tune Time	Ronnie Mansfield, songs	9:45
Tony Morse, news	Life Can Be Beautiful	Glenn Hardy, news		10am
Music for the Missus	Ma Perkins	Luncheon with Lopez	The Hollywood Fan Magazine	10:15
My True Story	Bernadine Flynn, news		Aunt Mary	10:30
	Young Dr. Malone	Music	Art Baker's Notebook	10:45
H. R. Baukhage, news	Two on a Clue	Cedric Foster, news	The Guiding Light	11am
The Mystery Chef	Rosemary	Jane Cowl, talk	Today's Children	11:15
News and Views	Perry Mason	Music / You're Never Too Old	The Woman in White	11:30
	Tena and Tim		Betty Crocker, cooking / Hymns of All Churches	11:45
The Coke Club, Morton Downey	Music	Broadway News	The Farm Reporter	12pm
Jay Burnett, news	Neighbors, Irene Beasley	The Johnson Family	Ma Perkins	12:15
John B. Kennedy, news	Bright Horizon	Mild and Mellow	Pepper Young's Family	12:30
Memories in Melody	Bachelor's Children	Gracious Living	The Right to Happiness	12:45
Time Views the News	House Party	Think Hard Now	Mary Noble, Backstage Wife	1pm
The Radio Parade			Stella Dallas	1:15
This Moving World	The American School of the Air	Music	Lorenzo Jones	1:30

DAYTIME — WINTER, 1945

Sunday

	ABC	CBS	MBS	NBC
1:45				Sam Ballet, sports
2pm	Mary Small's Revue	The Prudential Family Hour	Let's Face the Issue	NBC Symphony Orchestra
2:15				
2:30	The Metropolitan Opera Auditions		The Shadow	
2:45		William L. Shirer, news		
3pm	The Radio Hall of Fame	The Adventures of Ozzie and Harriet	Quick as a Flash	The Catholic Hour
3:15				
3:30		I Was There	Upton Close, news	News
3:45			Dick Brown, news	Report from the Battlefield
4pm	Drew Pearson, news	The Kate Smith Hour	Cleveland Symphony Orchestra	The Lucky Strike Program, Jack Benny
4:15	Don Gardiner, news			
4:30	National Vespers			The Fitch Bandwagon
4:45				

DAYTIME — WINTER, 1945

Monday-Friday

ABC	CBS	MBS	NBC	
The Blue Newsroom Review		The Handy Man	Young Widder Brown	1:45
What's Doing Ladies	The Strange Romance of Evelyn Winters	Today on the Coast	When a Girl Marries	2pm
	Sandra Martin		Portia Faces Life	2:15
Between the Lines	Meet the Missus		Just Plain Bill	2:30
The Frances Scully Show		Radio Tour	Front Page Farrell	2:45
The Three o'Clock News	The Housewives' Protective League	Philip Keyne Gordon, news	The Road of Life	3pm
Footlight Echoes		Nancy Young, talk	The Dreft StarPlayhouse	3:15
Music	Talk / Jimmy Carroll Sings		Rosemary	3:30
Easy Listenin'	The World Today	Bill Hay's Bible Readings	A Woman of America	3:45
General Junius Pierce, comment	Potluck Party	Fulton Lewis Jr., news	Dr. Kate	4pm
Raymond Gram Swing, news	News	Music	News of the World	4:15
Music	Open House / The American Melody Hour / Easy Aces /		Talk	4:30
Hop Harrigan	Mr. Keen, Tracer of Lost Persons / Friday on Broadway	Frolics		4:45

DAYTIME — WINTER, 1945

Saturday

	ABC	CBS	MBS	NBC
8am	The Breakfast Club	Let's Pretend	Larry Meiser, news	K. C. Jamboree
8:15			Rainbow House	
8:30		The Billie Burke Show		Smilin' Ed's Buster Brown Gang
8:45			Bill's Wax Shop	
9am	What's Cooking	The Armstrong Theater of Today	Hello, Mom	News
9:15				Consumer Time
9:30	Lois Long, shopping	Stars Over Hollywood	The Swap Shop	Alex Drier, news
9:45	Collins Calling			County Medical Association Talks
10am	News	Grand Central Station	Glenn Hardy, news	The Club
10:15	Popular Profiles		Health Talk	The Hollywood Fan Magazine
10:30	Mirandy	Syncopation Piece	Luncheon with Lopez	The Baxters
10:45	News			The War Telescope
11am	The Metropolitan Opera	Mary Lee Taylor, cooking	The Clinic Forum	The Opportunity Theater
11:15				
11:30		Carolina Hayride	Hollywood Open House	Serenade
11:45				
12pm		The Land is Bright	Broadway News	The Farm Reporter
12:15			Kelley Klassics	James Abee, news
12:30		Syncopation Piece		Music
12:45		Jobs for Tomorrow		
1pm		Report from Washington		Doctors Look Ahead
1:15		Destination Tomorrow	Felix de Cola, songs	
1:30		Assignment Home	Music for a Half Hour	Music on Display
1:45				

DAYTIME — WINTER, 1945

Saturday

	ABC	CBS	MBS	NBC
2pm		Philadelphia Symphony Orchestra	News	Grand Hotel
2:15			Rotary Internal	
2:30		Harry James Orchestra	The Clinic Forum	News
2:45	Hello Sweetheart, Nancy Martin			Tin Pan Alley
3pm	The Music Room	Music	The Halls of Montezuma	Since Pearl Harbor
3:15		The People's Platform		I Sustain the Wings
3:30			Hawaii Calls	Rupert Hughes, news
3:45	Labor USA	The World Today		Religion in the News
4pm	News	Afternoon Dance	The American Eagle in Britain	Traffic Tribunal
4:15	Music			John W. Vandercook, news
4:30	Curtain Calls	The Eddie Oliver Show	Flying High	On the Scouting Trail
4:45				

EVENING — SPRING, 1945

Sunday

	ABC	CBS	MBS	NBC
5pm	General Junius Pierce, comment	American Rhapsody	A. L. Alexander's Mediation Board	The Charlie McCarthy Show
5:15	Footlight Favorites			
5:30	The Jerry Wayne Show	The Art Baker Show		The Eddie Braken Show
5:45		Ned Calmer, news (5:55 PM)	Gabriel Heatter, news	
6pm	Walter Winchell's Jergens Journal	The Radio Reader's Digest	Steel Horizons	The Manhattan Merry-Go-Round
6:15	Hollywood Mystery Time			
6:30		The Texaco Star Theater, James Melton	Cedric Foster, news	The American Album of Familiar Music
6:45	Jimmy Fidler, gossip		Dorothy Thompson, news	
7pm	The Life of Riley	Take It or Leave It	Earl Wilson's Broadway Column	The Hour of Charm
7:15			Music	
7:30	One Foot in Heaven	The Baby Snooks Show	Anita Ellis Sings	The Old Gold Comedy Theater of the Air
7:45			This Changing World	
8pm	The Greenfield Village Choir	Crime Doctor	The Music Depreciation Hour	The Great Gildersleeve
8:15	Raymond Moley, news	Songs (8:55 PM)		
8:30	The Quiz Kids	Blondie	The Northwestern Reviewing Stand	The Standard Symphony Hour
8:45				
9pm	Sam Hayes, news	The Adventures of Bill Lance	Glenn Hardy, news	
9:15	Music of the Americas		Rex Miller, news	
9:30	Rodriguez and Sutherland, news	Romance of the Ranchos	The Human Adventure	The Lucky Strike Program, Jack Benny
9:45	Washington Inside and Out			
10pm	Soldiers of the Press	The Ten o'Clock Wire	The US Air Force Band	The Richfield Reporter
10:15	Al Roth Orchestra	Talk		The Chapel Quartet
10:30	News	We Deliver the Goods	Music	Inside the News
10:45	The Weekend Feature Section			News

EVENING — SPRING, 1945

Monday

ABC	CBS	MBS	NBC	
Terry and the Pirates	A Man Called Jordan	Sam Hayes, news	H. V. Kaltenborn, news	5pm
Dick Tracy	Through a Woman's Eyes	The Adventures of Superman	Alvin Wilder, news	5:15
Jack Armstrong, the All-American Boy	Harry W. Flannery, news	Tom Mix and His Ralston Straightshooters	The Voice of Firestone	5:30
Captain Midnight	Truman Bradley, news	The Nightly News Wire		5:45
Earl Godwin, news	The Lux Radio Theater	Gabriel Heatter, news	Tonight at Hoagy's	6pm
Peter de Lima, news		Real Stories from Real Life		6:15
Spotlight Bands		The Better Half	Information, Please	6:30
Short Story (6:55pm)				6:45
Guy Lombardo Orchestra	The Lady Esther Screen Guild	Anita Ellis Sings	The Carnation Contented Hour	7pm
		Lowell Thomas, news		7:15
The World Peace Forum	The Bob Hawk Show	The Lone Ranger	Dr. I. Q., the Mental Banker	7:30
				7:45
Ted Malone from England	The Jack Kirkwood Show	Sherlock Holmes	The Chesterfield Supper Club	8pm
Lum and Abner	Heddy Hopper's Hollywood		Fleetwood Lawton, news	8:15
Hawthorne House	Burns and Allen	Michael Shayne, Private Detective	The Cavalcade of America	8:30
	Wallace Sterling, news (8:55pm)			8:45
Blind Date	The Whistler	Glenn Hardy, news	The Bell Telephone Hour	9pm
		Cecil Brown, news		9:15
Rodriguez and Sutherland, news	Vox Pop	Mutual Musicale	The American Way	9:30
Allen Prescott, talk				9:45
George Fisher, gossip	The Ten o'Clock Wire	Fulton Lewis Jr., news	The Richfield Reporter	10pm
Martha Mears, songs	John Cohee, news	News	The Unseen Enemy	10:15
Sam Balter, sports	The World's Most Honored Music	The Johnson Family	Inside the News	10:30
What's New	Organ Recital	Music	The Voice of a Nation	10:45

EVENING — SPRING, 1945

Tuesday

	ABC	CBS	MBS	NBC
5pm	Terry and the Pirates	A Man Named Jordan	Sam Hayes, news	H. V. Kaltenborn, news
5:15	Dick Tracy	Through a Woman's Eyes	The Adventures of Superman	Alvin Wilder, news
5:30	Jack Armstrong, the All-American Boy	Harry W. Flannery, news	Tom Mix and His Ralston Straightshooters	A Date with Judy
5:45	Captain Midnight	Truman Bradley, news	The Nightly News Wire	
6pm	Earl Godwin, news	Inner Sanctum Mysteries	Gabriel Heatter, news	The Molle' Mystery Theater
6:15	Peter de Lima, news		Jimmy Fidler, gossip	
6:30	Spotlight Bands	This is My Best	The American Forum of the Air	Fibber McGee and Molly
6:45	Short Story (6:55pm)			
7pm	Raymond Gram Swing, news	Service to the Front		The Pepsodent Show, Bob Hope
7:15	News		Lowell Thomas, news	
7:30	One Man's Family	Newsreel	Red Ryder	The Raleigh Room, Hildegarde
7:45				
8pm	Ted Malone from England	The Jack Kirkwood Show	The Count of Monte Cristo	The Chesterfield Supper Club
8:15	Lum and Abner	Music That Satisfies		Fleetwood Lawton, news
8:30	The Alan Young Show	Theater of Romance	The Roy Rogers Show	The Purple Heart Show, Ginny Simms
8:45		Wallace Sterling, news (8:55pm)		
9pm	Rodriguez and Sutherland, news	Big Town	Glenn Hardy, news	Everything for the Boys, Dick Haymes
9:15	Music		Rex Miller, news	
9:30	Murder Will Out	Edwin C. Hill, news	The Mysterious Traveler	The Bullocks Show
9:45		Tapestries of Life		
10pm	George Fisher, gossip	The Ten o'Clock Wire	Fulton Lewis Jr., news	The Richfield Reporter
10:15	Music	John Cohee, news	News	George Polk, news
10:30	Sam Balter, sports	Congress Speaks	The Johnson Family	Inside the News
10:45	Freddy Martin Orchestra	Behind the Scenes at CBS	Music	The Voice of a Nation

EVENING — SPRING, 1945

Wednesday

ABC	CBS	MBS	NBC	
Terry and the Pirates	A Man Named Jordan	Sam Hayes, news	H. V. Kaltenborn, news	5pm
Dick Tracy	Through a Woman's Eyes	The Adventures of Superman	Alvin Wilder, news	5:15
Jack Armstrong, the All-American Boy	Harry W. Flannery, news	Tom Mix and His Ralston Straightshooters	Major H. S. Turner, comment	5:30
Captain Midnight	Truman Bradley, news	The Nightly News Wire	Louis Lochner, news	5:45
Earl Godwin, news	Songs By Sinatra	Gabriel Heatter, news	Time to Smile, Eddie Cantor	6pm
Peter de Lima, news		Real Stories from Real Life		6:15
Spotlight Bands	Which is Which	Brownstone Theater	Mr. District Attorney	6:30
Short Story (6:55PM)				6:45
The Ice Box Follies, Niles and Prindle	Great Moments in Music	The Feeling is Mutual	Kay Kyser's College of Musical Knowledge	7pm
		Lowell Thomas, news		7:15
Rhumba Revue	Let Yourself Go, Milton Berle	The Lone Ranger		7:30
				7:45
Ted Malone from England	The Jack Kirkwood Show	The Main Line	The Chesterfield Supper Club	8pm
Lum and Abner	Music That Satisfies		Fleetwood Lawton, news	8:15
Counterspy	Dr. Christian	Music	The Gay Mrs. Featherstone	8:30
	Wallace Sterling, news (8:55PM)			8:45
The Evelyn Bigsby Show	The Jack Carson Show	Glenn Hardy, news	Mr. and Mrs. North	9pm
Music		Cecil Brown, news		9:15
Rodriguez and Sutherland, news	The Adventures of Ellery Queen	Arch Oboler's Plays	The Skippy Hollywood Theater	9:30
Allen Prescott, talk				9:45
George Fisher, gossip	The Ten o'Clock Wire	Fulton Lewis Jr., news	The Richfield Reporter	10pm
Martha Mears, songs	John Cohee, news	News	The American Scene	10:15
Sam Balter, sports	The World's Most Honored Music	The Johnson Family	Inside the News	10:30
Freddy Martin Orchestra	Organ Recital	Music	The Voice of a Nation	10:45

EVENING — SPRING, 1945

Thursday

	ABC	CBS	MBS	NBC
5pm	Terry and the Pirates	A Man Named Jordan	Sam Hayes, news	H. V. Kaltenborn, news
5:15	Dick Tracy	Through a Woman's Eyes	The Adventures of Superman	Alvin Wilder, news
5:30	Jack Armstrong, the All-American Boy	Harry W. Flannery, news	Tom Mix and His Ralston Straightshooters	Major H. S. Turner, comment
5:45	Captain Midnight	Truman Bradley, news	The Nightly News Wire	Elmer Patterson, news
6pm	The Man from G-2	Major Bowes' Original Amateur Hour	Gabriel Heatter, news	The Kraft Music Hall, Bing Crosby
6:15			Real Stories from Real Life	
6:30	Spotlight Bands	Meet Corliss Archer	The Treasure Hour of Song	The Bob Burns Show
6:45	Short Story (6:55PM)			
7pm	Fred Waring Orchestra	The First Line of Defense	Music	Abbott and Costello
7:15			Lowell Thomas, news	
7:30	The March of Time	Romance, Rhythm and Ripley	Red Ryder	The Rudy Vallee Show
7:45				
8pm	Earl Godwin, news	The Jack Kirkwood Show	Bulldog Drummond	The Chesterfield Supper Club
8:15	Lum and Abner	Music That Satisfies		Fleetwood Lawton, news
8:30	America's Town Meeting of the Air	Death Valley Sheriff	Hercule Poirot	Maxwell House Coffee Time, Frank Morgan
8:45		Wallace Sterling, news (8:55PM)		
9pm		Suspense	Glenn Hardy, news	The Birdseye Open House, Dinah Shore
9:15			Rex Miller, news	
9:30	The Thrifty Theater of the Air	The Citizens Forum	Wings Over the Nation	Noah Webster Says
9:45				
10pm	George Fisher, gossip	The Ten o'Clock Wire	Fulton Lewis Jr., news	The Richfield Reporter
10:15	Music	John Cohee, news	News	Music
10:30	Sam Balter, sports	Sports	The Johnson Family	Inside the News
10:45	Freddy Martin Orchestra	Organ Recital	Music	The Voice of a Nation

EVENING — SPRING, 1945

Friday

ABC	CBS	MBS	NBC	
Terry and the Pirates	A Man Named Jordan	Sam Hayes, news	H. V. Kaltenborn, news	5pm
Dick Tracy	Through a Woman's Eyes	The Adventures of Superman	Alvin Wilder, news	5:15
Jack Armstrong, the All-American Boy	Harry W. Flannery, news	Tom Mix and His Ralston Straightshooters	Major H. S. Turner, comment	5:30
Captain Midnight	Truman Bradley, news	The Nightly News Wire	Elmer Patterson, news	5:45
Earl Godwin, news	Money on the Line	Gabriel Heatter, news	Waltz Time	6pm
Peter de Lima, news		Real Stories from Real Life		6:15
Spotlight Bands	Those Websters	Double or Nothing	People Are Funny	6:30
Short Story (6:55PM)				6:45
Sammy Kaye Orchestra	The Durante - Moore Show	The Feeling is Mutual	Amos 'n' Andy	7pm
		Lowell Thomas, news		7:15
The Tom Breneman Show	Stage Door Canteen	The Lone Ranger	The Colgate Sports Newsreel, Bill Stern	7:30
			Cabbages and Kings	7:45
This is Your FBI	The Jack Kirkwood Show	Madison Square Garden Boxing	The Chesterfield Supper Club	8pm
	Erskine Johnson's Hollywood		Fleetwood Lawton, news	8:15
Stars of the Future	It Pays to Be Ignorant		Duffy's Tavern	8:30
	Wallace Sterling, news (8:55PM)			8:45
The Weird Circle	The Aldrich Family	Glenn Hardy, news	Furlough Fun	9pm
		Cecil Brown, news		9:15
Rodriguez and Sutherland, news	The Adventures of the Thin Man	Freedom of Opportunity	The Sealtest Villiage Store, Davis and Haley	9:30
Allen Prescott, talk				9:45
George Fisher, gossip	The Ten o'Clock Wire	Fulton Lewis Jr., news	The Richfield Reporter	10pm
Martha Mears, songs	John Cohee, news	News	Matt Weinstock, talk	10:15
Sam Balter, sports	The World's Most Honored Music	The Johnson Family	Inside the News	10:30
The Doctors Talk It Over	Organ Recital	Songs to Remember	The Voice of a Nation	10:45

EVENING — SPRING, 1945

Saturday

	ABC	CBS	MBS	NBC
5pm	News	Pabst Blue Ribbon Time, Danny Kaye	News	Sports
5:15	The Army Exhibition Program		The Canary Pet Shop	News
5:30	Boston Symphony Orchestra	Harry W. Flannery, news	Music	Everybody's Favorite
5:45		Truman Bradley, news	News	Elmer Patterson, news
6pm		Your Hit Parade	The Symphony of America	The National Barn Dance
6:15				
6:30	Spotlight Bands		Calling All Detectives	Can You Top This
6:45	Quick Quiz (6:55 PM)	Saturday Night Serenade		
7pm	The Andy Russell Show		The Quiz of Two Cities	The Judy Canova Show
7:15		The Mayor of the Town		
7:30	The Green Hornet		Red Ryder	Grand Ole Opry
7:45		The Story Teller		
8pm	Early American Dance Music	America in the Air	The Chicago Theater of the Air	Truth or Consequences
8:15				
8:30	Leland Stowe, news	The FBI in Peace and War		Gaslight Gaieties
8:45	News	Bob Trout, news (8:55 PM)		
9pm	Meet Your Navy	This is My Story	Glenn Hardy, news	News
9:15			Dreamboat	This Happened in '55
9:30	The Fighting AAF	That's a Good Idea	The Frank Observer	
9:45		Don't You Believe It	Songs of Good Cheer	This is My Country
10pm	News	The Ten o'Clock Wire	The Frank Observer	Sick's Star Final
10:15	Organ Recital	The Hollywood Barn Dance		
10:30	Freddy Martin Orchestra		Music	BBC Calling
10:45		Talk		News

DAYTIME — SPRING, 1945

Sunday

	ABC	CBS	MBS	NBC
8am	AAF Symphonic Flight	The Blue Jacket Choir	The Wesley Radio League	The Eternal Light
8:15				
8:30	The Hour of Faith	Invitation to Learning	The Voice of Prophecy	Successful Gardening
8:45				News
9am	The Blue Network War Journal	The Salt Lake Tabernacle Choir	The Pilgrim Hour	The University of Chicago Round Table
9:15		Woman Power		
9:30	News	Transatlantic Call	The Lutheran Hour	Echoes and Encores
9:45	The Master Radio Canaries			
10am	John B. Kennedy, news	The CBS Church of the Air	Glenn Hardy, news	Layman's Views of the News
10:15	Music		Commander Scott	Collins Calling
10:30	Sammy Kaye's Sunday Serenade	News	Sweetheart Time	Musical Milestones
10:45		Edward R. Murrow, news		Modern Music
11am	News	Stradivari Orchestra	The Band Concert	Harvest of Stars
11:15	Behind the War News			
11:30	The Remember Hour	World News Today	Bill Cunningham, news	The Westinghouse Program, John C. Thomas
11:45			Dale Carnegie, inspirational	
12pm	Kay's Canteen	New York Philharmonic Orchestra	Broadway News	World's News Parade
12:15			The Home Town Parade of States	
12:30	Miss Hattie		Memory Music	The Army Hour
12:45				
1pm	Darts for Dough		Your America	
1:15				
1:30	The Eight to the Bar Ranch, Andrew Sisters	The Electric Hour, Nelson Eddy	Name That Song	Peter de Lima, news

DAYTIME — SPRING, 1945

Monday-Friday

ABC	CBS	MBS	NBC	
The Breakfast Club	The Gene Baker Show	Arthur Gaeth, news	The Johnny Murray Show	*8am*
	Valiant Lady	The Korn Kobblers	Between the Lines	*8:15*
	The Light of the World	The Quiz Wizard / Take It Easy Time	Ben Claasen Music	*8:30*
	Aunt Jenny's Real Life Stories	Lanny and Ginger, songs	David Harum	*8:45*
Glamor Manor, Cliff Arquette	Kate Smith Speaks	William Lang, news	Edward Jorgerson, news	*9am*
	Big Sister	The Coke Club, Morton Downey	Larry Smith, news	*9:15*
Breakfast at Sardi's	The Romance of Helen Trent	Time Out	News	*9:30*
	Our Gal Sunday	Tune Time	Ronnie Mansfield, songs	*9:45*
Tony Morse, news	Life Can Be Beautiful	Glenn Hardy, news		*10am*
Music for the Missus	Ma Perkins	Luncheon with Lopez	The Hollywood Fan Magazine	*10:15*
My True Story	Bernadine Flynn, news		Aunt Mary	*10:30*
	Young Dr. Malone	The John J. Anthony Program	Art Baker's Notebooks	*10:45*
H. R. Baukhage, news	Two on a Clue	Cedric Foster, news	The Guiding Light	*11am*
Ethel and Albert	Rosemary	Jane Cowl, talk	Today's Children	*11:15*
News and Views	Perry Mason	Music / You're Never Too Old	The Woman in White	*11:30*
	Tena and Tim		Betty Crocker, cooking / Hymns of All Churches	*11:45*
The Mystery Chef	Neighbors, Irene Beasley	Broadway News	The Farm Reporter	*12pm*
The Gospel Singer	News	The Johnson Family	Ma Perkins	*12:15*
John B. Kennedy, news	Bright Horizon	Mild and Mellow	Pepper Young's Family	*12:30*
Memories in Melody	Bachelor's Children	Gracious Living	The Right to Happiness	*12:45*
Time Views the News	House Party	Think Hard Now	Mary Noble, Backstage Wife	*1pm*
The Radio Parade		Talk	Stella Dallas	*1:15*
This Moving World	The American School of the Air	George Olsen Orchestra	Lorenzo Jones	*1:30*

DAYTIME — SPRING, 1945

Sunday

	ABC	CBS	MBS	NBC
1:45				Edward Jorgenson, news
2pm	Mary Small's Revue	The Prudential Family Hour	Let's Face the Issue	NBC Symphony Orchestra
2:15				
2:30	The Charlotte Greenwood Show		The Shadow	
2:45		William L. Shirer, news		
3pm	The Radio Hall of Fame	The Adventures of Ozzie and Harriet	Quick as a Flash	The Catholic Hour
3:15				
3:30		I Was There	Upton Close, news	News
3:45			Dick Brown, news	Report from the Battlefield
4pm	Drew Pearson, news	The Kate Smith Hour	Cleveland Symphony Orchestra	The Lucky Strike Program, Jack Benny
4:15	Don Gardiner, news			
4:30	National Vespers			The Fitch Bandwagon
4:45				

DAYTIME — SPRING, 1945

Monday-Friday

ABC	CBS	MBS	NBC	
The Blue Newsroom Review		Tempo	Young Widder Brown	1:45
What's Doing Ladies	The Strange Romance of Evelyn Winters	This Changing World	When a Girl Marries	2pm
	Sandra Martin	Today on the Coast	Portia Faces Life	2:15
Sunny Side of the Street	Meet the Missus		Just Plain Bill	2:30
The Frances Scully Show		Radio Tour	Front Page Farrell	2:45
The Three o'Clock News	The Housewives' Protective League	Philip Keyne Gordon, news	The Road of Life	3pm
Footlight Echoes		Nancy Young, talk	Joyce Jordan, MD	3:15
Music	Talk / Jimmy Carroll Sings		A Woman of America	3:30
	The World Today	Bill Hay's Bible Readings	Aunt Mary	3:45
Taylor Grant, news	Potluck Party	Fulton Lewis Jr., news	One Woman's Secret	4pm
Raymond Gram Swing, news	Music	Rex Miller, news	News of the World	4:15
General Junius Pierce, comment	Open House / The American Melody Hour / Easy Aces /	Tommy Harris Time	Art Baker's Notebook	4:30
Hop Harrigan	Mr. Keen, Tracer of Lost Persons / Friday on Broadway	Frolics		4:45

DAYTIME — SPRING, 1945

Saturday

	ABC	CBS	MBS	NBC
8am	The Breakfast Club	Let's Pretend	Larry Meiser, news	K. C. Jamboree
8:15			Rainbow House	
8:30		The Billie Burke Show		Smilin' Ed's Buster Brown Gang
8:45			Bill's Wax Shop	
9am	What's Cooking	The Armstrong Theater of Today	Hello, Mom	News
9:15				Consumer Time
9:30	Lois Long, shopping	Stars Over Hollywood	Virginia Spencer, songs	Alex Drier, news
9:45	Collins Calling			Ronnie Mansfield, songs
10am	News	Grand Central Station	Glenn Hardy, news	
10:15	Popular Profiles		Health Talk	The Hollywood Fan Magazine
10:30	Mirandy	Syncopation Piece	The Clinic Forum	The Baxters
10:45	News			News
11am	Music	Mary Lee Taylor, cooking		TBA
11:15				
11:30	News	News	Hollywood Open House	The Grantland Rice Story
11:45	News	Carolina Hayride		
12pm	Taylor Made Melodies	The Land is Bright	Broadway News	The Farm Reporter
12:15			Kelley Klassics	The War Telescope
12:30		Talk		Home is What You Make It
12:45		The Builders of Victory		Rhapsody
1pm	The Saturday Concert	Report from Washington		Doctors Look Ahead
1:15		Destination Tomorrow	Felix de Cola, songs	
1:30		Assignment Home	Music for a Half Hour	Music on Display
1:45				

DAYTIME — SPRING, 1945

Saturday

	ABC	CBS	MBS	NBC
2pm	News	Philadelphia Symphony Orchestra	News	Grand Hotel
2:15	A Date with the Duke		Sports	
2:30	The Fitzgeralds, talk	Harry James Orchestra	The Return of Nick Carter	Since Pearl Harbor
2:45				Tin Pan Alley
3pm	The Music Room	Welcome Home	The Halls of Montezuma	On the Scouting Trail
3:15		The People's Platform		
3:30	The Canary Pet Shop		Hawaii Calls	Rupert Hughes, news
3:45	Labor USA	The World Today		Religion in the News
4pm	News	Afternoon Dance	The American Eagle in Britain	Traffic Tribunal
4:15	What's New			John W. Vandercook, news
4:30	The Land of the Lost	The Western Air Theater	Flying High	Our Foreign Policy
4:45				

EVENING — SUMMER, 1945

Sunday

	ABC	CBS	MBS	NBC
5pm	News	The Park Concert	A. L. Alexander's Mediation Board	The Frances Langford Show
5:15	Footlight Favorites			
5:30	The Fighting AAF	The Art Baker Show		Tommy Dorsey Orchestra
5:45		Ned Calmer, news (5:55PM)	Gabriel Heatter, news	
6pm	Walter Winchell's Jergens Journal	The Radio Reader's Digest	Steel Horizons	The Manhattan Merry-Go-Round
6:15	Hollywood Mystery Time			
6:30		The Texaco Star Theater, James Melton	Double or Nothing	The American Album of Familiar Music
6:45	Jimmy Fidler, gossip			
7pm	One Foot in Heaven	Take It or Leave It	Brownstone Theater	The Hour of Charm
7:15				
7:30	Freddy Martin Orchestra	I Was There	What Happened in '55	Meet Me at Parky's
7:45			This Changing World	
8pm	The Greenfield Village Choir	Crime Doctor	Leave It to Mike	Music
8:15	Song Time	Songs (8:55PM)		
8:30	The Quiz Kids	Blondie	Murder is My Hobby	The Standard Symphony Hour
8:45				
9pm	Sam Hayes, news	The Adventures of Bill Lance	Glenn Hardy, news	
9:15	Evelyn Bigsby, news		Rex Miller, news	
9:30	Rodriguez and Sutherland, news	Romance of the Ranchos	Boston Blackie	The Haunting Hour
9:45	Washington Inside and Out			
10pm	Soldiers of the Press	The Ten o'Clock Wire	The US Air Force Band	The Richfield Reporter
10:15	Al Roth Orchestra	Lymon Breeson, talk		The Chapel Quartet
10:30	News	We Deliver the Goods	Music	Inside the News
10:45	The Weekend Feature Section			News

EVENING — SUMMER, 1945

Monday

ABC	CBS	MBS	NBC	
Terry and the Pirates	Knox Manning, news	Sam Hayes, news	H. V. Kaltenborn, news	5pm
Dick Tracy	Through a Woman's Eyes	The Adventures of Superman	Alvin Wilder, news	5:15
Jack Armstrong, the All-American Boy	Nelson Pringle, news	Tom Mix and His Ralston Straightshooters	The Voice of Firestone	5:30
News	Truman Bradley, news	The Nightly News Wire		5:45
Rex Maupin Orchestra	The Marlin Hurt and Beulah Show	Gabriel Heatter, news	Tonight at Hoagy's	6pm
		Real Stories from Real Life		6:15
The Jack Berch Show	The Sea Has a Story	Spotlight Bands	The Rise' Stevens Show	6:30
Sports				6:45
Tokyo Calling	The Lady Esther Screen Guild Theater	Now It Can Be Told	The Carnation Contented Hour	7pm
		News		7:15
Reunion, USA	The Bob Hawk Show	The Lone Ranger	Dr. I. Q., the Mental Banker	7:30
				7:45
Pick and Pat	A Man Named Jordan	Michael Shayne, Private Detective	The Chesterfield Supper Club	8pm
Peter de Lima, news	Heddy Hopper, gossip		Fleetwood Lawton, news	8:15
Hawthorne House	Money on the Line	Professor Broadway	Tommy Dorsey Orchestra	8:30
	Wallace Sterling, news (8:55PM)			8:45
Blind Date	The Whistler	Glenn Hardy, news	The Bell Telephone Hour	9pm
		Cecil Brown, news		9:15
Rodriguez and Sutherland, news	Vox Pop	Jimmy Fidler, gossip	The American Way	9:30
Music		News		9:45
George Fisher, gossip	The Ten o'Clock Wire	Fulton Lewis Jr., news	The Richfield Reporter	10pm
Charlie Chan	John Cohee, news	News	The Unseen Enemy	10:15
Sam Balter, sports	Open House	The Johnson Family	Inside the News	10:30
American Radio		So the Story Goes	The Old Corral	10:45

EVENING — SUMMER, 1945

Tuesday

	ABC	CBS	MBS	NBC
5pm	Terry and the Pirates	Know Manning, news	Sam Hayes, news	H. V. Kaltenborn, news
5:15	Dick Tracy	Through a Woman's Eyes	The Adventures of Superman	Alvin Wilder, news
5:30	Jack Armstrong, the All-American Boy	Nelson Pringle, news	Tom Mix and His Ralston Straightshooters	A Date with Judy
5:45	News	Truman Bradley, news	The Nightly News Wire	
6pm	Guy Lombardo Orchestra	Columbia Presents Corwin	Gabriel Heatter, news	The Navy Hour
6:15	Short Story (6:55pm)		Real Stories from Real Life	
6:30	Radie Harris, gossip	The Doctor Fights	The American Forum of the Air	The Victor Borge Show
6:45	Sports Roundup			
7pm	George Olsen Orchestra	Service to the Front		A Man Called X
7:15			News	
7:30	County Fair	The Hollywood Preview	Red Ryder	An Evening with Romberg
7:45				
8pm	Pick and Pat	A Man Named Jordan	The Count of Monte Cristo	The Chesterfield Supper Club
8:15	Peter de Lima, news	The Danny O'Neill Show		Fleetwood Lawton, news
8:30	The Alan Young Show	Theater of Romance	The Falcon	The Purple Heart Show, Ginny Simms
8:45		Wallace Sterling, news (8:55pm)		
9pm	Rodriguez and Sutherland, news	Big Town	Glenn Hardy, news	Everything for the Boys, Dick Haymes
9:15	Music		Rex Miller, news	
9:30	Murder Will Out	Edwin C. Hill, news	The Adventures of Nero Wolfe	Universe on Parade
9:45		Tapestries of Life		
10pm	George Fisher, gossip	The Ten o'Clock Wire	Fulton Lewis Jr., news	The Richfield Reporter
10:15	Charlie Chan	John Cohee, news	News	Navy Waves
10:30	Sam Balter, sports	Music	The Johnson Family	Inside the News
10:45	Freddy Martin Orchestra		So the Story Goes	The Old Corral

EVENING — SUMMER, 1945

Wednesday

ABC	CBS	MBS	NBC	
Terry and the Pirates	Know Manning, news	Sam Hayes, news	H. V. Kaltenborn, news	5pm
Dick Tracy	Through a Woman's Eyes	The Adventures of Superman	Alvin Wilder, news	5:15
Jack Armstrong, the All-American Boy	Nelson Pringle, news	Tom Mix and His Ralston Straightshooters	The Voice of a Nation	5:30
News	Truman Bradley, news	The Nightly News Wire	Louis Lochner, news	5:45
Curtain Time	Crime Photographer	Gabriel Heatter, news	Wednesday with You	6pm
Short Story (6:55PM)		Real Stories from Real Life		6:15
Music	Detect and Collect	Spotlight Bands	Mr. District Attorney	6:30
Sports Roundup				6:45
Counterspy	Great Moments in Music	The Human Adventure	Kay Kyser's College of Musical Knowledge	7pm
				7:15
Jobs for the G. I.	G. I. Laffs	The Lone Ranger		7:30
				7:45
Pick and Pat	A Man Named Jordan	The Main Line	The Chesterfield Supper Club	8pm
Peter de Lima, news	The Danny O'Neil Show		Fleetwood Lawton, news	8:15
The Fishing and Hunting Club	Dr. Christian	Music	The Gay Mrs. Featherstone	8:30
	Wallace Sterling, news (8:55PM)			8:45
Dark Venture	The Saint	Glenn Hardy, news	Mr. and Mrs. North	9pm
		Cecil Brown, news		9:15
Mrs. Music	The Adventures of Ellery Queen	Arch Oboler's Plays	McGregor Presents	9:30
Time Out				9:45
George Fisher, gossip	The Ten o'Clock Wire	Fulton Lewis Jr., news	The Richfield Reporter	10pm
Charlie Chan	John Cohee, news	News	Music	10:15
Sam Balter, sports	The Merry Life of Mary Christmas	The Johnson Family	Inside the News	10:30
Freddy Martin Orchestra		So the Story Goes	The Old Corral	10:45

EVENING — SUMMER, 1945

Thursday

	ABC	CBS	MBS	NBC
5pm	Terry and the Pirates	Knox Manning, news	Sam Hayes, news	H. V. Kaltenborn, news
5:15	Dick Tracy	Through a Woman's Eyes	The Adventures of Superman	Alvin Wilder, news
5:30	Jack Armstrong, the All-American Boy	Nelson Pringle, news	Tom Mix and His Ralston Straightshooters	The Voice of a Nation
5:45	News	Truman Bradley, news	The Nightly News Wire	Elmer Patterson, news
6pm	Peter de Lima, news	Morton Gould Orchestra	Gabriel Heatter, news	The Kraft Music Hall, Bing Crosby
6:15	Music		Real Stories from Real Life	
6:30	Navy Recruiting Programe	Meet Corliss Archer	The Treasure Hour of Song	Philo Vance
6:45	Sports Roundup			
7pm	One Foot in Heaven	The First Line of Defense	Now It Can BeTold	Mystery in the Air
7:15			News	
7:30	The March of Time	Romance, Rhythm and Ripley	Red Ryder	The American Scene
7:45				
8pm	Pick and Pat	A Man Named Jordan	Bulldog Drummond	The Chesterfield Supper Club
8:15	Earl Godwin, news	The Danny O'Neill Show		Fleetwood Lawton, news
8:30	America's Town Meeting of the Air	Maisie	Hercule Poirot	The Family Party
8:45		Wallace Sterling, news (8:55 PM)		
9pm		Suspense	Glenn Hardy, news	The Adventures of Topper
9:15			Rex Miller, news	
9:30	News and Views	The Citizens Forum	The Shadow	Noah Webster Says
9:45				
10pm	George Fisher, gossip	The Ten o'Clock Wire	Fulton Lewis Jr., news	The Richfield Reporter
10:15	Charlie Chan	John Cohee, news	News	Music
10:30	Sam Balter, sports	Sports	The Johnson Family	Inside the News
10:45	Your OPA	Organ Recital	So the Story Goes	The Old Corral

EVENING — SUMMER, 1945

Friday

ABC	CBS	MBS	NBC	
Terry and the Pirates	Knox Manning, news	Sam Hayes, news	Richard Harkness, news	5pm
Dick Tracy	Through a Woman's Eyes	The Adventures of Superman	Alvin Wilder, news	5:15
Jack Armstrong, the All-American Boy	Nelson Pringle, news	Tom Mix and His Ralston Straightshooters	The Voice of a Nation	5:30
News	Truman Bradley, news	The Nightly News Wire	Elmer Patterson, news	5:45
Peter de Lima, news	The Jerry Wayne Show	Gabriel Heatter, news	Waltz Time	6pm
Music		Real Stories from Real Life		6:15
The Sheriff	Those Websters	Music	People Are Funny	6:30
Short Story (6:55PM)				6:45
The Man from G-2	The Ray Bolger Show	Now It Can Be Told	Dunninger, the Mentalist	7pm
		News		7:15
The Green Hornet	Harry James Orchestra	The Lone Ranger	The Colgate Sports Newsreel, Bill Stern	7:30
			Cabbages and Kings	7:45
This is Your FBI	A Man Named Jordan	Madison Square Garden Boxing	The Chesterfield Supper Club	8pm
	The Danny O'Neill Show		Fleetwood Lawton, news	8:15
The Weird Circle	It Pays to Be Ignorant		Correction, Please	8:30
	Wallace Sterling, news (8:55PM)			8:45
The Spade Cooley Show	The Aldrich Family	Glenn Hardy, news	The Night Editor	9pm
		Cecil Brown, news	The Pleasure Parade	9:15
Rodriguez and Sutherland, news	The Adventures of the Thin Man	Freedom of Opportunity	The Sealtest Villiage Store, Jack Haley	9:30
Allen Prescott, talk				9:45
George Fisher, gossip	The Ten o'Clock Wire	Fulton Lewis Jr., news	The Richfield Reporter	10pm
Charlie Chan	John Cohee, news	News	Matt Weinstock, talk	10:15
Sam Balter, sports	Dance Orchestra	The Johnson Family	Inside the News	10:30
The Doctors Talk It Over		So the Story Goes	The Old Corral	10:45

EVENING — SUMMER, 1945

Saturday

	ABC	CBS	MBS	NBC
5pm	News	The Land is Bright	News	News
5:15	Music		News	News
5:30	Gilbert and Sullivan Music	Nelson Pringle, news	The Symphony of America	Everybody's Favorite
5:45		Truman Bradley, news		Elmer Patterson, news
6pm		Your Hit Parade	Radio Auction	The National Barn Dance
6:15				
6:30	Flight to the Pacific		Calling All Detectives	Can You Top This
6:45	Quick Quiz (6:55 PM)	Saturday Night Serenade		
7pm	Hoosier Hop		The Quiz of Two Cities	I Sustain the Wings
7:15		Assignment Home		
7:30	Senior Swing		Red Ryder	Grand Ole Opry
7:45		The Story Teller		
8pm	Early American Dance Music	America in the Air	The Chicago Theater of the Air	Favorites
8:15				
8:30	Kogen Orchestra	Twelve Players		The Younger Generation
8:45	News	Bob Trout, news (8:55 PM)		
9pm	The American Way	This is My Story	Glenn Hardy, news	The American Forum
9:15	Freddy Martin Orchestra		News	
9:30	Music	That's a Good Idea	Music	News
9:45		Don't You Believe It	Songs of Good Cheer	This is My Country
10pm	Showcase	The Ten o'Clock Wire	Wings Over the Nation	Sick's Star Final
10:15	Music	The Hollywood Barn Dance		
10:30	Freddy Martin Orchestra		Music	BBC Calling
10:45		Talk		News

DAYTIME — SUMMER, 1945

Sunday

	ABC	CBS	MBS	NBC
8am	War News	The Blue Jacket Choir	The Wesley Radio League	The Eternal Light
8:15	Music			
8:30	The Hour of Faith	Invitation to Learning	The Voice of Prophecy	Successful Gardening
8:45				News
9am	World News	The Salt Lake Tabernacle Choir	The Pilgrim Hour	The Atlantic Spotlight
9:15	News	Woman Power		
9:30	The Voice of the Army	Transatlantic Call	The Lutheran Hour	Echoes and Encores
9:45	The Master Radio Canaries			
10am	John B. Kennedy, news	The CBS Church of the Air	Glenn Hardy, news	Layman's Views of the News
10:15	News		Commander Scott	Collins Calling
10:30	Sammy Kaye's Sunday Serenade	News	Sweetheart Time	Musical Milestones
10:45		Edward R. Murrow, news		Modern Music
11am	Washington Story	Stradivari Orchestra	The Band Concert	Jo Stafford and Lawrence Brooks, songs
11:15	Behind the War News			
11:30	The Remember Hour	World News Today	Bill Cunningham, news	The Westinghouse Program, John C. Thomas
11:45			Mysteries of Crooked Square	
12pm	Musical Bouquet	New York Philharmonic Orchestra	Broadway News	World's News Parade
12:15			The Home Town Parade of States	
12:30	National Vespers		Memory Music	One Man's Family
12:45				
1pm	Darts for Dough		Your America	The Army Hour
1:15				

DAYTIME — SUMMER, 1945

Monday-Friday

ABC	CBS	MBS	NBC	
The Breakfast Club	News	The Jan Murray Show	Fred Waring Orchestra	*8am*
	Valiant Lady		Between the Lines	*8:15*
	The Light of the World	Success Stories / Take It Easy Time	Miranda, songs	*8:30*
	Aunt Jenny's Real Life Stories	Cliff Edwards, songs	David Harum	*8:45*
Glamor Manor, Cliff Arquette	Kate Smith Speaks	William Lang, news	Edward Jorgerson, news	*9am*
	Big Sister	The Coke Club, Morton Downey	Larry Smith, news	*9:15*
Breakfast at Sardi's	The Romance of Helen Trent	Time Out	News	*9:30*
	Our Gal Sunday	The Mystery Chef	Ronnie Mansfield, songs	*9:45*
Tony Morse, news	Life Can Be Beautiful	Glenn Hardy, news		*10am*
Between the Bookends	Ma Perkins	Music	The Hollywood Fan Magazine	*10:15*
My True Story	Bernadine Flynn, news		The Homemaker's Club	*10:30*
	Young Dr. Malone	The John J. Anthony Program	Art Baker's Notebooks	*10:45*
H. R. Baukhage, news	Two on a Clue	Cedric Foster, news	The Guiding Light	*11am*
Ethel and Albert	Rosemary	The Mystery Chef	Today's Children	*11:15*
The Gospel Singer	Perry Mason	Queen for a Day	The Woman in White	*11:30*
News	Tena and Tim		Betty Crocker, cooking / Hymns of All Churches	*11:45*
John B. Kennedy, news	Neighbors, Irene Beasley	Broadway News	The Farm Reporter	*12pm*
Charles Bennett, news	The House of Seven Gables	The Johnson Family	Ma Perkins	*12:15*
Ladies, Be Seated	A Woman's Life	Mild and Mellow	Pepper Young's Family	*12:30*
	Bachelor's Children	Music	The Right to Happiness	*12:45*
Time Views the News	House Party	Frolics	Mary Noble, Backstage Wife	*1pm*
The Radio Parade		Bill Hay's Bible Reading	Stella Dallas	*1:15*

DAYTIME — SUMMER, 1945

Sunday

	ABC	CBS	MBS	NBC
1:30	The Eight to the Bar Ranch, Andrew Sisters	The Electric Summer Hour	Time for Crime	These Make History
1:45			Harvey Harding, songs	News
2pm	Mary Small's Revue	The Prudential Family Hour	Father Brown Mysteries	NBC Symphony Orchestra
2:15				
2:30	The Charlotte Greenwood Show		The Return of Nick Carter	
2:45		William L. Shirer, news		
3pm	The Philco Summer Hour	The Silver Theater	The Abbott Mysteries	The Catholic Hour
3:15				
3:30	The Ice Box Follies, Niles and Prindle	Report to the Nation	Cedric Foster, news	News
3:45			Music	Music
4pm	Drew Pearson, news	Men of Vision	The Better Half	Wayne King Orchestra
4:15	Don Gardiner, news			
4:30	Songs	Music	The Ken Carson Show	The Fitch Bandwagon
4:45				

DAYTIME — SUMMER, 1945

Monday-Friday

ABC	CBS	MBS	NBC	
This Moving World	Feature Story	Music	Lorenzo Jones	1:30
Betty Crocker, cooking / Hymns of All Churches	Songs		Young Widder Brown	1:45
What's Doing Ladies	The Strange Romance of Evelyn Winters	This Changing World	When a Girl Marries	2pm
	Service Time	Today on the Coast	Portia Faces Life	2:15
Best Sellers	Meet the Missus		Just Plain Bill	2:30
		The Korn Kobblers	Front Page Farrell	2:45
The Three o'Clock News	The Housewives' Protective League	Philip Keyne Gordon, news	The Road of Life	3pm
Walkie Talkie		Nancy Young, talk	Joyce Jordan, MD	3:15
The Frances Scully Show	Talk and Music		A Woman of America	3:30
	The World Today	Elsa Maxwell, comment	Aunt Mary	3:45
Taylor Grant, news	Potluck Party	Fulton Lewis Jr., news	One Woman's Secret	4pm
Raymond Gram Swing, news	News	Rex Miller, news	News of the World	4:15
General Junius Pierce, comment	Open House / The American Melody Hour / Easy Aces /	Sketchbook	Art Baker's Notebook	4:30
Louise Masser, news	Mr. Keen, Tracer of Lost Persons / Friday on Broadway			4:45

DAYTIME — SUMMER, 1945

Saturday

	ABC	CBS	MBS	NBC
8am	The Breakfast Club	Easy Does It	Larry Meiser, news	K. C. Jamboree
8:15			Rainbow House	
8:30		The Billie Burke Show	Navy Recruiting Program	Smilin' Ed's Buster Brow Gang
8:45			Bill's Wax Shop	
9am	What's Cooking	The Armstrong Theater of Today	Hello, Mom	News
9:15				Consumer Time
9:30	The National Farm and Home Hour	Stars Over Hollywood	Virginia Spencer, songs	Alex Drier, news
9:45				Ronnie Mansfield, songs
10am	News	Grand Central Station	Glenn Hardy, news	
10:15	Popular Profiles		Health Talk	Treasury Salute
10:30	Mirandy	News and Views	The Clinic Forum	The Baxters
10:45	News			News
11am	Music		Music	Musicana
11:15		Mary Lee Taylor, cooking		Talk
11:30	News	Let's Pretend		Sky High
11:45	Allen Prescott, talk			
12pm	Taylor Made Melodies	Your Marine Corps	Broadway News	The Farm Reporter
12:15			Kelley Klassics	The War Telescope
12:30		Public Affairs		Home is What You Make It
12:45		Ten from Tokyo		Rhapsody
1pm	NBC Symphony Orchestra	Ted Husing, sports	Memo for Tomorrow	Butler Handen
1:15		Music	Felix de Cola, songs	
1:30		Jack Kerr, news	Music for a Half Hour	World of Melody
1:45		Horse Racing		Sports

DAYTIME — SUMMER, 1945

Saturday

	ABC	CBS	MBS	NBC
2pm	News	We Deliver the Goods	News and Views	Grand Hotel
2:15	A Date with the Duke			
2:30		George Olsen Orchestra	Coke Session	John W. Vandercook, news
2:45				Tin Pan Alley
3pm	The Music Room	Welcome Home	The Halls of Montezuma	Saturday Session
3:15				Rhapsody of the Rockies
3:30	The Canary Pet Shop	Syncopation Piece	Hawaii Calls	Rupert Hughes, news
3:45	Labor USA	The World Today		The Art of Living
4pm	News	Afternoon Dance	Music	Our Foreign Policy
4:15	American Radio			
4:30	The Land of the Lost	The Todds	Opinion Requested	Traffic Tribunal
4:45		Ona Munson, comment		The Band Parade

EVENING — FALL, 1945

Sunday

	ABC	CBS	MBS	NBC
5pm	The Ford Sunday Evening Hour	The Marlin Hurt and Beulah Show	A. L. Alexander's Mediation Board	The Charlie McCarthy Show
5:15				
5:30		The Art Baker Show		The Fred Allen Show
5:45		Ned Calmer, news (5:55PM)	Gabriel Heatter, news	
6pm	Walter Winchell's Jergens Journal	Request Performance	The Human Adventure	The Manhattan Merry-Go-Round
6:15	Hollywood Mystery Time			
6:30		The Texaco Star Theater, James Melton	Double or Nothing	The American Album of Familiar Music
6:45	Jimmy Fidler, gossip			
7pm	The Theater Guild of the Air	Take It or Leave It	This Changing World	The Hour of Charm
7:15			Music	
7:30		The Baby Snooks Show	What's the Name of That Song	Meet Me at Parky's
7:45				
8pm	Playhouse Favorites	Crime Doctor	Raising Your Husband	The Great Gildersleeve
8:15	Song Time	Surprise Theater (8:25PM)		
8:30	The Quiz Kids	Blondie	Boston Blackie	The Standard Symphony Hour
8:45				
9pm	Sam Hayes, news	The Adventures of the Thin Man	Glenn Hardy, news	
9:15	Evelyn Bigsby, news		Rex Miller, news	
9:30	Eastside Serenade	Romance of the Ranchos	Jimmy Fidler, gossip	The Lucky Strike Program, Jack Benny
9:45			Music	
10pm	Hit Tunes	The Ten o'Clock Wire	California Melodies	The Richfield Reporter
10:15	Music	Dr. Sterling, health		The Chapel Quartet
10:30	Success Story	Talk	Music	Inside the News
10:45		Music		Show Time

EVENING — FALL, 1945

Monday

ABC	CBS	MBS	NBC	
Terry and the Pirates	Knox Manning, news	Sam Hayes, news	H. V. Kaltenborn, news	5pm
Dick Tracy	Through a Woman's Eyes	The Adventures of Superman	News	5:15
Jack Armstrong, the All-American Boy	Harry W. Flannery, news	Captain Midnight	The Voice of Firestone	5:30
News	Truman Bradley, news	Tom Mix and His Ralston Straightshooters		5:45
Washington Story	The Lux Radio Theater	Gabriel Heatter, news	Tonight at Hoagy's	6pm
		Real Stories from Real Life		6:15
Public Affairs		Spotlight Bands	Information, Please	6:30
Sports				6:45
Public Affairs	The Lady Esther Screen Guild Theater	Radio Auction	The Carnation Contented Hour	7pm
				7:15
Reunion, USA	The Bob Hawk Show	The Lone Ranger	Dr. I. Q., the Mental Banker	7:30
				7:45
Lum and Abner	The Jack Kirkwood Show	Michael Shayne, Private Detective	The Chesterfield Supper Club	8pm
Hedda Hopper, gossip	The Jack Smith Show		Fleetwood Lawton, news	8:15
Hawthorne House	Joanie's Tea Room	Sherlock Holmes	The Cavalcade of America	8:30
	Carroll Alcott, news (8:55 PM)			8:45
The Man from G-2	The Whistler	Glenn Hardy, news	The Bell Telephone Hour	9pm
		Rex Miller, news		9:15
Symposium	Vox Pop	The Inside of Sports	Light Opera	9:30
The Hobby Hour		Henry J. Taylor, news		9:45
George Fisher, gossip	The Ten o'Clock Wire	Fulton Lewis Jr., news	The Richfield Reporter	10pm
Charlie Chan	Talk	News	Art Baker's Notebook	10:15
Raymond Gram Swing, news	The Symphonette	The Johnson Family	Inside the News	10:30
Rainbow Rendezvous		So the Story Goes	Show Time	10:45

EVENING — FALL, 1945

Tuesday

	ABC	CBS	MBS	NBC
5pm	Terry and the Pirates	Kurt Manning, news	Sam Hayes, news	News and Views
5:15	Dick Tracy	Through a Woman's Eyes	The Adventures of Superman	
5:30	Jack Armstrong, the All-American Boy	Harry W. Flannery, news	Captain Midnight	A Date with Judy
5:45	News	Truman Bradley, news	Tom Mix and His Ralston Straightshooters	
6pm	Guy Lombardo Orchestra	Inner Sanctum Mysteries	Gabriel Heatter, news	Amos 'n' Andy
6:15			Real Stories from Real Life	
6:30	Radie Harris, gossip	This is My Best	The American Forum of the Air	Fibber McGee and Molly
6:45	Sports			
7pm	Public Affairs	Stafford Brooks, talk		The Pepsodent Show, Bob Hope
7:15			Upton Close, news	
7:30	County Fair	The Hollywood Preview	Red Ryder	The Raleigh Room, Hildegarde
7:45				
8pm	Lum and Abner	The Jack Kirkwood Show	The Count of Monte Cristo	The Chesterfield Supper Club
8:15	Manchester Boddy, news	The Jack Smith Show		Fleetwood Lawton, news
8:30	The Alan Young Show	Theater of Romance	The Falcon	Johnny Presents
8:45		Carroll Alcott, news (8:55 PM)		
9pm	Dark Venture	Big Town	Glenn Hardy, news	The Bullocks Show
9:15			Rex Miller, news	
9:30	Murder Will Out	Congress Speaks	The Inside of Sports	The American Way
9:45			News	
10pm	George Fisher, gossip	The Ten o'Clock Wire	Fulton Lewis Jr., news	The Richfield Reporter
10:15	Charlie Chan	News	News	Two in Love
10:30	Raymond Gram Swing, news	Edwin C. Hill, news	The Johnson Family	Inside the News
10:45	The Doctors Talk It Over	Behind the Scenes at CBS	So the Story Goes	Show Time

EVENING — FALL, 1945

Wednesday

ABC	CBS	MBS	NBC	
Terry and the Pirates	Kurt Manning, news	Sam Hayes, news	H. V. Kaltenborn, news	5pm
Dick Tracy	Through a Woman's Eyes	The Adventures of Superman	News	5:15
Jack Armstrong, the All-American Boy	Harry W. Flannery, news	Captain Midnight	The Voice of a Nation	5:30
News	Truman Bradley, news	Tom Mix and His Ralston Straightshooters	Elmer Patterson, news	5:45
One Foot in Heaven	Songs By Sinatra	Gabriel Heatter, news	Time to Smile, Eddie Cantor	6pm
		Real Stories from Real Life		6:15
Story Review	Maisie	Spotlight Bands	Mr. District Attorney	6:30
Sports				6:45
Counterspy	Great Moments in Music	Hercules Poirot	Kay Kyser's College of Musical Knowledge	7pm
				7:15
Jobs for G.I.s	The N-K Musical Showroom, Andrew Sisters	The Lone Ranger		7:30
				7:45
Lum and Abner	The Jack Kirkwood Show	The Main Line	The Chesterfield Supper Club	8pm
Manchester Boddy, news	The Jack Smith Show		Fleetwood Lawton, news	8:15
The Fishing and Hunting Club	Dr. Christian	The Fresh Up Show, Bert Lahr	An Evening with Romberg	8:30
	Carroll Alcott, news (8:55PM)			8:45
One Way Street	The Jack Carson Show	Glenn Hardy, news	Mr. and Mrs. North	9pm
War Town		Rex Miller, news		9:15
Spade Cooley Orchestra	The Adventures of Ellery Queen	The Inside of Sports	The Skippy Hollywood Theater	9:30
		Spike Jones Orchestra		9:45
George Fisher, gossip	The Ten o'Clock Wire	Fulton Lewis Jr., news	The Richfield Reporter	10pm
Charlie Chan	News	News	The Kenny Baker Show	10:15
Raymond Gram Swing, news	The Symphonette	The Johnson Family	Inside the News	10:30
Freddy Martin Orchestra		So the Story Goes	Show Time	10:45

EVENING — FALL, 1945

Thursday

	ABC	CBS	MBS	NBC
5pm	Terry and the Pirates	Knox Manning, news	Sam Hayes, news	News
5:15	Dick Tracy	Through a Woman's Eyes	The Adventures of Superman	News
5:30	Jack Armstrong, the All-American Boy	Harry W. Flannery, news	Captain Midnight	The Voice of a Nation
5:45	News	Truman Bradley, news	Tom Mix and His Ralston Straightshooters	Elmer Patterson, news
6pm	The Hobby Hour	Music Millions Love	Gabriel Heatter, news	The Kraft Music Hall, Bing Crosby
6:15	Design for Death		Real Stories from Real Life	
6:30	Detect and Collect	Hobby Lobby	The Treasure Hour of Song	The Bob Burns Show
6:45				
7pm	Curtain Time	The First Line of Defense	The Land of the Lost	Abbott and Costello
7:15				
7:30	Your AEF	The Powder Box Theater	Red Ryder	The Rudy Vallee Show
7:45	Sports			
8pm	Lum and Abner	The Jack Kirkwood Show	Bulldog Drummond	The Chesterfield Supper Club
8:15	Earl Godwin, news	The Jack Smith Show		Fleetwood Lawton, news
8:30	America's Town Meeting of the Air	The FBI in Peace and War	Rogue's Gallery	Maxwell House Coffee Time, Burns and Allen
8:45		Carroll Alcott, news (8:55PM)		
9pm		Suspense	Glenn Hardy, news	The Birdseye Open House, Dinah Shore
9:15			Rex Miller, news	
9:30	Mystery House	The Citizen's Forum	Inside of Sports	Noah Webster Says
9:45			Music	
10pm	George Fisher, gossip	The Ten o'Clock Wire	The Legion Stadium Fights	The Richfield Reporter
10:15	Charlie Chan	News		Mayor Bowron, comment
10:30	Raymond Gram Swing, news	Talk	The Johnson Family	Inside the News
10:45	Freddy Martin Orchestra	Organ Recital	So the Story Goes	Show Time

EVENING — FALL, 1945

Friday

ABC	CBS	MBS	NBC	
Terry and the Pirates	Knox Manning, news	Sam Hayes, news	H. V. Kaltenborn, news	5pm
Dick Tracy	Through a Woman's Eyes	The Adventures of Superman	News	5:15
Jack Armstrong, the All-American Boy	Harry W. Flannery, news	Captain Midnight	The Voice of a Nation	5:30
News	Truman Bradley, news	Tom Mix and His Ralston Straightshooters	Elmer Patterson, news	5:45
Famous Jury Trials	The Ginny Simms Show	Gabriel Heatter, news	People Are Funny	6pm
		Real Stories from Real Life		6:15
The Sheriff	Those Websters	Spotlight Bands	Waltz Time	6:30
				6:45
Madison Square Garden Boxing	The Durante - Moore Show	Leave It to Mike	The Molle' Mystery Theater	7pm
		News		7:15
	Pabst Blue Ribbon Town, Danny Kaye	The Lone Ranger	The Colgate Sports Newsreel, Bill Stern	7:30
			Cabbages and Kings	7:45
Blind Date	The Jack Kirkwood Show	The Adventures of Nero Wolfe	The Chesterfield Supper Club	8pm
	The Jack Smith Show		Fleetwood Lawton, news	8:15
This is Your FBI	It Pays to Be Ignorant	Freedom of Opportunity	Duffy's Tavern	8:30
	Carroll Alcott, news (8:55pm)			8:45
Roundup Time	The Aldrich Family	Glenn Hardy, news	The Night Editor	9pm
		Rex Miller, news	Latin Serenade	9:15
Spade Cooley Orchestra	Kate Smith Sings	Inside of Sports	The Haunting Hour	9:30
		Henry J. Taylor, news		9:45
George Fisher, gossip	The Ten o'Clock Wire	Fulton Lewis Jr., news	The Richfield Reporter	10pm
Charlie Chan	News	News	The Kenny Baker Show	10:15
Raymond Gram Swing, news	The Symphonette	The Johnson Family	Inside the News	10:30
Freddy Martin Orchestra		So the Story Goes	Show Time	10:45

EVENING — FALL, 1945

Saturday

	ABC	CBS	MBS	NBC
5pm	Woody Herman Orchestra	The Three B's	News	Tommy Dorsey Orchestra
5:15			The Canary Pet Shop	
5:30	What's the Score	Harry W. Flannery, news	Music	News
5:45	Swing Music	Bob Garred, news		Elmer Patterson, news
6pm	Musical Playground	Your Hit Parade	Leave It to the Girls	The National Barn Dance
6:15				
6:30	Boston Symphony Orchestra		The Whisper Men	Can You Top This
6:45		Saturday Night Serenade		
7pm			The Quiz of Two Cities	The Judy Canova Show
7:15		Report to the Nation		
7:30	Dick Tracy		Red Ryder	Grand Ole Opry
7:45		The Story Teller		
8pm	Win, Place or Show	The Dick Haymes Show	The Chicage Theater of the Air	Truth or Consequences
8:15				
8:30	Salute to the Fleet	The Mayor of the Town		The Life of Riley
8:45		Carroll Alcott, news (8:55PM)		
9pm	Gangbusters	Navy Day	Glenn Hardy, news	The Adventures of Bill Lance
9:15			News	
9:30	The Green Hornet	That's a Good Idea	Dance Orchestra	The Family Party
9:45		Don't You Believe It	The Frank Parker Show	
10pm	Dance Orchestra	The Ten o'Clock Wire	You Were There	News
10:15		The Hollywood Barn Dance	Organ Recital	News
10:30	Freddy Martin Orchestra		Dance Orchestra	This is My Country
10:45		Talk		Show Time

DAYTIME — FALL, 1945

Sunday

	ABC	CBS	MBS	NBC
8am	War News	The Blue Jacket Choir	The Wesley Radio League	The Eternal Light
8:15	The Chapel Quartet			
8:30	The Hour of Faith	Invitation to Learning	The Voice of Prophecy	News Roundup
8:45				
9am	It Happened During the Week	The Salt Lake Tabernacle Choir	The Pilgrim Hour	The University of Chicago Round Table
9:15	News	Woman Power		
9:30	Music	Transatlantic Call	The Lutheran Hour	Echoes and Encores
9:45				
10am	John B. Kennedy, news	The People's Platform	Glenn Hardy, news	Layman's Views of the News
10:15	Orson Welles, comment		Commander Scott	The Home Town Parade
10:30	Sammy Kaye's Sunday Serenade	News	Sweetheart Time	Musical Milestones
10:45		Edward R. Murrow, news		Modern Music
11am	Washington Inside and Out	Stradivari Orchestra	The Band Concert	Harvest of Stars
11:15	General Junius Pierce, comment			
11:30	The Remember Hour	Hollywood Star Time	News	The Westinghouse Program, John C. Thomas
11:45			Dale Carnegie, inspirational	
12pm	Musical Bouquet	New York Philharmonic Orchestra	Broadway News	The Sheaffer Parade
12:15			Ilka Chase, talk	
12:30			Vera Holly Sings	One Man's Family
12:45				
1pm	Darts for Dough		Murder is My Hobby	The Army Hour
1:15				

DAYTIME — FALL, 1945

Monday-Friday

ABC	CBS	MBS	NBC	
The Breakfast Club	News	Arthur Gaeth, news	Fred Waring Orchestra	*8am*
	Valiant Lady	The Korn Kobblers		*8:15*
	The Light of the World	Take It Easy Time	Dr. Paul	*8:30*
	Aunt Jenny's Real Life Stories	Victor Lindlahr, health	David Harum	*8:45*
Glamor Manor, Cliff Arquette	Kate Smith Speaks	William Lang, news	Edward Jorgerson, news	*9am*
	Big Sister	The Coke Club, Morton Downey	Music	*9:15*
Breakfast at Sardi's	The Romance of Helen Trent	Time Out	Living It in Hollywood	*9:30*
	Our Gal Sunday	The Mystery Chef	Ronnie Mansfield, songs	*9:45*
Tony Morse, news	Life Can Be Beautiful	Glenn Hardy, news	Mirandy	*10am*
Between the Bookends	Ma Perkins	Something to Talk About	What You Say	*10:15*
My True Story	Bernadine Flynn, news	Music	The Hollywood Fan Magazine	*10:30*
	Young Dr. Malone	The John J. Anthony Program	Art Baker's Notebook	*10:45*
H. R. Baukhage, news	Two on a Clue	Cedric Foster, news	The Guiding Light	*11am*
Ethel and Albert	Perry Mason	Music	Today's Children	*11:15*
Music	Rosemary	Queen for a Day	The Woman in White	*11:30*
News	Tena and Tim		Hymns of All Churches	*11:45*
John B. Kennedy, news	Try 'n' Find Me	Broadway News	The Farm Reporter	*12pm*
Memories in Melody	News	The Johnson Family	Ma Perkins	*12:15*
Ladies, Be Seated	A Woman's Life	Mild and Mellow	Pepper Young's Family	*12:30*
	Bachelor's Children	Frolics	The Right to Happiness	*12:45*
The Jack Berch Show	House Party	Billboard	Mary Noble, Backstage Wife	*1pm*
The Radio Parade		Bill Hay's Bible Reading	Stella Dallas	*1:15*

DAYTIME — FALL, 1945

Sunday

	ABC	CBS	MBS	NBC
1:30	Jones and I	The Electric Hour, Nelson Eddy	The Nebbs	These Make History
1:45				Music
2pm	Mary Small's Revues	The Prudential Family Hour	The Shadow	NBC Symphony Orchestra
2:15				
2:30	The Charlotte Greenwood Show	Gene Autry's Melody Ranch	The Return of Nick Carter	
2:45		William L. Shirer, news		
3pm	The Radio Hall of Fame	The Adventures of Ozzie and Harriet	Quick as a Flash	The Catholic Hour
3:15				
3:30	Phil Davis' Sunday Party	Money on the Line	Cedric Foster, news	News
3:45			Fulton Lewis Jr., news	The Melody Parade
4pm	Drew Pearson, news	I Was There	Opera	The Lucky Strike Program, Jack Benny
4:15	Don Gardiner, news			
4:30	The Hollywood Music Hall	My Story		The Fitch Bandwagon
4:45				

DAYTIME — FALL, 1945

Monday-Friday

ABC	CBS	MBS	NBC	
News	The Strange Romance of Evelyn Winters	This Changing World	Lorenzo Jones	1:30
Hymns of All Churches	Background for Living	Tello-Test Quiz	Young Widder Brown	1:45
What's Doing Ladies	The American School of the Air	Smile Time	When a Girl Marries	2pm
		Tomorrow's Calendar	Portia Faces Life	2:15
Best Sellers	Meet the Missus	Weight in Gold	Just Plain Bill	2:30
			Front Page Farrell	2:45
Walkie Talkie	The Housewives' Protective League	Philip Keyne Gordon, news	The Road of Life	3pm
News		Nancy Young, talk	Joyce Jordan, MD	3:15
The Frances Scully Show	Talk / Jimmy Carroll Sings		Aunt Mary	3:30
Easy Listenin'	The World Today	Elsa Maxwell, news	A Woman of America	3:45
Taylor Grant, news	Easy Aces	Fulton Lewis Jr., news	One Woman's Secret	4pm
Raymond Gram Swing, news	News	Rex Miller, news	News of the World	4:15
General Junius Pierce, comment	Talk and Music / Open House / The American Melody Hour /	Erskine Johnson, gossip	Art Baker's Notebook	4:30
Hop Harrigan	Mr. Keen, Tracer of Lost Persons	Talk and Music		4:45

DAYTIME — FALL, 1945

Saturday

	ABC	CBS	MBS	NBC
8am	The Breakfast Club	Let's Pretend	Larry Meiser, news	G.I.'s Abroad
8:15			Music	Jamboree
8:30		The Billie Burke Show	Bill's Wax Shop	Smilin' Ed's Buster Brown Gang
8:45				
9am	Galen Drake, talk	The Armstrong Theater of Today	The House of Mystery	News
9:15	Mirandy			Victory Chest
9:30	Home and Garden	Stars Over Hollywood	Music	Alex Drier, news
9:45				Music
10am	Music	Grand Central Station	Glenn Hardy, news	The National Farm and Home Hour
10:15	The Vagabonds Quartet		Al Williams, news	
10:30		News and Views	The Clinic Forum	The Hollywood Fan Magazine
10:45	Sports			Sports
11am		Mary Lee Taylor, cooking	Music	
11:15				
11:30		Give and Take		
11:45				
12pm		Sports	Broadway News	
12:15			Music	
12:30				
12:45				
1pm				
1:15			Felix DeCola Orchestra	
1:30	News		Coke Session	
1:45	A Date with the Duke			

DAYTIME — FALL, 1945

Saturday

	ABC	CBS	MBS	NBC
2pm	The Saturday Concert	Philadelphia Symphony Orchestra	News	
2:15			Sports	
2:30				John W. Vandercook, news
2:45				Tin Pan Alley
3pm	Music	Welcome Home		Our Foreign Policy
3:15				
3:30		Syncopation Piece		Jamborree
3:45	Labor USA	The World Today		
4pm	Jobs after Victory	The Textron Theater		Youth on Parade
4:15	American Radio			
4:30	Horse Racing	The First Nighter Program		Horse Racing
4:45				

Bear Manor Media

Classic Cinema.
Timeless TV.
Retro Radio.
WWW.BEARMANORMEDIA.COM

www.ingramcontent.com/pod-product-compliance
Lightning Source LLC
Chambersburg PA
CBHW050425240426
43661CB00055B/2270